The Euro Area and the Financial Crisis

The financial crisis of 2007–10 has presented a number of key policy challenges for those concerned with the long-term stability of the euro area. It has shown that price stability as provided by the European Central Bank is not enough to guarantee financial stability, and exposed fault lines in governance and deficiencies in the architecture of the financial supervisory and regulatory framework. This book addresses these and other issues, including why the crisis affected some countries more than others, whether the euro is still attractive for new EU states and what policy changes and structural reforms, both macro and micro, should be undertaken to ensure its future viability. Written by a team of leading academic and central bank economists, the book also includes chapters on the cross-country incidence of the crisis, the Irish crisis and ECB monetary policy during the crisis, and studies on Spain, the Baltics, Slovakia and Slovenia.

MIROSLAV BEBLAVÝ has an unusual blend of academic and political experience. He is a Senior Research Fellow at the Brussels think tank, Centre for European Policy Studies and, at the same time, Member of the Slovak Parliament. He is also Associate Professor of Public Policy at the Comenius University in Bratislava, Slovakia. In the past, he served as a junior minister in his country's government, created an influential think tank and worked for a range of multilateral development institutions as a consultant in Europe, Africa and the Caucasus.

DAVID COBHAM is Professor of Economics at Heriot–Watt University. He is a specialist in monetary policy who has worked on the UK, on French and Italian monetary policy, on European monetary integration and on monetary policy and exchange rate regimes in the Middle East and North Africa. He is the editor or co-editor of a number of books on European monetary integration and monetary policy, including *The Travails of the Eurozone* (2007) and *Twenty Years of Inflation Targeting: Lessons Learned and Future Prospects* (2010).

L'UDOVÍT ÓDOR is an advisor to the Prime Minister and Minister of Finance in Slovakia. In the past, he served as a member of the Bank Board at the National Bank of Slovakia and Executive Director responsible for research. He also worked as a Chief Economist at the Ministry of Finance of the Slovak Republic. He played an important role in institutional and structural reforms in Slovakia including the euro adoption in 2009.

The Euro Area and the Financial Crisis

Edited by

Miroslav Beblavý, David Cobham
and Ľudovít Ódor

NÁRODNÁ BANKA SLOVENSKA
EUROSYSTÉM

CAMBRIDGE
UNIVERSITY PRESS

CAMBRIDGE UNIVERSITY PRESS
Cambridge, New York, Melbourne, Madrid, Cape Town,
Singapore, São Paulo, Delhi, Mexico City

Cambridge University Press
The Edinburgh Building, Cambridge CB2 8RU, UK

Published in the United States of America by Cambridge University Press, New York

www.cambridge.org
Information on this title: www.cambridge.org/9781107014749

© Cambridge University Press 2011

First published 2011

A catalogue record for this publication is available from the British Library

Library of Congress Cataloguing in Publication data
The Euro area and the financial crisis / edited by Miroslav Beblav´y, David
Cobham, and Ľudov´ıt O´ dor.
    p.   cm.
"This volume brings together the papers and panel contributions presented at
the conference on 'The Euro Area and the Financial Crisis', held in Bratislava
from 6 to 8 September 2010" – Introd.
Includes bibliographical references and index.
ISBN 978-1-107-01474-9
1. Monetary policy – European Union countries. 2. Euro.
3. Global Financial Crisis, 2008–2009. I. Beblav´y, Miroslav.
II. Cobham, David P. III. O´dor, Ludov´ıt. IV. Title.
HG925.E8677   2011
330.9405611 – dc23   2011027489

ISBN 978-1-107-01474-9 Hardback

Contents

Figures

Tables

Boxes

Contributors

BISWAJIT BANERJEE, Haverford College

MIROSLAV BEBLAVÝ, Comenius University

WENDY CARLIN, UCL and CEPR

LAURENT CLERC, Banque de France

DAVID COBHAM, Heriot–Watt University

BORIS COURNÈDE, OECD

AURELIJUS DABUŠINSKAS, Bank of Estonia

DANIELE FRANCO, Banca d'Italia

VÍTOR GASPAR, Banco de Portugal

ANGEL GAVILÁN, Banco de España

STEFAN GERLACH, Goethe University and CEPR

FRANCESCO GIAVAZZI, Bocconi University, CEPR and NBER

PABLO HERNÁNDEZ DE COS, Banco de España

THOMAS F. HUERTAS, EBA and FSA

JUAN F. JIMENO, Banco de España

DAMJAN KOZAMERNIK, Bank of Slovenia

PHILIP R. LANE, Trinity College Dublin and CEPR

JACQUES MÉLITZ, Heriot–Watt University, CREST–INSEE and CEPR

DIEGO MOCCERO, OECD

BENOÎT MOJON, Banque de France

EWALD NOWOTNY, Österreichische Nationalbank

L'UDOVÍT ÓDOR, Ministry of Finance, Slovakia (formerly National Bank of Slovakia)

THORVARDUR TJÖRVI ÓLAFSSON, Central Bank of Iceland and University of Aarhus

ATHANASIOS ORPHANIDES, Central Bank of Cyprus and CEPR

THÓRARINN G. PÉTURSSON, Central Bank of Iceland

MARTTI RANDVEER, Bank of Estonia

JUAN A. ROJAS, Banco de España

LUIGI SPAVENTA, University of Rome and CEPR

ZDENĚK TŮMA, Charles University

DAVID VÁVRA, OGResearch

STEFANIA ZOTTERI, Banca d'Italia

Abbreviations and acronyms

ABS	Asset Backed Securities
AIB	Allied Irish Banks
BCBS	Basel Committee on Banking Supervision
BEA	Bureau of Economic Analysis (US)
BEPGs	Broad Economic Policy Guidelines (EU)
BIS	Bank for International Settlements
BLS	Bank Lending Survey (ECB)
bp	basis point
CBA	cost-benefit analysis
CCA	common currency area
CDS	credit default swaps
CEBS	Committee of European Banking Supervisors
CEE	Central and Eastern Europe
CESEE	Central, Eastern and Southeastern Europe
CPI	consumer prices index
DGECFIN	Directorate General for Economic and Financial Affairs (EU)
DGSD	Deposit Guarantee Schemes Directive (EU)
DSGE	Dynamic Stochastic General Equilibrium
EBA	European Banking Authority
ECB	European Central Bank
ECOFIN	Economic and Financial Affairs Council
EDIRF	European Deposit Insurance and Resolution Fund
EDP	Excessive Deficit Procedure (EU)
EEA	European Economic Area
EFSA	European Financial Stability Agency
EFSF	European Financial Stability Facility
EFSM	European Financial Stability Mechanism
EIB	European Investment Bank
EIU	Economic Intelligence Unit (EU)
ELA	emergency liquidity assistance
ELG	Eligible Liabilities Guarantee (Ireland)

EMS	European Monetary System
EMU	European Monetary Union (Economic and Monetary Union)
EONIA	Euro Overnight Index Average
ERB	exchange rate-based
ERM II	Exchange Rate Mechanism II (since 1999)
ESAs	European Supervisory Authorities
ESM	European Stabilisation Mechanism
ESRB	European Systemic Risk Board
ESRI	Economic and Social Research Institute (Ireland)
EU	European Union
FDI	foreign direct investment
FDIC	Federal Deposit Insurance Corporation (US)
FDICIA	Federal Deposit Insurance Corporation Improvement Act (US)
FPC	Fiscal Policy Committee
FRB	Federal Reserve Board
FSA	Financial Services Authority (UK)
FSB	Financial Stability Board (EU)
FSC	Fiscal Stability Charge
FX	foreign exchange
GDI	gross disposable income
GDP	gross domestic product
HICP	harmonised index of consumer prices
HP	Hodrick–Prescott
IADB	Inter-American Development Bank
IFS	*International Financial Statistics* (IMF)
IMF	International Monetary Fund
INBS	Irish Nationwide Building Society
INE	Instituto Nacional de Estadística (Spain)
IPN	Inflation Persistence Network
IT	inflation targeting
LIBOR	London Interbank Offered Rate
LOLR	lender of last resort
MAR	mean absolute revision
NAMA	National Asset Management Agency (Ireland)
NATO	North Atlantic Treaty Organisation
NPR	notice of proposed rule-making (FDIC)
NPRF	National Pension Reserve Fund (Ireland)
NTMA	National Treasury Management Agency (Ireland)
OBR	Office for Budget Responsibility (UK)
OCA	optimum currency area

OECD	Organisation for Economic Cooperation and Development
OIS	overnight indexed swap
OLG	overlapping generations
ONS	Office for National Statistics (UK)
PCAR	prudential capital assessment review
PCE	personal consumption expenditures
PLT	price-level targeting
PPF	production possibilities frontier
PPP	purchasing power parity
PV	present value
REER	real effective exchange rate
RFE	Federal Planning Bureau (Belgium)
RPI	retail price index
RPIX	retail price index excluding interest payments
RWAs	risk-weighted assets
SGP	Stability and Growth Pact
SITC	Standard International Trade Classification
SME	small and medium-sized enterprise
SRR	special resolution regime (UK)
SVAR	structural vector autoregression
TAF	Term Auction Facility (ECB)
TARP	Troubled Asset Relief Program (US)
TFEU	Treaty on the Functioning of the European Union
TFP	total factor productivity
TPO	temporary public ownership
UIP	uncovered interest parity
ULC	unit labour cost
VAR	vector autoregression
VAT	value added tax
WPI	wholesale price index

1   Introduction

*Miroslav Beblavý, David Cobham and L'udovít Ódor**

This volume brings together the papers and panel contributions presented at the conference on 'The Euro Area and the Financial Crisis', held in Bratislava from 6 to 8 September 2010. The conference was hosted by the National Bank of Slovakia and jointly organised by the National Bank of Slovakia, Heriot–Watt University in Edinburgh and Comenius University in Bratislava. The event was characterised by intensive discussions between central bankers, academics and policy-makers from all over Europe, which contributed directly and indirectly to the authors' revisions of their papers. The basic question was: What are the implications of the financial crisis and the great recession for the future of the euro area?

The book begins in Chapter 2 with the keynote contribution by Governor Athanasios Orphanides on the issues surrounding financial stability in Europe. Part I addresses the experience of the crisis. Thorvardur Ólafsson and Thórarinn Pétursson try in Chapter 3 to identify the factors that caused the depth and duration of the crisis to be larger in different countries. Philip Lane in Chapter 4 focuses on the Irish case. Angel Gavilán, Pablo Hernández de Cos, Juan F. Jimeno and Juan A. Rojas in Chapter 5 examine the Spanish case. Aurelijus Dabušinskas and Martti Randveer in Chapter 6 consider the varying experiences of the Baltic countries. Part II considers the issue of accession to the euro area by countries in Central, Eastern and Southeastern Europe (CESEE). Biswajit Banerjee, Damjan Kozamernik and L'udovít Ódor in Chapter 7 analyse the different strategies for entry to the euro used by Slovakia and Slovenia. Miroslav Beblavý in Chapter 8 investigates whether euro entry was associated with significant rises in prices (especially for non-tradable goods and services) in Slovakia. And in the first panel contributions Governor Ewald Nowotny in Chapter 9 and Zdeněk Tůma, together with

* We would like to express our thanks to the discussants and all the other participants in the conference, and to Martin Šuster of the National Bank of Slovakia, for their contributions to the conference and to the book.

David Vávra, discuss in Chapter 10 whether and how CESEE countries should accede to the euro.[1] Part III looks at the future of the euro area. Francesco Giavazzi and Luigi Spaventa in Chapter 11 argue that much more attention needs to be paid to current account deficits within the European Monetary Union (EMU). Daniele Franco and Stefania Zotteri in Chapter 12 consider the role that national fiscal rules could play in avoiding future problems. Thomas F. Huertas in Chapter 13 discusses mechanisms for 'bail-in' as an alternative to future bail-outs of financial institutions. Laurent Clerc and Benoît Mojon in Chapter 14 review the conduct of monetary policy in the euro area since the inception of the euro and the challenges that the Eurosystem has faced since the financial crisis. Boris Cournède and Diego Moccero in Chapter 15 assess the contribution that a price-level (as opposed to an inflation) target could make to the operation and performance of monetary policy. This is followed by contributions by Wendy Carlin, Vítor Gaspar, Stefan Gerlach and Jacques Mélitz to the second panel (Chapters 16–19), on how to restore confidence in the euro project.

Despite the different backgrounds of the contributors, there was a significant measure of convergence, and five important observations emerge. The first is the need to reshape and strengthen EU governance. Governor Orphanides made it clear in Chapter 2 that alongside the important topic of better prudential regulation and supervision attention should be paid to governance issues, notably crisis resolution. The financial crisis found the member states and their financial frameworks largely unprepared, which led to chaotic resolution mechanisms and huge costs for taxpayers. Orphanides calls for a unified EU resolution mechanism based on three principles: limited moral hazard, fair burden-sharing and cost-effectiveness.

The crisis also showed that one of the pillars of the monetary union – the 'no bail-out' principle – was more wishful thinking than credible threat for financial institutions and member states. Several participants argue that this problem needed to be fixed, but there is no clear consensus on how to do this. Huertas (Chapter 13) argues that EU countries cannot continue to support large financial institutions, and advocates 'bail-in' rather than bail-out: he explores the creation of buffers at systemically important financial institutions in the form of subordinated debt which in case of emergency would be automatically converted into capital. This would place the primary burden not on taxpayers but on the creditors of financial institutions. Mélitz in his panel contribution (Chapter 19)

---

[1] Dr Tůma was unable to attend the conference but kindly submitted his views shortly afterwards.

argues there is no need for no bail-out rules in EMU. Instead, as with the states of the US, a national government could simply be allowed to default, while policy should be limited to the construction and operation of EMU-wide prudential rules for banks backed up by ECB powers to act as lender of last resort. Gerlach in his panel contribution (Chapter 18) takes the failure of no bail-out rules as given and proposes a mechanism that credibly promises a rescue, but at unattractive terms. Such a mechanism would replace the temporary European Financial Stability Facility (EFSF) and would contain significant automatic write-downs (of 20–30 per cent) and strict conditionality, including pre-approval of budgets.

The second key observation to emerge was a challenge to the models scholars have traditionally used to think about monetary unions, with the most heated debates concentrated on the issue of fiscal policy coordination. Several contributors put much more emphasis than the traditional model on the issue of countries' current account deficits. In particular, Giavazzi and Spaventa (Chapter 11) argue that an important mistake was made in the downgrading of the problem of current account deficits: although monetary union eliminates the threat of currency devaluation, high current account deficits can cause substantial problems if the proceeds of external borrowing are not used for 'productive purposes'. In other words, using external resources to finance investments in nontradables or domestic consumption can lead to problems in meeting the intertemporal budget constraint. The high level of the former (investment in construction and housing) made economic success fragile in Ireland and Spain, while the latter (borrowing for consumption) resulted in increasing stress in Greece and Portugal.

This general argument, with its emphasis on country-specific conditions, is broadly consistent with the individual country studies by Lane (Chapter 4) and Gavilán et al. (Chapter 5). Lane argues that the long Irish expansion actually involved two distinct periods: a 'Celtic Tiger' output boom fuelled by high productivity increases in the second half of the 1990s, and then a property-driven boom period concentrated mainly in the non-tradable sector in the 2000s. He considers the arguments that EMU membership may have contributed to the Irish boom–bust cycle, but emphasises instead the lack of appropriate policies in banking regulation and fiscal stabilisation, and the positive contributions of EMU membership. Gavilán et al. use a small open-economy model to discuss the reasons for the emergence of a large current account deficit during the period of strong Spanish growth before the crisis. Their analysis highlights the decline in interest rates due to Spain's participation in EMU, and the demographic changes resulting from the large inflow of immigrants. Given these factors, in their model alternative fiscal policies would have made little difference, while structural reform in labour and product markets would have improved the growth rate but intensified the external deterioration in the short run.

There is also some common ground here in the more general chapter by Ólafsson and Pétursson (Chapter 3), which attempts to explain the cross-country variation in post-crisis experience using a wide variety of pre-crisis explanatory variables. They find that high preceding domestic inflation and macroeconomic imbalances, including large current account deficits, are crucial in determining the incidence and severity of the crisis, while larger banking systems were associated with longer and deeper cuts in consumption and with a higher risk of banking or currency crisis. Exchange rate flexibility tended to make the contraction shorter and shallower, but it also increased the risk of crisis. EMU membership, on the other hand, did not entail the negative effects associated with unilateral exchange rate pegs. In addition, Carlin's panel contribution (Chapter 16) emphasises the issue of relative price levels as between the different countries of the euro area: because nominal exchange rates cannot be adjusted such differentials (which would show up in current account imbalances) have to be reversed and eliminated (not just contained).

The third observation concerns fiscal policy. Bringing the problem of current account deficits to the forefront does not mean that fiscal policy problems are less relevant than before. On the contrary, several contributors highlighted the need to strengthen the Stability and Growth Pact (SGP) and increase the effectiveness of national fiscal frameworks. Gaspar in his panel contribution (Chapter 17), who also highlights the challenges posed by demographic trends in the EU, argues that both market discipline (operating through interest rate differentials) and the SGP have failed to ensure appropriate behaviour by national fiscal authorities. Major adjustments in the governance of the euro area are therefore called for; these will include higher financial penalties and stronger conditionality on financial support to countries in difficulty. Gerlach in his panel contribution (Chapter 18) stresses the importance of incorporating more automaticity in the SGP and replacing the existing inadequate market discipline by incentives for governments to act with restraint: he calls for a mechanism of graduated sanctions. Franco and Zotteri (Chapter 12) discuss the fiscal policy reforms which have been introduced or are under consideration in different EU countries, with particular reference to current and ongoing German and French reforms and to fiscal rules. Such national reforms need to be complementary to any changes at the EU or euro area level, but they can contribute to fiscal discipline and facilitate stabilisation. However, they need to be supported by public opinion. Carlin in her panel contribution (Chapter 16) suggests a further task for fiscal policy: she proposes the use of fiscal policy not just to stabilise the price level but to ensure optimal relative prices *vis-à-vis* the rest of the monetary union.

The fourth observation is that the crisis has uncovered some of the weaknesses of the conventional monetary policy framework. Policymakers on both sides of the Atlantic found themselves in a difficult situation after hitting the effective lower bound for nominal interest rates. They had to chart unknown waters using non-standard monetary policy measures, including quantitative and credit easing. Some of the contributors tried to identify gaps in the conduct of monetary policy and analysed the costs and benefits of changes in the standard flexible inflation targeting (IT) regime. Clerc and Mojon (Chapter 14) investigate whether the build-up of financial fragility was a consequence of monetary policy and whether it would be worth incorporating financial stability issues into the conduct of such policy. Although their modelling suggests that higher interest rates in the run-up to the crisis would have had relatively small effects on house prices, they suggest that the ECB should widen its monitoring of asset prices as well as money and credit and should stand ready to take decisions based on that monitoring even when consumer prices seem securely stable. They also discuss the potential conflict between the ECB's price stability target and its liquidity management operations intended to ensure financial stability. Cournède and Moccero (Chapter 15) ask whether there is a case for price-level targeting (PLT) instead of inflation targeting. If bygones are not bygones the risk of hitting a zero lower bound is reduced. Moreover, when an economy is near that bound PLT is preferable to, for example, raising the inflation target. There is a growing body of literature that finds some other aspects of PLT appealing, including lower volatility of inflation and hence nominal policy rates, lower inflation risk premia in long-term rates and higher capital accumulation. On the other hand moving to PLT is not without costs. The main concerns are that there is little practical experience of PLT, there are question marks over the transition from inflation targeting (credibility issues) and agents might not be sufficiently forward-looking.

The final observation is that there is no optimal one-size-fits-all euro adoption strategy and much depends on the set-up of the foreign capital inflow-based catching-up growth model. Banerjee, Kozamernik and Ódor (Chapter 7) compare the successful paths by which Slovakia and Slovenia joined the euro area. The starting positions of these two countries were very distinct and there were also substantial differences in the conduct of monetary policy before euro adoption. While Slovenia preferred stable exchange rates and more administrative control over the process, Slovakia allowed for significant exchange rate appreciation and deep structural reforms which resulted in a high productivity growth differential *vis-à-vis* the euro area. This also confirms the importance of investments in productive uses if one relies on external financing. Dabušinskas and Randveer (Chapter 6) compare the impact of the financial crisis on the Baltic countries, which were hit particularly hard. They had experienced a prolonged boom period but then suffered falls of one-fifth in consumption. According to Dabušinskas and Randveer the high cyclical volatility of these countries can be explained mainly by the strong procyclical developments in the financial sector. Foreign capital inflows via the financial sector were significantly higher in the Baltic countries than in most other new EU member states. In addition, the choice of exchange rate regime (currency board or fixed exchange rate regime) could have created overconfidence.

All this illustrates that the catching-up model based on foreign financing is not without risks and the policy options need to be selected with care. The crisis brought mixed feelings about the attractiveness of euro area membership for new member states. On the one hand – as Ólafsson and Pétursson showed in Chapter 3 – euro area membership served as a shelter against the excessive volatility of financial markets. On the other hand, the problems in Greece illustrate that membership of the elite club is not a panacea and if the internal problems of the union are not solved the future of the euro is uncertain. This brings additional arguments for opponents of euro adoption in many new member states and lowers the motivation to meet the Maastricht criteria in the near future. Tůma and Vávra in their panel contribution (Chapter 10) argue that 'the provision of long-term nominal stability is the only tangible economic benefit of the euro project'. This may be enough to justify adoption by the fixed exchange rate economies of Southeastern Europe, but not enough for the independent monetary policy countries of Central and Eastern Europe (though these countries may have sufficient political reasons for joining the euro). On the other hand, Nowotny in his panel contribution (Chapter 9) argues that the euro will remain an attractive option for potential entrants, but he emphasises that participation implies a commitment to structural reforms which will enable the economy to function without recourse to competitiveness-improving devaluations.

On one of the more specific issues of euro adoption, Beblavý (Chapter 8) provides an analysis of whether in the Slovakian case there were faster or exceptional price rises associated with the introduction of euro notes and coin (of the kind typical of popular beliefs about the euro in many existing member countries). The answer turns out to be 'no', in the sense that Slovakian entry to the euro occurred at a time of actual and perceived disinflation. However, there is some evidence of faster inflation in certain non-tradables around the time of entry. More generally, Beblavý emphasises that countries are likely to experience euro adoption in quite different ways, which implies that Slovakia's experience here cannot be generalised.

In the four months between the conference itself and the submission of this book to Cambridge University Press, the European Union, the ECB and the euro area countries have taken – often after much debate – a number of measures to strengthen the coordination and credibility of monetary, fiscal and financial policies, in a process which is still continuing. We have not attempted to cover these innovations here, and most of the chapters were finalised in October or November 2010 (the only exception is Lane's Chapter 4 on Ireland which takes the story up to the end of December). At this stage it is clear that some important issues remain unresolved. Moreover, as conference participants broadly agreed, while better policies can reduce the probability or magnitude of future crises, it will not be possible to completely prevent them. We believe that the way in which events and policy changes work out will be consistent with the analyses and propositions put forward in this book. But there will, of course, be plenty of scope for further critical work in this area.

2   Towards a new architecture for financial stability in Europe

Athanasios Orphanides

As crises often do, the global financial crisis we have been experiencing has highlighted key policy challenges that were insufficiently attended to in the past and has focused minds on needed improvements. In Europe, the crisis has exposed fault lines in governance and deficiencies in the architecture of the financial supervisory and regulatory framework. The need for more effective micro- and macro-prudential regulation and supervision, but also for better coordination between the two as well as among regulators, has been underlined. The crisis has confirmed that central banks can play an important role in safeguarding financial stability, but also demonstrated that a mandate to maintain price stability is not sufficient to ensure financial stability, strengthening the case that central banks need to be armed with the appropriate policy tools to enhance their contribution to financial stability.

The crisis has prompted critical thinking about the EU economic and financial policy frameworks and the need for a new supervisory architecture. The severe economic cost suffered as a result of the crisis, and the acknowledgement of the need to limit the likelihood of future costly occurrences, has provided an important opportunity for the development of an improved financial stability framework for Europe and highlighted the urgency of the need for a comprehensive crisis management regime. Not that this was not understood earlier. The lack of harmonisation in the European legal and supervisory framework and its potential cost in managing crises were known. Nevertheless, perhaps due to the complications and political sensitivities involved in addressing crisis management, and perhaps owing to other policy priorities, undue reliance was arguably given to the role of crisis prevention, avoiding prickly issues such as how potential losses associated with the efficient resolution of a cross-border financial institution were allocated.

In the European context the financial crisis has illustrated not only the deficiencies of the current EU cross-border arrangements, but also that a fragmented approach towards crisis management and resolution is insufficient to deal with these shortcomings. I take for granted the desirability of further integration of our economy across member states, and further enhancement and cross-border development of the financial industry in Europe. This is imperative to raise efficiency and more fully exploit the benefits of a common market, even more so in the euro area, where member states have tied their fortunes together more closely by adopting the common European currency. The economic benefits of integration are unquestionable, but realising the great potential presented by our union also makes it necessary to place greater emphasis on comprehensive EU-wide solutions towards enhancing financial stability in Europe.

Against this background, I would like to thank Narodna Banka Slovenska (the National Bank of Slovakia) for the invitation to address this conference on 'The Euro Area and the Financial Crisis'. I focus on a few issues related to the question of how the financial supervision architecture in Europe could be strengthened in order to secure financial stability. Namely, I discuss elements of micro- and macro-prudential policy tools for enhancing regulation and supervision, and also the development of a crisis management framework in Europe. I also present some pertinent thoughts on governance. Before proceeding, however, I should note that the views I express are my own and do not necessarily reflect those of my colleagues on the Governing Council of the European Central Bank (ECB).

Financial stability is a multifaceted concept. It involves the stability of the whole financial system, comprising financial institutions, financial intermediaries and financial markets. The latest international financial crisis has been associated with a serious weakening and, in some cases, failure of financial institutions, together with stress in credit markets and in the funding of financial institutions. These inflicted heavy costs on real economies and their taxpayers in many countries, including in the EU.

In light of the cost to the real economy associated with financial instability as well as the threat to public finances, the desirability of policies that reduce the occurrence of future crises as well as policies that contain the damaging effects of actual crises is clearly evident. This entails two main elements: first, prudential regulation and supervision policies and, second, a crisis management and resolution framework. The two elements are interrelated because the effectiveness of prudential supervision crucially depends on the incentives of financial institutions and thus on the likely costs incurred by the management and other stakeholders of a financial institution in case it needs to be resolved during a crisis.

This is the notion that endgames matter.[1] For cross-border institutions, EU governance issues may need to take a central role.

As already mentioned, the crisis has highlighted weaknesses in prudential regulation and supervision. It has demonstrated a general underappreciation of systemic risks in micro-prudential supervision and highlighted the need for a more system-wide macro-prudential approach towards supervisory oversight to ensure overall stability in the financial system. But what further prudential tools should be developed, or how should existing tools be enhanced? A number of sometimes competing proposals have been put forward by policy-makers, regulators, academics and the financial services industry to be included in preventive policies.[2] These proposals entail specific prudential policy instruments aimed at mitigating the build-up of systemic risk. Systemic risk – that is, the risk of serious disruption in the provision of financial services to the economy – arises from linkages both within the financial system and through its interaction with the real economy across the cycle. Macro-prudential policies are needed to address the cyclical aspect of systemic risk, noting that in 'good times' financial imbalances tend to build up as leverage increases and financial institutions become overexposed to risks, ultimately raising the probability of triggering system-wide instability. Prudential tools can be used to counter an excessive build-up of these risks in the financial system as a whole.

Higher prudential requirements regarding capital and liquidity would enhance the resilience of credit institutions to shocks and adverse market developments. A leading role in the construction of a harmonised global framework for the achievement of this objective rests with the Basel Committee on Banking Supervision (BCBS). In December 2009, the BCBS approved for consultation a package of proposals to strengthen global capital and liquidity regulations (Basel Committee on Banking Supervision, 2009b). These proposals are aimed at raising the quality, consistency and transparency of bank capital (predominance of common equity, phasing out of hybrid Tier 1 and abolishing Tier 3); introducing a simple capital-to-asset ratio (leverage ratio); introducing measures to promote the build-up of capital buffers in good times (countercyclical capital buffers); restrictions on dissipating capital when buffers are depleted (capital conservation measures); and strengthening the risk coverage of the capital framework (by increasing capital requirements for counterparty credit risk arising from derivatives, repos and securities financing activities).

[1] This is discussed in detail in Claessens, Herring and Schoenmaker (2010).
[2] See, e.g., International Monetary Fund (2010a).

Prudential regulation could also limit the build-up of liquidity risk, which proved neglected in various supervisory frameworks before the crisis. Quantitative liquidity ratios or standards that limit reliance on volatile non-core funding and prevent excessive build-up of maturity mismatches could be introduced, while other potentially volatile liability components such as foreign currency deposits should have adequate liquidity coverage and maturity matches.

Improving liquidity and capital standards should discourage excessive leverage and enhance the resilience of financial institutions during all phases of the business cycle. Adjusting regulation according to business cycle considerations may also better smooth risks across time. One approach towards that end is that of expected loss provisioning as against the current incurred loss approach, in line with the dynamic provisioning practised by banks in Spain. Indeed, in 2009 the European Commission started consultations with a view to adopting dynamic provisioning across the EU.

Additional macro-prudential tools could limit the build-up of more structural vulnerabilities that contribute to systemic risk. Such policies and monitoring could aim *inter alia* to address the build-up of financial imbalances in the economy relating to the raising of leverage in specific sectors. Early detection of signs of overheating of particular financial or property markets would be a case in point. Efforts aimed at affecting imbalances could include measures to attempt to directly reduce mortgage or credit demand from specific economic sectors. Prudent collateral policies could be used – for example, by setting minimum margins on collateral and/or capping loan-to-value ratios. There is some uncertainty regarding the effectiveness of loan-to-value ratios and margin requirements in reducing risk-taking, as financial institutions may attempt to evade, in part, such regulations. Nonetheless, there are examples where these tools appear to have had an effect in dampening risk-taking. A recent example I am personally familiar with is the reduction in the loan-to-value ratios in the real estate sector in Cyprus in July 2007, near the peak of a rapid run-up in real estate prices and fast credit growth in that sector. Raising the shock-absorbing capacity of lending in real estate with a stricter loan-to-value regulation before the crisis erupted was one of the factors that contributed to the maintenance of stability on the island in 2008 and 2009, years that proved quite difficult for other banking systems in Europe.

Shortcomings in regulation and supervision reflected in inadequate macro- and micro-prudential policies have been identified as major factors contributing to the international financial crisis. In Europe, rules and regulations for the financial sector are made at the country level and are not fully aligned across the euro area, despite the existence of some common directives. And even when rules and regulations are similar, national differences in interpretation and rigour of application have resulted in a fragmented and highly decentralised supervisory structure across Europe that is much too micro and institutionally focused.

The crisis has revealed not only the need for more effective micro- and macro-prudential regulation and supervision, but also the need for better coordination between the micro and macro parts, especially in providing timely information. Considering the important informational synergies between micro-prudential supervision and systemic risk analysis, bringing micro-supervision under the same roof as other central bank functions seems very appropriate. Central banks can benefit from, and rely on, extended access to supervisory information and intelligence, especially on systemically relevant intermediaries, in order to better assess the risks and vulnerabilities of the financial system as a whole. Overall, a lesson of the crisis is that greater central bank involvement in regulation and supervision pertaining to credit and finance should contribute to better management of overall economic stability.[3]

In Europe, the need to strengthen the macro-prudential orientation of financial supervision has led to an important new initiative at the EU level. It was decided by the European Council in June 2009, in line with the de Larosière (2009) report, to entrust macro-prudential supervision to a new body, the European Systemic Risk Board (ESRB), with the objective of increasing the focus on systemic risk within the framework of financial supervision. Institutionally and at the EU level, the ESRB should be in a favourable position to undertake system-wide risk assessments with a policy designed to detect areas of emerging financial imbalances and related structural vulnerabilities. The ESRB can provide policy recommendations based on its risk assessments, which can be converted into effective policy actions via the use of the macro-prudential tools and measures outlined above.

To enhance micro-prudential supervision in Europe, new European Supervisory Authorities (ESAs) are currently being set up which, among other things, will help coordination and convergence of the content and implementation of regulatory standards. The ESAs that are being created include the European Banking Authority (EBA), which combines the advantages of a European-wide framework for financial supervision with the expertise of micro-prudential supervision bodies at the national level that are closest to the institutions operating in their jurisdictions. However, in certain cross-border emergency situations, the tools for

---

[3] See, e.g., Orphanides (2009 and 2010).

coordinated effective action by national supervisors may be insufficient, and this points to the need to build a comprehensive cross-border framework to strengthen the EU's financial crisis management.[4]

It is recognised that close cooperation between the ESRB and the new ESAs in establishing the link between macro- and micro-prudential supervision would be useful for strengthening financial stability in Europe. For example, the ESRB together with the newly established EBA could conduct EU-wide stress tests on a regular basis to assess the resilience of financial institutions to adverse shocks.

Apart from the task of integrating macro- with micro-prudential supervision and regulation, an urgently needed convergence of supervisory standards across Europe is required, with supervisors addressing problems through European rather than national approaches. While the creation of a supranational financial supervisory authority for Europe does not currently appear to enjoy strong support, efforts should be made to help the existing highly decentralised system of supervision to become sufficiently effective that it can act as one in dealing with crisis prevention and management.

Effective prudential supervision can help prevent the occurrence of a crisis. But to contain the economic and budgetary cost of a crisis once it materialises and swiftly restore financial stability requires effective crisis management mechanisms. A transparent pre-agreed crisis management framework also reduces the moral hazard for banks, thereby contributing to reducing the risk of a financial crisis. The presence of a legal authority for prompt action and clear rules about how potential losses are allocated affects incentives and actual behaviour long before difficulties arise, and indeed might effectively discourage excessive risk-taking. There are serious weaknesses in policies and procedures relating to crisis management in Europe. Indeed, the de Larosière report called for 'a coherent and workable framework for crisis management in the EU'. But little progress has been made towards a comprehensive European crisis framework focusing on early intervention by supervisors, bank resolution and more formal procedures for the rapid winding-up of insolvent financial institutions. EU bodies have been working on developing a crisis management framework and the European Commission has indicated to the G20 that it will set out its 'orientations' for a crisis management framework in October 2010. At the same time the EU has called for the Financial Stability Board (FSB), in cooperation with the BCBS, to provide concrete policy recommendations to reduce the moral hazard posed by systemically important

---

[4] See, e.g., European Commission (2009).

financial institutions by the time of the G20 November 2010 Seoul Summit.

The crisis has provided a fresh opportunity for the EU to build a crisis management framework consistent with the regulatory and supervisory frameworks improving coordination between policy-makers and taking account of the potential problems of moral hazard, burden-sharing and allocation of costs. The development of a comprehensive crisis management framework would also appear to be in line with EU citizens' support for stronger supervision by the EU of the activities of the most important international financial groups. According to the Spring 2010 Eurobarometer public opinion poll, 75 per cent of Europeans agreed that stronger coordination of economic and financial policies among EU member states would be effective as a means of combating the crisis (Council of the European Union, 2010a). I note that the strongest support, 89 per cent, was registered in Slovakia, while Cyprus, at 87 per cent, tied for second place with Belgium.

In the euro area stability framework, liquidity matters clearly lie within the mandate of the ECB, which exercises a rigorous European approach. As a result, there is already in place a mechanism for dealing with liquidity crises and, indeed, the experience since the beginning of the turbulences in August 2007, which were originally manifested in the money markets, serves as evidence of the effectiveness of the ECB in alleviating liquidity issues. In contrast, solvency matters are addressed exclusively by national institutions, which may have differences on what constitutes a systemic threat, in identifying potential insolvency and about how and when public resources should be employed. As numerous observers have pointed out, and experience during the crisis has painfully confirmed, crisis management involving cross-border institutions in such a decentralised system is a highly inefficient and difficult task. The failure of Fortis in September 2008 highlighted conflicting national interests and the inability of governments in the Benelux region – arguably the most integrated region in the euro area – to find an efficient way to resolve a cross-border concern.

Accordingly, the greatest difficulty, perhaps, is associated with developing a framework for crisis management for dealing with problems involving cross-border financial groups that should have procedures for early intervention, bank resolution and insolvency. At present, there is no common approach in Europe for early public intervention in the case of a troubled financial institution. The absence of such a mechanism increases moral hazard on the part of the management of institutions that may find themselves in trouble. There is a need for supervisory authorities to have a stronger set of tools which they can use in intervening at an early stage to avoid the failure of an institution, or at least limit its problems. While

many stakeholders are in favour of minimum rather than maximum harmonisation, a credible threat of early intervention provides incentives for
financial institutions to guard their capital and thereby reduces systemic
risks and moral hazard problems. The absence of such mechanisms leaves
policy-makers with only bad choices during a crisis and often proves very
costly to taxpayers.

Where early intervention fails to deal with the problems of a distressed bank the second pillar, 'bank resolution', involves reorganising
the troubled bank in the most cost-efficient manner for the economy
and society, before it becomes insolvent. Resolution measures that might
be taken by the competent authorities include, for example, transfer of
assets/liabilities, a bridge bank, or a good bank/bad bank split designed
to preserve the value of remaining assets and facilitate, if possible, their
quick return to productive use. An appropriate legal framework is needed
for resolution, especially since resolution measures may impinge on
shareholder rights (under company or other laws). Moreover, resolution
measures entail costs, which need to be financed, ideally by the financial
industry itself. However, controversy surrounds the concrete means of
financing and burden-sharing as well as the level of authority (EU or
national) to be responsible for bank resolution. A global consensus is
emerging that shareholders and uninsured creditors of a bank should be
the first to bear the costs of its distress, in line with the principle 'the
polluter pays'. A key issue is how to credibly implement this attractive
idea.

A European resolution authority, as argued for example by Fonteyne
et al. (2010), could be created and be given the mandate and tools to
resolve large cross-border bank problems, particularly in a cost-effective
manner. To deal with the financing of bank resolution measures and,
ultimately, the use of public money to support ailing banks, the Commission has suggested the establishment of bank resolution funds by
member states to be funded *ex ante* by a levy on banks. Together with the
G20, they have asked specifically for the International Monetary Fund
(IMF) to study this funding proposal (G20 Pittsburgh Summit, 2009).
However, the resolution funds could be used as insurance against failure
or to bail out failing banks, thus creating a moral hazard problem.

Fonteyne et al. (2010) contend that a resolution framework needs to
include a European Deposit Insurance and Resolution Fund (EDIRF)
that is pre-funded by the financial industry through deposit insurance
premiums and systemic levies, so as to minimise the costs of crisis management to government budgets. The authors argue further that the
crisis management and resolution framework for the European banking
system should be designed to implement and achieve commonly agreed

principles and objectives. There should be *ex ante* agreement on these objectives and principles to allow rapid decision-making in crisis situations with countries agreeing to a third party, such as a European resolution authority, largely managing financial crises for them.

In this context it may be recalled that on 9 October 2007, the EU's Economic and Financial Affairs Council (ECOFIN) adopted a set of common principles for the management of any cross-border financial crisis (Council of the European Union, 2007), which were later endorsed by the financial supervisory authorities and central banks as part of the 1 June 2008 Crisis Management Memorandum of Understanding (Council of the European Union, 2008). Key elements of these principles are that:

- The objective of crisis management is to protect the stability of the financial system in all countries involved and in the EU as a whole, and is not to prevent bank failures
- Crisis management should minimise potential harmful economic impacts at the lowest overall collective cost
- Direct budgetary net costs should be shared among affected member states on the basis of equitable and balanced criteria.

While these principles are sound, the crisis has demonstrated that non-binding commitments or understandings insufficiently guarantee their consistent implementation, to the detriment of mutual trust and cooperation and, consequently, crisis outcomes. In this context, it is noted that in April 2010 the EU and euro area member states, together with the IMF, agreed on a loan to Greece, with participation of euro area members, to be ratified by their respective parliaments. However, last month the parliament of one euro area member state voted overwhelmingly against contributing to the agreed loan. This decision highlighted the challenge of successfully achieving cohesiveness and solidarity between the member states within the EU, despite the public support for stronger coordination of economic and financial policies reflected in the Spring 2010 Eurobarometer survey mentioned earlier.

This underlines the need for strong, binding and institutionalised arrangements for EU crisis management, putting the principles agreed upon on an operational basis. Cost-minimisation needs to be defined more precisely, with cost-effectiveness representing a major challenge, as avoiding or minimising costs is the best way to preclude disagreements about their distribution or burden-sharing between EU member states: cost-effectiveness is also essential to deal with moral hazard and 'too-big-to-fail' or 'too-big-to-save' financial institutions. Indeed, it is argued that only a cost-effective resolution offers a credible threat of failure and exit (Čihák and Nier, 2009). And cost-effectiveness in arranging a deal with a failing cross-border bank should comprise no losses to insured depositors, minimal losses to deposit guarantee systems, minimal collateral damage to the economy and minimal or no costs to government budgets.

In the case of insolvency proceedings, where resolution measures cannot return the distressed bank or part of it to viability, these proceedings should ensure an orderly wind down. However, insolvency regimes differ substantially across the twenty-seven EU countries and initiatives to promote their harmonisation are required. In particular, there are major differences between EU members in bankruptcy legislation and procedures. The European Commission's initiative to establish a group of experts on insolvency law is commendable, but harmonisation of insolvency regimes, while certainly feasible, will be difficult.

Alternatively, the Basel Committee on Banking Supervision (2009a) argues that contingent resolution plans ('living wills') could be an effective tool in crisis contingency preparedness for large and complex financial groups. These institutions would be required to devise detailed and regularly updated plans for dissolution that need to be approved by the supervisory authority. In principle, these plans would also 'specify formulas for loss-sharing among international subsidiaries of the bank (such loss-sharing arrangements would be preapproved by regulators in countries where subsidiaries are located)' (Calomiris, 2009: 10). It is important also that supervisors should have the power to require a banking group to formulate an acceptable winding-down plan, so that the living will puts in place all the conditions, *ex ante*, that would allow a wider range of options beyond having the whole bank rescued.

For the euro area the crisis demonstrated the need for greater cooperation and coordination between member states and, moreover, raised questions about euro area governance. Which European institutions are ultimately in charge of surveillance and collective action in times of stress, and how can member states be disciplined to adhere to agreed policies? Is it sufficient for the Van Rompuy task force on euro area governance (Council of the European Union, 2010b) to concentrate on enforcement and strengthening of existing EMU provisions? Or are there more macro-surveillance problems that go beyond weak enforcement in the fiscal area? In this respect, the European Commission has proposed that macro-surveillance go 'beyond the budgetary dimension to address other macro economic imbalances' (European Commission, 2010).

Some commentators contend that euro area governance has been characterised by a lack of policy coherence, with most member states not gearing domestic policies, particularly wage-setting, to euro area policy management.[5] Even under the SGP, member states have demonstrated little ownership of fiscal targets to which they were committed. Certainly, the crisis has exposed fault lines in the governance of the euro area, and much is expected of the Van Rompuy task force on multiple fronts, including strengthening surveillance of budgetary policies and more effective corrective measures, improving surveillance of competitiveness developments and the correction of imbalances. In particular, there are three pillars on which stronger governance may rely in order to reinforce compliance of national authorities with the rules of the Treaty and the SGP. First, reinforcing the SGP through, for example, more effective fiscal surveillance, a wider spectrum of sanctions, strengthening the independence of fiscal surveillance, etc. Second, addressing imbalances in competitiveness through, for example, less strict surveillance of countries which perform well and stricter oversight for member states with excessive vulnerabilities. Third, establishing a permanent framework for crisis management that will minimise moral hazard problems and at the same time provide a credible arrangement for countries in true need. Within this framework a euro area crisis management institution could be developed.

The crisis has provided an opportunity to construct a comprehensive crisis management regime that can replace the current patchwork of limited financial stability arrangements based largely on national interests. And, as outlined earlier, it is recommended that institutional arrangements for resolving the problems of large cross-border banks should give authority to a pan-European institution backed by largely private *ex ante* funding arrangements. Furthermore, in extending financial assistance to member states – such as under the European Financial Stability Facility (EFSF) created in May 2010 to address tensions in the euro area sovereign debt markets and from unsustainable financial imbalances – there is a need to strengthen institutional arrangements and legal obligations so that member states can show greater cohesiveness in fully honouring their commitments and providing funding and loan guarantees for assistance to financially distressed members.

At this stage of the crisis, and while efforts are still in progress to strengthen the framework for surveillance, corrective measures and mutual support, it is critical for all governments in the EU, and in particular in the euro area, to show their support for a European approach. It would be especially unfortunate, in light of the strong support exhibited by the citizens of Europe for stronger European economic

---

[5] See the discussion in Bini Smaghi (2010), Gaspar (2010), International Monetary Fund (2010b) and Pisani-Ferry (2010).

governance, if this strengthening is not achieved within a reasonable time-frame.

The crisis has brought to the forefront the need to build a European financial supervisory architecture. There has been progress in developing the institutional framework for micro- and macro-prudential supervision, including the recent process of creating pan-EU financial supervisory authorities. Progress in establishing prudential tools, especially more appropriate capital and liquidity requirements, for contributing to crisis prevention, has been more limited. But it is in the construction of a comprehensive European crisis management and resolution framework where there is a real deficiency, and where much work needs to be undertaken.

In my remarks I have provided some thoughts on the way forward for building a crisis management framework, which needs to address problems of moral hazard, burden-sharing and cost-effectiveness and, moreover, problems of policy coordination between the various financial authorities in Europe. Inevitably, such discussion leads to issues of economic governance in Europe on which I have posed some questions and furnished some further considerations. An extended discussion on the most effective ways to improve regulation and monitoring as well as facing potential future crises has been going on for some time in European and international fora. It is also apparent that an integrated approach to prevention management and conflict resolution is crucial to ensure financial stability.

In closing, I note that it is virtually impossible to avert future crises without an unwelcome change in the core elements of the philosophy of our economic system based on the free market ideology and the fundamental principles of free movement of labour, capital, goods and services. It is, however, feasible to work towards a framework that supports economic efficiency and growth while it reduces the frequency and the cost of future crises. Building this framework should be one of our main present tasks.

References

Basel Committee on Banking Supervision (2009a). *Report and Recommendations of the Cross-Border Bank Resolution Group*, Bank for International Settlements, September
  (2009b). *Strengthening the Resilience of the Banking Sector – Consultative Document*, Bank for International Settlements, 17 December
Bini Smaghi, L. (2010). 'The financial and fiscal crisis: a euro area perspective', speech delivered at Le Cercle, Brussels, 18 June

Calomiris, C. (2009). 'Prudential bank regulation: what's broke and how to fix it', April, mimeo

Čihák, M. and E. Nier (2009). 'The need for special resolution regimes for financial institutions – the case of the European Union', IMF Working Paper, No. **09/200**

Claessens, S., R. J. Herring and D. Schoenmaker (2010). *A Safer World Financial System: Improving the Resolution of Systemic Institutions', Geneva Reports on the World Economy*, 12, Geneva: International Centre for Monetary and Banking Studies

Council of the European Union (2007). *Conclusions of the 2822nd Council Meeting of Economic and Financial Affairs*, Luxembourg, 9 October

   (2008). *Memorandum of Understanding on Cooperation Between the Financial Supervisory Authorities, Central Banks and Finance Ministries of the European Union on Cross-Border Financial Stability*, Brussels, 1 June

   (2010a). 'Spring 2010 Eurobarometer: EU citizens favour stronger European economic governance', Brussels, 26 August

   (2010b). *Task Force on Euro Area Governance*, Spring

de Larosière, J. (2009). *Report of the High-Level Group on Financial Supervision in the EU*, Brussels, 25 February

European Commission (2009). *Proposal for a Regulation of the European Parliament and of the Council Establishing a European Banking Authority*, Brussels

   (2010). 'Surveillance of euro area competitiveness and imbalances', *European Economy*, **1/2010**

Fonteyne, W., W. Bossu, L. Cortavarria-Checkley, A. Giustiniani, A. Gullo, D. Hardy and S. Kerr (2010). 'Crisis management and resolution for a European banking system', IMF Working Paper, No. **10/70**

G20 Pittsburgh Summit (2009). Leaders' Statement, 24–25 September

Gaspar, V. (2010). 'Euro area governance and the global crisis', keynote opening address at the Fifth Pan-European Conference on EU Politics, organised by the European Consortium for Political Research at Universidade Fernando Pessoa and Faculty of Economics of Porto University, 23 June

International Monetary Fund (2010a). 'Central banking lessons from the crisis', IMF Policy Paper, 27 May

   (2010b). 'Euro Area Policies: 2010 Article IV Consultation – Staff Report', July

Orphanides, A. (2009). 'Dealing with crises in a globalised world: challenges and solutions', panel remarks at the Twelfth Annual International Banking Conference 'The International Financial Crisis: Have the Rules of Finance Changed?', 25 September

   (2010). 'Monetary policy lessons from the crisis', Central Bank of Cyprus Working Paper, No. **2010–1**

Pisani-Ferry, J. (2010). 'Euro-area governance: what went wrong? How to repair it?' *Bruegel Policy Contribution*, **2010/05**

Part I

The experience of the crisis

3 Weathering the financial storm: the importance of fundamentals and flexibility

*Thorvardur Tjörvi Ólafsson and Thórarinn G. Pétursson**

1 Introduction

The recent global financial tsunami has had economic consequences that have not been witnessed since the Great Depression. But while some countries suffered a particularly large contraction in economic activity on top of a system-wide banking and currency collapse, others came off relatively lightly. This chapter aims to explain this difference in cross-country experience by means of a non-structural econometric analysis using a variety of potential pre-crisis explanatory variables in a cross-section of forty-six medium-to-high-income countries. The severity of the macroeconomic impact is measured in terms of the depth and duration of the contraction in both output and consumption. Potential pre-crisis explanatory variables are chosen to reflect propagation channels for the global crisis typically mentioned in the literature, i.e. a financial channel, a trade channel, a macro channel and an institutional channel, although we offer some new variables that have not been included in such analyses before as far as we know. As another contribution to the analysis of the current crisis, we also use cross-country ordered probit regressions to identify the main determinants of the probability of domestic systemic banking or currency crises during the current crisis period.

* This chapter was prepared for the conference 'The Euro Area and the Financial Crisis', at the National Bank of Slovakia, Bratislava, 6–8 September 2010, under the auspices of the National Bank of Slovakia, the Heriot–Watt University of Edinburgh and the Comenius University of Bratislava. We are grateful to the conference participants, and especially the discussant on the original paper, Atanas Christev, for helpful comments and suggestions. We are also grateful to David Cobham for fruitful discussions on the project and to Francis Breedon, Már Gudmundsson, Andrew Rose and participants at a seminar in the Central Bank of Iceland for helpful comments on earlier versions of the chapter. Finally, we would like to thank Luc Laeven and Fabio Valencia who kindly shared an update of their banking crises database and Helga Gudmundsdóttir for helping with data. All remaining errors and omissions are ours. The views expressed do not necessarily reflect those of the Central Bank of Iceland.

Our results suggest that the macro channel played a prominent role, as domestic macroeconomic imbalances and vulnerabilities are found to be crucial in determining the incidence and severity of the crisis. An especially important pre-crisis macroeconomic indicator, which seems to capture factors that are important in explaining the extent of the crisis along many different dimensions, is the rate of inflation in the run-up to the crisis. We also find evidence suggesting the importance of financial factors. In particular, we find that large banking systems tended to be associated with a deeper and more protracted consumption contraction and a higher risk of a systemic banking or currency crisis. Our results suggest that greater exchange rate flexibility coincided with a smaller and shorter contraction, but at the same time increased the risk of a banking and currency crisis. We also find that countries with exchange rate pegs outside the European Monetary Union (EMU) were hit particularly hard, while inflation targeting seemed to mitigate the crisis. Finally, we find some evidence suggesting a role for international real linkages and institutional factors.

Several recent papers attempt to explain the cross-country variation in the impact of the global crisis. For example, the findings in Berkmen *et al.* (2009) suggest that private sector leverage, credit growth, exchange rate flexibility, trade composition and the fiscal position are important in explaining the cross-country variation in output growth forecast revisions. Lane and Milesi-Ferretti (2011) show that current account deficits, credit and output growth rates and exposure to trade and production of traded goods are all important predictors for the impact of the crisis on post-crisis output and domestic demand (including consumption) growth rates. Other papers are more sceptical about the importance of initial conditions. Using output growth, stock price and exchange rate changes and revisions to country's credit ratings as crisis indicators, Rose and Spiegel (2009a, 2009b) find that initial conditions have limited predictive power. Only pre-crisis asset price changes and current account deficits are found to be robust crisis predictors, while there is weaker evidence for a role of pre-crisis credit growth. Claessens *et al.* (2010) are also somewhat sceptical concerning the importance of initial conditions, although they find that credit growth, mortgage debt, asset price appreciation, current account deficits and trade openness can predict the severity of the output contraction and the post-crisis development of a financial stress index.

Our results, however, give us reason to be more optimistic about the predictive power of initial conditions in the current crisis, in terms of both explaining a significant share of the cross-country variation in the depth and duration of the crisis and in providing quite sharp predictions of the incidence of banking and currency crises. This therefore suggests that country-specific initial conditions played an important role in determining the economic impact of the crisis and, in particular, that countries with sound fundamentals and flexible economic frameworks were better able to weather the financial storm. We find that these results are robust to various alterations in the empirical set-up.

The remainder of the chapter is organised as follows. Section 2 discusses the country sample, our crisis measures and the potential explanatory variables used in the analysis. Section 3 presents the empirical results, with regard to both the real-economy effects of the crisis and the probability of a banking and currency crisis. Results from some sensitivity analyses are also reported. The section ends with an interpretation of the key results from the chapter. Section 4 concludes.

2   The data

2.1   The country sample

This section describes the country sample analysed in this chapter. Since the incidence of the crisis and occurrences of domestic banking and currency crises were much higher in higher-income countries, the focus is on countries in the upper half of the income spectrum. Thus, the aim is to include countries of similar income levels and size as OECD member countries. Hence, countries with PPP-adjusted *per capita* GDP lower than the poorest OECD member country (Turkey) and PPP-adjusted GDP level lower than the smallest OECD member country (Iceland) are excluded.[1] This gives a sample of sixty-four countries in total from the 227 countries recorded in the *CIA World Factbook* for the period 2006–8. After eliminating countries with missing data, we are left with forty-six countries, i.e. all the current thirty-three OECD member countries, plus Bulgaria, Croatia, Cyprus, Estonia, Hong Kong, Latvia, Lithuania, Malta, Romania, Russia, South Africa, Taiwan and Thailand.

Thus, the analysis includes all the twenty-seven EU member countries, six other European countries and thirteen countries outside of Europe. There are twenty-seven industrial countries and nineteen emerging market economies, of which twelve are in Central and Eastern Europe (CEE). Finally, the analysis includes seven very small open economies, i.e. countries with populations below 2.5 million.

The sample also includes countries with a wide array of monetary policy frameworks. Thus, there are the sixteen EMU countries, four countries pegging their currency to the euro within the ERM II framework and

---

[1] There is, however, one exception: Malta is included although its GDP level falls just short of Iceland's level, in order to add one observation of a very small, open economy.

Table 3.1: *Country sample*

Australia	France	Lithuania	Slovakia
Austria	Germany	Luxembourg	Slovenia
Belgium	Greece	Malta	Spain
Bulgaria	Hong Kong	Mexico	Sweden
Canada	Hungary	Netherlands	Switzerland
Chile	Iceland	New Zealand	Taiwan
Croatia	Ireland	Norway	Thailand
Cyprus	Israel	Poland	Turkey
Czech Republic	Italy	Portugal	UK
Denmark	Japan	Romania	US
Estonia	Korea	Russia	
Finland	Latvia	South Africa	

four other unilateral exchange rate pegs. There are also twenty-two countries with a floating exchange rate, of which nineteen follow an explicit inflation targeting (IT) regime.[2] The analysis therefore includes a country sample with a wide range of monetary frameworks. Table 3.1 gives an overview of the sample.

2.2   Crisis indicators

There is no single, optimal way to measure economic losses due to financial crises and the results from this chapter and the other papers referred to in the Introduction clearly show the need to look at many different crisis indicators. Various measures have therefore been put forward in the literature. While most papers focus on various measures of output loss, this chapter also focuses on consumption loss, which we think is important as it is clear that a special feature of this crisis is the unusually prominent role played by the highly indebted household sector in propagating and amplifying the financial shock, with an exceptionally large consumption contraction occurring in many countries.

Following Cecchetti, Kohler and Upper (2009), we measure the depth of the output (consumption) contraction as the log-difference of the seasonally adjusted GDP (consumption) level between its peak in the period from 2007Q1 to 2008Q4 and the level in 2009Q4 (our final data

---

[2] Information on monetary regimes is based on the IMF *de facto* classification of exchange rate regimes and monetary policy frameworks from 23 February 2009 (using data from 31 April 2008), but updating the framework in Slovakia to reflect its EMU membership from January 2009.

observation).[3] We also focus on the duration of the crisis with the aim of analysing whether the same factors explain the depth and duration of the crisis or whether different factors play a role in explaining the cross-country variation in the speed of recovery. We measure the duration of output (consumption) contractions as the number of quarters with negative quarter-on-quarter growth in seasonally adjusted GDP (consumption) from 2008Q3 to 2009Q4. The starting point is chosen to capture the effects of the global crisis once it entered panic mode in September 2008, so as to avoid capturing normal business cycle adjustments unrelated to the crisis. Of course, it can be argued that tighter financial conditions due to the emerging global crisis from mid 2007 played a part in reinforcing the downturn in activity and bringing some advanced economies into recession at an earlier stage, but we choose to focus our duration analysis on the impact of the crisis once it entered panic mode in late 2008.[4]

We also want to analyse the cross-country variation in the probability of a banking and currency crisis. The incidence of systemic banking crises is based on an updated version of the database in Laeven and Valencia (2008), generously provided by the authors, in addition to our own elaboration. They categorise ten countries from our country sample to have experienced a systemic banking crisis during the global crisis: Austria, Belgium, Denmark, Germany, Iceland, Ireland, Luxembourg, the Netherlands, the UK and the US. We add Latvia, Russia and Switzerland (which Laeven and Valencia had as borderline cases at the time of our correspondence) to the list, on the basis of significant stress in the banking sectors of these countries and the extent of policy interventions. Hence, there are thirteen incidences of systemic banking crises in our country sample.

Using the Bank for International Settlements' (BIS) nominal effective exchange rate indices, we follow the Laeven and Valencia (2008) definition of currency crises (see also Frankel and Rose, 1996). We categorise a country as having experienced a currency crisis if the annual average of the nominal effective exchange rate depreciated by 30 per cent or more

---

[3] Other measures were also considered, for example the difference between the 2007Q1–2008Q4 peak and the trough in 2008Q4–2009Q4 as well as the difference between the level in 2008Q3 and the trough in 2008Q4–2009Q4. The results were very similar (with correlations between the measures all above 0.9). The Working Paper version contains a more detailed discussion on the pros and cons of our approach.

[4] We also considered other measures of duration, with similar results. Two examples were the number of quarters below peak and the number of quarters before two consecutive quarters of positive quarter-on-quarter growth, respectively. The correlations between these two measures, on the one hand, and the measure chosen, on the other, are very high (above 0.8) for both output and consumption contractions.

in 2008–9 and if this depreciation is also at least a 10 percentage points increase in the rate of depreciation compared to the two-year period before. Given this definition, only two countries experienced a currency crisis between 2008 and 2009, Iceland and Korea, and therefore only Iceland experienced a twin crisis (see the appendix on p. 52 for more detail).[5]

The real-economy crisis indicators are positively correlated, but not overwhelmingly so: the correlations range from 0.39 between the duration of output and consumption loss to 0.78 between the depth of output and consumption loss. The correlations between the banking and currency crises incidences and the correlations of those indicators with the real-economy indicators are all well below 0.3.

2.3   Potential pre-crisis explanatory variables

We use a range of variables to analyse which factors played a role in determining the depth and duration of the contraction in activity, on the one hand, and the probability of a banking and currency crisis, on the other. In a broad sense, they can be categorised into four general channels from which the crisis was transmitted throughout the world economy: a financial channel, a trade channel, a macro channel and a channel reflecting institutional factors. To avoid possible endogeneity problems, all of our explanatory variables are measured at pre-crisis values, with most dated in 2006 or 2007 or values obtained from time series data with a cut-off point in 2007 or earlier. These variables and their motivation are further discussed below, but more detail and some descriptive statistics can be found in the Working Paper version of the chapter (Ólafsson and Pétursson, 2010, www.sedlabanki.is/?PageID=238). A detailed list of variable definitions and sources can be found in the appendix on p. 52.

Economic structure: The first set of explanatory variables includes two measures of economic size and development. First, we include *per capita* income to control for the concentration of the economic impact of the crisis on the more advanced economies (cf. Claessens *et al.*, 2010; Lane and Milesi-Ferretti, 2011), but also as a possible proxy for other economic and institutional factors that are probably positively correlated

---

[5] The Icelandic króna depreciated by roughly 48 per cent in total between 2007 and 2009, while the Korean won fell by 30 per cent. Expanding the criteria to other countries with large depreciations in both 2008 and 2009 would include next the pound sterling (22 per cent depreciation between 2007 and 2009) and the Romanian lei (19 per cent depreciation between 2007 and 2009). We decided, however, to stick to the stricter criteria as we found no supporting evidence suggesting that a currency crisis occurred in the UK during 2008–9.

with income. We also include the GDP level, to reflect the fact that small countries were hit particularly hard by the crisis (cf. Rose and Spiegel, 2009a), through the build-up of large imbalances, greater exposure to the collapse in global trade and less ability to absorb large shocks.

Financial structure and development: As a second set of explanatory variables we include three different measures of financial structure and development. It is often argued that the level of financial sophistication reached during the years prior to the crisis, even if it did not trigger the crisis, at least served to exacerbate it and propagate it across different financial markets and around the world through rising moral hazard problems, opaque and complicated financial instruments and the inability of financial regulators to effectively regulate the financial system. This is especially true if deep and large markets merely reflect the ability of domestic agents to increase their leverage and hence contribute to greater imbalances through asset price bubbles and unsustainable balance sheet expansion (cf. Dell'Ariccia, Detragiache and Rajan, 2008; Claessens *et al.*, 2010). Large banking systems, with significant cross-border operations, can also serve to exacerbate the transmission of the global crisis to the domestic economy (cf. Davis, 2008; Claessens *et al.*, 2010), and may increase the risk of regulatory capture or stretch both the ability of domestic regulators to deal with such large and complex banking systems and the fiscal and monetary resources to support them in times of need (cf. Buiter and Sibert, 2008; Demirgüç-Kunt and Serven, 2009).[6] At the same time, deeper financial markets may be more able to absorb shocks and diversify risk and therefore support the recovery from the crisis than thin markets with few financial instruments for hedging risk which may even disappear completely during crisis periods. The question of the sign of these effects is therefore ultimately an empirical one. To capture these effects we use the ratio of broad money (M2) to GDP as a measure of financial deepening, the ratio of total assets of the five largest banks to GDP as a measure of the size of the banking system and the ratio of stock market capitalisation to GDP as a measure of the size of the domestic stock market.

---

[6] Due to data limitations, we could not include detailed banking system data often mentioned in the discussion as having played a role in the current crisis, such as banking interconnectedness, cross-currency funding needs and currency and maturity mismatches present in banking systems in the run-up to the crisis. Another potentially important pre-crisis condition missing due to data limitations is data on interbank turnover, which could capture the serious market disruption that occurred in many countries and differentiate more clearly between different types of market structures that could have played a role in the propagation of the crisis.

International real linkages: The financial crisis literature stresses the importance of international trade as a key channel of crisis contagion. With the global recession causing a sharp decline in global demand, the spill-over effects can be expected to be greater in countries with closer ties to the global economy (cf. Levchenko, Lewis and Tesar, 2009; Rose and Spiegel, 2009b). We therefore add as a third set of explanatory variables five different measures of macroeconomic exposure to external shocks through trade linkages. We include trade openness and the correlation between the domestic and global output gaps to capture the effects of trade intensity, the share of manufacturing exports in total merchandise exports to capture possible additional effects through the composition of trade and measures of trade diversification and concentration to capture the possible effects of trade patterns on the transmission of the global shock to the domestic economy.

International financial linkages: The fourth set of explanatory variables captures the extent of countries' linkages with the international financial system. Closer financial links are likely to have enhanced the spill-over of the financial shock to domestic financial systems (cf. Davis, 2008; Rose and Spiegel, 2009b). But it can also be argued that stronger ties to the global financial system may facilitate a more rapid recovery from the crisis through greater access to global finance once the crisis hit. Following Kose, Prasad and Terrones (2009), we measure financial openness by the sum of foreign assets and liabilities as a share of GDP (a higher ratio can imply greater exposure to global financial disruptions but, as pointed out by Lane and Milesi-Ferretti, 2011, can also reflect a more internationally diversified asset portfolio which can mitigate a domestic financial crisis). We also include a measure of the extent of capital inflows in the run-up to the crisis (with greater inflows creating greater risks of sudden reversals of capital flows).[7] Finally, we include an indicator variable for participation in the US Federal Reserve's extraordinary US dollar liquidity swap facilities in the autumn of 2008, with participation in this 'global security net' potentially easing US dollar liquidity shortage problems and therefore facilitating smoother domestic cash market operations and easing fears of potential banking and currency crises.

---

[7] We follow Forbes and Chinn (2004) and measure these capital inflows using foreign direct investment (FDI) inflows. These might not be the inflows most vulnerable to these types of reversals, but we were not able to obtain data for the whole-country sample on portfolio flows or bank loans, which are probably more vulnerable, as pointed out by Tong and Wei (2009). Dooley, Fernandez-Arias and Kletzer (1994), however, question this view and find that high levels of FDI tend to be associated with highly variable capital inflows.

Underlying economic volatility: The fifth set of variables includes three measures of underlying economic volatility. In general, greater economic volatility can reflect frequent or large shocks, or poor success in dealing with shocks, e.g. due to weak institutions and lack of credibility. Greater underlying volatility could therefore be expected to make countries more vulnerable to the global crisis. To capture these effects we include the standard deviation of domestic output gaps. We also include the standard deviation of nominal exchange rates, with a more volatile exchange rate possibly reflecting underlying instability in the economy, high and volatile inflation and the lack of credibility and transparency of monetary policy (e.g. Kuttner and Posen, 2000). A more volatile exchange rate may, however, also reflect greater exchange rate flexibility that can help mitigate economic shocks and facilitate a more rapid recovery through improved competitiveness of the domestic economy due to depreciation of the domestic currency.[8] But not all currency movements serve to facilitate economic adjustment. As a final variable capturing underlying economic volatility, we therefore also add a measure of the non-fundamental part of exchange rate volatility from Pétursson (2010).

Economic imbalances and vulnerabilities: The sixth set of initial conditions includes variables capturing macroeconomic conditions just before the crisis hit. The idea is that the larger the macroeconomic imbalances, the more vulnerable the economy is to adverse changes in financial and economic conditions. This is a well-known characteristic of financial crises. Barajas, Dell'Ariccia and Levchenko (2009) show, for example, that large macroeconomic imbalances tend to increase the probability of a crisis. They also find that the larger the imbalances, the longer the contraction following the crisis tends to be. To capture these imbalances in the run-up to the crisis, we include inflation (with higher inflation possibly reflecting greater demand pressures, less anchored inflation expectations, poorer policy institutions and less ability to use monetary stimulus to mitigate the crisis), the current account balance (with larger deficits increasing the vulnerability to sudden capital flow reversals), financial leverage (with higher leverage increasing the vulnerability of domestic balance sheets to sudden asset price reversals and refinancing risk), two measures of the underlying vulnerabilities of the fiscal authority (with higher budget deficits reducing the fiscal space to mitigate the crisis and higher government debt possibly exacerbating the crisis through rising

---

[8] This shock-absorber role of a flexible exchange rate may be limited in practice, however, if currency mismatches are widespread, as non-financial private sector or public sector balance sheets will be dealt a heavy blow by the depreciation, causing widespread repayment problems and write-downs of banks' assets. Data limitations prevent us from including these currency mismatches in the analysis.

risk premia) and central bank foreign reserves (with low levels of reserves limiting the ability of the monetary authority to support the domestic currency and provide liquidity support during the US dollar liquidity shortage).[9]

Institutional factors: One can expect countries with stronger institutions to be better able to cope with crisis situations and in general to deliver a more stable macroeconomic environment (cf. Acemoglu *et al.*, 2003), which may also make countries less vulnerable to crisis as discussed on p. 31. The seventh set of initial conditions therefore includes ten variables capturing different institutional aspects. We include four different measures of institutional quality and four measures of market flexibility. We also include two indicator variables capturing past crisis experience. It is often argued that countries that have experienced such crises in the past tend to learn from earlier mistakes and prevent such vulnerabilities from building up again. But, at the same time, recurring crises may reflect weak institutions and lack of credibility, which means a long time to recover. Hence, past crisis experience can make countries more vulnerable to rapid loss of confidence once a new crisis occurs.

Monetary and exchange rate regimes: It is often argued that the exchange rate regime played a key role in the current crisis. Thus, some have argued that euro membership was crucial in preventing a complete collapse in Ireland, Malta and some of the Southern European countries, while others have argued that the flexible exchange rate regime played a key role in the banking collapse and large contraction in activity experienced in Iceland. On the other hand, some have highlighted the benefit of a flexible exchange rate for supporting the post-crisis recovery, while others have argued that the strong focus on inflation control that comes with the IT regime played an important detrimental role in the build-up of vulnerabilities in the run-up to the financial crisis in some of the IT countries, with Iceland a particular case in point. We therefore also include indicator variables capturing different monetary and exchange rate regimes within the country sample with the aim of analysing to what extent different regimes played a role in the crisis after controlling for the initial conditions discussed on pp. 28–32.[10]

---

[9] See, for example, Fratzscher (2009), and Obstfeld, Shambaugh and Taylor (2009). The size of foreign reserves was, however, to a certain extent made less important for countries with access to international swap lines. Of the main international centres, the euro area, the UK, Switzerland and Australia would have depleted a substantial fraction of their foreign currency reserves if they had had to provide foreign currency liquidity out of their reserves without the use of central bank swap lines, according to Allen and Moessner (2010).

[10] For example, Berkmen *et al.* (2009) find evidence that countries with exchange rate pegs experienced a more severe contraction than countries with more flexible exchange

3   Empirical results

In this section, we move on to analyse the relevance of different initial conditions in explaining the depth and duration of the output and consumption contraction, using cross-country regressions, and the probability of systemic banking and currency crises, using cross-country probit regressions. Subsections 3.1 and 3.2 report the main results, while subsection 3.3 reports some sensitivity analysis. The economic interpretation of the main results is relegated to subsection 3.4.

Note that the explanatory variables pre-date the crisis and the analysis is therefore an attempt to identify what factors were important in predicting the depth and duration of the contraction and whether countries experienced a banking or a currency crisis, or both. Furthermore, with the large number of potential explanatory variables included in this study and limited guidance from theory on exactly what factors to include, we necessarily had to undertake some experimentation before arriving at the preferred baseline specifications presented. Thus, all the potential variables were tested but only those found to be statistically significant at conventional levels were retained.

3.1   The real-economy effects of the crisis

Tables 3.2–3.5 present the main results, i.e. the preferred baseline specifications and the marginal contributions of additional dummy variables for different monetary and exchange rate regimes. As the tables show, we are able to explain up to three-quarters of the cross-country variation in output and consumption loss with a limited set of pre-crisis indicators. Thus, we immediately obtain the important result that initial conditions have mattered in this crisis, in contrast to the conclusions drawn by Rose and Spiegel (2009a, 2009b) and Claessens *et al.* (2010).[11]

The depth of the contraction
The macro channel seems to have played a particularly important role in determining the depth of the real-economy contraction during the current crisis, through both macroeconomic volatility and macroeconomic

---

rate regimes. Against this, the results in Coulibaly (2009) indicate that countries within currency unions are less likely to experience a currency crisis.

[11] As Tables 3.2–3.5 show, we are only able to explain one-third to half of the cross-country variation in crisis duration. That we are able to explain less of the country variation in crisis duration than crisis depth probably reflects the fact that the variation in duration across countries is smaller than the variation in depth. Again, this may reflect the fact that the crisis is still being played out in some countries and greater variation in the duration of the crisis can be expected once the crisis is fully completed.

Table 3.2: *Regression results for the depth of the output contraction*

	Specification				
	(1)	(2)	(3)	(4)	(5)
Constant	−0.093	−0.096	−0.086	−0.089	−0.084
	(0.002)	(0.001)	(0.002)	(0.002)	(0.004)
	[0.001]	[0.001]	[0.001]	[0.001]	[0.002]
Output correlation	0.066	0.063	0.055	0.069	0.060
	(0.030)	(0.048)	(0.055)	(0.023)	(0.050)
	[0.023]	[0.021]	[0.042]	[0.016]	[0.044]
Output volatility	2.981	3.016	2.941	2.754	2.909
	(0.001)	(0.001)	(0.001)	(0.002)	(0.001)
	[0.002]	[0.001]	[0.001]	[0.003]	[0.002]
Exchange rate variability	−0.905	−0.872	−0.700	−0.866	−0.794
	(0.002)	(0.003)	(0.012)	(0.002)	(0.007)
	[0.013]	[0.019]	[0.047]	[0.012]	[0.025]
Inflation rate	1.562	1.553	1.406	1.453	1.463
	(0.000)	(0.000)	(0.000)	(0.000)	(0.000)
	[0.002]	[0.002]	[0.002]	[0.003]	[0.003]
Financial leverage	0.023	0.024	0.028	0.022	0.025
	(0.012)	(0.012)	(0.002)	(0.017)	(0.008)
	[0.001]	[0.001]	[0.004]	[0.011]	[0.002]
EMU dummy		0.005			
		(0.661)			
		[0.617]			
Inflation targeting dummy			−0.025		
			(0.014)		
			[0.022]		
Exchange rate peg dummy				0.019	
				(0.200)	
				[0.263]	
Floating exchange rate dummy					−0.014
					(0.200)
					[0.148]
R^2	0.726	0.728	0.766	0.738	0.738
Standard error	0.032	0.033	0.030	0.032	0.032

Notes: Numbers in parenthesis are p-values based on conventional standard errors, while numbers in brackets are p-values based on robust (White) standard errors.

imbalances in the run-up to the crisis. This is especially true for inflation which seems to capture factors that were crucial in determining how large the contraction in output and consumption turned out to be. The baseline results (specification (1) in Tables 3.2 and 3.3) suggest that a

Table 3.3: *Regression results for the depth of the consumption contraction*

	Specification				
	(1)	(2)	(3)	(4)	(5)
Constant	−0.089	−0.081	−0.081	−0.083	−0.077
	(0.000)	(0.002)	(0.000)	(0.000)	(0.001)
	[0.000]	[0.000]	[0.000]	[0.000]	[0.002]
Size of banking system	0.013	0.013	0.013	0.013	0.013
	(0.004)	(0.003)	(0.002)	(0.001)	(0.004)
	[0.000]	[0.000]	[0.003]	[0.002]	[0.006]
Inflation rate	2.368	2.291	2.403	1.811	2.320
	(0.000)	(0.000)	(0.000)	(0.000)	(0.000)
	[0.001]	[0.001]	[0.000]	[0.001]	[0.000]
Current account balance	−0.248	−0.261	−0.219	−0.240	−0.222
	(0.009)	(0.007)	(0.017)	(0.003)	(0.017)
	[0.032]	[0.031]	[0.046]	[0.019]	[0.047]
Past banking crisis	0.033	0.029	0.040	0.031	0.039
	(0.094)	(0.148)	(0.039)	(0.064)	(0.046)
	[0.018]	[0.033]	[0.005]	[0.011]	[0.008]
EMU dummy		−0.014			
		(0.415)			
		[0.190]			
Inflation targeting dummy			−0.032		
			(0.034)		
			[0.040]		
Exchange rate peg dummy				0.078	
				(0.000)	
				[0.002]	
Floating exchange rate dummy					−0.027
					(0.081)
					[0.099]
R^2	0.704	0.708	0.735	0.794	0.726
Standard error	0.050	0.050	0.048	0.042	0.049

Notes: Numbers in parenthesis are p-values based on conventional standard errors, while numbers in brackets are p-values based on robust (White) standard errors.

1 percentage point higher inflation prior to the crisis was associated with a 1.6 percentage point deeper contraction in output and a 2.4 percentage point deeper contraction in consumption, respectively. The baseline results also suggest that output volatility had a sizeable effect, with a 1 percentage point higher standard deviation in the output gap associated with a 3 percentage point larger output contraction. There are also effects

from private sector leverage, with a 10 percentage point higher leverage relative to GDP associated with a 0.2 percentage point deeper contraction in output. However, a more flexible exchange rate seems to have contributed to a smaller output contraction: a 1 percentage point higher standard deviation of the effective nominal exchange rate was associated with a 0.9 percentage point smaller contraction in output. The macro channel also had an effect on the consumption contraction through the current account balance, with the baseline results in Table 3.3 implying that a 10 percentage point better current account position leading to the crisis was associated with a 2.5 percentage point smaller consumption contraction.

There is also a role for the trade and financial channels in determining the extent of the output and consumption contractions. Thus, closer ties to the world economy, in the form of a 0.1 higher correlation of the domestic and world business cycle, were associated with a 0.7 percentage point deeper output contraction, while countries with bigger banking systems tended to have a larger consumption contraction: a country with a banking system that was 100 percentage points of GDP larger than the average country tended to have a 1.3 percentage point larger contraction in consumption. In addition, we find that countries which had experienced a systemic banking crisis in the past tended to have a 3.3 percentage point larger consumption contraction compared to countries which had not experienced such a crisis in the past thirty years.

Finally, our results suggest that countries with some kind of unilateral exchange rate pegs were hit particularly hard by the crisis, while we find no significant additional effects for the EMU countries. Countries with floating exchange rates came out better, in particular if they also had a formal inflation target. Thus, countries outside EMU with an exchange rate peg experienced an almost 8 percentage point larger contraction in consumption compared to other countries, while countries with an inflation target tended to have a 2.5 percentage point smaller contraction in output and 3.2 percentage point smaller contraction in consumption.

The duration of the contraction

We also find that the macro channel played a key role in determining the duration of the crisis (specification (1) in Tables 3.4 and 3.5). Again, we find that higher inflation in the run-up to the crisis is reflected in a more protracted economic impact, with a 1 percentage point higher inflation being associated with a contraction in output roughly 0.3 quarters longer and a contraction in consumption 0.5 quarters longer, respectively. Higher government debt prior to the crisis also seems to have been associated with a longer output contraction: a 10 percentage point higher

Table 3.4: *Regression results for the duration of the output contraction*

	Specification				
	(1)	(2)	(3)	(4)	(5)
Constant	2.465	2.548	2.598	2.477	2.432
	(0.000)	(0.000)	(0.000)	(0.000)	(0.002)
	[0.001]	[0.001]	[0.001]	[0.001]	[0.004]
Trade openness	−0.719	−0.740	−0.749	−0.794	−0.717
	(0.040)	(0.034)	(0.037)	(0.024)	(0.044)
	[0.048]	[0.013]	[0.023]	[0.014]	[0.025]
Financial openness	0.030	0.033	0.029	0.029	0.030
	(0.000)	(0.000)	(0.000)	(0.000)	(0.001)
	[0.000]	[0.000]	[0.000]	[0.000]	[0.000]
Capital inflows	7.220	7.812	7.144	6.932	7.288
	(0.002)	(0.001)	(0.003)	(0.003)	(0.003)
	[0.001]	[0.000]	[0.000]	[0.000]	[0.001]
Exchange rate variability	−26.148	−30.116	−25.069	−25.895	−26.507
	(0.001)	(0.000)	(0.002)	(0.001)	(0.001)
	[0.001]	[0.000]	[0.000]	[0.000]	[0.000]
Inflation rate	30.110	30.825	28.886	26.172	30.412
	(0.001)	(0.001)	(0.002)	(0.005)	(0.002)
	[0.001]	[0.000]	[0.001]	[0.003]	[0.000]
Government debt	1.382	1.587	1.313	1.561	1.389
	(0.014)	(0.007)	(0.025)	(0.007)	(0.016)
	[0.002]	[0.003]	[0.020]	[0.004]	[0.013]
Past currency crisis	0.730	0.793	0.737	0.726	0.735
	(0.039)	(0.026)	(0.040)	(0.037)	(0.042)
	[0.061]	[0.036]	[0.061]	[0.061]	[0.055]
EMU dummy		−0.457			
		(0.205)			
		[0.156]			
Inflation targeting dummy			−0.124		
			(0.701)		
			[0.682]		
Exchange rate peg dummy				0.649	
				(0.151)	
				[0.146]	
Floating exchange rate dummy					0.040
					(0.905)
					[0.898]
R^2	0.494	0.515	0.495	0.521	0.494
Standard error	0.930	0.922	0.941	0.916	0.942

Notes: Numbers in parenthesis are p-values based on conventional standard errors, while numbers in brackets are p-values based on robust (White) standard errors.

Table 3.5: *Regression results for the duration of the consumption contraction*

	Specification				
	(1)	(2)	(3)	(4)	(5)
Constant	2.195	2.187	2.371	2.271	2.443
	(0.000)	(0.000)	(0.000)	(0.000)	(0.000)
	[0.000]	[0.000]	[0.000]	[0.000]	[0.000]
Exchange rate variability	−20.742	−20.643	−16.695	−19.857	−15.916
	(0.022)	(0.035)	(0.074)	(0.024)	(0.093)
	[0.012]	[0.017]	[0.033]	[0.018]	[0.044]
Inflation rate	46.381	46.391	43.983	37.925	42.350
	(0.000)	(0.000)	(0.000)	(0.001)	(0.000)
	[0.000]	[0.000]	[0.000]	[0.000]	[0.000]
EMU dummy		0.012			
		(0.977)			
		[0.977]			
Inflation targeting dummy			−0.535		
			(0.175)		
			[0.127]		
Exchange rate peg dummy				1.038	
				(0.058)	
				[0.017]	
Floating exchange rate dummy					−0.547
					(0.168)
					[0.120]
R^2	0.358	0.358	0.386	0.411	0.386
Standard error	1.237	1.252	1.224	1.198	1.223

Notes: Numbers in parenthesis are *p*-values based on conventional standard errors, while numbers in brackets are *p*-values based on robust (White) standard errors.

debt ratio was associated with a contraction in output 0.1 quarters longer. Just as with the depth of the crisis, we find that greater exchange rate variability tended to be associated with a more rapid recovery: a 1 percentage point higher standard deviation in the nominal exchange rate was associated with a contraction in output 0.3 quarters shorter and a contraction in consumption 0.2 quarters shorter. We also find some role for the financial channel in determining the length of the output contraction. Thus, the more financially open countries tended to experience a somewhat longer contraction, although the effects are quite small. For example, increasing our measure of financial openness by 100 percentage points of GDP lengthens the contraction in output by 0.03 quarters. There are also negative effects from the extent of capital inflows: increasing the ratio of capital inflows to GDP by 10 percentage points is associated with a contraction in output 0.7 quarters longer. However, we find that countries more open to trade experienced a shorter output contraction: increasing the share of trade to GDP by 10 percentage points reduces the duration of the output contraction by 0.1 quarters. The results also indicate that countries which have experienced a currency crisis in the past tended to have a contraction in output 0.7 quarters longer than countries which had not experienced such a crisis in the past thirty years.

Finally, we find no additional effects from the monetary and exchange rate regime dummies, except that countries with unilateral exchange rate pegs experienced a 1 quarter longer consumption contraction than countries with floating exchange rates or a peg within EMU.

3.2   The probability of a banking and currency crisis

To estimate the probability of a systemic banking or currency crisis, we estimate a multivariate ordered probit model. Tables 3.6–3.8 report the results for a banking, currency and twin crisis, respectively.[12] Since probit coefficients are difficult to interpret, we report the marginal effects measured as the effects of a one-unit change in the regressors on the probability of a crisis, evaluated at the mean of the data.[13] However, for binary regressors, we report the effect of a change from 0 to 1 on the probability of a crisis. For the twin-crisis specification, we only report the marginal effects on the probability of a banking or currency crisis, as the marginal effects on the probability of a twin crisis were extremely small, with twin crises found to be highly unlikely in this dataset. The marginal effects on the probability of no crisis were therefore practically identical (but with opposite signs) to the marginal effects of either a banking or currency crisis. Tables 3.6–3.8 also report some diagnostic statistics, including success in correctly predicting a crisis (using a cut-off point of 50 per cent) and a measure of improvement over a simple constant-probability model (a probit model which only includes a constant).

[12] For the banking and currency crisis specifications, the indicator variable takes on the value 1 if a banking (currency) crisis occurs and 0 otherwise. For the twin-crisis specification the indicator variable takes on the value 0 if neither a banking nor currency crisis occurs, 1 if either a banking or currency crisis occurs and 2 if a twin crisis occurs. We also tried separating the banking and currency crisis incidence in the crisis indicator (thus allowing four mutually exclusive outcomes: no crisis, a banking crisis, a currency crisis and a twin crisis). The results obtained were very similar to those reported. In particular, the same variables remained significant in both specifications.
[13] For single-digit percentages the unit change is measured as a rise of 1 percentage point, while for double-digit or higher percentages the unit change is a rise of 10 percentage points. For GDP *per capita* the unit change is a rise of $1,000.

Table 3.6: *Probit estimates of the likelihood of a banking crisis*

	Specification				
	(1)	(2)	(3)	(4)	(5)
Constant	−18.358	−22.200	−30.500	−19.932	−30.594
	(0.002)	(0.002)	(0.003)	(0.009)	(0.007)
Log of GDP *per capita*	4.050	4.895	6.972	4.526	7.213
	[2.25]	[2.14]	[0.66]	[1.31]	[0.74]
	(0.006)	(0.005)	(0.003)	(0.019)	(0.013)
Size of banking system	0.645	0.694	1.108	0.604	0.802
	[0.98]	[0.83]	[0.29]	[0.48]	[0.23]
	(0.001)	(0.000)	(0.019)	(0.000)	(0.001)
Inflation rate	81.585	96.780	133.488	78.020	126.755
	[12.41]	[11.63]	[3.46]	[6.19]	[3.58]
	(0.001)	(0.001)	(0.009)	(0.007)	(0.004)
Size of foreign reserves	−3.214	−2.770	−4.772	−6.001	−4.501
	[−4.89]	[−3.33]	[−1.24]	[−4.76]	[−1.27]
	(0.053)	(0.083)	(0.017)	(0.065)	(0.016)
EMU dummy		0.586			
		[8.18]			
		(0.414)			
Inflation targeting dummy			−2.276		
			[−8.10]		
			(0.018)		
Exchange rate peg dummy				1.684	
				[32.39]	
				(0.126)	
Floating exchange rate dummy				−1.538	
				[−5.78]	
				(0.047)	
Log-likelihood	−11.706	−11.437	−8.592	−10.491	−10.031
Pseudo R^2	0.573	0.582	0.686	0.617	0.634
Cases correct	37	39	41	41	39
% gain	0.308	0.462	0.615	0.615	0.462

Notes: Numbers in brackets are marginal effects of a one-unit change in the explanatory variables on the probability of a banking crisis (× 100 to convert into percentages), evaluated at the mean of the data, except when reporting the marginal effects for the dummy variables, in which case the numbers are the effects of a change from 0 to 1 on the probability of a banking crisis. Numbers in parenthesis are *p*-values based on robust (Hubert–White) standard errors. Cases correct show the number of cases predicted correctly by each model, using a cut-off point of 50 per cent, while the % gain shows the % of incorrect cases predicted by a simple constant-probability specification corrected by each model.

Table 3.7: *Probit estimates of the likelihood of a currency crisis*

	Parameter estimate	Marginal effect	p-value
Constant	−20.558	−	0.004
log of GDP *per capita*	5.471	2.10E-7	0.002
Size of banking system	1.040	1.10E-7	0.005
Exchange rate variability	62.843	6.63E-7	0.003
Fiscal balances	−40.440	−4.27E-7	0.005
Central bank independence	−13.353	−1.41E-7	0.016
Past banking crisis	7.402	0.89	0.003
Log-likelihood	−3.075		
Pseudo R^2	0.626		
Cases correct	45		
% gain	0.500		

Notes: The table reports the marginal effects of a one-unit change in the explanatory variables on the probability of a currency crisis ($\times$ 100 to convert into percentages), evaluated at the mean of the data, except when reporting the marginal effects for 'Past banking crisis', in which case the number is the effect of a change from 0 to 1 on the probability of a currency crisis. The p-values are based on robust (Hubert–White) standard errors. Cases correct show the number of cases predicted correctly by the model, using a cut-off point of 50 per cent, while the % gain shows the % of incorrect cases predicted by a simple constant-probability specification corrected by the model.

Before proceeding to individual results, it is important to note that the estimation results for the incidence of currency crisis need to be interpreted with some caution as the frequency of such crises is very low in the country sample (two currency crises and one twin crisis). These results should therefore be considered merely indicative. This is much less of a problem for the estimation of a banking crisis, where there are thirteen crisis observations (28 per cent of the sample).

Determinants of a banking crisis

The variables that significantly predict a systemic banking crisis are reported in Table 3.6. First, higher GDP *per capita* is associated with a higher probability of a banking crisis. This finding simply reflects the fact that there was a higher frequency of banking failures in the current financial crisis among higher-income countries and it therefore has no obvious structural implication. More interestingly, a larger banking system prior to the crisis is found to have been associated with a higher probability of a banking crisis. The marginal effect in the baseline specification (specification (1)) suggests that a 10 percentage point increase in the ratio of banking system assets to GDP increased the probability of a banking crisis by 1 percentage point. Higher pre-crisis inflation is also

Table 3.8 *Probit estimates of the likelihood of a banking, currency, or twin crisis*

	Specification				
	(1)	(2)	(3)	(4)	(5)
Log of GDP *per capita*	5.490	5.458	5.696	6.103	5.822
	[4.38]	[4.40]	[4.22]	[4.12]	[4.21]
	(0.000)	(0.000)	(0.001)	(0.001)	(0.003)
Financial deepening	−0.471	−0.463	−0.556	−0.633	−0.558
	[−1.03]	[−1.02]	[−1.14]	[−1.17]	[−1.11]
	(0.023)	(0.038)	(0.055)	(0.029)	(0.059)
Size of banking system	0.545	0.544	0.554	0.506	0.542
	[1.19]	[1.20]	[1.13]	[0.94]	[1.07]
	(0.002)	(0.002)	(0.006)	(0.001)	(0.006)
Exchange rate variability	29.566	29.093	31.827	31.700	32.462
	[6.47]	[6.43]	[6.47]	[5.87]	[6.44]
	(0.017)	(0.023)	(0.014)	(0.013)	(0.017)
Inflation rate	56.909	56.163	56.876	46.700	56.964
	[12.45]	[12.41]	[11.54]	[8.65]	[11.29]
	(0.014)	(0.020)	(0.023)	(0.015)	(0.032)
Fiscal balances	−14.814	−15.154	−14.233	−20.175	−14.995
	[−3.24]	[−3.35]	[−2.89]	[−3.74]	[−2.97]
	(0.010)	(0.006)	(0.010)	(0.008)	(0.010)
Threshold level 1	22.633	22.447	23.188	24.449	23.560
	(0.000)	(0.000)	(0.001)	(0.000)	(0.002)
Threshold level 2	27.539	27.319	28.100	28.860	28.515
	(0.000)	(0.000)	(0.001)	(0.000)	(0.002)
EMU dummy		−0.097			
		[−2.11]			
		(0.883)			
Inflation targeting dummy			−0.505		
			[−9.84]		
			(0.495)		
Exchange rate peg dummy				1.291	
				[36.00]	
				(0.151)	
Floating exchange rate dummy					−0.448
					[−8.81]
					(0.527)
Log-likelihood		−14.185	−14.176	−13.831	−13.294	−13.907
Pseudo R^2		0.555	0.555	0.566	0.583	0.564

Table 3.8: (*cont.*)

	Specification				
	(1)	(2)	(3)	(4)	(5)
Cases correct	39	39	40	41	40
% gain	0.500	0.500	0.571	0.643	0.571

Notes: Numbers in brackets are marginal effects of a one-unit change in the explanatory variables on the probability of a banking or a currency crisis (× 100 to convert into percentages), evaluated at the mean of the data, except when reporting the marginal effects for the dummy variables, in which case the numbers are the effects of a change from 0 to 1 on the probability of a banking or a currency crisis. The marginal effects on the probability of a twin crisis are extremely small and therefore not reported. The marginal effects on the probability of no crisis are therefore practically the same as the marginal effects on the probability of either banking or currency crisis, but with reversed signs. Numbers in parenthesis are *p*-values based on robust (Hubert–White) standard errors. Cases correct show the number of cases predicted correctly by each model, using a cut-off point of 50 per cent, while the % gain shows the % of incorrect cases predicted by a simple constant-probability specification corrected by each model.

associated with a higher probability of a banking crisis: the baseline specification suggests that a 1 percentage point higher inflation in the run-up to the crisis raised the probability of a banking crisis by 12 percentage points. Finally, a higher level of foreign reserves relative to GDP is found to decrease the probability of a banking crisis, with the marginal effects suggesting that a 10 percentage point higher ratio of reserves to GDP reduced the probability of a banking crisis by almost 5 percentage points.

Table 3.6 also reports the effects of adding dummy variables for different monetary regimes. The dummy variables for EMU membership and countries with unilateral exchange rate pegs are not found to be significant, but the dummy variables for IT countries and floating exchange rate countries are found significant at the 5 per cent critical level. The results suggest that the probability of a banking crisis was 8 percentage points lower for the IT countries than for the non-IT countries, other things equal, while the probability was almost 6 percentage points lower for the floating exchange rate countries in general. Note also that the original regressors remain highly significant although the marginal effects decline somewhat when the regime dummies are added.

Determinants of a currency crisis

Table 3.7 reports the variables that significantly predict a currency crisis. It should, however, be noted from the outset that with only two observations of currency crisis, these results by and large pick up the difference between Iceland and Korea, on the one hand, and the whole-country sample, on the other. Sweeping conclusions cannot therefore be drawn. That said, we again find that GDP *per capita* needs to be included as a control variable. A larger banking system is also associated with a higher probability of a currency crisis. There are also positive effects on the probability of a currency crisis from greater exchange rate flexibility and higher fiscal deficits prior to the crisis. However, better institutions, as reflected in greater central bank independence and lower incidence of past banking crises, are found to be associated with a lower proba-bility of a currency crisis in the current episode. With the probability of a currency crisis extremely low, the marginal effects of changes in the explanatory variables are found to be very small, as shown in Table 3.7. Furthermore, note that we are not able to add the regime dummies as the maximum likelihood procedure breaks down with the probit model perfectly predicting the binary variable.

Determinants of a twin crisis
Finally, Table 3.8 reports the significant variables predicting a twin crisis. As for the previous two crisis variables, GDP *per capita* is needed as a control variable. The size of the banking system and the level of inflation are positively associated with a twin crisis, with similar marginal effects as those found for the baseline specification on the probability of a banking crisis in Table 3.6. Greater exchange rate variability and higher fiscal deficits are also associated with a higher probability of a currency crisis, as in the findings in Table 3.7, with a 1 percentage point increase in these variables raising the probability of a banking or currency crisis by 6 and 3 percentage points, respectively. However, a 10 percentage point increase in financial deepening is found to have reduced the probability of a banking or currency crisis by roughly 1 percentage point. Finally, none of the regime dummies is found to be significant.

Estimated banking and currency crisis probabilities
The probit models are quite successful in predicting the banking and currency crises correctly. The three baseline specifications (specification (1)) predict the incidences correctly in 80–98 per cent of the cases (using a cut-off point of 50 per cent), sometimes with some improvements when the regime dummies are added. The baseline specifications also show a significant improvement over a simple constant-probability alternative, with the percentage gain ranging from 30 to 50 per cent. The models are also generally able to make a sharp distinction between crisis and

non-crisis countries: the crisis probabilities lie above 90 per cent or below 10 per cent in 59–91 per cent of the cases and above 80 per cent and below 20 per cent in 76–96 per cent of the cases.

The banking crisis regression in Table 3.6 correctly predicts a banking crisis in Belgium, Iceland, Ireland, Latvia, Luxembourg, the Netherlands and Switzerland with close to 100 per cent probability and in the UK with the slightly lower probability of 70 per cent. The model predicts a banking crisis in Austria and the US with just short of 50 per cent probability, and assigns an even lower probability to a banking crisis in Denmark (34 per cent), Russia (23 per cent) and Germany (18 per cent). There are also a few cases of false warnings: the model predicts a banking crisis in Sweden with a 70 per cent probability and a banking crisis in Estonia, Hungary and Norway with a probability just above 50 per cent.[14] A somewhat smaller probability is assigned to a crisis in Spain (31 per cent).[15] However, only four (Denmark, Germany, Russia and Sweden) of the residuals are found to be significantly different from zero.

The currency crisis regression in Table 3.7 predicts a currency crisis in Iceland with a 93 per cent probability, but fails to predict the currency crisis in Korea (only 15 per cent probability). It also incorrectly assigns quite a high probability of a currency crisis in Israel (43 per cent) and Bulgaria (23 per cent) – but only the prediction errors for Korea and Israel are found to be significant at the 95 per cent critical level.

Finally, the probit specification for the twin crisis in Table 3.8 is better able to predict the banking crisis in Austria, Russia, the UK and the US than the banking crisis specification in Table 3.6, but seems less certain about the crisis in Latvia. For other countries, the crisis predictions are very similar to those from the banking crisis specification. Of the false banking crisis predictions, the high probabilities of a banking crisis in Hungary and Sweden remain, but the probabilities for Estonia, Norway and Spain decline substantially. Against this, the model incorrectly predicts a crisis in Bulgaria with a 54 per cent probability. Furthermore, the

---

[14] Allen and Moessner (2010) doubt that Sweden and Denmark could have provided effective support to their banks in the absence of swap lines from the Fed after the Lehmans failure and from the ECB a little later, as the necessary provision of foreign currency liquidity would have used up most of their reserves. Swedish banks in Estonia received support from their mother companies and the Swedish Riksbank set up swap lines with their Estonian counterpart. Hungary did turn to the IMF and the EU for considerable support and the ECB and Swiss National Bank set up swap facilities with the Hungarian central bank to provide commercial banks within the country with access to euro and Swiss franc liquidity.

[15] Problems among Spanish saving banks became clear in May 2010, outside of our sample period, when the Bank of Spain seized control of CajaSur and merger plans among the remaining Cajas intensified.

false currency crisis in Israel has disappeared. Finally, the model predicts the twin crisis in Iceland correctly, with a 79 per cent probability.

3.3   Robustness tests

We try various alterations to the empirical set-up to test how robust our results are. First we try retaining the GDP level and GDP *per capita* as controls throughout to capture the greater incidence of the crisis in higher-income countries and smaller countries, as discussed on pp. 28–29. In no case does the inference on other explanatory variables change. With a relatively large number of small countries in our sample, it could also be the case that the small countries are given unduly large weights in the empirical findings, thus somewhat blurring how the global crisis spread from its epicentre in the US to other large countries. To test for the sensitivity of our results to a possible small-country bias we therefore re-estimate all the regressions using weighted least squares, with the log of GDP as a scaling variable. However, we find that our results are insensitive to this and in no case is the inference altered. Neither does adding different country group dummy variables, capturing different regions and continents, different income and size groups, and different country types (see the Working Paper version of the chapter for more detail).

We also re-estimate all the baseline regressions, dropping one observation at a time, and check whether the explanatory variables continue to be significant. We find that they do in almost all cases. There are, however, four exceptions: dropping Hong Kong from the sample makes foreign reserves insignificant in the bank crisis equation, dropping Luxembourg from the sample makes financial openness insignificant in the output duration equation and financial deepening insignificant in the twin-crisis equation, and dropping Norway from the sample makes fiscal balances insignificant in the twin-crisis equation. We also do a similar sensitivity analysis for the regime dummies. The inference on the IT and exchange rate peg dummies is found to be robust to variations in the country sample, whereas the dummy variable for floating exchange rate countries becomes marginally insignificant in the consumption loss equation in some cases. However, leaving out Iceland in the consumption loss equation results in a highly significant dummy variable for floating exchange rate countries.

3.4   Interpreting the results

In this section we offer an interpretation of the key results of our chapter. Before proceeding it should, however, be emphasised that this study is not a general analysis of financial, banking, or currency crises, but focuses only on the current crisis and its consequences. Therefore, some of the results found in this chapter may be specific to this crisis and may not generalise to others. However, there are some interesting results worth highlighting that may be relevant to understanding not only this crisis but financial crises in general, and may have some important policy implications.

One of the most striking results we obtain is how strong the effects of inflation just prior to the crisis seem to be, with the inflation effect generally the most significant of all the initial conditions. Thus, countries with higher inflation tended to experience a deeper and more protracted contraction, and were more vulnerable to the risk of systemic banking and currency crises. We believe that this inflation effect captures the degree of macroeconomic imbalances in the run-up to the crisis and the policy constraints that countries faced in their response to it. The scope for monetary policy easing and its transmission to the real economy is affected by current inflationary pressures and the extent to which inflation expectations are sufficiently anchored. Countries with higher inflation in the run-up to the crisis were therefore likely to be in a less favourable position to use monetary stimulus measures to counteract the economic impact of the global crisis than countries where inflation was already well anchored.[16]

Looking at other measures of economic imbalances and vulnerabilities, the general story emerges that the greater the macroeconomic imbalances in the run-up to the crisis, the more painful it turned out to be. Higher private sector leverage, larger current account deficits,[17] more output volatility, or lower foreign reserves all seemed to contribute in one way or another to a deeper contraction and an increased risk of a systemic banking crisis. It is interesting to note that the level of foreign reserves

[16] This finding on the importance of inflation could be interpreted as being at odds with the recent recommendation of the IMF's chief economist, Olivier Blanchard, and his co-authors (Blanchard, Dell'Ariccia and Mauro, 2010), who suggest that higher inflation targets, and therefore higher average inflation, make crisis responses easier by increasing the scope for lowering interest rates to counteract the crisis. Our results suggest that higher inflation in the run-up to this crisis made it worse, not better, and these results seem robust to different crisis measures and various robustness checks. In particular, it is worth emphasising that they are not driven by a few observations of extremely high inflation (the highest observed inflation in our sample is 10 per cent and the average inflation rate across the country sample is 3.4 per cent).

[17] Interestingly, we find that higher current account deficits tend to exacerbate the consumption contraction but have no effects on the output contraction. This seems logical as higher current account deficits call for an adjustment in domestic demand, with a net export adjustment (especially through import compression), reducing the effect on output.

did not have any significant effect on the probability of a currency crisis. Instead, we find that lower reserves increased the risk of a banking crisis, which may reflect the interaction between very large banking systems and the limited ability of the domestic monetary authority to provide foreign currency liquidity services, often pointed out as a major vulnerability during the current crisis. We note, however, that the effect of reserves is not robust to the exclusion of Hong Kong from the country sample and that the interaction between access to central bank swap lines and actual reserve holdings can be difficult to control for.

We also find that the fiscal position played a role. Thus, we find that greater government debt in the run-up to the crisis coincided with a longer output contraction. This seems logical: the worse the debt position of the government, the less the fiscal space for supporting the recovery after the crisis hit. We also find that larger fiscal deficits prior to the crisis tended to increase the risk of a banking or currency crisis. Again, this seems logical: larger deficits tend to go hand in hand with higher risk premia which would presumably rise sharply once the crisis hit and exacerbate uncertainty that could eventually lead to panic and a full-blown currency crisis. The significance of this effect depends, however, on the inclusion of Norway in the country sample.

Furthermore, we also find that the size of the banking system played an important role. First, we find that the larger the banking system, the larger the consumption contraction tended to be. This is consistent with the interpretation that once the crisis hit, governments needing to support large banking systems had less fiscal space to support domestic demand. It can also reflect households' increased dependence on credit for consumption financing in countries with larger banking systems. We also find that larger banking systems increased the probability of banking and currency crises. However, our results suggest that a more developed financial system reduced the risk of a banking or currency crisis. This last finding, however, is not robust to excluding Luxembourg from the country sample.

We find mixed results on whether stronger ties to the global economy through trade and finance exacerbated the crisis or not. Thus, stronger trade and financial linkages coincided with a larger and longer output contraction, as the global financial panic and the sudden reversal of capital inflows and subsequent sharp contraction in global demand hit especially hard those countries which relied more heavily on these capital flows or were more open to trade. The significant effect of financial openness on the persistence of the output contraction is, however, very much driven by the extremely large external balance sheet of Luxembourg, and excluding Luxembourg from the sample leaves this effect insignificant. Thus, any interpretation of a causal link between financial openness and exposure to the global crisis will need to take account of the sensitivity to this large outlier. The significance of capital inflows, however, remains when Luxembourg is excluded from the sample. At the same time, we find that countries more open to trade recovered faster from the crisis. This probably reflects the fact that these countries benefited more from the relatively rapid reversal in global demand (especially in Asia) in 2009 than countries less open to trade.

We also find some mixed results on the role of exchange rate flexibility. While our results suggest that greater exchange rate flexibility reduced both the depth and the duration of the contraction, it increased the risk of a banking or currency crisis. Thus, exchange rate flexibility facilitated the economic adjustment to the crisis through greater relative price flexibility, but at the same time made countries more vulnerable to a banking or currency crisis. Flexibility was thus a double-edged sword in this sense. This is further corroborated by the effects of different unilateral exchange rate regime dummies: we find that countries with unilateral exchange rate pegs had a particularly large and protracted consumption contraction. This, however, only applies to countries with exchange rate pegs outside a monetary union: we find no evidence that EMU membership led to additional negative effects of the crisis comparable to the effects we find for the unilateral peg countries. At the same time we find that countries with a formal inflation target (and sometimes floating exchange rates in general) tended to have smaller contractions and were less likely to have systemic banking crises.[18]

We also find that countries that have experienced a banking or currency crisis in the past tended to have deeper and longer consumption contractions and were more likely to suffer currency crises. Thus, learning from past crises does not seem to have helped in the current crisis or, at least, seems to have been outweighed by the possible negative effects of past crisis experience on the credibility of current institutions to deal with the crisis. The importance of sound institutions is also suggested by our finding that greater central bank independence reduced the probability of a currency crisis. Other institutional factors are not found to be significant, however.

Our results indicate a non-significant role for some variables which have been widely discussed as having played an important role in

---

[18] This is consistent with Carvalho Filho (2010), who also finds beneficial effects of IT during the current crisis.

determining the economic impact of the crisis. Especially, it is note-worthy that we find no role for access to the Fed's dollar liquidity facility in the likelihood of a systemic banking crisis. The establishment of central bank swap lines has been widely praised for having effectively relieved US dollar liquidity stresses in money and foreign exchange swap markets and having prevented global financial instability from becoming much more serious (see e.g. Allen and Moessner, 2010). Our results should, how-ever, not be interpreted as rejecting the importance of these international facilities since we cannot measure what the outcome would have been in their absence. We could also be overlooking the role played by access to central bank swap lines in limiting the scale of a systemic banking cri-sis, as our measurement of banking crises does not make any distinction between a banking crisis and a total banking system collapse. Neither do we find a role for our three measures of trade structure (the share of man-ufacturing exports, trade diversification and trade concentration), which might turn out to be important if the country sample were expanded to include more developing countries.

While our finding that exchange rate flexibility seems to facilitate the real adjustment to the crisis while at the same time increasing the risk of currency crisis is plausible, a comment with respect to the apparent lack of a separate effect of EMU membership is also in order. For example, it is important to keep in mind that the pre-crisis initial conditions are unlikely to be exogenous to the exchange rate regime in a given country. In addition, within a monetary union it is probable that a larger share of external debt and the current account deficit would be in domestic cur-rency and thus less likely to be a source of vulnerability. Furthermore, it seems obvious that EMU membership protected countries against a cur-rency crisis and may thus have helped mitigate the real impact of the crisis through that channel (cf. Cecchetti, Kohler and Upper 2009, who find that output losses tend to be much higher in currency crisis episodes). Finally, as previously mentioned, our measure of banking crises does not discriminate between the size of different banking crises in our sample. It could, for example, be argued that the large banking collapse in Iceland could have been contained to some extent had Iceland been a member of EMU, with stronger institutional support – for example, through the greater ability of the ECB to provide liquidity support.

4   Conclusions

The goal of this chapter is to try to identify which factors were important in determining the macroeconomic impact of the recent global finan-cial crisis, and why some countries experienced systemic banking and currency crises while others escaped more lightly. We do this by identifying a broad set of potential pre-crisis explanatory variables in a cross-section of forty-six medium-to-high-income countries, framed within four possible channels through which the crisis spread out from financial markets through the real economy all over the world: a financial channel, a trade channel, a macro channel and an institutional channel.

We find an important role for the macro channel in the propagation of the shock and the extent of the crisis, through various measures of pre-crisis macroeconomic imbalances and vulnerabilities. Thus, we find that countries which, in the run-up to the crisis, had higher inflation, larger current account deficits, a more leveraged private sector, greater output volatility, or a poorer fiscal position tended to experience some combination of a deeper or more protracted contraction in output or consumption, and were more likely to experience a systemic banking or currency crisis.

We also find an important role for the financial channel. Thus, countries with relatively large banking systems or stronger global financial linkages tended to experience a deeper or longer contraction in output or consumption. In addition we find that large banking systems significantly increased the probability of a systemic banking or currency crisis.

Our results on the trade channel are mixed. While we find that countries with business cycles that were closely connected to the global business cycle experienced a deeper output contraction, we also find that the output contraction tended to be shorter in those countries that were more open to trade.

We also get mixed results for the role of exchange rate flexibility. We find that greater exchange rate flexibility was associated with a smaller and shorter contraction, while at the same time increasing the probability of a currency crisis or a combination of a systemic banking and currency crisis. We also find that countries with unilateral exchange rate pegs had particularly large and protracted consumption contractions, while no comparable evidence is found for EMU countries. This suggests that countries with exchange rate pegs outside a monetary union were particularly vulnerable in the current financial crisis. We also find that countries with a formal inflation target (and sometimes floating exchange rates in general) tended to have a smaller contraction and were less likely to have a systemic banking crisis.

Finally, we find that past experience of a systemic banking or currency crisis had no beneficial effect during this crisis. In fact, our results suggest that past-crisis countries tended to have a deeper and longer contraction and were more likely to suffer a currency crisis. We conclude that the possible positive learning effects from past crises are outweighed by loss of credibility resulting from past crisis experience. We also find some tentative evidence suggesting the importance of institutional quality, in that countries with more independent central banks were less likely to experience a currency crisis.

The policy implications of these results seem clear and perhaps uncontroversial. Thus, the key factors in escaping this global crisis relatively unscathed seem to have been to maintain sound macroeconomic conditions, i.e. prevent large economic imbalances from building up, and stop the banking system getting too large relative to the economy. Our results suggest that economies that achieved this were better able to absorb the financial shock and were faster to recover from the crisis. Exchange rate flexibility also seems to have helped to reduce the real-economy impact and expedite the recovery, but increased the risk of a currency crisis at the same time. Exchange rate flexibility, jointly with a formal inflation target, however, seems to have helped to reduce the risk of a systemic banking crisis. Although we find no significant effects of EMU membership, the fact that the additional negative effects of unilateral exchange rate pegs are not found in the case of EMU countries suggests that fixed exchange rates through euro membership mitigated the negative effects of exchange rate pegs in the crisis. EMU membership may also have helped by preventing the occurrence of currency crises and reducing the size of possible banking crises within member countries.

Appendix: the data

Data definitions and sources are set out in Table 3.A1.

Table 3.A1: *Data definitions and sources*

Variable	Description	Source
Dependent variables		
Depth of output contraction	Log difference of seasonally adjusted GDP level from peak in 2007Q1–2008Q4 to 2009Q4	Eurostat, Reuters/EcoWin, local central banks and Global Insight
Depth of consumption contraction	Log difference of seasonally adjusted private consumption level from peak in 2007Q1–2008Q4 to 2009Q4	Eurostat, Reuters/EcoWin, local central banks and Global Insight
Duration of output contraction	Numbers of quarters with negative quarter-on-quarter growth in seasonally adjusted GDP from 2008Q3 to 2009Q4	Eurostat, Reuters/EcoWin, local central banks and Global Insight

Table 3.A1: (*cont.*)

Variable	Description	Source
Duration of consumption contraction	Numbers of quarters with negative quarter-on-quarter growth in seasonally adjusted private consumption from 2008Q3 to 2009Q4	Eurostat, Reuters/EcoWin, local central banks and Global Insight
Banking crisis	Indicator variable for a systemic banking crisis: defined as 1 if a country's corporate and financial sectors experience a large number of defaults and financial institutions and corporations face great difficulties repaying contracts on time leading to a rise in non-performing loans and an almost complete exhaustion of aggregate banking system capital and 0 otherwise	Laeven and Valencia (2008) updated database and authors' own elaboration
Currency crisis	Indicator variable for a currency crisis: defined as 1 if the annual average of the nominal effective exchange rate depreciated by 30 per cent or more in 2008–9 and if this depreciation is also at least a 10 percentage points increase in the rate of depreciation compared to the two-year period before and 0 otherwise	Effective exchange rates from the BIS database
Economic structure		
GDP level	GDP level in 2008 (PPP-adjusted billion US$)	*CIA World Factbook* (www.cia.gov/ publications/factbook)
GDP *per capita*	GDP *per capita* in 2008 (PPP-adjusted thousand US$)	*CIA World Factbook* (www.cia.gov/ publications/factbook)
Financial structure and development		
Financial deepening	Broad money (M2) as a share of GDP in 2007	IMF/IFS and local central banks
Size of banking system	Total assets of the five largest banks in each country as a share of GDP in 2007	The Banker (2008) database
Stock market capitalisation	Market value of publicly traded stocks as a share of GDP in 2007	*CIA World Factbook* (www.cia.gov/ publications/factbook)
International real linkages		
Trade openness	Imports and exports as a share of GDP in 2007	IMF/IFS

(*cont.*)

Table 3.A1: (*cont.*)

Variable	Description	Source
Output correlation	Correlation of cyclical part of seasonally adjusted domestic GDP and world output 1985Q1–2007Q4 (or time period available, using the HP filter to generate trend GDP). For France, Germany, Italy, Japan, the United Kingdom, and the United States world output is measured using world output excluding each of these countries	Eurostat, Reuters/EcoWin, local central banks and Pétursson (2010)
Manufacturing exports share	Share of manufacturing exports (SITC 5 to 8, less 667 and 68) in total merchandise exports in 2006	UN/UNCTAD database (www.unctad.org/ Handbook)
Trade diversification	A modified Finger–Kreinin index of trade similarities, measuring to what extent a country's trade structure in 2006 differs from that of the average country; index ranging from 0 to 1, with higher numbers indicating a bigger difference from the world average	UN/UNCTAD database (www.unctad.org/ Handbook)
Trade concentration	A Herfindahl–Hirschman index measuring the degree of market concentration in country's trade in 2006; index ranging from 0 to 1, with higher numbers indicating greater market concentration in trade	UN/UNCTAD database (www.unctad.org/ Handbook)

International financial linkages

Variable	Description	Source
Financial openness	Sum of foreign assets and liabilities as a share of GDP in 2007	Lane and Milesi-Ferretti (2006) updated database
Capital inflows	FDI inward flows as share of GDP in 2007	UN/UNCTAD database (www.unctad.org/ Handbook)
Access to US$ liquidity	Indicator variable for participation in the US Fed liquidity program in 2008: defined as 1 if a country participated in the liquidity program and 0 otherwise	McGuire and von Peter (2009)

Underlying economic volatility

Variable	Description	Source
Output volatility	Standard deviation of cyclical component of seasonally adjusted GDP in 1985Q1–2007Q4 (or time period available, using the HP filter to generate trend GDP)	Eurostat, Reuters/EcoWin and local central banks

Table 3.A1: (*cont.*)

Variable	Description	Source
Exchange rate variability	Standard deviation of quarterly changes in effective nominal exchange rates in 1994–2007	Effective exchange rates from the BIS database
Exchange rate noise	A measure of the standard deviation of the exchange rate risk premium, i.e. the present value (PV) of the rational expectations deviation from the uncovered interest rate parity condition in effective exchange rates estimated for the period 1990Q1–2005Q4 and available for all the countries except, Bulgaria, Croatia, Romania and Russia	Pétursson (2010)

Economic imbalances and vulnerabilities

Variable	Description	Source
Inflation rate	Average consumer price inflation in 2007	Eurostat, Reuters/EcoWin and local central banks
Current account balance	Current account balance as a share of GDP in 2007	IMF/IFS
Size of foreign reserves	Foreign reserves as a share of GDP in 2007	IMF/IFS
Financial leverage	Ratio of domestic credit to domestic deposits in 2007	IMF/IFS
Fiscal balance	General government balance as a share of GDP in 2007	IMF/IFS, Eurostat, Reuters/EcoWin, local central banks and statistical offices
Government debt	General government debt as a share of GDP in 2007	IMF/IFS, Eurostat, Reuters/EcoWin, local central banks and statistical offices

Institutional factors

Variable	Description	Source
Government effectiveness	A measure of government governance quality; index from 2007 ranging from −2.5 to 2.5, with higher values indicating more effective governments	World Bank database (http://info.worldbank.org/governance/wgi/index.asp)
Regulatory quality	A measure of regulatory quality; index from 2007 ranging from −2.5 to 2.5, with higher values indicating greater regulatory quality	World Bank database (http://info.worldbank.org/governance/wgi/index.asp)
Legal structure and security of property rights	A measure of quality of legal system covering judicial independence, impartiality of courts, protection of property rights, military interference in rule of law, integrity of legal	Economic Freedom Network (www.freetheworld.com/2008/2008Dataset.xls)

(*cont.*)

Table 3.A1: (*cont.*)

Variable	Description	Source
	system, legal enforcement of contracts and restrictions on sale of real property; index from 2006, ranging from 0 to 10, with higher values indicating greater quality of legal system	
Central bank independence	A measure of central bank overall independence; index ranging from 0 to 1, with higher values indicating greater independence	Fry *et al.* (2000)
Credit market regulations	A measure of regulatory burden in the domestic credit market; index from 2006 ranging from 0 to 10, with lower values indicating greater regulatory burden	Fraser Institute database on economic freedom (www.freetheworld.com/ 2008/2008Dataset.xls)
Labour market regulations	A measure of regulatory burden in the domestic labour market; index from 2006 ranging from 0 to 10, with lower values indicating greater regulatory burden	Fraser Institute database on economic freedom (www.freetheworld.com/ 2008/2008Dataset.xls)
Business regulations	A measure of regulatory burden in general business activities; index from 2006 ranging from 0 to 10, with lower values indicating greater regulatory burden	Fraser Institute database on economic freedom (www.freetheworld.com/ 2008/2008Dataset.xls)
Economic freedom index	Overall economic freedom index, weighing together subindices covering size of government, legal structure, access to sound money, freedom of international trade and regulation of markets; index from 2006 ranging from 0 to 10, with higher values indicating greater economic freedom	Fraser Institute database on economic freedom (www.freetheworld.com/ 2008/2008Dataset.xls)
Past banking crisis	Indicator variable for past banking crisis: defined as 1 if it has experienced a banking crisis in the past thirty years and 0 otherwise	Laeven and Valencia (2008)
Past currency crisis	Indicator variable for past currency crisis: defined as 1 if it has experienced a banking crisis in the past thirty years and 0 otherwise	Laeven and Valencia (2008)

References

Acemoglu, D., S. Johnson, J. Robinson and Y. Thaicharoen (2003). 'Institutional causes, macroeconomic symptoms: volatility, crises and growth', *Journal of Monetary Economics*, 50: 49–123

Allen, W. A. and R. Moessner (2010). 'Central bank co-operation and international liquidity in the financial crisis of 2008–9', BIS Working Paper, No. 310

Barajas, A., G. Dell'Ariccia and A. Levchenko (2009). 'Credit booms: the good, the bad, and the ugly', unpublished manuscript

Berkmen, P., G. Gelos, R. Rennhack and J. P. Walsh (2009). 'The global financial crisis: explaining cross-country differences in the output impact', IMF Working Paper, No. 09/280

Blanchard, O., G. Dell'Ariccia and P. Mauro (2010). 'Rethinking macroeconomic policy', IMF Staff Position Note, No. 10/03

Buiter, W. H. and A. Sibert (2008). 'The Icelandic banking crisis and what to do about it: the lender of last resort theory of optimal currency areas', CEPR *Policy Insight*, No. 26

Carvalho Filho, I. (2010). 'Inflation targeting and the crisis: an empirical assessment', IMF Working Paper, No. 10/45

Cecchetti, S. G., M. Kohler and C. Upper (2009). 'Financial crisis and economic activity', National Bureau of Economic Research Working Paper, No. 15379

Claessens, S., G. Dell'Ariccia, D. Igan and L. Laeven (2010). 'Cross-country experiences and policy implications from the global financial crisis', *Economic Policy*, 61: 267–93

Coulibaly, B. (2009). 'Currency unions and currency crises: an empirical assessment', *International Journal of Finance and Economics*, 14: 199–221

Davis, E. P. (2008). 'Liquidity, financial crises and the lender of last resort – How much of a departure is the sub-prime crisis?', in P. Bloxham and C. Kent (eds.), *Lessons from the Financial Turmoil of 2007 and 2008*, Reserve Bank of Australia

Dell'Ariccia, G., E. Detragiache and R. Rajan (2008). 'The real effects of banking crises', *Journal of Financial Intermediation*, 17: 89–112

Demirgüç-Kunt, A. and L. Serven (2009). 'Are the sacred cows dead? Implications of the financial crisis for macro and financial policies', World Bank Policy Research Working Paper, No. 4807

Dooley, M., E. Fernandez-Arias and K. Kletzer (1994). 'Recent private capital inflows to developing countries: Is the debt crisis history?', National Bureau of Economic Research Working Paper, No. 4792

Forbes, K. J. and M. D. Chinn (2004). 'A decomposition of global linkages in financial markets over time', *Review of Economics and Statistics*, 86: 705–22

Frankel, J. A. and A. K. Rose (1996). 'Currency crashes in emerging markets: an empirical treatment', *Journal of International Economics*, 41: 351–66

Fratzscher, M. (2009). 'What explains global exchange rate movements during the financial crisis?', European Central Bank Working Paper, No. 1060

Fry, M., D. Julius, L. Mahadeva, S. Roger and G. Sterne (2000). 'Key issues in the choice of monetary policy frameworks', in L. Mahadeva and G. Sterne (eds.), *Monetary Policy Frameworks in a Global Context*, London: Routledge

Kose, A., E. Prasad and M. Terrones (2009). 'Does openness to international financial flows raise productivity growth?', *Journal of International Money and Finance*, 28: 554–80

Kuttner, K. N. and A. S. Posen (2000). 'Inflation, monetary transparency, and G3 exchange rate volatility', Institute for International Economics Working Paper, No. 00–6

Laeven, L. and F. Valencia (2008). 'Systemic banking crises: a new database', IMF Working Paper, No. 08/224

Lane, P. R. and G. M. Milesi-Ferretti (2006). 'The external wealth of nations Mark II: revised and extended estimates of foreign assets and liabilities, 1970–2004', IMF Working Paper, No. 06/69

  (2011). 'The cross-country incidence of the global crisis', *IMF Economic Review*, 59: 77–110

Levchenko, A. A., L. Lewis and L. L. Tesar (2009). 'The collapse of international trade during the 2008–2009 crisis: in search for a smoking gun', Paper prepared for the *IMF Economic Review* Special Issue: Economic Linkages, Spillovers and the Financial Crisis

McGuire, P. and G. von Peter (2009). 'The US dollar shortage in global banking and the international policy response', BIS Working Paper, No. 291

Obstfeld, M., J. C. Shambaugh and A. M. Taylor (2009). 'Financial instability, reserves and central bank swap lines in the panic of 2008', *American Economic Review*, 99: 480–6

Ólafsson, T. T. and T. G. Pétursson (2010). 'Weathering the financial storm: the importance of fundamentals and flexibility', Central Bank of Iceland Working Paper, No. 51

Pétursson, T. G. (2010). 'Inflation control around the world: why are some countries more successful than others?', in D. Cobham, Ø. Eitrheim, S. Gerlach and J. F. Qvigstad (eds.), *Twenty Years of Inflation Targeting: Lessons Learned and Future Prospects*, Cambridge University Press

Rose, A. K. and M. M. Spiegel (2009a). 'Cross-country causes and consequences of the 2008 crisis: early warning', Federal Reserve Bank of San Francisco Working Paper, No. 2009–17

  (2009b). 'Cross-country causes and consequences of the 2008 crisis: international linkages and American exposure', National Bureau of Economic Research Working Paper, No. 15358

The Banker (2008). *Top 1000 World Banks*, London: The Financial Times

Tong, H. and S. Wei (2009). 'The composition matters: capital inflows and liquidity crunch during a global economic crisis', IMF Working Paper, No. 09/164

4   The Irish crisis

*Philip R. Lane**

1   Introduction

Ireland is in the midst of a severe crisis. While the global financial crisis has affected all economies to varying degrees, it has been especially severe in Ireland with a cumulative nominal GDP decline of 21 per cent from 2007Q4 to 2010Q3. This ranks Ireland among the worst-affected countries in terms of output performance during this period (Lane and Milesi-Ferretti, 2011).

Allied to this economic shock, Ireland has also experienced a severe fiscal deterioration. After a long period of running surpluses, the fiscal balance shifted from positive territory in 2007 to baseline deficits of 11–12 per cent of GDP in 2009 and 2010. Much of this fiscal deficit is structural in nature, such that the resumption of economic growth on its own is not sufficient to restore fiscal sustainability. In addition, the one-off cost of recapitalising the banking system pushed the overall general government deficit to 14.5 per cent of GDP in 2009 and 32 per cent of GDP in 2010, leading to rapid growth in the overall level of public debt.

The main factor behind these developments has been the devastating boom–bust cycle in the Irish property market. Since the property boom was financed through aggressive lending by the Irish banking system, the decline in property prices and the collapse in construction activity has resulted in severe losses in the Irish banking system. In turn, this has contributed to the economic crisis through a credit squeeze and the fiscal crisis, both directly through the costs of recapitalising the banking system and indirectly through the loss of asset-driven revenues.

* This chapter is a revised version of a paper prepared for the conference on 'The Euro Area and the Financial Crisis' at the National Bank of Slovakia, Bratislava, 6–8 September 2010, under the auspices of the National Bank of Slovakia, the Heriot–Watt University of Edinburgh and the Comenius University of Bratislava. I thank my discussant Wendy Carlin and conference participants for helpful feedback. I am grateful to Niamh Devitt, Peter McQuade and Donal Mullins for helpful research assistance. This chapter is part of an IRCHSS-sponsored research project on 'An Analysis of the Impact of European Monetary Union on Irish Macroeconomic Policy'.

The scale of these problems meant that the sovereign spread on Irish debt rose sharply in 2010, with doubts concerning whether the government could achieve the triple play of restoring economic growth, fiscal sustainability and a healthy banking system. In the end, this resulted in a shift to official sources of funding in November 2010, with a three-year deal agreed with the International Monetary Fund (IMF) and the EU.

The primary goal of this chapter is to describe what went wrong in Ireland, which is covered in section 2. I review the Irish government's management of the crisis since 2007 in section 3. Next, I reflect on the role of Ireland's membership of EMU during this episode in section 4. Section 5 concludes.

2   The boom and bust in Ireland

It is important to appreciate that there was a genuine Irish 'economic miracle', with very rapid output, employment and productivity growth during the 1994–2000 period. This period can be interpreted as an accelerated convergence phase, with Ireland catching up with the European frontier after a long period of underperformance (Honohan and Walsh, 2002). In particular, major policy mistakes in the late 1970s had led to an unstable macroeconomic situation that resulted in a sustained phase of economic stagnation.

This period of stagnation came to an end with a sharp fiscal correction which was launched in 1987 with the agreement of the main political parties and accompanied by a new social partnership approach that provided a strong social consensus behind a cooperative approach to rebuilding the economy on a pro-business platform (see also Lane, 2000). While the economy performed well in the late 1980s (supported by the boom in major export markets such as the UK and the US), this was temporarily halted by the 1992–3 European recession and currency crisis. Accordingly, the sustained period of uninterrupted economic growth really only began in 1994.

The remarkable economic performance during the 1990s was underpinned by multiple factors. The 1987 fiscal adjustment had delivered a stable fiscal situation, while the stagnation during the mid 1980s had eliminated the high inflation that had plagued Ireland in the late 1970s and early 1980s. Participation rates in second-level and third-level education had sharply increased throughout the 1970s and 1980s, such that new entrants into the labour force had far higher human capital levels than those leaving the labour force through retirement.

These positive domestic trends were accompanied by a favourable shift in the nature of world production and world trade. In particular, the rise of the 'weightless' economy, in which 'high-value, low-weight' sectors such as computers and pharmaceuticals were increasingly important, meant that Ireland's peripheral geographic status became less of a barrier to export-oriented production. The result was a boom in inward foreign direct investment (FDI), primarily from American multinational firms. In part, these firms selected Ireland as a platform for exporting to the newly unified European single market. However, a substantial proportion of the exports were also directed towards other regions, including exports back to the US home market.

With FDI providing an engine for productivity growth, domestic components of domestic demand also picked up, such that the economic expansion was very broad in its nature. Employment grew quickly with little pressure on wage rates, since there was an overhang of high unemployment, a very low initial level of female participation in the labour force and a large stock of Irish workers overseas that were ready to return home.

While house prices began to grow strongly from around 1994, much of the initial growth could be justified by low initial property values (in the wake of the 1992–3 currency crisis) and the rapid growth in income levels. Moreover, credit expansion during the 1990s was also relatively restrained (Kelly, 2010).

The rapid pace of economic growth was reinforced during 1999–2000 by the sharp devaluation of the euro against the dollar, which boosted Irish exports. In addition, interest rates fell in Ireland once entry into EMU was confirmed in 1997. While Ireland undertook a revaluation in the spring of 1998 prior to the formation of EMU, this was very small in scale. Moreover, Ireland had attained full employment by this stage and strong upward pressure on wage rates became evident.

There was also substantial fiscal expansion during 2000–1, with a rapid increase in public spending and substantial cuts in taxation. While the ratio of public spending to GDP declined considerably during the rapid growth of the late 1980s, the timing of the fiscal expansion was procyclical. Accordingly, the initial years of EMU saw rapid growth but also a big surge in inflation, with Ireland appreciating against its fellow member states (Honohan and Lane, 2003).

The international recession in 2001 marked a turning point for the Irish economy. The expectation at the time was that Ireland would return to a more 'normal' European growth path, since the spare capacity in the labour force had been eliminated and the real appreciation meant that the marginal gains to foreign investors were diminishing (at least in labour-intensive sectors such as assembly or call centres).

This projection was wrong. Rapid economic growth resumed in 2003 and was maintained through 2007. However, the flavour of this boom was very different to the 'Celtic Tiger' years. In particular, it was dominated

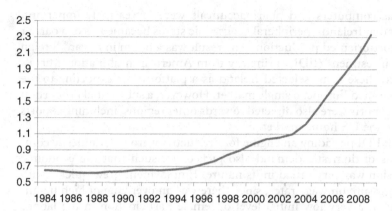

Figure 4.1: Ratio of private credit to GDP, 1984–2008

Note: Ratio of private credit by deposit money banks and other financial institutions to GDP.

Source: World Bank Financial Development Database.

by a surge in construction activity, with the economy driven by a boom in investment in housing and commercial property. In turn, the positive wealth effect from rising property prices fed into strong growth in private consumption. With tax revenues from asset-related sources very strong, the government was also able to fund a strong pace of public expenditure growth, while maintaining a budget surplus and enjoying a rapid decline in the debt-to-GDP ratio.

The result was strong growth in employment but with little productivity growth. While FDI still grew, it was increasingly targeted at higher-value activities that required relatively little by way of unskilled labour, even if this sector was an important source of demand for higher-skilled workers.

The expansion in property investment was fuelled by rapid credit expansion, with the ratio of private credit to GDP sharply increasing during 2003–7 (see also Kelly, 2010). Figure 4.1 shows the acceleration in credit expansion during this period.

This expansion encompassed an increase in credit provision to the household sector but also to a small group of property developers. These property magnates acquired large and complex portfolios that included the building of new housing estates, retail outlets and office buildings. There was also intense competition to redevelop prime sites in Dublin, looking to replace existing structures with higher-density complexes. At the peak of the boom, such sites were acquired at astronomical values.

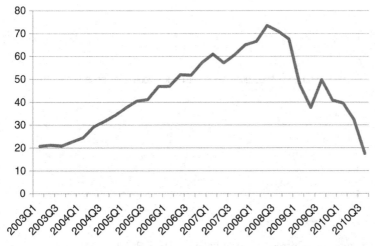

Figure 4.2: Net foreign liabilities of the Irish banking system, 2003–10
Note: Net foreign liabilities of domestic banking sector, expressed as a ratio to GDP.
Source: Author's calculations, based on data from the Central Bank of Ireland.

In addition to these domestic activities, many of these developers were also aggressive in international acquisitions, in the London prime real estate sector, the US and emerging Europe. (Irish households were also highly active in foreign property purchases, both holiday homes and buy-to-let properties.)

Much of the credit growth was provided by local banks. In turn, these banks relied increasingly on international wholesale markets for funding, with a mix of short-term interbank funds and international bond issues. However, there was also significant expansion by the local affiliates of UK-headquartered funds. The increased competition in the market contributed to very low loan spreads and a loosening of loan documentation standards. Figure 4.2 illustrates the extraordinary expansion in the net foreign liabilities of the core Irish banks during this period.

Some standard feedback mechanisms amplified the boom. The collateral cycle played an important role, with rising property prices improving the net worth of domestic investors, which in turn enabled extra leverage and a further impetus to the property market. In related fashion, the high profitability of the domestic banking system enabled an expansion in the balance sheets of these institutions, with a major increase in net external liabilities. The overall current account balance shifted from near

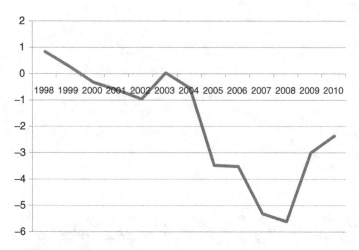

Figure 4.3: Current account balance, 1998–2010
Note: Ratio of current account to GDP.
Source: Author's calculations based on data from Ireland's Central Statistics Office.

zero in 2003 to a deficit close to 6 per cent of GDP in 2007, as shown in Figure 4.3.

The boost to tax revenues from asset-related sources enabled the government to add to domestic demand, including via a heavy programme of public investment. A new twist was the role played by inward migration from the new member states from 2004 onwards. Inward migration helped to limit labour cost pressures in the construction sector, while the boost to population growth also added to investor confidence that the underlying demand for housing would continue to grow.

Finally, the demand-led nature of the boom also contributed to a high rate of domestic inflation. Since this meant that the short-term real interest rate was low, it boosted borrowing and investment demand. In addition, it also boosted tax revenues due to the non-indexation of the tax system.

There were clear signs that the property sector had passed its peak by the autumn of 2006. However, the hope was that there would be a soft landing by which the decline in property prices and construction-related activity would be gradual in nature and could be offset by expansion in other areas. Indeed, economic activity continued to be strong during 2007 such that the risk of a sharp crash did not seem immediate, even if the historical cross-country evidence signalled that the likelihood of a large decline in house prices was substantial (Kelly, 2007).

As it turned out, the final trigger for the economic collapse was the shift in international financial markets during 2007 and 2008. By early 2008, the Irish banks found it more difficult to maintain funding in the international wholesale markets and, at the same time, there was a more rapid pull back by domestic investors from the property market. This period of stress culminated in a full-scale crisis in September 2008, with commercial funding for the Irish banks drying up in the wake of the disruption of international credit markets after the collapse of Lehmans. Since then, Ireland has grappled with a triple crisis, with a severe decline in economic activity, massive losses in the banking system and rapid deterioration in the fiscal position.[1] We turn to the management of the crisis in section 3.

3   Crisis management

3.1   The economic crisis

In relation to the real economy, the recession in Ireland in 2008–9 was driven by a dramatic decline in construction investment, with the sudden reversal in Ireland's fortunes also inducing a pull back in domestic consumption. In contrast to many other advanced economies, the export sector was a stabilising factor, with the decline in output concentrated in the domestically oriented sectors of the economy. In a mirror image to the boom period, negative feedback mechanisms kicked in. Banks pulled in lending, which in turn amplified the downturn in the property sector. The increase in bad loans further curtailed the supply of credit by Irish banks. The decline in domestic demand also put downward pressure on the price level, with deflation contributing to the decline in tax revenues and an increase in the real burden of debt. Deflation was also partly driven by the sharp depreciation of sterling against the euro, in view of the importance of imports from the UK in Irish consumption, which constituted a terms of trade gain for Ireland. Between September 2008 and November 2010, the cumulative decline in the consumer prices index (CPI) was 6.2 per cent.

The recession has led to a sharp increase in unemployment, which climbed from 4.6 per cent in 2007 to 13.3 per cent in 2010. In addition, participation rates dropped and net emigration resumed, so that the total fall in employment was about 12 per cent. With the decline in domestic

---

[1] The crisis in Ireland has other dimensions, including the damage to Ireland's international reputation and a loss of confidence among the domestic population in the political and administrative systems. I do not address these broader problems in this chapter.

demand, the current account has sharply improved, from 5.6 per cent of GDP in 2008 to 2.4 per cent of GDP in 2010.

3.2   *The fiscal crisis*

The downturn in domestic spending and the decline in transactions in the property market meant that tax revenues fell very quickly, to the extent that the government had to introduce a series of measures to obtain other sources of tax revenue and limit public expenditure growth.

This included the introduction of graduated income levies, which had the effect of sharply increasing the marginal income tax rate for middle- and high-earners. For public sector workers, pay levels were *de facto* reduced by the introduction of a public sector pension levy, while a recruitment freeze was also implemented. Further measures were taken in the 2010 budget (announced in December 2009), including further sizeable reductions in public sector pay levels, a reduction in social benefit levels and a contraction in spending commitments.

These measures limited the scale of the decline in the fiscal situation. Even so, the underlying weak state of the economy and the collapse of the tax base meant that the baseline fiscal deficits in 2009 and 2010 were still extraordinarily large at 11–12 per cent of GDP, even before taking into account the one-off costs of recapitalising the banking system.

A sizeable proportion of the deficit is structural in nature. A key problem is that elevated revenues from asset-related sources during the boom were in part deployed to reduce more stable types of tax revenue (see also Lane, 2007). In particular, the direct tax burden on low- and middle-earners was significantly reduced during this period. In addition, the Irish tax base is quite narrow, with no significant role for sources such as annual property taxes or local-level taxes. Accordingly, a major challenge is to expand the tax base.

On the spending side, public pay levels and social benefit payments had been increased quite sharply during the good years. The initial phase of fiscal adjustment has already rolled back some of these gains. However, a 2010 agreement with public sector unions means that nominal levels of public sector pay will not be further reduced (barring exceptional circumstances), with savings to be obtained from a combination of a recruitment freeze and productivity reforms in the delivery of public services. A saving grace is that the decline in the construction sector means that the cost of public investment projects has greatly declined, allowing cuts in nominal investment spending far in excess of the decline in real spending.

The fiscal tightening measures are certainly a procyclical force that has contributed to the scale of the recession. It would have been better to have run larger surpluses during the good years and even accumulated a liquid rainy-day fund that might have been deployed as a buffer against the impact of the severe negative economic shock (Lane, 1997; Lane, 1998a; Lane, 2010).

Taken together, the cumulative size of the discretionary fiscal tightening over 2008–10 amounts to €14.6 billion, which is 9.3 per cent of 2010 GDP. In November 2010, the government announced a four-year fiscal plan for 2011–14 which would involve a further €15 billion in discretionary fiscal tightening. In turn, this four-year plan forms the basis for the fiscal component of the EU/IMF deal, which is further discussed on p. 73. Under current IMF forecasts, this fiscal austerity package is projected to stabilise the debt-to-GDP ratio by 2014 at 124 per cent of GDP.

3.3   The banking crisis

In addition to the baseline fiscal problem, the sovereign balance sheet in Ireland has been further strained by the government's role in resolving the crisis in the banking sector. At the end of September 2008, the most immediate concern was to stabilise the banking system. At the time, the belief was that the main problem was the loss of market liquidity. Accordingly, the Irish government sought to improve the funding situation by guaranteeing the vast bulk of its liabilities for a two-year period (deposits, senior debt and dated subordinated debt). This was followed later in 2008 by the provision of extra capital for the banking system, as it became clear that losses on property-related loans would be greater than previously calculated. (However, these initial capital injections would prove small relative to subsequent estimates of the underlying scale of potential losses.) In April 2009, the Irish government also established the National Asset Management Agency (NAMA), with the mandate to purchase the universe of development-related loans (above a certain value) from the banks.

This triple-track strategy had an internal coherence, even if the execution of the strategy was problematic in several respects.[2] One basic problem was that the initial guarantee of liabilities was too broad (Honohan, 2010a). By guaranteeing existing senior bonds and some types of

---

[2] Other approaches to resolving the banking crisis were also debated. For instance, the pre-emptive nationalisation of the banking system was advocated by many domestic economists and also raised by the 2009 IMF Article IV mission.

subordinated debt, the capacity to allocate some part of the ultimate loan losses to bondholders was compromised, raising the taxpayer cost of resolving the banking crisis.

In relation to asset transfers, the aim was to cleanse bank balance sheets by transferring development-related loans to NAMA, since this category was the main source of uncertainty concerning total loan losses. During 2009–10, NAMA purchased most of these loans at a steep average discount, such that the transfer also forced the banks to crystallise the losses on these loans. Under the guidance of EU rules, the discount has been applied on a loan-by-loan basis. Accordingly, there were substantial transaction costs involved, since each individual loan had to be individually assessed. Moreover, the cumbersome nature of this approach meant that the transfer of loans took place slowly, which inhibited the goal of a rapid cleansing of bank balance sheets. (Under the EU/IMF deal, the remaining transfers to NAMA do not require loan-by-loan appraisal.)

While the asset transfer approach had the virtue of transparency, it also meant that the banks required substantial upfront recapitalisation programmes. Only one bank (Bank of Ireland) was able to raise significant new private capital, such that the State has ended up with extensive control of the Irish banking system. In turn, the high recapitalisation costs led to a sharp increase in gross government debt and increased the riskiness of the sovereign debt profile, in view of the ongoing uncertainties regarding ultimate losses in the banking sector.

While all banks have suffered considerable losses, the most extreme losses (relative to the size of loan books) were incurred by two marginal banks that have been revealed to have had very weak corporate governance. The biggest offender has been Anglo-Irish Bank, which was nationalised in early 2009. While it had little presence in the retail deposit market, this bank had grown very rapidly through aggressive property-related lending which was largely funded on wholesale markets. The losses at this bank have been by far the largest contributor to the overall losses in the Irish banking system. In addition, a smaller mutual bank (Irish Nationwide Building Society, INBS) has also incurred catastrophic property-related losses. However, the losses at the two main commercial banks (Bank of Ireland and Allied Irish Banks, AIB) and the tail-risk exposures of these banks to further deterioration in the economy has meant that the entire banking system has been compromised.

While the public capital injections into Bank of Ireland and AIB may be viewed as financial investments that may ultimately yield a return, the capital poured into Anglo-Irish Bank and INBS is effectively a write-off. The capital transfers to Anglo-Irish Bank and INBS pushed the overall

2009 general government balance to 14.5 per cent of GDP and the 2010 balance to 32 per cent of GDP.

3.4   The EU/IMF deal

The Irish government ultimately requested assistance from the EU and IMF in November 2010. There were several triggers for this decision. In relation to the banking system, the expiry of the State guarantee in September 2010 led to an exit of private sector funders that had committed funding under the guarantee. In turn, this resulted in a marked increase in the reliance of the Irish banks on liquidity support from the ECB and the extraordinary liquidity assistance facility of the Irish central bank. Apparently, the view from the ECB was that this liquidity support could only be maintained if the process of downsizing the Irish banking system were accelerated and the capital ratios of the Irish banks further improved as a buffer against tail-risk losses.

In addition, the projected level of property-related losses had increased over the summer of 2010, with the discounts on the second tranche of loan transfers to NAMA greater than expected. In addition, the new management team at Anglo-Irish Bank decided to make extra provisions on non-NAMA loans, requiring further capital injections into Anglo-Irish Bank.

These extra capital requirements contributed to increased market concerns about the sustainability of the fiscal position. More generally, the surprise nature of the extra provisions underlined the extent of the uncertainty surrounding estimates of total loan losses in the Irish banking system and this tail risk pushed up the spread on Irish sovereign debt (Figure 4.4).

Furthermore, a downward revision to the 2009 GDP data was announced in June 2010 and the publication of lower growth forecasts in the IMF Article IV report in July 2010 led to a reassessment of the scale of the adjustment that would be needed to achieve a sustainable fiscal position. In part, these lower GDP forecasts related to a more pessimistic view of the impact of the financial crisis on the medium-term trend growth rate for the economy. However, an additional factor was a greater recognition that the adjustment process would involve a sustained real depreciation, in which the growth in the GDP deflator would be negative in the short term and only increase slowly over the medium term, such that the five-year projection for nominal GDP was much lower than previously estimated.

The total financial package under the EU/IMF deal is valued at €85 billion, which is about 54 per cent of 2010 GDP for Ireland. However,

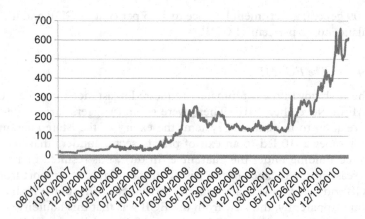

Figure 4.4: Spread between ten-year bonds: Ireland over Germany, 2007–10

Note: Yield spread on ten-year government bonds.
Source: Author's calculations based on data from Global Financial Data.

€17.5 billion of the total is domestically sourced, from the assets held by Ireland's sovereign wealth fund (the National Pension Reserve Fund, NPRF) and the cash balances held by the agency responsible for managing the national debt (the National Treasury Management Agency, NTMA). The external component of €67.5 billion is evenly split, with €22.5 billion from the European Commission's European Financial Stability Mechanism (EFSM), €22.5 billion from the IMF and €22.5 billion from the European Financial Stability Facility (EFSF) and bilateral loans (from the UK, Sweden and Denmark).

In terms of composition, the intention is that €50 billion can provide funding to the Irish State, such that Ireland need not rely on the bond markets to fund its fiscal deficit or roll over existing debt over the next three years. In relation to the banking system, €10 billion is to be drawn down to provide extra capital to the Irish banking system (€8 billion) and fund credit enhancements that are intended to allow the Irish banks to sell packages of risky loans to private investors (€2 billion). The final €25 billion is contingent funding that can be drawn down if it turns out that the Irish banking system requires yet further capital in the coming years.

The agreed programme involves discretionary fiscal tightening of €15 billion over 2011–14, with €6 billion of this total to take place in 2011. Under an optimistic growth scenario, this might deliver a budget deficit-to-GDP ratio in 2014 that is just under the 3 per cent limit. However, the programme recognises that a lower growth path would not see the 3 per cent target achieved by 2014. Under that scenario, the programme envisages that further tightening will be required in 2015 in order to achieve the 3 per cent target.

The combined interest rate across the different funding lines is of the order of 5.8 per cent per annum for a 7.5 year loan. While this is in line with standard IMF funding conditions, it is arguable that the European component of the funds could have been priced at a lower rate. While it is certainly important that such official funding contains a premium to discourage moral hazard, the 300 basis point premium built into this funding rate makes it more difficult to achieve fiscal sustainability. This limits the degree of solidarity across EU partners, while also increasing the risk facing other European governments in view of the potential contagion from doubts about the sustainability of the Irish sovereign position. Although the context is quite different, it is striking that the December 2010 agreement between Iceland and the UK and Dutch governments on the Icesave debt specifies an interest rate of 3.2 per cent over a long repayment period, with the interest rate calculated to approximate the cost of funds for the creditor governments. Similarly, the balance of payments support provided by the European Commission to EU member countries outside the euro area (Hungary, Latvia) does not carry a similar penalty premium.

In terms of structural reforms, the main objective under the deal is to de-risk the banking system (see also Honohan, 2010c; Honohan, 2011). This involves several elements. First, the extra capital injections are intended to increase core Tier 1 capital ratios to 12 per cent. Second, the level of risky loans held by the banks are to be reduced through the transfer of extra property loan tranches to NAMA and the sale of loan packages to private investors. (As indicated above, the sale of loan packages to private investors will be supported by €2 billion in credit enhancements to limit the risk exposure that would otherwise deter private investors.) Third, the banks will be further downsized through the disposal of affiliates and other non-core assets. Fourth, the winding down of the main disaster banks (Anglo-Irish Bank and INBS) will be accelerated. Fifth, the €25 billion in contingent funding provides an additional buffer in the event of extra loan losses.

Finally, these financial measures will be accompanied by a more extensive third-party assessment of the quality of the loan books. While the Irish central bank published a prudential capital assessment review (PCAR) in March 2010 that set out conservative provisions for loan losses (this was updated in September 2010), the level of uncertainty about loan quality means that further information disclosure is necessary in order to improve market understanding of the likely distribution of loan losses. Furthermore, the role of third-party assessors in examination of the loan books is seen as important in guaranteeing the rigour of the 2011 PCAR exercise. If it turns out that the review signals that extra bank capital is advisable, this is allowed for under the terms of the EU/IMF funding.

Taken together, the goal is that these banking sector reforms will result in a smaller, less-risky and better-capitalised banking system. In turn, these changes improve the sustainability of the ECB liquidity provisions and also increase the likelihood that the Irish banks can return to the private wholesale funding markets.

An important issue in the negotiation of the deal was the appropriate scale of burden-sharing by bank bondholders in the recapitalisation of the Irish banking system. If the holders of bonds issued by the Irish banks absorbed some of the losses, the fiscal burden would be lightened. There are about €32 billion of non-guaranteed bank bonds outstanding, consisting of €12 billion of subordinated debt and €20 billion of senior debt. These are bonds that were issued before the introduction of the September 2008 guarantee (which has now expired) but have not yet reached their maturity dates. In addition, there are €25 billion of guaranteed senior bonds that were issued under the 2009 Eligible Liabilities Guarantee (ELG) scheme for new debt issuance.[3] (A small amount of new non-guaranteed bonds has also been issued.)

The EU/IMF deal envisages that holders of subordinated debt will not be repaid in full. There is currently a bond exchange programme for the Anglo-Irish subordinated debt which offers the bondholders 20¢ on the euro. Over the last two years, there have been other voluntary exchange programmes for subordinated debtholders in several banks, with an estimated €7 billion obtained in discounts. (It is arguable that these earlier exchange programmes were premature in that the appropriate level of discount could not be properly determined before the full systemic evaluation of prospective loan losses had taken place.)

However, it also seems that there was serious discussion of writing down the value of some non-guaranteed senior bonds as part of the EU/IMF negotiations. While the legal tradition in Ireland has been to view senior bonds as *pari passu* with depositors, it seems that there may be legal options to break that link. For instance, in situations in which the scale of State capital injections exceeds the pre-crisis level of capital, it may be possible to argue that senior bondholders should have no legitimate expectation of full repayment.

---

[3] The main focus of the debate is on the non-guaranteed bonds, since a restructuring of guaranteed bonds would have broader implications for sovereign debt.

However, no agreement was reached for restructuring the non-guaranteed senior bonds. Media reports indicate that European policy-makers took the view that the restructuring of senior debt would create a new precedent in European banking that could severely disrupt bank funding markets. However, the counter-argument is that a set of objective criteria could be developed that would clearly delimit the scenarios under which some types of senior debt should be written down, thereby limiting the scope for contagion.

Indeed, the working document of European Commission (2011) identifies a range of possible criteria, even if the scope of the European Commission report is restricted to the design of future bank bond contracts, rather than to altering the payoffs on existing bank debt. Moreover, to the extent that the restructuring of senior bank bonds improves the sovereign fiscal position, it might even be a calming influence on sovereign debt markets. At the time of writing (January 2011) the ultimate treatment of the non-guaranteed senior bank bonds remains an unresolved issue and is set to feature in the political debate surrounding the upcoming general election in Ireland.

In terms of other structural reforms, the main priority is to improve the operation of the labour market in order to facilitate a reversal in the sharp increase in unemployment (much of it now long term) since the onset of the crisis. The minimum wage (set at the peak of the boom) has been reduced by 12 per cent, while there has been a further 4 per cent decline in unemployment benefits. In addition, more vigorous labour market activation policies are envisaged under the plan and other types of rigidities in the wage-setting system will be targeted. In relation to product markets, there are aspirations to reduce monopoly rents in sheltered sectors (such as the legal and medical professions) and boost productivity in the public sector.

However, the growth payoff from such reforms may occur with a long lag and cannot be relied on to improve growth substantially within the period of the deal. Similarly, public sector reform has the potential to boost efficiency considerably, but the overall growth payoff will only occur over a long period. Accordingly, it is not realistic to expect a sizeable direct short-term growth payoff.

Overall, the EU/IMF deal provides an environment in which Ireland can make progress in resolving its crisis. However, there are considerable implementation challenges in delivering the planned fiscal adjustment (see also Beetsma, Giuliodori and Wierts, 2009). In addition, the cost of restructuring the banking system remains uncertain and depends on the ability to sell bank assets at prices above fire-sale values.

Both the debt dynamics and the health of the banking sector are dependent on the rate of nominal GDP growth in the coming years.

In this regard, there is considerable uncertainty about the path for GDP. The Irish Finance Ministry and the main local economic forecaster (the Economic and Social Research Institute, ESRI) are relatively optimistic about the speed of output growth, pointing to the capacity for a small open economy to rely on export-driven growth and the high current levels of precautionary savings that should fall once uncertainty declines and consumer confidence recovers. Against that view, the cross-country historical evidence is that output growth is typically very slow after major banking crises, even if these historical examples do not precisely match the current Irish conditions (Reinhart and Reinhart, 2010).

Having reviewed the course of events in Ireland, we now turn to asking some general questions about the lessons to be drawn from the Irish experience in relation to the impact of EMU on member countries.

4   Ireland and EMU

At a surface level, it is possible to argue that membership of EMU has directly contributed to the boom–bust cycle in Ireland.[4] First, Ireland entered EMU at the peak of the 'Celtic Tiger' output boom, with full employment only recently achieved and the emergence of shortages in the labour market. Accordingly, the initial conditions for Ireland were quite different than for the aggregate euro area economy.

A standard prescription in this case is to revalue the exchange rate prior to entering the monetary union, such that price-level pressures in the economy are diverted into nominal exchange rate appreciation rather than a differential post-entry inflation rate. While Ireland undertook a small revaluation in spring 1998, this was inadequate given the scale of the boom.[5] Accordingly, the undervalued conversion rate between the Irish pound and the euro contributed to the inflationary pressures in Ireland in the early years of EMU.

Second, the creation of EMU itself represented an asymmetric shock. In particular, while the core member countries had experienced a convergence in interest rates long before the formation of EMU, there was a substantial decline in interest rates for peripheral member countries such as Ireland, Portugal, Spain and Greece in the late 1990s. For these countries, a history of devaluations meant that there was a substantial country-risk premium in interest rates. Moreover, the smaller countries

---

[4] This section draws on Lane (2009).
[5] Slovakia revalued by 15 per cent in 2008 before it joined EMU at the beginning of 2009.

suffered from a low level of liquidity in their money and currency markets, such that a liquidity premium was also incorporated into the level of interest rates in these countries. Accordingly, EMU represented a major economic shock for them, since devaluation risk and currency liquidity risk were eliminated. As such, holding fixed other factors, households, firms and governments in these countries now faced a permanent reduction in the cost of capital. In turn, this triggered an expenditure boom in these countries (see also Fagan and Gaspar, 2007).

Third, by virtue of its greater involvement in extra-EMU trade, Ireland was more affected by shifts in the external value of the euro than was the case for other member countries. In particular, the sharp depreciation of the euro against the dollar during 1999–2002 represented a positive differential shock for Ireland *vis-à-vis* the rest of the euro area, since the strong economic linkages between Ireland and the US meant that Irish competitiveness was boosted by more than in other countries. This contributed to the already strong aggregate demand conditions in Ireland during that period and the positive inflation differential between Ireland and the rest of the euro area (Honohan and Lane, 2003). More recently, the rapid depreciation of sterling against the euro during the Autumn of 2008 affected the Irish economy more than other regions in the euro area.

Fourth, the effective segmentation of national banking systems that remained even after the formation of EMU meant that shifts in market structure in the Irish banking system posed a challenge for the domestic financial regulator. In particular, aggregate credit growth in Ireland was boosted by the rise of Anglo-Irish Bank as an aggressive lender to property developers, which in turn induced a relaxation of lending standards by other participants in the Irish loans market (Honohan, 2009, 2010a, 2010b). In similar fashion, greater competition from the affiliates of UK banks further contributed to rapid domestic credit growth. In turn, this domestic credit boom contributed to faster expansion in Irish aggregate demand relative to other members of the euro area and increased country-specific risks in the banking system.

Fifth, there have been major shifts in government spending and taxation in Ireland relative to other members of the euro area since 1999. Membership of a monetary union is perfectly consistent with a wide range of variation in terms of the ratios of government spending and tax revenues to GDP. However, the timing of the fiscal expansion was procyclical in nature, such that fiscal policy tended to amplify cyclical divergences between Ireland and the rest of the euro area economy.[6]

---

[6] Lane (1998b) and Hunt (2005) analyse the long-standing procyclical pattern in Irish fiscal policy.

Sixth, the asymmetric liberalisation of EU labour markets to migrants from the new member states in 2004 represents a further idiosyncratic shock. In particular, Ireland was the only member of the euro area to open its labour market to workers from Central and Eastern Europe (CEE) and only the UK and Sweden adopted a similar approach among the existing members of the EU. The scale of post-liberalisation migration far exceeded *ex ante* expectations, acting as another structural shock for the Irish economy that was not shared by its fellow members of the euro area.

Taken together, these country-specific factors meant that macroeconomic stability in Ireland required effective national stabilisation policies. However, there was a failure to regulate the banking sector to guard against systemic risk factors. This was especially problematic under EMU, since access to the area-wide financial markets meant that the scope for Irish banks to take on too much risk was amplified. Moreover, the operation of fiscal policy was insufficiently counter-cyclical. These twin policy weaknesses both failed to curb the boom and exacerbated the scale of the crisis.

The weaknesses in banking regulation have been extensively analysed in two major reports that were commissioned by the Irish government (Honohan, 2010a; Regling and Watson, 2010). As a follow-on to these reports, a banking inquiry has been established to further probe into these regulatory failures. This should prove helpful in establishing in more detail the factors that contributed to the banking crisis. However, major required reforms have already been implemented, with new senior appointments at the central bank and a reorganisation of the system of financial regulation.

In relation to fiscal policy, there were both macroeconomic and microeconomic weaknesses (see also Lane, 2010). While budget surpluses were run during the boom period, these were relatively small and the scale of the structural deficit was systematically underestimated (by both domestic and international agencies). On net, the fiscal position was fundamentally fragile, despite appealing headline numbers. In relation to microeconomics, the tax system during the boom period provided excessive incentives to invest in property – and these distortions amplified the cycle.

Accordingly, the lesson is that the fiscal system needs to be redesigned in order to be more robust in the event of future shocks. A broader tax base should help to provide a more stable platform for tax revenues, while the setting of tax rates should be counter-cyclical or at least acyclical. In relation to the fiscal balance, the crisis has illustrated that a small open economy such as Ireland should run much bigger surpluses during boom periods in order to provide fiscal space during downturns. An important

current debate is whether formal fiscal rules and a role for an independent fiscal council can facilitate a more counter-cyclical pattern for fiscal
policy (Lane, 2010). Indeed, the EU/IMF deal includes a commitment to
introduce a Fiscal Responsibility Law and a Budgetary Advisory Council
in the first half of 2011.

The failure to implement appropriate national stabilisation problems
meant that Ireland took excessive macroeconomic risks during the early
years of EMU. In turn, membership of a currency union limits the range
of options that can be pursued in emerging from the current crisis. However, along some dimensions, membership of the euro area has also provided considerable stability during this crisis period. Most directly, the
Irish banks have heavily relied on the liquidity provided by the ECB as a
substitute for the loss of access to private wholesale funders. In addition,
highly indebted Irish households have benefited from low ECB interest
rates during the crisis.

Had Ireland not joined the euro, the foreign liabilities of the banking system would most likely have been in foreign currency and the
banking crisis would have been amplified by a parallel currency crisis.
Moreover, an independent currency would not have offered a guarantee against the onset of the mid 2000s credit boom. This credit boom
affected many non-EMU economies in Europe (Iceland, CEE) and many
countries have experienced the problems associated with currency over-
shooting that can act to amplify the impact of credit booms, only to be
followed by a deeper crash with currency depreciation exacerbating balance sheet problems. Moreover, even under an independent monetary
policy, it is not clear that the central bank would have been able to neuter
the housing boom solely through its interest rate policy, in view of the
weak relation between interest rates and housing prices and the potential
output costs of targeting asset prices ahead of real indicators (Dokko
et al., 2011).

Of course, there are some attractions to an 'immaculate' devaluation by
which a one-off realignment of the Irish real exchange rate could provide
a boost to exports. However, as is exhaustively documented by Eichengreen (2010), there are considerable financial and logistical disruptions
associated with seeking to exit the euro. In view of Ireland's very deep
level of international financial and economic integration, these transition
costs might be especially high.

Moreover, the longer-term attractions of an independent currency
remain open to question, for the reasons given above. Such problems
would be especially severe for a new currency created in the wake of exit-
ing EMU, since the credibility of the new monetary regime and its anti-
inflation commitment would be queried by the markets. Accordingly,

the monetary regime for a new Irish currency would likely require an initial phase of relatively high interest rates.

In terms of the broader reform of the institutional framework for the euro area, the failures in domestic macroeconomic policy and financial regulation during the pre-crisis period mean that the proposals by the European Commission for tighter surveillance are welcome in terms of reducing the risk of future crisis episodes.

However, the absence of an EU-wide special resolution regime for failing banks has made it more difficult and more costly to resolve the Irish banking crisis. In relation to future crises, the types of proposals currently being developed by the European Commission should help (for instance, in allowing for the bailing-in of senior unsecured bondholders in the event of severe bank losses) but these are too late to be helpful in resolving the current crisis. More broadly, the creation of the European Systemic Risk Board (ESRB) and the associated European Supervisory Authorities (ESAs) should help in monitoring European-wide risks in the financial system.

While the creation of the EFSF has facilitated the funding of the EU/IMF programme for Ireland, the size of the penalty premium built into the interest cost is arguably too stiff for a fund that is built on the principles of solidarity and common financial interests among members of the euro area, since it is sufficiently high to non-trivially increase the risk that the sovereign will ultimately run into repayment difficulties. Furthermore, the EFSF can only provide loans to member governments. In terms of promoting financial stability, a more flexible mechanism that could also offer tail-risk insurance might have been better suited to tackling the underlying fiscal exposure of the Irish government in relation to resolving the Irish banking crisis (see also Honohan, 2011).

The current proposals for the permanent European Stabilisation Mechanism (ESM) that will replace the EFSF in 2013 do not extend the remit of the ESM to include this type of risk-sharing mechanism. However, the greater clarity about the potential for burden-sharing by bondholders under the ESM should prove helpful in providing greater market discipline in relation to future fiscal management. However, the uncertainty about the transition towards the ESM arrangements is a source of instability in dealing with the current sovereign debt crisis.

5   Conclusions

The 2003–7 property-driven boom has proven to be very costly for Ireland, resulting in a deep recession, a severe fiscal crisis and the near-collapse of the banking system. While the frothy state of international financial markets and the underpricing of risk certainly played a role in fuelling the boom, the primary responsibility for curbing excesses lay with domestic policy-makers. In this regard, there was a twin failure, with the financial regulator losing control of systemic financial risk while fiscal policy was insufficiently counter-cyclical.

By the same token, although the 2007–8 international financial crisis was the proximate trigger for the hard landing in the domestic property market, the unwinding of the boom was bound to happen at some point, even if the nature of the inevitable adjustment might have been different under alternative realisations.

At a domestic level, a primary lesson from the Irish crisis is that it reaffirms the principle that rigorous discipline in fiscal policy and financial regulation is essential if membership of a currency union is to be compatible with macroeconomic and banking stability. At an EU level, the Irish crisis has highlighted the costs of the incomplete institutional design of the monetary union and the importance of deep-level reforms to both reduce the probability of future crises and to increase the resilience of the European banking system in the event of a crisis.

References

Beck, T., A. Demirgüç-Kunt and R. Levine (2000). 'A new database on financial development and structure', *World Bank Economic Review*, **14**: 597–605

Beetsma, R., M. Giuliodori and P. R. Wierts (2009). 'Budgeting versus implementing fiscal policy in the EU', *Economic Policy*, **24**: 753–804

Dokko, J., B. Doyle, M. T. Kiley, J. Kim, S. Sherlund, J. Sim and S. Van Den Heuvel (2011). 'Monetary policy and the global housing bubble', *Economic Policy*, **66**: 237–87

Eichengreen, B. (2010). 'The breakup of the euro area', in A. Alesina and F. Giavazzi (eds.), *Europe and the Euro*, University of Chicago Press

European Commission (2011). 'Technical details of a possible EU framework for bank recovery and resolution', DG Internal Market and Services Working Document

Fagan, G. and V. Gaspar (2007). 'Adjusting to the euro', ECB Working Paper, No. **716**

Honohan, P. (2009). 'Resolving Ireland's banking crisis', *Economic and Social Review*, **40**(2): 207–32

  (2010a). *The Irish Banking Crisis – Regulatory and Financial Stability Policy 2003–2008*, Central Bank of Ireland

  (2010b). 'Euro membership and bank stability: friends or foes?', *Comparative Economic Studies*, **52**: 133–57

  (2010c). 'Financial regulation: risk and reward', Speech to International Financial Services Summit, 10 November

  (2011). 'Restoring Ireland's credit by reducing uncertainty', IIEA Speech, 7 January

Honohan, P. and P. R. Lane (2003). 'Divergent inflation rates under EMU', *Economic Policy*, **37**: 58–94

Honohan, P. and B. Walsh (2002). 'Catching up with the leaders: the Irish hare', *Brookings Papers on Economic Activity*: 1–79

Hunt, C. (2005). 'Discretion and cyclicality in Irish budgetary management 1969–2003', *Economic and Social Review*, **36**: 295–321

Kelly, M. (2007). 'On the likely extent of falls in Irish house prices', *Quarterly Economic Commentary*, Summer: 42–54

(2010). 'Whatever happened to Ireland?', CEPR Discussion Paper, No. **7811**

Lane, P. R. (1997). 'EMU: macroeconomic risks', *Irish Banking Review*, Spring: 24–34

(1998a). 'Irish fiscal policy under EMU', *Irish Banking Review*, Winter: 2–10

(1998b). 'On the cyclicality of Irish fiscal policy', *Economic and Social Review*, **29**: 1–16

(2000). 'Disinflation, switching nominal anchors and twin crises: the Irish experience', *Journal of Policy Reform*, **3**: 301–26

(2007). 'Fiscal policy for a slowing economy', in *Budget Perspectives 2008*, Economic and Social Research Institute

(2009). 'European Monetary Union and macroeconomic stabilisation policies in Ireland', Report Prepared for National Economic and Social Council

(2010). 'A new fiscal framework for Ireland', *Journal of the Statistical and Social Inquiry Society of Ireland*, **39**: 144–65

Lane, P. R. and G. M. Milesi-Ferretti (2011). 'The cross-country incidence of the global crisis', *IMF Economic Review*, **59**: 77–110

Regling, K. and M. Watson (2010). *A Preliminary Report on the Sources of Ireland's Banking Crisis*, Dublin: Government Publications

Reinhart, C. and V. R. Reinhart (2010). 'After the fall', in *Macroeconomic Challenges: The Decade Ahead*, Federal Reserve Bank of Kansas City Economic Policy Symposium, forthcoming, www.kansascityfed.org/publications/research/escp/escp-2010.cfm

5 The crisis in Spain: origins and developments

Angel Gavilán, Pablo Hernández de Cos,
Juan F. Jimeno and Juan A. Rojas

1 Introduction

The impact of the crisis on the Spanish economy, although qualitatively similar to that in other countries, shows some important quantitative differences. First, the cumulative decline in GDP (−4.5 per cent) has not been as large. Secondly, the banking sector started the crisis with more solid portfolios, as Spanish banks were kept away from the 'toxic assets' that initiated the first phase of the crisis, and has not imposed too much stress on public finances. Thirdly, despite the mild decrease in GDP, cumulative employment losses (−9.4 per cent) and the increase of unemployment (almost 12 percentage points) have been extremely high, due to some peculiarities of the Spanish labour market. Finally, after a decade of fiscal consolidation in which there was a long period of running fiscal surpluses and the debt-to-GDP ratio was brought below 40 per cent, there has been a severe deterioration in the fiscal position, with a deficit of 11.1 per cent in 2009. Despite the low debt-to-GDP ratio and the government commitment to restore fiscal soundness by 2013, Spain was temporarily among the 'collateral victims' of the Greek debt crisis. While the problems of the banking system seem currently under control, Spain faces the policy dilemma of restoring competitiveness and growth within a monetary union – that is, without control of the exchange rate and interest rates – at the same time as running down the volume of private debt accumulated before the crisis and that of public debt which increased sharply in response to the effects of the crisis.

Understanding this sequence of events and the policy options to restore growth requires revisiting the driving factors of the long expansion during the pre-crisis period and the impact of alternative policies. The pre-crisis expansionary phase was mostly driven by two factors: (1) a significant expansion of credit, which was induced by the fall in interest rates that followed Spain's entry into the European Monetary Union (EMU) and, more broadly, by a pervasive relaxation in the conditions of access to credit, and (2) the large immigration inflows into Spain over the period that substantially modified the demographic structure of the Spanish population.[1]

During the expansion some imbalances built up: the Spanish economy became increasingly more dependent on external financing over the period. Despite a move toward fiscal consolidation by the public sector, private sector indebtedness rose sharply due to the fall in interest rates and the overall expansion of credit, which led to an investment boom, much of which materialised in the housing sector. Moreover, the price-competitiveness of the Spanish economy also deteriorated significantly, due to very low productivity growth and the existence of important distortions in the domestic labour and product markets.

The goal of this chapter is to account for these developments. In order to organise the discussion, we use a structural model of the Spanish economy that accommodates the main demographic and economic developments that sustained the expansion and the imbalances which characterised the initial conditions under which the Spanish economy had to cope with the global financial crisis.[2] The chapter is organised as follows. Section 2 sets out the main facts with respect to the macroeconomic evolution of the Spanish economy during the expansionary phase. Section 3 addresses the role played by demographic developments and interest rates in shaping the Spanish macroeconomic evolution over the period of analysis. Section 4 discusses to what extent alternative fiscal and structural policies could have changed the path of the economy during this period. Finally, Section 5 concludes and proposes some extensions to model the financial crisis and analyse its transmission in an economy with the same initial conditions as those of the Spanish economy in 2007.

2   From EMU accession to the crisis

The expansionary phase was mostly fuelled by two factors: the fall in interest rates and the expansion of credit, and the large immigration inflows into Spain over the period. Although fiscal policy was in surplus and public debt was falling, the current account went into large and increasing deficits over the period which significantly deteriorated

---

[1] Estrada, Jimeno and Malo de Molina (2009) provides the main facts regarding the macroeconomic performance of the Spanish economy during the period 1990–2007. Suárez (2010) describes the strengths and weaknesses of Spain's long growth cycle, the real and financial imbalances accumulated towards its end, the troubles faced at the current stage and some ongoing structural reforms intended to revive growth.

[2] See Gavilán *et al.* (2011).

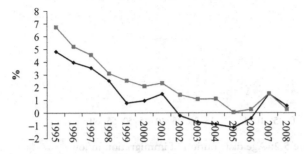

Figure 5.1: *Ex post* real interest rates, 1995–2008

the international investment position of the country. In this section, we document these facts.[3]

2.1 Interest rates

Figure 5.1 gives the evolution of *ex post* real long-term and short-term interest rates in Spain. As observed in Figure 5.1, despite a slight increase after 2005 the fall in interest rates during the period was truly remarkable: between 1995 and 2005 long-term (short-term) rates fell by around 7 (6) percentage points. Nominal convergence in the run-up to EMU, lax monetary policy since the early 2000s, the anchoring of inflation expectations and a positive inflation differential in Spain are behind that large decrease.[4] As shown by Fagan and Gaspar (2008) this resembles the macroeconomic performance of other catching-up economies which entered EMU from an initial position of relatively high nominal interest rates.

2.2 Immigration

Immigration inflows were another important factor behind the expansionary process in the Spanish economy. In Spain, traditionally an

---

[3] The data come from the OECD *Economic Outlook*, except those for the Spanish current account balance and international investment position (Banco de España). Population data are from Instituto Nacional de Estadística (INE).

[4] Indeed, it is controversial to what extent this fall truly resembles a reduction in the cost of financing. For some (see, for instance, Blanco and Restoy, 2007 and Gimeno and Marqués, 2008) the reduction in inflation uncertainty explains a great deal of the decline in real interest rates, so that the actual real cost of financing might have decreased significantly less than that indicated by *ex post* real rates.

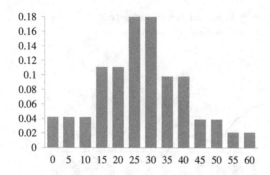

Figure 5.2: Age distribution of immigration inflows

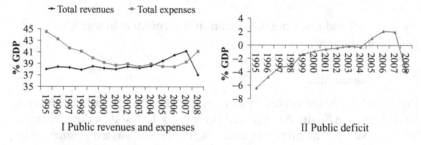

I Public revenues and expenses   II Public deficit

Figure 5.3: Public finances, 1995–2008

out-migration country, these inflows reached a significant scale in the years immediately before the creation of EMU and, since then, they have intensively transformed the Spanish population. Thus, foreign population residing in Spain increased from 0.35 million (1 per cent of total population) in 1995 to 5.22 million (11 per cent of total population) in 2008. In addition, these inflows have modified the age distribution in the Spanish population and reduced the dependency ratio since, as is usual in international migration flows, the age distribution of the immigrants that have entered Spain has been younger than that of natives (see Figure 5.2).

2.3   Fiscal consolidation

As is clear from Figure 5.3, up to 2007 fiscal consolidation in Spain was achieved through both a reduction in expenditures and an increase in revenues. Thus, the public deficit, which was around 6.5 per cent of GDP in 1995, gradually disappeared, turning into a surplus of almost 2 per cent of GDP in 2007. In 2008, however, with the arrival of the global

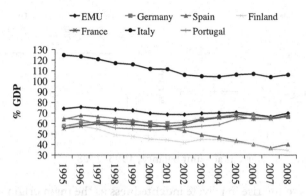

Figure 5.4: Public debt, 1995–2008

Figure 5.5: External imbalance, 1995–2008

financial crisis, government disbursements increased again, revenues fell and the public deficit reached 4 per cent of GDP. Overall, the process of fiscal consolidation over this period contributed to a considerable reduction of public debt, which decreased from 63.3 per cent of GDP in 1995 to 39.7 per cent in 2008. As shown in Figure 5.4, Spain significantly outperformed other EMU countries on this account.

2.4   External imbalance

As shown in Figure 5.5, the Spanish current account balance as a percentage of GDP fell almost monotonically during the 1995–2008 period and led to a very pronounced deterioration in the share of net foreign assets in GDP, which decreased from around −22 per cent in 1995 to around −80 per cent in 2008. The increase in current account deficits over this period, despite the process of consolidation of public accounts,

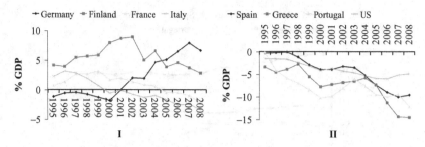

Figure 5.6: Current account balance, 1995–2008

clearly points to the rise in private indebtedness as the main origin of this external imbalance.

In a cross-country comparison (Figure 5.6), it is evident that the increasing Spanish dependence on external financing over this period is truly remarkable, comparable only to that of Portugal and Greece and more pronounced than that of the US. It also contrasts with the situation of other countries in EMU. Thus, while Germany and Finland exhibited sizeable current account surpluses, France and Italy showed considerably less deterioration in their current account balance than that of Spain.

3   Accounting for the expansion, measuring the imbalances

In order to frame the macroeconomic performance of the Spanish economy since accession to EMU, we rely on a structural model to guide us in the interpretation of the sources of growth during the pre-crisis period and in the evaluation of alternative policies. Without such a theoretical reference, it is not possible either to provide a quantitative assessment of the factors driving the expansion or to define a useful concept of 'imbalances' to discuss the nature of the adjustment process.[5]

Here our theoretical framework is an overlapping generations (OLG) model, along the lines of Auerbach and Kotlikoff (1987), Rojas (2005) and Storesletten (2000) of a small open economy within a monetary union, enriched with monopolistic competition in the product and labour

---

[5] Among the new initiatives of the von Rompuy EU task force on economic governance there is the strengthening of macroeconomic surveillance of member countries. As an example of a 'surveillance report' see European Commission (2010). Typically, these surveillance exercises provide very rich and detailed descriptive information about the macroeconomic situation of each country but are still a bit short on interpretation, since they lack a reference model with which the macroeconomic indicators could be confronted and, hence, interpreted.

market (see Gavilán *et al.*, 2011) and calibrated to replicate the main facts of the Spanish economy. The demographic structure of the model is very detailed, as immigration flows are one of the main shocks hitting the Spanish economy over this period. Thus, individuals differ on age, nationality, age upon arrival to Spain in the case of immigrants and skills. Together with population, the path of real interest rates is taken as exogenous. Fiscal policy is pinned down by a rule stating that the labour tax rate is adjusted to penalise large changes of this rate and deviations of the public debt ratio over GDP from the reference level of the Stability and Growth Pact (SGP) in the euro area (60 per cent). This rule captures the relative short-run stability of labour taxes over short time horizons observed in the data, and the long-run notion that the aging of the Spanish population will require tax adjustment in order to avoid excessive debt increases. In this set-up, forward-looking individuals will take into account that any change in fiscal policy will have implications for the dynamics of public debt and consequently for the evolution of labour taxes in the future.

One natural question to ask is to what extent immigration and the real interest rate can account for the evolution of the main macroeconomic variables during the expansion period. Of course, taking immigration flows as exogenous could be controversial, as the increase in employment attracted immigrants. A more fundamental explanation has to rely on other exogenous shocks (to technology or preferences) or, as in Martin and Ventura (2010), on a shock to investor sentiment that led to the collapse of a bubble or a pyramid scheme in financial markets. Other aspects of the expansion, such as the role played by the construction sector and the housing boom, can be explained by the more favourable conditions for the expansion of credit in these sectors, as their outputs are natural assets to pledge as collateral (see, for instance, Arce, Campa and Gavilán, 2008). We discuss alternative modelling strategies further in section 5 of the chapter.

We now return to the question of to what extent the large decline in interest rates and the intense demographic changes observed in the Spanish economy after 1998 can explain the evolution of the main macro-aggregates in this country over the period 1998–2008. Our approach here is to compare the actual evolution of the Spanish economy with the model's predictions under the path of interest rates and demographic changes that took place during the period 1998–2008.[6] This comparison

---

[6] Any simulation from the model requires postulating the paths of interest rates, immigration flows and fertility and mortality rates long into the future. For more details, see Gavilán *et al.* (2011).

Table 5.1: *Role of demographic changes, 1998–2008*

	Data		Model	
	1998 (%)	2008 (%)	1998 (%)	2008 (%)
Investment/GDP	23.5	29.3	23.4	26.9
Public debt/GDP	64.1	39.5	64.1	53.8
Foreign assets/GDP	−31.7	−80.6	−31.7	−44.9

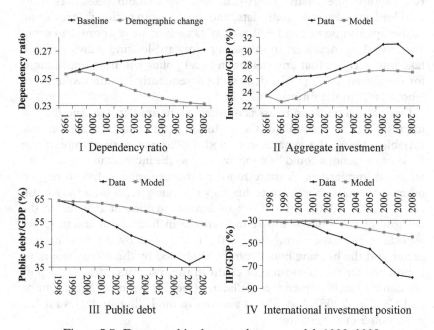

Figure 5.7: Demographic changes: data vs. model, 1998–2008

is presented in Figure 5.7 and Table 5.1. The expansion of the working-age population leads to a rise in aggregate employment, aggregate investment and, consequently, GDP. In particular, the observed demographic changes would have been responsible, on their own, for 60 per cent of the observed expansion in aggregate investment. The impact of these demographic changes is also strong in terms of the public accounts. In particular, the share of public debt in GDP gets significantly reduced from 64.1 per cent in 1998 to 53.8 per cent in 2008. This corresponds to 42 per cent of the improvement observed in this variable in the data

Table 5.2: *Role of interest rates and demographic changes, 1998–2008*

	Data		Model	
	1998 (%)	2008 (%)	2008 (Scenario 1) (%)	2008 (Scenario 2) (%)
Investment/GDP	23.5	29.3	27.4	30.1
Public debt/GDP	64.1	39.5	41.3	40.1
Foreign assets/GDP	−31.7	−80.6	−63.9	−77.3

and it has to do mostly with the increase in tax revenues associated with the expansion of economic activity.

As for the impact of demographic developments on the external imbalance of the economy (measured as the ratio of net foreign assets to GDP) the aforementioned increase in investment, together with minor changes in aggregate savings, impacts negatively on the current account and leads to a deterioration in the economy's international investment position: 27 per cent of the deterioration in the ratio of net foreign assets to GDP observed in Spain over the period 1998–2008 could be explained by the demographic changes hitting the economy.

Regarding the contribution of the fall in interest rates, it is important to distinguish between two alternative scenarios, one in which the fall in interest rates observed over the period 1998–2008 is transitory, so that by 2010 the interest rate gets back to its 1998 level, staying constant afterwards; and another in which the fall in interest rates is permanent – that is, rather than returning to their 1998 level, interest rates increase slightly between 2008 and 2010 and then stay constant at 1.5 per cent. Adding these changes in interest rates to the demographic evolution has two main effects. First, it contributes to a further expansion in aggregate investment and, via a reduction in the debt burden, to a stronger improvement in public debt (Table 5.2). It turns out that the former effect dominates so that the fall in interest rates leads to a further deterioration of the economy's international investment position. Naturally, all these effects are larger when the fall in interest rates is permanent rather than transitory. Thus, the model delivers a better description of the evolution of the ratios of public debt and of net foreign assets to GDP in the Spanish economy over the period 1998–2008 (Figure 5.8).

In short, the developments in interest rates and demographic variables observed in the Spanish economy over this period would have been responsible for much of the observed improvement in public accounts in Spain (93 per cent assuming that the observed change in interest rate

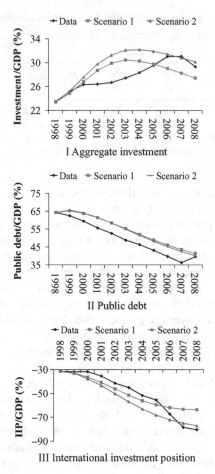

Figure 5.8: Demographic and interest rate changes: data vs. model, 1998–2008

is temporary, and 97 per cent if it is permanent) and much of the deterioration of its external imbalance (66 per cent in the former case and 93 per cent in the latter).

Obviously, these results are conditional upon a path for productivity growth. The fact that external finance served mostly to finance investment in the construction, non-traded sector, is perceived by some, for instance Giavazzi and Spaventa (2010), as a violation of the intertemporal budget constraint and, hence, as an 'external imbalance'. The path of productivity growth which would be required to justify the current account deficits accumulated during this period was, indeed, substantially above the rate of growth of productivity during the 1995–2006 period (see Banco de España, 2006). Nevertheless, these results confirm that large current account deficits do not always need to signal an 'external imbalance'.

4   **Measuring the role of fiscal policy and structural reforms**

As shown in section 3, much of the investment boom, the consolidation of the public accounts and the increase in external indebtedness observed in the Spanish economy over the period 1998–2008 can be rationalised as the natural reaction of the economy to the observed developments in interest rates and demographic variables. However, it could be argued that alternative policies could have been adopted to prevent such a large accumulation of private indebtedness. In this context, two of the most appealing ones are a deeper fiscal consolidation and the correction of labour and product market distortions during the expansionary period.

With respect to fiscal policy, rather than assuming, as in the simulation exercises described above, that government consumption represents a constant fraction of GDP (17.3 per cent) in each period, we now consider two alternative fiscal policy scenarios. In these scenarios government consumption stays constant, in *per capita* terms, at its 1998 level for ten (Scenario 1) and twenty (Scenario 2) years.

Given that, as mentioned on p. 92, GDP increases in the model over the period of analysis in response to interest rate and demographic developments, these fiscal policy scenarios imply, in practice, a temporary reduction in the share of government expenditure to GDP, this being more permanent in Scenario 2. Namely, in Scenario 1 (Scenario 2) this share decreases smoothly from 17.3 per cent in 1998 to 15.8 per cent (14.8 per cent) in 2008 (2018).

The impact of such a policy relies very much on agents' expectations of future productivity, taxes and public expenditures. Despite consumers having finite horizons, given the postulated fiscal policy rule most changes in the path of government expenditures are reflected in tax changes that affect current generations. Hence, although a lower level of less government consumption over the period 1999–2008 would have led to a stronger improvement in the public accounts by 2008 than that in the benchmark case, this fiscal tightening would have helped very little in attenuating the build-up of the economy's external imbalance over this period. In particular, the transitory tightening of government

Table 5.3: *Role of fiscal policy*

	Model (year 2008)		
	Benchmark (%)	Fiscal scenario 1 (%)	Fiscal scenario 2 (%)
Investment/GDP	27.4	27.5	28.0
Public debt/GDP	41.3	36.7	36.9
Foreign assets/GDP	−63.9	−63.0	−75.9

consumption, given a temporary fall in interest rates, would have reduced the size of this imbalance by only 1 percentage point by 2008 (Table 5.3). Under a permanent fall in interest rates, the more permanent tightening of fiscal policy would even have increased that imbalance.

The intuition for this result is straightforward. Certainly, a reduction in government consumption leads to an improvement in the public accounts and this, by itself, attenuates the economy's need for external financing. However, to the extent that households anticipate that the reduction in the share of public debt to GDP is going to imply a reduction in labour income taxes in the future (once the fiscal rule operates), they immediately modify their labour and consumption profiles so that current private borrowing increases. This increase therefore counteracts the fall in public financing needs and, depending on the temporal dimension of the fiscal tightening, it may even imply a stronger deterioration in the economy's external imbalance.

As for the corrections of product and labour market imperfections, we study the reaction of our model economy to a decrease of 2 percentage points in the labour and product market mark-ups.[7] Not surprisingly, reducing the inefficiencies in these markets leads, compared to the benchmark, to an expansion of economic activity, with increases in aggregate investment and employment, and to an improvement in external competitiveness. According to the model, the positive effects of the same 2 percentage point reduction in the mark-up are larger if the reform is carried out in the product market rather than in the labour market. Namely, with a product market reform, GDP, employment and the terms of trade would have been 1.5 per cent higher, 0.7 per cent higher and 0.3 per cent lower, respectively, by 2008, than with a labour market

---

[7] The calibration of the model considers a 20 per cent (10 per cent) mark-up in the labour (product) market. These values fall within the typical range for these parameters considered in the literature for the Spanish economy. See, for instance, Andrés, Ortega and Vallés (2008).

Table 5.4: *Role of labour and product market distortions*

	Model (year 2008)		
	Benchmark (%)	Labour market reform (%)	Product market reform (%)
Investment/GDP	27.4	27.6	28.4
Public debt/GDP	41.3	38.0	36.6
Foreign assets/GDP	−63.9	−65.0	−68.4

reform. In the long run, these differences persist: GDP, employment and the terms of trade would have been 1.6 per cent higher, 0.6 per cent higher and 0.3 per cent lower, respectively, with a 2 percentage point decrease in the product market mark-up than with the same decrease in the labour market mark-up.

The impact that these structural reforms would have had on the Spanish public accounts and on the economy's external imbalance over the period 1998–2008 is summarised in Table 5.4. Due to the expansion of economic activity, the consolidation of the public accounts over this period would have been deeper with the reforms. The external imbalance of the economy, however, would have been higher by 2008 if the reforms had been carried out. The reason for this result is that, as in the case of fiscal policy, households anticipate lower taxes and a more efficient economy in the future. Thus, in order to smooth consumption, they increase current private borrowing which, together with the increase in aggregate investment, dominates the improvement in the public accounts and then leads to higher external indebtedness.

Thus, a structural reform in the product market (like the one considered in this section) could have achieved a short-run reduction (over the 1998–2008 period) in the ratio of public debt to GDP similar to that achieved with the fiscal tightening. This, together with the fact that the long-term positive effects of structural reforms on GDP, employment, investment and competitiveness are absent with alternative fiscal policy experiments, emphasises the role of structural reforms as a powerful instrument for pursuing improvements in the economy's public accounts, not only for the period 1998–2008 but also for the future. In this sense, as mentioned above, the fact that these reforms may lead to a worsening of the economy's external imbalance in the short run should not be worrisome. The worsening arises naturally from (1) increased investment (once inefficiencies have been reduced) and (2) households' consumption smoothing behaviour, as a response to the fact that in the future the economy will be wealthier, having less distorted product and labour markets.

5   Concluding remarks

The emergence of a huge current account deficit was one of the main characteristics of developments in the Spanish economy during the period of robust economic growth prior to the current crisis. This chapter tries to disentangle the main drivers behind this upswing. To this end, we calibrate a small open-economy model for Spain that replicates relatively well the main features of the Spanish economy during the last decade. According to this model two main factors turn out to be particularly relevant in explaining these developments: first, the decline in interest rates derived from Spain's participation in EMU; and, second, the far-reaching demographic change brought about by huge immigration flows.

Apart from the role of these two factors, which have already been emphasised by the existing literature, our chapter investigates the role played by economic policies in the build-up of the Spanish external imbalance. First, considerable attention has been given in the related literature to the potential role fiscal policy might play in the reduction of this imbalance. In this chapter, the role of fiscal policy is analysed by means of two counterfactual scenarios that try to measure what the external imbalance would have been if significantly tighter fiscal policies had been applied during the last decade. This restrictive fiscal policy is simulated through lower public expenditure growth than that observed in the data. Our results show that the role that a tightening of fiscal policy could have played in the reduction of the Spanish external imbalance would have been very limited and would have depended on the temporal dimension of this tightening. A transitory change in fiscal policy would have reduced the economy's external imbalance only very slightly, by affecting public savings without significantly distorting private ones. Instead, a permanent fiscal tightening would have had a negative effect on the economy's net foreign assets, as it would have distorted optimal decisions by forward-looking agents and would have reduced private savings.

Second, we investigate the role played by labour and product market reforms in the correction of this imbalance. This is relevant insofar as the Spanish economy experienced a progressive increase in its prices and costs relative to those of its main competitors during the economic boom, which may have had an effect on net exports, and there is evidence that this rise in relative prices and wages is related to labour market rigidities and insufficient competition in some markets. Our results show that, if structural reforms in labour and product markets had been adopted in the Spanish economy over the period 1998–2008, the expansion of economic activity, investment and employment would have been stronger than the one observed over that period. The external competitiveness of the economy would also have improved relative to a non-reform scenario and the improvement in the public accounts would have been larger. These reforms would, however, have implied a further deterioration of the Spanish external imbalance over the 1998–2008 period. Increased investment, once market distortions had been reduced, and reduced private savings, as households which anticipated lower taxes and a more efficient economy in the future tried to smooth their consumption, would be responsible for this further deterioration. Nevertheless, it is worth mentioning that, despite this short run effect on the economy's external imbalance, in this model structural reforms, besides improving GDP, employment, investment and competitiveness in the long run, constitute a very effective policy instrument for achieving fiscal consolidation.

The framework set out in this chapter could also be used to analyse the different policy options faced by the Spanish economy after the crisis. Indeed, the economic crisis has dramatically changed the outlook for the Spanish economy. It has helped to correct, at least partially, the current account deficit but it has brought about a huge public deficit and a dramatic increase in unemployment. Different policy options could be appropriate for confronting these problems. We plan to analyse the consequences and trade-offs of these different policy options and their implications for the dynamics of the external imbalance in the future.

References

Andrés, J., E. Ortega and J. Vallés (2008). 'Competition and inflation differentials in EMU', *Journal of Economic Dynamics and Control*, 32(3): 848–74
Arce, Ó., J. M. Campa and A. Gavilán (2008). 'Asymmetric collateral requirements and output composition', Banco de España Working Paper, No. **0837**
Auerbach, A. J. and L. J. Kotlikoff (1987). *Dynamic Fiscal Policy*, Cambridge University Press
Banco de España (2006). *Informe Anual*
Blanco, R. and F. Restoy (2007). 'Have real interest rates really fallen that much in Spain?', Banco de España Working Paper, No. **0704**
Estrada, A., J. F. Jimeno and J. L. Malo de Molina (2009). 'The Spanish economy in EMU: the first ten years', Banco de España Occasional Paper, No. **0901**
European Commission (2010). 'Surveillance of intra-Euro-Area competitiveness and imbalances', *European Economy*, 1
Fagan, G. and V. Gaspar (2008). 'Macroeconomic adjustment to monetary union', ECB Working Paper, No. **946**

Gavilán, Á., P. Hernández de Cos, J. F. Jimeno and J. Rojas (2011). 'Fiscal policy, structural reforms and external imbalances: a quantitative evaluation for Spain', Working Paper, No. 1107, Banco de España
Giavazzi, F., and L. Spaventa (2010). 'Why the current account may matter in a monetary union', Chapter 11 in this volume
Gimeno, R. and J. M. Marqués (2008). 'Uncertainty and the price of risk in a nominal convergence process', Banco de España Working Paper, No. 0802
Martin, A. and J. Ventura (2010). 'Theoretical notes on bubbles and the current crisis', CEPR Discussion Paper, No. 8038
Rojas, J. A. (2005). 'Life-cycle earnings, cohort size effects and social security: a quantitative exploration', *Journal of Public Economics*, **89**: 465–85
Storesletten, K. (2000). 'Sustaining fiscal policy through immigration', *Journal of Political Economy*, **108**: 300–23
Suárez, J. (2010). 'The Spanish crisis: background and policy challenges', CEPR Discussion Paper, No. 7909

6   The financial crisis and the Baltic countries

*Aurelijus Dabušinskas and Martti Randveer**

1   Introduction

After several years of very strong economic growth, the Baltic countries have witnessed one of the deepest recessions in the world. In an historical context, the expected cumulative output loss associated with this Baltic recession is almost twice the size of the losses suffered by the hardest-hit countries in the 1997–8 Asian crisis, and in the case of Latvia comes close to the size of the US output decline during the Great Depression.

Despite many similarities in structural characteristics (including fixed exchange rate arrangements) and macroeconomic developments prior to the crisis, the Baltic countries have shown clear differences in their ability to cope with the common negative shocks associated with the global economic crisis. Estonia has been more successful than its Baltic neighbours in withstanding the impact of the financial crisis, and will join the euro area from 2011. Resilience to the crisis has been weakest in Latvia, which is dependent on financial support from the International Monetary Fund (IMF) and the EU and has a more uncertain economic outlook.

Our chapter is motivated by the following three questions. First, why was the cyclical volatility in the Baltic countries so large? Second, why did the financial crisis have such a strong negative impact on the Baltic economies? And, finally, what explains the differences in the individual countries' ability to deal with the common negative shock? To set the stage for addressing the first two questions, in section 2 we compare the last economic cycle in the Baltic countries with historical business cycle episodes in OECD countries and some emerging market economies. In addition, we discuss a number of similarities and differences in several macroeconomic, economic policy and structural variables among the three Baltic countries. In section 3, we look at various causes and

* We would like to thank Liina Kulu and Priit Jeenas for research assistance and Karsten Staehr and Dmitry Kulikov for discussions and helpful comments.

mechanisms that have amplified the business cycle in the Baltic countries: procyclical developments in the financial sector, fiscal policy, labour market developments, etc. Section 4 discusses two key economic policy issues: (1) high uncertainty about the actual cyclical position of the Baltic economies in real time and (2) the main policy measures that have been undertaken by the Baltic countries to counter cyclical fluctuations. The analysis of the impact of the financial crisis would be incomplete if we concentrated only on the post-crisis period. Therefore we also focus on the years preceding the recession. Section 5 concludes.

The contribution of the chapter is two-fold. First, it contributes to the comparative analysis of the Baltic countries prior to and after the onset of the global financial crisis (see, for instance, Brixiova, Morgan and Worgötter, 2009; Brixiova, Vartia and Worgötter, 2009; Becker *et al.*, 2010; European Commission, 2010; Gardo and Martin, 2010). Second, it is related to the literature that analyses the determinants of the depth of the recent recession in different countries (see Berglöf *et al.*, 2009; Blanchard, Faruqee and Das, 2010; IMF, 2010; Lane and Milesi-Ferretti, 2011).

2   Descriptive and comparative evidence

In this section, we compare the latest business cycle of the Baltic States with economic fluctuations in OECD countries and some emerging market economies during the last fifty years. In addition, we look at the similarities and differences in several macroeconomic, economic policy and structural variables between the three Baltic countries. The aim of the intra-Baltic comparison is to shed light on the potential reasons for differences in the crisis outcomes within the region.

2.1   *Comparison with previous recessions in OECD countries and selected emerging markets*

To identify and date business cycles, we employ the method developed by Bry and Boschan (1971) and Harding and Pagan (2002) that has recently been used by Claessens *et al.* (2008). It determines cyclical turning points in the log-level of a series, whereby a cycle starts with a peak, ends with the next peak and consists of two phases in between – a contraction (from peak to trough) and an expansion (from trough to peak). Specifically, a peak is reached in the quarterly time series y_t at time t if

$$\{[(y_t - y_{t-2}) > 0, \ (y_t - y_{t-1}) > 0] \text{ and}$$
$$[(y_{t+2} - y_t) < 0, \ (y_{t+1} - y_t) < 0]\};$$

whereas a trough is achieved at time t if

$$\{[(y_t - y_{t-2}) < 0, (y_t - y_{t-1}) < 0] \text{ and}$$
$$[(y_{t+2} - y_t) > 0, (y_{t+1} - y_t) > 0]\}.$$

The algorithm also assumes that the minimum duration of the full cycle is five quarters and that the contractionary and expansionary phases last at least two quarters each. To identify countries' business cycles, we have applied this algorithm to their GDP series.

We consider a sample of all OECD countries[1] and selected emerging market economies,[2] and we split it into two groups: (1) advanced countries and (2) emerging market economies. The former consists of the OECD countries except the Czech Republic, Hungary, Korea, Mexico, Poland, Slovakia and Turkey, which in the following analysis appear in the emerging markets group. Accordingly, our sample includes twenty-three advanced countries and eighteen emerging market economies.

Our data consist of quarterly series for the period 1960Q1–2007Q4 obtained from the IMF's *International Financial Statistics* (IFS). In particular, we focus on fourteen macroeconomic variables: output (GDP), private consumption, investment, government consumption, exports, imports, net exports, employment, unemployment, net foreign capital inflows, bank credit, real interest rates, share prices and CPI-based real effective exchange rates. Most of the variables are seasonally adjusted;[3] GDP and its components are in constant prices, and credit and share prices are deflated by GDP deflators.

Altogether we identify 133 recessions, ninety-three in advanced economies and forty in emerging markets. In addition to the number of countries in our sample, an important determinant of the number of cyclical episodes we can analyse is data availability (which is better for advanced countries). Table 6.A1 (in the appendix, see p. 126) presents the number of recessionary episodes for each of our variables and shows that our data are more complete for GDP components, financial variables and external variables, but considerably less so for labour market indicators.

Figure 6.1 illustrates average macroeconomic developments four years before and three years after the quarter, denoted by t, when the level

---

[1] Australia, Austria, Belgium, Canada, Czech Republic, Denmark, Finland, France, Germany, Greece, Hungary, Iceland, Ireland, Italy, Japan, Korea, Luxembourg, Mexico, Netherlands, New Zealand, Norway, Poland, Portugal, Slovakia, Spain, Sweden, Switzerland, Turkey, UK, US.

[2] Argentina, Brazil, Chile, Colombia, Indonesia, Jordan, Malaysia, Philippines, Russia, South Africa, Thailand. We tried to include emerging market economies that are financially open. The sample of countries was also constrained by data availability.

[3] Output, private consumption, investment, government consumption, exports, imports, net exports, employment, unemployment and bank credit.

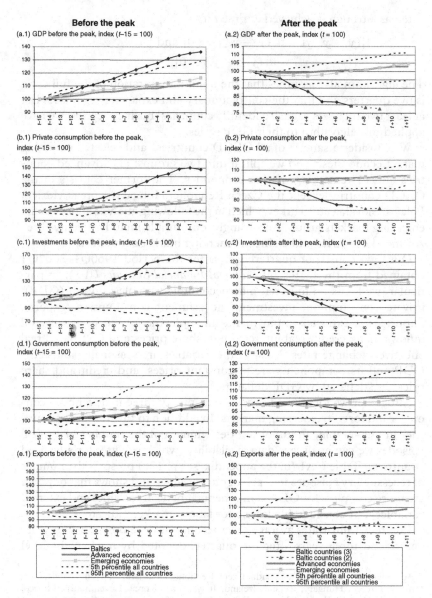

Figure 6.1: Comparison with previous recessions

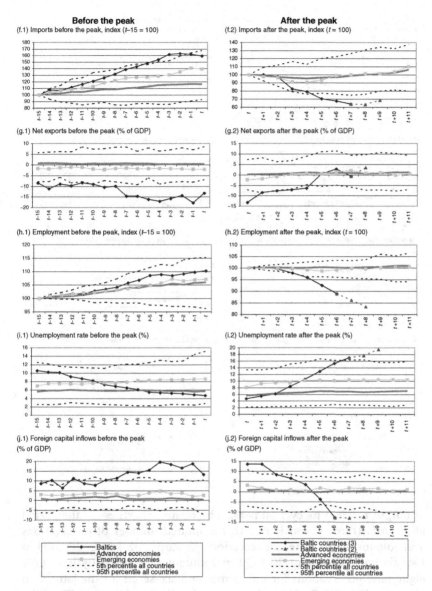

Figure 6.1: (cont.)

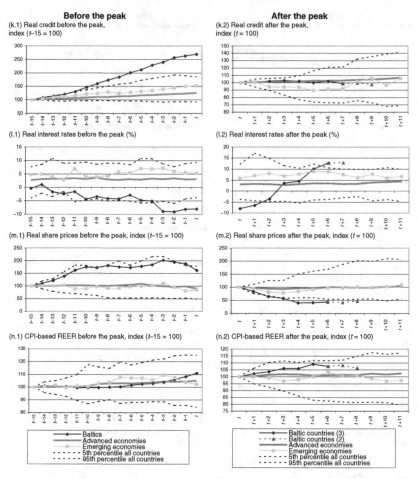

Figure 6.1: (*cont.*)

of output reached its cyclical peak. The relative shortness of the period afterwards (three years) is due to the limited number of observations available for the most recent recession. As output peaked in 2007Q4 in Estonia and Latvia and 2008Q2 in Lithuania, we currently have only eight–nine observations for the former and six–seven for the latter.[4] In all cases, Figure 6.1 shows the (unweighted) average dynamics of the variables considered for advanced countries, emerging economies and

---

[4] The Baltic economies are represented by unweighted averages. As the Lithuanian series are shorter after the peak, the last two observations in Figure 6.1 are based on the Estonian and Latvian data.

the Baltic States. To capture the overall variation in the data, it also reports the 5th and 95th percentiles for the whole sample.

It immediately follows from Figure 6.1 that the Baltic business cycle has been very pronounced, in both its upswing and its downturn. In terms of output dynamics, for example, both phases of the cycle fall well beyond the 95th and 5th percentiles of the respective phases of past economic cycles.

In many other respects, the latest macroeconomic experience of the Baltic economies conforms well with the business cycle typical of emerging markets. That includes high volatility of macroeconomic variables, sudden stops in capital inflows, consumption volatility exceeding output volatility, counter-cyclical trade balances and counter-cyclical real interest rates that, in addition, lead the cycle.[5] Except for the real interest rate leading the cycle, we find that the same patterns characterise the Baltic economies as well.[6]

The main driver of output changes in the Baltic States was an initial boom and a subsequent steep decline in domestic demand. Both private consumption and investment exceeded the 95th percentile during expansion and declined below the 5th percentile afterwards. The largest swings in private consumption – in fact, the most pronounced ones among all other episodes in our data – took place in Latvia. In addition, changes in private consumption in all three Baltic States, during both phases of the cycle, were stronger than the respective changes in their output levels.

The Baltic States also stand out for the extent of the external vulnerabilities that emerged during the boom. Both trade deficits and foreign capital inflows were significantly higher than the average for emerging

[5] See, for example, Neumeyer and Perri (2005) and Aquiar and Gopinath (2007). A quick look at the data from our sample of emerging countries confirms these facts: (1) the volatility of macroeconomic variables is higher than in advanced economies, (2) net foreign capital inflows drop after a cyclical peak, (3) real interest rates increase after the peak, (4) trade balances improve in recessions. However, we do not find clear evidence that the real interest rates lead the cycle and, in contrast with the experience of the Baltic States during the last cycle, consumption volatility is not significantly higher than the volatility in economic growth.

[6] At first glance, the recent economic cycle of the Baltic economies also resembles the stylised boom–bust cycle that was typically observed after exchange rate-based (ERB) inflation stabilisation programmes in Latin American countries (Calvo and Vegh, 1999). Though qualitatively the two cycles are indeed alike, a crucial distinction between the two phenomena is their timing. The stylised ERB boom–bust cycle is intrinsically linked to the initiation of a stabilisation programme. Its boom phase starts with the programme and typically lasts for up to three years, after which an economic slowdown takes place, regardless of whether the programme is successful or not. Hence, the ERB cycle describes typical post-stabilisation dynamics over the time horizon of about five years. By contrast, the Baltic economic cycle we discuss in the chapter occurred more than ten years after the inflation stabilisations in these countries.

market economies. In international comparisons another remarkable feature is the speed at which these imbalances changed as the crisis struck.
A sudden stop in foreign capital inflows meant that over a little more than
one year capital inflows of around 15 per cent of GDP turned into outflows exceeding 10 per cent of GDP. Similarly, the initial trade deficit of
about 15 per cent of GDP turned into a small surplus. Both changes were
considerably larger than the average for emerging market economies.

In international comparisons, the dynamics of financial variables in
the Baltic States have been quite extraordinary as well. The cumulative
change in real interest rates, which were highly negative before the crisis
and turned positive during the recession, exceeded 15 percentage points,
which is well above the typical adjustment in emerging markets. The
dynamics of credit showed some qualitative differences, however. Before
the crisis, the rise in the stock of credit in the Baltic States was one
of the largest internationally, but its decline was slower than average in
emerging markets.

The significant decline in output is also reflected in labour market
variables. The decline in employment and the increase in unemployment
are both much larger in the Baltic States than those experienced by
emerging or advanced economies in past downturns.

However, there are two characteristics of the Baltic business cycle
that do not corroborate the picture of the atypically high volatility of
these economies. First, growth in government consumption before the
recession was close to the average in advanced and emerging countries
under similar cyclical circumstances, indicating that fiscal policy was not
a strong contributor to the boom, at least not via public consumption.
Second, our proxy for international cost competitiveness – the CPI-based
real effective exchange rate – did not appreciate unusually strongly during
the expansionary phase. For most of the period, the appreciation was
lower than the average for emerging market economies. Yet, in contrast
to other countries' experience, the real effective exchange rate continued
to appreciate for over a year after the start of the recession before reversing
its trend.

2.2   Comparison of the Baltic States

In international comparisons, the Baltic economies are often grouped
together as they are similar structurally (e.g. in terms of size, openness,
exchange rate regime, rapid financial integration and labour market flexibility) and their macroeconomic developments have largely followed the
same path. However, their individual ability to deal with the impact of the
global economic crisis has differed. Estonia and Lithuania, for example,

have withstood the financial shock more successfully than Latvia. To improve our understanding of this variation in resilience, we next document some differences among the Baltic economies. We begin from macroeconomic developments and then focus on economic policies and structural characteristics.

All three Baltic countries experienced high volatility in their macroeconomic variables (see Figure 6.2), but cyclical fluctuations were somewhat stronger in Latvia than in Estonia and Lithuania. That is more evident in the case of external and competitiveness indicators and some of the financial variables.

Judging by the extent of trade imbalances and capital inflows, prior to the crisis Latvia displayed the highest level of external vulnerabilities among the Baltic economies. During the boom, its trade deficit reached 15 per cent of GDP compared to about 10 per cent of GDP in Estonia and Lithuania. The sudden stop and the subsequent outflow of capital as well as the forced improvement in the trade balance were larger in Latvia as well. During the recession, the net foreign capital flows to Latvia, relative to its GDP, changed by an astonishing 35 percentage points; in Estonia and Lithuania the change was close to 20 percentage points.

Furthermore, rapid growth during 2004–7 had the strongest impact on Latvian prices and wages, resulting in the highest appreciation of the real exchange rate in the region. The largest difference in this regard is shown by the unit labour cost-based real effective exchange rate, which over 2004–8 appreciated by 85 per cent in Latvia, but only by 25 per cent and 40 per cent in Lithuania and Estonia, respectively.

The higher volatility of the Latvian cycle was also evident in some of our financial variables. Fluctuations in the real interest rate and house prices were more pronounced in Latvia than in Estonia and Lithuania.

As regards economic policies, the main difference among the Baltic countries concerns fiscal policy. Though it is difficult to identify the exact reasons why, fiscal discipline has been consistently stronger in Estonia: during the expansionary phase, the Estonian fiscal balance was on average 2.5–3 percentage points higher than that of its neighbours. An even larger difference emerged in 2009, when fiscal deficits widened to 9 per cent of GDP in Latvia and Lithuania but remained slightly under 2 per cent of GDP in Estonia. An important additional reason for containing the deficit in the latter case was the Estonian intention to join the euro area in 2011.

Another, though related, feature of Estonian fiscal policy prior to the crisis was the accumulation of sizeable fiscal reserves, amounting to about 10 per cent of GDP, that could be used to finance the deficits of 2008 and

106   *Aurelijus Dabušinskas and Martti Randveer*

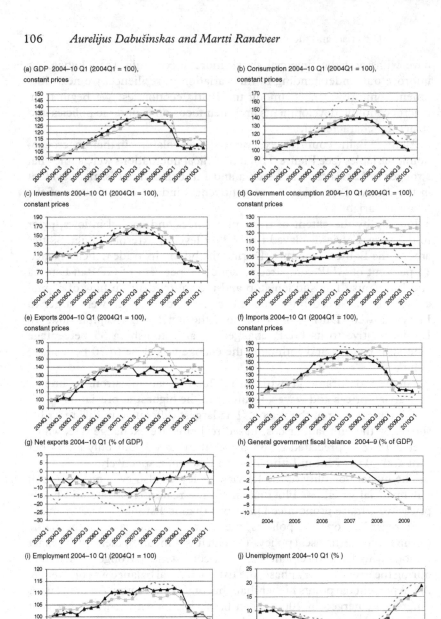

Figure 6.2: Comparison of the Baltic States, 2004–9 or 2004–10

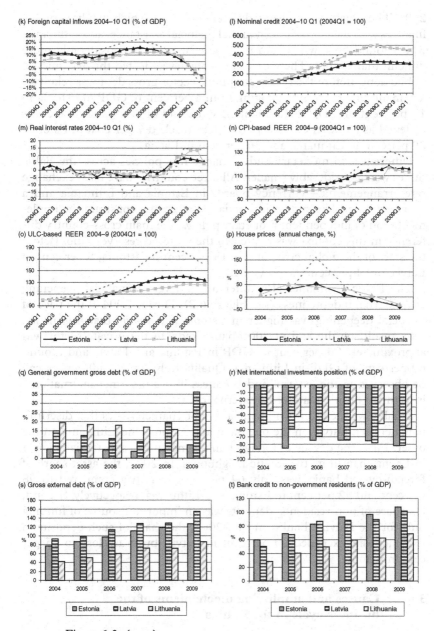

Figure 6.2: (cont.)

2009. The situation was clearly different in Latvia, which stabilised public finances with the help of international financial assistance, and Lithuania, which found borrowing from the financial markets considerably more difficult than before. These developments have affected the dynamics of public debt. Before the recession, public sector gross debt was relatively low in all three countries, ranging from 4 per cent of GDP in Estonia to 17 per cent of GDP in Lithuania. By the end of 2009, the differences widened as the level of gross public debt reached 7 per cent in Estonia, 29 per cent in Lithuania and 36 per cent in Latvia.

Differences in monetary and exchange rate policies across the Baltic States were considerably smaller. All three countries have fixed exchange rate arrangements – currency boards in Estonia and Lithuania and a currency board-like system in Latvia – that greatly constrain the implementation of independent monetary policy. The main cross-country difference in this context was related to the required reserves ratio. Before the start of the global crisis, it was 15 per cent in Estonia, 8 per cent in Latvia and 4 per cent in Lithuania.

The Baltic economies also differ in the level of financial deepening and external indebtedness (see Figure 6.2). During 2004–9 the pace of financial deepening was higher in Estonia and Latvia than Lithuania. As a result, by the end of 2007 bank credit to the private sector was approximately 90 per cent of GDP in Estonia and Latvia and around 60 per cent of GDP in Lithuania. Qualitatively similar differences can be observed in the external indebtedness indicators – net international investment position and gross external debt.

Finally, we mention two financial sector characteristics that discriminate between Latvia on the one hand and Estonia and Lithuania on the other. First, the degree of foreign bank ownership is substantially lower in Latvia than in its two Baltic neighbours. In 2008, the asset share of foreign-owned banks was only 64 per cent in Latvia compared to 98 per cent and 92 per cent in Estonia and Lithuania, respectively. Second, the share of non-residents' deposits was an important source of funding only for the Latvian banks. In mid-2008, the share of such deposits in total deposits exceeded 40 per cent in Latvia, but was close to 15 per cent in Estonia.

3   Causes and amplifying mechanisms of the business cycle in the Baltics

In section 2, we demonstrated that in international and historical perspective the recent economic cycle of the Baltic States was indeed very pronounced. After experiencing one of the strongest expansions right

Table 6.1: *Correlation between output gap and financial variables: EU countries, 2004–9 (correlation coefficients)*

	Foreign capital inflows	Real interest rates	Credit gap
Latvia	0.90	−0.86	0.76
Lithuania	0.80	−0.71	0.73
Estonia	0.78	−0.86	0.70
Slovenia	0.77	−0.05	0.51
Hungary	0.71	−0.19	0.51
Spain	0.69	0.00	0.56
Poland	0.50	−0.46	0.64
Ireland	0.46	−0.15	0.80
Cyprus	0.44		−0.36
Greece	0.44	0.29	0.86
UK	0.30		
Denmark	0.22		0.45
Italy	0.01	0.72	0.57
Slovakia	−0.03	0.24	0.42
Luxembourg	−0.18	−0.18	0.53
Portugal	−0.19	0.13	−0.29
Belgium	−0.22	−0.33	0.57
Czech Republic	−0.26	0.50	0.43
Malta	−0.26		−0.03
Netherlands	−0.28	−0.20	0.33
Finland	−0.50	−0.01	0.72
Austria	−0.52	0.58	0.42
France	−0.53	−0.52	0.69
Germany	−0.74	0.07	−0.02
Unweighted average	0.14	−0.10	0.46

Note: The output gaps and the cyclical component of credit are calculated by the HP filter. The real interest rate is the difference between the nominal interest rate on long-term government bonds and the GDP deflator inflation. The data are quarterly.
Source: Eurostat, own calculations.

before the global financial crisis, these countries witnessed the steepest economic contraction in the world. In this section we look into the causes and mechanisms that amplified the Baltic cycle. In this regard, we discuss five factors: the contribution of the financial sector; the role of fiscal and monetary policies; labour market developments; external trade shocks; and the workings of the competitiveness channel.

The most obvious explanation for the high cyclical fluctuation of the Baltic economies is very strong procyclical behaviour of the financial sector. Table 6.1 reports correlation coefficients between output gaps and several financial variables (credit, real interest rates and net foreign capital inflows) for EU countries. According to it, the co-movement

Table 6.2: *Structure of foreign capital inflows: the Baltic countries, 2004–9 (% of GDP)*

	2004	2005	2006	2007	2008	2009
FDI	3.9	7.3	5.6	5.0	3.3	0.6
Portfolio investments	2.8	−5.9	−2.9	−1.8	1.3	−2.1
Other investments	4.6	10.7	18.4	15.5	5.8	−6.3
Total capital inflows	11.4	12.2	21.2	18.7	10.4	−7.8

Source: ECB.

between the financial variables and the cyclical component of output in the Baltic countries has been much stronger than in other EU countries. That is especially true for foreign capital inflows and real interest rates. As mentioned earlier, foreign capital inflows in the Baltic countries were exceptionally large during the expansion but reversed during the recession; likewise, real interest rates were negative before the cyclical peak and increased sharply afterwards. A co-movement between credit and output gaps is also clearly evident, but it has been of a similar magnitude in several other EU countries as well.

In terms of composition, changes in foreign capital inflows were mainly driven by the category 'other investments', most of which is bank loans and cross-border deposits (Table 6.2).[7] Indeed, the difference between capital inflows to the Baltic States and to Central European countries (Poland, Czech Republic, Hungary, Slovakia) is accounted for by the size of other investments. While the level of foreign direct investment (FDI) as a share of GDP was largely similar in both country groups, the size of capital inflows via the financial sector was considerably higher in the Baltic countries.

The exceptionally high banking sector-intermediated capital inflows during the boom years had many causes. According to Bakker and Gulde (2010), high capital inflows to the EU new member states in general could be explained by the overall optimism about the region and expectations of its convergence to Western European income levels; strategic considerations by foreign investors in gaining market access; and the favourable global environment with abundant liquidity and low risk aversion. Though these considerations apply to the Baltic experience as well,

---

[7] As the banking sector in Estonia and Lithuania is dominated by foreign banks, these flows consisted mostly of credit from parent banks. In Latvia, where domestic bank ownership is higher, domestic banks attracted substantial funds from abroad in the form of syndicated loans and non-resident deposits. However, credit from parent banks was the most important for Latvia as well.

they cannot fully explain why the share of foreign capital that the Baltic countries received via the banking sector was substantially higher than in the case of Central European countries. We suggest, therefore, that in addition to the above factors, high capital inflows via the financial sector and the associated rapid credit expansion in the Baltic economies were caused by a combination of (1) proximity to the Nordic countries; (2) business strategies adopted by foreign banks operating in the Baltic markets; (3) the relatively small size of the Baltic economies; and (4) the operation of the real interest rate channel.

The major Nordic (mostly Swedish) banks had already gained a significant market share in Estonia in the second half of the 1990s and soon thereafter established a strong position in Lithuania and Latvia as well. Swedish banks were among the first in the EU to start an active expansion of retail banking activities abroad (Riksbank, 2007). In the process, they competed for market share aggressively[8] and came to treat the Baltic markets quite similarly to their home ones. Specifically, nominal interest rates and other loan conditions in the Baltic countries were set almost at the same level as in the Nordic countries. Favourable lending conditions enabled very high credit growth, which was to a large extent financed by loans from parent banks.[9] The expansion was also supported by high profitability. For example, in 2007 profits from operations in the Baltic countries accounted for over a third of the total profits of Swedbank, a Nordic bank with the strongest presence in the Baltics, whereas in terms of assets its exposure to the region was only 15 per cent.[10]

The increase in credit supply was further supported by positive trends in asset markets, especially the real estate market.[11] Rapidly expanding lending volumes increased liquidity and asset prices, which increased the value of collateral. This in turn minimised loan losses: during 2005–7 the share of non-performing loans in the Baltic countries was significantly lower than in other new EU member countries. The perception of low credit risk further facilitated lending, which was made possible by capital transfers from parent banks.

---

[8] For example, in Estonia, the strong credit growth during the latter part of the expansion appeared to have been prolonged by foreign banks with smaller market shares, who actively tried to increase their market position by, *inter alia*, relaxing the lending standards.

[9] By the end of 2007, the Baltic country banks' liabilities to non-residents were roughly half of their total liabilities.

[10] With regard to credit developments in Estonia, Brixiova, Vartia and Worgötter (2009) argued that Nordic banks might have taken increased risks in Estonia because compared to total portfolios their exposure in Estonia was relatively small. In principle, this argument could be extended to the Baltic countries as a whole.

[11] The cumulative (nominal) house price growth over the 2004–7 period was 180 per cent in Estonia, 210 per cent in Lithuania and 360 per cent in Latvia (ECB, 2010).

Table 6.3: *Changes in credit portfolios: selected Nordic banks on group level and Estonia, 2008Q3–2010Q4 (%)*

	Group level	In Estonia
Danske	−6.8	−20.4
Nordea	7.5	11.5
SEB	−3.5	−8.6
Swedbank	−3.3	−10.2

Note: The changes in credit in Estonia are calculated before loan provisions.
Source: Bank of Estonia and financial reports of Swedbank, SEB, Danske Bank and Nordea Bank.

The rapid expansion in domestic demand was also supported by the dynamics of real interest rates. Highly credible exchange rate arrangements and favourable credit risk assessments of the Baltic countries resulted in a high degree of nominal interest rate convergence. As demand pressures increased and inflation accelerated, real interest rates turned negative. This and the associated positive wealth effects from asset price inflation further increased domestic demand and lending. The combination of optimistic expectations, high risk tolerance and a fear of losing market share made banks reluctant to tighten lending standards in response to increases in their overall level of risk in the Baltic countries. In a similar manner, the rapidly increasing debt burden of domestic borrowers and the associated risks did not have a strong and rapid impact on credit demand.

The reversal of capital inflows and credit contraction that followed the deepening of the global financial crisis in September 2008 reflected an interplay of both credit supply and demand factors. The severity of these developments, however, had a lot to do with a high degree of external and financial vulnerabilities of the Baltic economies.

Capital inflows to the Baltic countries were dominated by banking sector intermediated financial flows, which suffered a stronger decline than other forms of foreign investment. A significant and sudden drop in these capital flows was related to rising global risk aversion and the drying up of interbank markets. Liquidity shortages and funding problems in parent banks, especially those leading to reductions in loan portfolios, were likely to affect the operations of their Baltic subsidiaries and branches as well. Notably, data on changes in the credit portfolios of the Nordic banks and their Estonian subsidiaries/branches show a clear link between changes in credit on the group and local levels (see Table 6.3). Bakker and Gulde (2010) report that, in response to the crisis, some foreign banks had advised their subsidiaries in the EU new member states that new credit would need to be financed by increases in local deposits rather than transfers from the parent banks. There were indications that similar changes in lending strategy were also implemented in several subsidiaries and branches in the Baltic countries.

In sum, it appears that the sudden stop in these previously robust capital inflows had a major impact on the credit supply and, by implication, economic activity in the Baltic countries. The importance of changes in the supply of credit is also emphasised by Ghosh (2009), who analysed credit developments in Hungary, Latvia and Poland and found that a credit crunch affected all of these countries.[12] Similarly, Takats (2010) argues that during the crisis changes in global cross-border lending were mostly driven by supply factors.

Even though net capital flows between parent banks and their Baltic subsidiaries and branches changed from inflows to outflows, foreign banks did not exit the market and their overall exposure to the Baltic economies did not decrease significantly. The volatility of capital inflows via the financial sector was actually higher in the category of cross-border flows related to non-resident deposits and syndicated loans (from foreign banks). Capital movements in both categories were more pronounced in Latvia, where domestic banks had financed themselves via non-resident deposits and syndicated loans. As mentioned earlier, the severity of the problem was exacerbated by the size of such liabilities and by uncertainty about the economic situation in Latvia.

Though the Nordic banks greatly contributed to the build-up of vulnerabilities during the boom, they also helped to stabilise the situation during the recession. The best evidence is the fact that despite a very strong economic contraction, there have not been serious problems with individual banks in either Estonia or Lithuania. Latvia, in contrast, was shaken by liquidity and solvency problems in one of its major banks in the autumn of 2008; that worsened the recession and certainly contributed to Latvia's need for international financial assistance, but the troubled bank was domestically, not foreign, owned.

The supply-side factors behind the drop in foreign capital inflows and domestic credit were later supplemented by a decrease in credit demand. The rapid slowdown in credit demand was the result of lower growth expectations, increased debt burdens (due to the fall in output), lower capacity utilisation, smaller incomes and profits and higher unemployment.

---

[12] Poland in 2008Q4, Latvia between 2008Q4 and 2009Q1, and Hungary between 2008Q4 and 2009Q2 (Ghosh, 2009).

Table 6.4: *Cyclically adjusted fiscal balance of general government, 2004–10 (% of GDP)*

	2010 forecast	2009	2008	2007	2006	2005	2004
EU (27 countries)	−5.6	−5.2	−3.2	−2.1	−2.2	−2.6	−2.9
Euro area (16 countries)	−5.1	−4.8	−2.9	−1.9	−2.0	−2.5	−2.9
Estonia	0.2	1.3	−4.1	−0.7	0.0	0.3	1.2
Latvia	−5.7	−6.3	−6.4	−4.5	−3.2	−1.5	−1.3
Lithuania	−6.1	−6.7	−5.7	−3.7	−2.1	−1.8	−2.5
Baltic countries (unweighted)	−3.9	−3.9	−5.4	−3.0	−1.8	−1.0	−0.9
Central Europe 5 (unweighted)	−4.6	−4.9	−4.7	−3.7	−5.1	−4.1	−3.7

Source: European Commission AMECO database.

As during the boom episode, procyclical developments in the financial sector since the start of the recession have been aggravated by counter-cyclical dynamics in real interest rates. The main factor behind the rise in real interest rates is the strong deceleration in inflation. The role of nominal rates is smaller because an increase in nominal interest rate spreads between the Baltics and the euro area was offset by decreases in the ECB policy rate and thus short-term money market rates. All in all, the increase in real interest rates and the negative wealth effect associated with asset price deflation have further dampened domestic demand and lending in the Baltic economies.

Fiscal policy

On the basis of our international comparison in section 2, we argued that fiscal policy was not among the primary reasons behind the recent cyclical volatility of the Baltic economies. First, during the 2004–7 expansion, the headline fiscal balances in Estonia, Latvia and Lithuania were relatively small (in absolute terms) and stable. Second, this conclusion is robust to taking into account the fact that the episode was characterised by increasingly positive output gaps and thus possibly deteriorating cyclically adjusted balances. According to the European Commission's estimates, over the 2004–7 period the cyclically adjusted (general government) balance weakened by about 3 percentage points of GDP in Latvia, 2 percentage points in Estonia and 1 percentage point in Lithuania (see Table 6.4). Such fiscal policy positions did not help to contain overheating, but their (direct) contributions to fuelling the booms could not have been very significant.

Table 6.5: *Impact of EU funds on the cyclically adjusted fiscal balance of general government: Estonia, 2005–10 (% of GDP)*

	2010 proj.	2009 proj.	2008 est.	2007	2006	2005
Cyclically adjusted balance	–0.3	–0.3	–4.6	–0.9	0.9	0.8
Transfers from EU	8.3	6.7	3.0	3.0	2.1	1.4
Transfers to EU	1.3	1.3	1.2	1.2	1.0	1.0
Cyclically adjusted balance corrected for net EU transfers	–7.3	–5.7	–6.4	–2.7	–0.2	0.3

Source: IMF Staff Report for the 2009 IV Article Consultation: Republic of Estonia: 12.

The onset of recession in 2008 worsened both headline and cyclically adjusted fiscal balances. The strongest counter-cyclical fiscal adjustment in 2008 was recorded by Estonia, where the cyclically adjusted fiscal balance weakened by $3\frac{1}{2}$ percentage points of GDP. In Latvia and Lithuania, the corresponding counter-cyclical fiscal impulse was close to 2 percentage points of GDP.

A strong further weakening of Latvian and Lithuanian headline fiscal balances took place in 2009 (by about 5 and $5\frac{1}{2}$ percentage points, respectively), but because of the rapid widening of negative output gaps, changes in the corresponding cyclically adjusted fiscal balances were small. As mentioned earlier, the situation was different in Estonia, where efforts to contain the fiscal deficit were stronger due to the plans to apply for euro area membership. As a result, the cyclically adjusted budget balance improved by $5\frac{1}{2}$ percentage points of GDP, in what constituted a very strong procyclical fiscal impulse. However, this procyclical impact of fiscal policy was greatly reduced by a rapid increase in net EU transfers (see Table 6.5). It can be expected that the frontloading of EU funds had similar counter-cyclical fiscal effects in Latvia and Lithuania as well.

Labour market

The cyclical volatility of the Baltic economies has also been influenced by labour market developments. A very important factor in this regard has been the opening of the EU15 labour markets to the citizens of the EU new member states. The entry of the Baltic countries to the EU in May 2004 led to a substantial increase in emigration to other EU countries. According to Randveer and Rõõm (2009), emigration to the (rest of the) EU from the Baltic States amounted to 0.2–0.3 per cent of their population in 2002–3 but increased to 1.3 per cent, 0.9 per cent and

0.5 per cent in Lithuania, Latvia and Estonia, respectively, in 2004–7.[13] As the latter was also a period of rapid economic expansion, high emigration flows tended to lower labour supply and put upward pressure on wages, thereby further accelerating domestic demand.[14]

With the start of the recession, emigration from the EU new member states to the EU15 has generally decelerated, but the tendencies show some differences across countries. In the UK and Ireland, the top two destination countries for such migration flows, the number of applications for social security numbers from the nationals of EU new member states in 2009 was half the number in 2007.[15] However, the number of applicants from Estonia and Lithuania remained broadly the same and the number of applicants from Latvia clearly increased. There is also evidence that emigration from Estonia to Finland, which is the main destination country for Estonia, slightly increased during 2007–9. These trends seem to support the argument that labour market integration has helped the Baltic economies to avoid even deeper recessions. More generally, however, the trends in emigration flows and their impact on the economies show that in the case of symmetric shocks labour market integration tends to exacerbate the cycle in the sender countries (this was quite evident during 2004–7, when there was an expansion in both sending and receiving countries), while in the case of asymmetric shocks it facilitates the adjustment.

External trade

All EU countries were affected by the strong decline in foreign trade that followed the collapse of Lehmans in 2008Q3. On average, imports by the ten main trading partners of each individual country in the EU27 decreased by 26 per cent (see Table 6.6). Because the Baltic countries trade intensively with each other and with Finland, Sweden and Russia, all of which recorded large declines in imports themselves, the plunge in

---

[13] The data on emigration flows from EU new member states to EU15 countries are incomplete and often unreliable.

[14] Although reliable estimates of the emigration effects on local wages are missing, close to a half of all firms covered by migration surveys conducted among Estonian firms in 2007 and 2008 agreed that emigration increased wages in the Estonian economy (Randveer and Rõõm, 2009).

[15] Right after the deepening of the financial crisis in the Autumn of 2008 there was news that many nationals from the Baltic countries had lost their jobs in EU15 and that gross emigration flows from the Baltics had decelerated. For example, the number of applicants for work permits from Lithuania dropped at the end of 2008 and the beginning of 2009. More recently, however, the number of Lithuanian applicants has recovered.

Table 6.6: *Decline in imports among the ten main trading partners of selected EU new member countries (% change in 2008Q4–2009Q3 compared to 2007Q4–2008Q3)*

	Decline in imports (%)
Estonia	–32.7
Latvia	–32.4
Lithuania	–30.2
Poland	–26.7
Slovakia	–26.4
Hungary	–26.1
Czech Republic	–25.3
Slovenia	–23.7
EU27	–25.9

Sources: Eurostat, IMF IFS database, own calculations.

the effective foreign demand for the Baltic economies was even larger than the above average. In 2008Q4–2009Q3 compared to 2007Q4–2008Q3, the drop in foreign effective demand for the Baltic countries amounted to 30–33 per cent. For comparison, the corresponding decline in foreign demand for the five Central European countries was only 24–27 per cent.

Competitiveness channel

Under fixed exchange rates and full capital mobility, the central mechanism of adjustment to real shocks is captured by the so-called competitiveness channel. In the background of the recent Baltic cycle, the competitiveness channel seems to have worked too slowly and with insufficient intensity to smooth out the very pronounced fluctuations.

To illustrate the workings of the competitiveness channel, suppose an economy is hit by a favourable demand shock that results in a positive output gap. This leads to an increase in prices and/or wages, and thereby to an appreciation of the real exchange rate. The strengthening of the real exchange rate lowers the country's competitiveness and pushes economic activity down until the positive output gap is closed.

The first link in the above mechanism, the impact of output gaps on real exchange rates, is quite clear in the recent dynamics of the Baltic economies (see Figure 6.3). The widening of positive GDP gaps in 2006 and 2007 was accompanied by an increase in the rate of real exchange rate appreciation. During the recession, when the large positive output

118   *Aurelijus Dabušinskas and Martti Randveer*

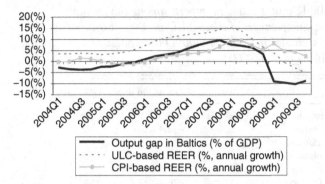

Figure 6.3: Output gap and REER indexes: Baltic States, 2004–9

Note: The output gap, CPI-based REER and ULC-based REER indexes for the Baltics are unweighted averages.

Sources: Eurostat, own calculations.

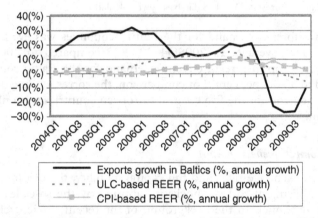

Figure 6.4: Merchandise export and REER indexes: Baltic States, 2004–9

Note: The output gap, CPI-based REER and ULC-based REER indexes for the Baltics are unweighted averages.

Sources: Eurostat, own calculations.

gap was replaced by a similarly large negative gap, the ULC-based real effective exchange rate (REER) depreciated, though the response of the CPI-based REER was slower and smaller.

The second link in the functioning of the competitiveness channel has been much weaker. Although real exchange rates appreciated quite strongly over 2006–8, their influence on the growth rate of merchandise exports was not strong, and the Baltic countries continued to enjoy high export growth until the end of 2008, when foreign trade contracted globally (see Figure 6.4). Although the CPI- and the ULC-based REER continued to appreciate until the second quarter of 2009, the impact of this appreciation on merchandise exports was not obvious. On the contrary, between the first half of 2008 and 2010 the drop in merchandise exports in the Baltic countries was slightly smaller than in the EU27. Therefore it appears that the competitiveness channel has not been strong enough to counter the causes that magnified the cyclical volatility of the Baltic economies.

4   Economic policy

As shown in section 2, the recent economic cycle of the Baltic countries has been so pronounced that it stands out in comparison to all peak-recession episodes that we could identify in the IMF IFS data going back to 1960. Since the intensity of the boom phase may explain the subsequent decline, it seems natural to ask why the Baltic policy-makers did not use economic policy aggressively enough to contain such an excessive boom. Instead, they seem to have tolerated a prolonged period of very substantial overheating, allowing a build-up of various imbalances and vulnerabilities that made the later recession worse.

In this section, we argue that the choice of the most appropriate economic policies during the Baltic boom was not as clear-cut as it may seem in retrospect. We build our argument in two steps. First, we show that throughout the boom years official 'real-time' output gap estimates – in this case, those published by the European Commission – considerably underestimated the 'true' extent of overheating in the Baltic economies. Second, we provide a short account of policies that the authorities of the Baltic countries actually implemented. Though restrictive, these measures were not sufficient to have a significant cooling impact on the then-buoyant Baltic economies.

4.1   *Accuracy of real-time output gap estimates and growth forecasts*

During the boom years, macroeconomic policy-making in the Baltic countries was greatly complicated by high uncertainty about the actual position of the Baltic economies relative to their potential. Though this sort of uncertainty is clearly not specific to the Baltic countries, the degree of uncertainty about their 'true' cyclical position was remarkably high. To illustrate this point, we make use of different vintages of output gap estimates available from the European Commission's economic forecasts. We show that, during the period 2004–9, output gap revisions were on average substantially larger for the Baltic than for other EU economies.

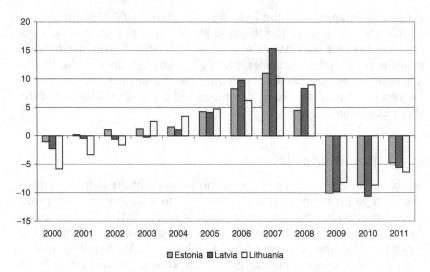

Figure 6.5: Output gaps (%): Baltics States July 2010 estimates, 2000–11
Source: AMECO database, July 2010.

We start by considering the latest vintage of output gap estimates[16] for the Baltic economies, which are depicted in Figure 6.5. As expected, Figure 6.5 reveals clear contours of the high volatility of the business cycle in the Baltic States. In all three countries, the level of economic activity started to exceed potential in about 2004, the year of EU accession. By 2007, the Baltic output gaps peaked at about 11 per cent and 10 per cent in Estonia and Lithuania, respectively, and 15 per cent in Latvia. In 2009, however, the economies contracted sharply, and all three output gap estimates became strongly negative, reaching −10 per cent in Estonia and Latvia, and −8 per cent in Lithuania.

The extent of overheating that these output gap measures imply for the period from 2005 to 2008 is striking, but it is important to realise that the definitive clarity of this policy-relevant message has a lot to do with the fact that Figure 6.5 refers to the most recent vintage of output gaps; these estimates were not available in 'real time'.

To illustrate how much difference that makes, we have constructed Figure 6.6, which plots different vintages of output gap estimates for 2007, the year of the largest positive output gaps reported according to Figure 6.5. The horizontal axis in Figure 6.6 indicates the years when different vintages of output gaps were published. Since the European Commission's economic forecasts are published twice a year, the letters

16 AMECO database, July 2010.

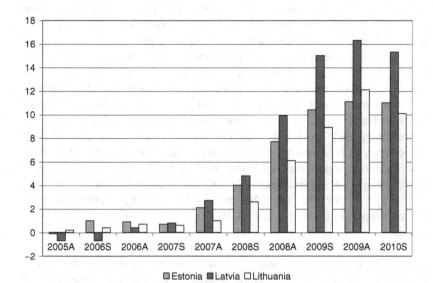

Figure 6.6: Output gap (%) for 2007: forecasts and estimates, 2005–10
Source: European Commission's Economic forecasts.

'S' and 'A' attached to the years on the horizontal axis indicate whether a given forecast was published in the spring or autumn, respectively. In total, we have ten different vintages of output gap estimates for 2007: from the projections published in the autumn of 2005 to the *ex post* estimates released in the spring of 2010.

Figure 6.6 paints a rather dramatic picture of the extent to which the overheating of the Baltic economies was underestimated throughout most of the boom years. First, Figure 6.6 shows very clearly that the double-digit output gaps of 2007 were completely unpredicted: even the 2007 Spring estimates were suggesting that the 2007 output gaps would be virtually zero. Second, the contemporaneous estimates, released in the autumn of 2007, were only marginally better. Though rightly adjusted upwards, the implied output gaps of 1–3 per cent were still 5–10 times smaller than the 'actual' figures – the latest available estimates of output gaps for 2007. Finally, it took more than a year – with interim assessments more or less doubling with each new estimation round – until in the spring of 2009, the output gap estimates for 2007 became similar to what they are today.

Such underestimation of overheating in the Baltic economies was not specific to 2007, however. We have compared the contemporaneous, or 'real-time', output gap estimates throughout the 2004–9 period with the latest available output gap estimates for the same years,[17] and the message is very clear: the contemporaneous output gap measures underestimated the 'true' gaps very substantially in all years but 2009.

To see how the accuracy of contemporaneous output gap estimates for the Baltic economies compared with that for other EU countries, we computed country-specific mean absolute revisions (MARs) between the real-time output gap estimates and their updates. We considered three different updates: the *ex post* measures published one and two years later, and the latest available ones. It turns out that, for all three types of revisions we consider, the average MAR across the three Baltic countries is about twice the average MAR across all EU countries. To give a specific example, the average MAR based on two-year revisions for the Baltic States is 4.4 percentage points, whereas the corresponding average for all EU countries is only 2.1 percentage points.

By construction, revisions in output gap estimates arise either because of updates in actual or forecast output series or because of changes in potential output estimates. Consequently, the relatively high level of uncertainty that has been characteristic of the Baltic output gap estimates must be related to instability or unpredictability in one or both of these components. Though we do not report the details here, our results show that output gap revisions have been driven by discrepancies on both sides – errors in output forecasts as well as changes in the assessments of output potential. All these uncertainties have greatly constrained the implementation of effective counter-cyclical economic policies in the Baltic countries.

4.2   Economic policy measures

Despite the high degree of uncertainty concerning the cyclical position of the Baltic economies during the growth phase, the authorities acknowledged that the economic boom involved a build-up of macroeconomic and financial vulnerabilities. Likewise, since the start of the recession it has been evident that the large drop in economic activity has pushed the Baltic economies below their potential. In this subsection we describe the most important economic policies that the Baltic policy-makers have used to stabilise their economies.

---

[17] As before, by contemporaneous or 'real-time' output gap estimates for a given year we mean estimates that were published in the autumn editions of forecasts of that same year.

During the growth phase, the main policy tools that were used to contain overheating included fiscal policy measures, changes in prudential regulation and changes in the banks' required reserve ratios. Fiscal measures were most actively used in Estonia, where the headline fiscal balance was kept in surplus throughout the whole growth phase, and thus accumulated fiscal reserves amounted to approximately 10 per cent of GDP by the end of the expansion in 2007. The budget surpluses and fiscal reserves were partly motivated by the desire to create fiscal buffers to better handle negative shocks and to contain demand pressures.

In addition, some more specific fiscal policy measures were tried to reduce incentives to borrow (European Commission, 2010). To decrease mortgage lending, Estonia reduced the tax deductibility of interest rate payments on mortgages; similarly, Lithuania introduced restrictions to limit the possibilities for residents with mortgage loans to benefit from tax relief. In 2007, the Latvian authorities started to require that banks would grant loans only on the basis of legally reported income, demand a 10 per cent minimum down payment and operate stricter loan-to-value requirements; the last two measures were later abolished, however.

The changes in prudential regulation were mainly focused on increasing the capital base of the banks. In Estonia, the risk weight on mortgage loans in the capital base calculation was increased from 50 per cent to 100 per cent in 2006. Similar measures were implemented in Lithuania, which also introduced restrictions on the inclusion of current-year profits into the capital base. In addition, commercial bank reserve requirements were raised in Estonia and Latvia. In Estonia, the required reserve ratio increased from 13 per cent to 15 per cent in 2006. In Latvia, the minimum reserve ratio was gradually raised from 4 per cent in 2004 to 8 per cent by the end of 2008.

The effectiveness of these policy measures was arguably quite low. For example, even though the Estonian headline fiscal policy position was continually better and its minimum reserve requirements higher than those in Latvia and Lithuania, these policy differences did not seem to matter much in terms of avoiding overheating-related problems. Likewise, Brixiova, Vartia and Worgötter (2009) argue that the measures adopted by the Bank of Estonia to cool the lending boom were mostly of a signalling nature and had minimal actual impact.

During the crisis, the scope for counter-cyclical policies in the Baltic countries was limited by the following considerations and policy constraints: the severity of the crisis, the decision to maintain the currency pegs, the limited fiscal policy space in Latvia and Lithuania, the conditions stipulated in the international financial assistance agreement with

Latvia and the firm commitment of the Estonian authorities to meeting the Maastricht criteria.

As regards fiscal policy, arguably the main factor that limited the possibilities of conducting counter-cyclical fiscal policies in the Baltic countries was the exceptionally large decrease in their output levels. Coupled with the weak cyclically adjusted fiscal positions of Latvia and Lithuania prior to the crisis, the economic reality of the Baltic States posed considerable risks that their fiscal deficits would soon become unsustainable. According to Purfield and Rosenberg (2010), under unchanged policies the 2009 deficits would have reached 16–18 per cent of GDP in Latvia and Lithuania and more than 10 per cent in Estonia. Financing such large fiscal deficits would have been extremely difficult given that during the crisis the Baltic countries' access to international financial markets was severely limited. In addition, very large fiscal deficits might have undermined confidence in the exchange rate regimes. In Estonia, which had sizeable fiscal reserves prior to the crisis, the determined efforts to fulfil the Maastricht fiscal deficit criterion also effectively eliminated any scope for counter-cyclical fiscal measures. In the case of Latvia, on the other hand, one of the main preconditions for the international financial assistance was the promise to strengthen fiscal policy discipline.

In the end, for one predominant reason or another, all three Baltic countries ended up implementing very sizeable fiscal consolidations.

5   Conclusions

Recent cyclical developments in the Baltic countries conform well with the main features of the typical economic cycle in emerging market economies: high volatility in macroeconomic variables, sudden stops in capital inflows, consumption volatility in excess of output volatility, counter-cyclical trade balances and counter-cyclical real interest rates.

One of the most distinguishing characteristics of the economic cycle in the Baltic countries has been the unusually high degree of volatility, which is clear from our comparison of the Baltic experience with previous business cycle episodes in OECD and selected emerging market countries. The Baltic economies especially stand out for the large fluctuations in their domestic demand components, and in external and financial variables. Among the indicators that have not exhibited high volatility are fiscal balances and some competitiveness variables.

Despite many similarities, the Baltic countries' ability to deal with the impact of the global financial crisis has been different. At least in some respects, Estonia seems to have been more resilient than its neighbours, whereas Latvia appears to have suffered the most. The main structural feature that made Latvia more susceptible to the global financial shock was its significantly larger share of domestically owned banks: Latvia was forced to ask for international financial assistance when its largest domestic bank ran into urgent liquidity and solvency problems in the Autumn of 2008. Latvia's situation was then aggravated by its larger external and financial vulnerabilities and the associated stronger expansion in domestic demand.

The cyclical volatility of the Baltic economies was mainly caused by the procyclical behaviour of their financial sectors. As compared to other EU countries the co-movements between the financial variables and the cyclical component of output have been much stronger in the Baltic countries. This is especially true for foreign capital inflows and real interest rates. Large capital inflows during the expansion and the associated rapid credit growth were among the main determinants of high growth prior to the onset of the financial crisis. The sudden stop in capital inflows during the financial crisis and the associated contraction in credit were significant reasons for the severity of the recession. The impact of these developments in capital flows and credit was strengthened by the counter-cyclical behaviour of real interest rates.

We argue that fiscal policy has not been among the primary reasons behind the volatility of the recent cycle. However, with hindsight we can see that during the growth phase the fiscal policy stance did not help to contain the overheating pressures, though its impact on further fuelling domestic economic activity was not very significant. During the recession public spending, with the help of increased net EU transfers, has been much more stable than other components of domestic demand.

The cyclical volatility of the Baltic economies has also been influenced by developments in their labour markets. During the growth phase the relatively large emigration from the Baltic countries was likely to decrease labour supply and put upward pressure on wages, thereby further accelerating the demand boom. The impact of labour mobility within the EU during the recession has not been clear-cut, but it appears that at least in Latvia labour market integration has helped to avoid an even deeper recession.

The negative shock to foreign trade at the end of 2008 had a stronger impact on the Baltic States than on the other EU new member countries because the decline in foreign effective demand for the Baltic countries was larger. Another potentially important adjustment channel – the competitiveness channel – has not been strong enough to counter the other causes and channels that have increased the cyclical volatility of the Baltic economies.

During the expansion, the conduct of macroeconomic policy in the Baltics was greatly complicated by high uncertainty about the actual position of the Baltic economies relative to their potential. Our calculations show that based on the real-time estimates of the output gap the extent of overheating was significantly underestimated until the end of the boom. The revisions to these variables have been much higher in the case of the Baltic States than other EU countries.

The initial momentum of the expansion in the Baltic countries was too strong for the authorities to lean against by using standard policy options. For example, this is evident in Estonia, where the headline fiscal position was clearly stronger and banks' minimum reserve requirements higher than in Latvia and Lithuania, but the impact of these policy measures did not have a clear differential effect in avoiding overheating pressures. On the other hand the experience with the recession in the Baltic countries has highlighted the importance of liquidity and capital buffers in the banking sector, the stabilising role of foreign bank ownership and the contribution of fiscal discipline in withstanding negative shocks.

Appendix

The number of recessions covered by different variables and country groups are shown in Table 6.A1.

Table 6.A1: *Number of recessions covered by different variables and country groups*

	Before the peak		After the peak	
	Advanced countries	Emerging countries	Advanced countries	Emerging countries
Economic growth	83	32	93	40
Private consumption	78	28	88	37
Investments	78	28	88	37
Government consumption	77	28	88	37
Exports	74	28	86	37
Imports	69	28	81	37
Net exports	76	31	88	37
Employment	27	12	36	15
Unemployment	25	10	35	16
Net foreign capital inflows	59	27	73	34
Bank credit	89	21	89	23
Real interest rates	72	13	84	20
Share prices	64	25	73	31
CPI-based REER	61	16	71	19

Note: The first row of the table shows the number of recessionary episodes identified using real GDP series. All other rows report the number of recessions for which data on other economic variables are available in our dataset.

References

Aquiar, M. and G. Gopinath (2007). 'Emerging market business cycles: the cycle is the trend', *Journal of Political Economy*, 115: 69–102

Bakker, B. B. and A.-M. Gulde (2010). 'The credit boom in the EU new member states: bad luck or bad policies?', IMF Working Paper, No. 130

Becker, T., D. Daianu, Z. Darvas, V. Gligorov, M. Landesmann, P. Petrovic, J. Pisani-Ferry, D. Rosati, A. Sapir and B. Weder di Mauro (2010). 'Whither growth in Central and Eastern Europe? Policy lessons for an integrated Europe', Bruegel Blueprint, No. 11

Berglöf, E., Y. Korniyenko, A. Plekhanov and J. Zettelmayer (2009). 'Understanding the crisis in emerging Europe', EBRD Working Paper, No. 109

Blanchard, O., H. Faruqee and M. Das (2010). 'The initial impact of the crisis on emerging market countries', *Brookings Papers on Economic Activity*, Spring: 263–307

Brixiova, Z., M. H. Morgan and A. Worgötter (2009). 'Estonia and euro adoption: small country challenges of joining EMU', OECD Economics Department Working Paper, No. 728

Brixiova, Z., L. Vartia and A. Worgötter (2009). 'Capital inflows, household debt and the boom–bust cycle in Estonia', OECD Economics Department Working Paper, No. 700

Bry, G. and C. Boschan (1971). *Cyclical Analysis of Time Series: Selected Procedures and Computer Programs*, New York: National Bureau of Economic Research

Calvo, G. A. and C. A. Vegh (1999). 'Inflation stabilisation and BOP crises in developing countries', in J. B. Taylor and M. Woodford (eds.), *Handbook of Macroeconomics*, 1c, Amsterdam: Elsevier

Claessens, S., A. M. Kose and M. Terrones (2008). 'What happens during recessions, crunches, and busts?', IMF Working Paper, No. 274

European Central Bank (ECB) (2010). *Convergence Report 2010*

European Commission (2010). 'Cross-country study: economic policy challenges in the Baltics', Occasional Paper, No. 58

Gardo, S. and R. Martin (2010). 'The impact of the global economic and financial crisis on Central, Eastern and South-Eastern Europe', ECB Occasional Paper, No. 114

Ghosh, S. (2009). 'Credit crunch or weak demand for credit?', *The World Bank EU10 Regular Economic Report October 2009*: 37–44

Harding, D. and A. Pagan (2002). 'Dissecting the cycle: a methodological investigation', *Journal of Monetary Economics*, 49: 365–81

IMF (2010). 'How did emerging markets cope in the crisis?', IMF Policy Paper, 15 June

Lane, P. R. and G. M. Milesi-Ferretti (2011). 'The cross-country incidence of the global crisis', IMF Working Paper, No. 171/10

Neumeyer, P. A. and F. Perri (2005). 'Business cycles in emerging economies: the role of interest rates', *Journal of Monetary Economics*, 52: 345–80

Purfield, C. and C. B. Rosenberg (2010). 'Adjustment under a currency peg: Estonia, Latvia and Lithuania during the global financial crisis 2008–2009', IMF Working Paper, No. 213

Randveer, M. and T. Rõõm (2009). 'The structure of migration in Estonia: survey-based evidence', Eesti Pank Working Paper, No. **1/2009**

Riksbank (2007). Financial Stability Report 2001: 1

Takats, E. (2010). 'Was it credit supply? Cross-border lending to emerging market economies during the financial crisis', *BIS Quarterly Review*, June: 49–56

Part II

Accession to the euro area

7 The road to euro adoption: a comparison of Slovakia and Slovenia

*Biswajit Banerjee, Damjan Kozamernik and L'udovít Ódor**

1 Introduction

Of the eight Central and East European (CEE) countries that became European Union (EU) members in May 2004, only Slovakia and Slovenia have adopted the euro so far. They reached this milestone by different means, illustrating that there is no one-size-fits-all euro adoption strategy. There were striking differences in the starting positions of the two countries when negotiations on EU membership began and in their macroeconomic policy frameworks prior to and during ERM II participation. Important differences were also present in the macroeconomic developments immediately after the adoption of the single currency and during the global financial crisis.

At the time of initiation of EU accession negotiations in March 1998, Slovenia had the highest GDP *per capita* (in purchasing power standards) among the eight CEEs, equivalent to 67 per cent of the EU15 average. Economic growth was strong, fiscal and external imbalances were relatively low and the public debt burden was modest, though inflation was in the high single-digits (Table 7.1). However, the Slovene economy was characterised by enormous structural rigidities. A large part of the economy was sheltered from competition, capital controls were extensive, financial contracts and wages were index-linked to inflation and the structure of budgetary spending was not conducive to policy shifts. Moreover, expected demographic trends were likely to increase fiscal pressures over the longer term because of increases in the old-age dependency ratio.

Slovakia was excluded from the first group of EU applicant states because the political landscape was deemed not to be in line with the

* The authors thank Mark Allen, David Cobham, Mark De Broeck, Michal Horvath, Peter Mooslechner and Juan Zalduendo for comments on an earlier version of the chapter.

Table 7.1: *Selected indicators at landmark dates, 1998–2007*

	Start of EU accession negotiations	Adoption of programme for ERM II entry and euro adoption	EU membership	ERM II entry	Convergence report	Euro adoption
Slovenia	March 1998	November 2003	May 2004	June 2004	May 2006	January 2007
GDP growth (%)	4.9 1997	2.8 2003	2.8 2003	2.8 2003	4.5 2005	5.8 2006
HICP inflation (%)*	8.4 February 1998	6.0 October 2003	4.8 April 2004	4.7 May 2004	2.4 April 2006	2.5 December 2006
General government balance (% of GDP)	-2.4 1997	-2.7 2003	-2.7 2003	-2.7 2003	-1.4 2005	-1.3 2006
Public debt (% of GDP)	20.8 1997	27.5 2003	27.5 2003	27.5 2003	27.0 2005	26.7 2006
Long-term interest rates (%)*		6.16 October 2003	4.83 April 2004	4.77 May 2004	3.73 April 2006	3.90 December 2006
Slovakia	February 2000	July 2003	May 2004	November 2005	May 2008	January 2009
GDP growth (%)	0.0 1999	4.6 2002	4.8 2003	6.7 2005	10.6 2007	6.2 2008
HICP inflation (%)*	11.0 January 2000	5.4 June 2003	8.6 April 2004	3.2 October 2005	2.4 April 2008	3.9 December 2008
General government balance (% of GDP)	-7.4 1999	-8.2 2002	-2.8 2003	-2.8 2005	-1.9 2007	-2.3 2008
Public debt (% of GDP)	47.9 1999	43.4 2002	42.4 2003	34.2 2005	29.3 2007	27.7 2008
Long-term interest rates (%)**		4.70 June 2003	5.06 April 2004	3.25 October 2005	4.46 April 2008	4.72 December 2008

Notes:
* 12-month average annual rate.
** Long-term interest rate for convergence purposes.
Sources: Bank of Slovenia, National Bank of Slovakia, Eurostat.

Copenhagen criteria, but accession negotiations were launched in February 2000 following a change of government in September 1998. At this juncture, Slovakia's GDP *per capita* was only 43 per cent of the EU15 average. Economic growth was on a sliding path, fiscal and external imbalances were large and inflation was in the double-digits. Moreover, corporate governance was weak and the health of the financial sector was generally fragile. Fiscal pressures arising from an aging population were also lurking, though to a lesser degree than in Slovenia.

In both countries, the policy strategy for euro adoption evolved concurrently with the preparations for EU membership, with the objective of entering the Eurozone at the earliest possible date. There was close coordination between the central bank and the Ministry of Finance, and combined programmes for ERM II entry and euro adoption were adopted by Slovakia in July 2003 and by Slovenia in November 2003. The bulk of the macroeconomic structural and policy changes triggered by EU accession requirements were completed before ERM II entry. Many of these requirements had short-term negative influences on inflation and fiscal performance, which complicated the task of meeting the Maastricht criteria on nominal convergence within the short time horizon chosen for euro adoption.

Since the Maastricht criteria were not designed with transition economies in mind, both countries faced other important policy challenges in meeting the criteria.[1] A key policy decision was the choice of a monetary policy framework that could overcome the impossible trinity of having at the same time a fixed exchange rate, unimpeded capital mobility and an independent monetary policy dedicated to domestic policy goals. The two countries went about this task pursuing different exchange rate regimes. Slovenia's monetary framework entailed a progressive fading out of depreciation in line with the disinflation process in the pre-ERM II phase, and relative stability around the central parity in the ERM II phase. In contrast, Slovakia followed a managed float regime throughout. There were also challenges in securing the desired fiscal consolidation and flexibility, primarily because socially oriented spending was a large share of total expenditure and subject to considerable inefficiencies, and additional budgetary pressures arose after EU accession mainly because of co-financing obligations, Schengen border-related expenses, losses of customs revenues from imports originating in the EU, and decreases in VAT receipts tied to the elimination of border customs controls with EU member countries. As a result, in both countries tax, pension and healthcare systems and labour markets needed substantial reform.

[1] See Schadler *et al.* (2005).

Slovenia entered ERM II soon after EU accession in June 2004 and adopted the euro in January 2007. Slovakia followed a little later, entering ERM II in November 2005 and adopting the euro in January 2009. Thus, both countries spent close to the minimum required period of two years in ERM II, and accomplished their euro adoption objective in nine years from the initiation of EU accession negotiations. There was broad-based political and social support in both Slovakia and Slovenia for the fast-track euro adoption objective. Thus, even when the governments changed shortly after ERM II entry – in October 2004 in Slovenia and in June 2006 in Slovakia – there was no material change to the basic approach and timetable for euro adoption.

In this chapter, we review and assess the policy strategies implemented by Slovakia and Slovenia to meet the Maastricht criteria and prepare the economy for life within the Eurozone, and discuss some of the dilemmas that arose during and after the process. On this basis, we draw some lessons that the experiences of these two countries offer to future Eurozone entrants.

2   Meeting the Maastricht inflation criterion

2.1   Inflation developments

Slovenia's inflation developments since the beginning of the preparations for EU membership and euro adoption can be divided into three broad phases. Inflation picked up in the second half of 1999 and remained sticky around 9 per cent during 2000 and the first half of 2001. In the subsequent period, inflation was on a downward path and bottomed out at 2 per cent in mid 2005 and fluctuated in the range of 2–3 per cent from then until mid 2007. Slovenia fulfilled the Maastricht inflation criterion in November 2005 (sixteen months after entering ERM II) and kept fulfilling it throughout 2006. However, within six months of Eurozone entry, inflation began to gather pace from the first half of 2007 and reached a peak of nearly 7 per cent in mid 2008. Thereafter, inflation came down sharply and the gap with the other euro area countries narrowed markedly, as the impact of the global financial crisis began to be felt (Figure 7.1).

In contrast with Slovenia, inflation developments in Slovakia were more volatile. Slovakia's inflation followed a broad downward trend from 2000, with periodic swings of varying magnitude and duration. In the first swing, inflation rose sharply in 2003Q1 and remained sticky around 8–9 per cent until 2004Q2. Subsequently, it declined to about 2.25 per cent in 2005Q3 but climbed again to a peak of 5 per cent in 2006Q3. The

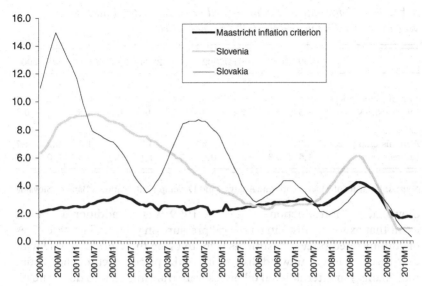

Figure 7.1: Twelve-month HICP inflation and the Maastricht inflation criterion, 2000–10 (%)
Source: Eurostat.

third upswing overlapped with the last stage of the ERM II period. From a low of 1.25 per cent in 2007Q3, inflation reached a peak of 4.5 per cent in 2008Q3. Still, the Maastricht inflation criterion was comfortably met. Inflation fell below the reference value in August 2007 (twenty months after ERM II entry), and the twelve-month average inflation over the reference period from April 2007 to March 2008 was a full percentage point lower than the reference value. Inflation in Slovakia following euro adoption in January 2009 was significantly below the euro area average.

2.2   Determinants of inflation

An important aspect of the inflation process in both Slovakia and Slovenia was the significant role played by changes in indirect taxes and upward adjustments in administered prices. They pushed up inflation considerably in the pre-ERM II period when most of the substantial changes and adjustments occurred, but their impact on inflation was present in subsequent years as well. In both countries, the programme of annual increases in excise taxes on cigarettes and tobacco, aimed at gradual harmonisation of these rates to EU levels, was an ongoing source of inflation and contributed between 0.5 and 2 percentage points annually. In

Table 7.2: *Contribution of administered price and indirect taxes to year-on-year inflation, 1999–2008 (percentage points)*

	1999	2000	2001	2002	2003	2004	2005	2006	2007	2008
Slovenia										
Administered prices	1.5	2.2	1.4	1.3	0.6	1.4	1.3	0.4	1.2	−0.9
Indirect taxes	2.3	0.6	1.3	1.7	0.7	0.4	−0.3	0.5	−0.1	0.2
Slovakia										
Administered prices	6.8	4.5	4.1	1.5	4.3	3.7	2.4	1.8	0.2	1.7
Indirect taxes	1.5	0.3	−0.1	0.4	2.5	1.1	0.0	0.3	0.0	0.2

Sources: Institute of Macroeconomic Analysis and Development, National Bank of Slovakia

Slovenia, the introduction of VAT in 1999 was an additional one-off event that exerted substantial upward pressure on prices.[2] The objectives of administered price adjustments were to bring these prices in line with cost-recovery levels, unwind distortions in the price structure and ensure that changes in international oil prices were transmitted into domestic oil prices. Their annual contributions to headline inflation were in the range of 0.6–2.2 percentage points in Slovenia and 0.2–6.8 percentage points in Slovakia (Table 7.2).

In both countries, the authorities were concerned about the negative influence that a rapid increase in administered prices could have on price formation in other sectors and on inflation expectations. They also considered many of the increases in administered prices to be unjustifiably high and a reflection of the ineffective functioning of regulatory bodies. Thus they adopted a policy of capping price increases and pressuring service providers for greater cost efficiency and saving.[3] In Slovenia, a key guideline from 2003 onward was that increases in non-fuel administered prices should not diverge substantially from increases in projected market-determined prices, which were on a decelerating path. During 2003–5, the government also lowered excise duties on fuel in several steps to the minimum level allowed by EU regulations in order to mitigate the impact of rising oil prices on domestic prices. Slovakia began to implement the policy of restraining administered price adjustments from 2006 after entering ERM II, and the authorities were particularly vigilant during 2007–8. Significantly, water supply and sewerage collection charges were reduced and electricity tariffs for households were frozen in 2007, and prices of natural gas and heat were kept unchanged in 2008.

[2] Slovakia had introduced VAT in 1993.
[3] As discussed on p. 141, the evidence does not suggest that the authorities were suppressing administered prices below cost-recovery levels.

With moderation in administered price adjustments, headline inflation in both countries slowed down.

Exchange rate developments accompanied disinflation during the pre-ERM II phase in Slovenia and contributed to disinflation during both pre-ERM II and ERM II phases in Slovakia. A steady slowdown in the pace of tolar depreciation from mid 2001 onward accompanied the falling inflation trend in Slovenia. With the exchange rate stabilising upon ERM II entry in June 2004, there was a further drop in underlying net inflation, reflecting mostly the negative output gap and the correspondingly low growth in unit labour costs. Also, the lagged effect of earlier depreciation faded and there seemed unlikely to be any further exchange rate effect on inflation beyond end-2004. Banerjee and Shi (2010) found that the impact of exchange rate changes on inflation in Slovenia was temporary and the pass-through incomplete, so that a faster stabilisation of the nominal exchange rate would have triggered a real appreciation and a corresponding loss in competitiveness.[4] In contrast, Slovakia experienced substantial trend nominal appreciation from 2002Q4 onward, particularly during the ERM II phase: the nominal effective exchange rate appreciated by 38 per cent during July 2002–May 2008, of which 20 per cent occurred after ERM II entry in November 2005. It appears that exchange rate shocks filtered through to prices slowly in Slovakia. A study by DG ECFIN staff (Cigan et al., 2008) found an exchange rate pass-through to the core harmonised index of consumer prices (HICP) of 17 per cent spread out over eight quarters, and estimated that exchange rate appreciation reduced average inflation in Slovakia in 2007 by more than 1 percentage point. The findings of an unpublished study by IMF staff (Dalgic, 2008) are broadly similar.

Wage settlement outcomes facilitated the disinflation process in both countries, and were especially important in Slovenia where considerable institutional rigidities prevailed and collective bargaining was centralised. In Slovenia, from 2001 onward, an explicit social contract weakened the wage indexation formula and the social partners abided by the guideline that real wage increases should lag productivity growth by at least 1 percentage point. In addition, the government took steps to ensure that increases in average wages in the public sector were below those in

---

[4] In estimating an error-correction model of inflation, Banerjee and Shi (2010) found that exchange rates changes affected inflation with a lag of one–two quarters, and that longer lags of exchange rate changes had no significant impact. Impulse-response analysis showed that a 1 per cent appreciation of the exchange rate would lead to a decrease in inflation of 0.24 per cent in the second quarter and 0.19 per cent in the third quarter, and have no impact thereafter. Similarly, Kozamernik and Žumer (2011) found a pass-through of roughly 40 per cent within a year by estimating a structural VAR.

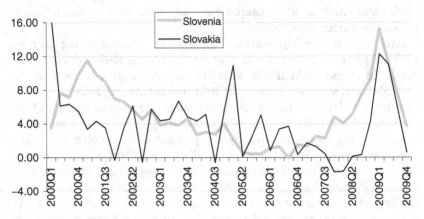

Figure 7.2: Unit labour costs, 2000–9 (year-on-year % change)
Source: Eurostat.

the private sector. Thus, the growth of nominal unit labour costs slowed down substantially (Figure 7.2). In Slovakia, collective bargaining was decentralised, the position of the trade unions was relatively weak and there was no formal wage indexation mechanism in place. Wage agreements were influenced by announced public sector wage decisions and by minimum wage adjustments, both of which were based on budget inflation assumptions and were moderate. Nominal compensation growth per employee fluctuated around 8–9 per cent from 2002 onward. Reflecting productivity developments, growth of nominal unit labour costs fluctuated between 3 and 4.5 per cent during 2002–5 and fell sharply in the ERM II phase in 2006 and 2007, when productivity growth surged.

To counter the risk of a pick-up in wage growth after euro adoption, the Slovak government, employers and trade unions signed an agreement in 2008 aimed at keeping real wage increases below productivity growth. This was an attempt to emulate the tripartite agreements that were prevalent in Slovenia in the period leading up to euro adoption. Ironically, tripartite wage agreements in Slovenia ended in 2006 just prior to Eurozone entry, and sectoral wage agreements between employers and unions became dominant. Following this change, the earlier pattern of real-wage increases lagging productivity gains was reversed in 2008–9.

The absence of demand-side pressures during the euro adoption process made it easier for Slovenia to meet the Maastricht inflation criterion. The reduction in inflation in Slovenia from mid-2001 to end-2005 closely tracked a decline in the output gap with a lag. With the economy growing significantly faster than the potential rate in 2006, the negative output

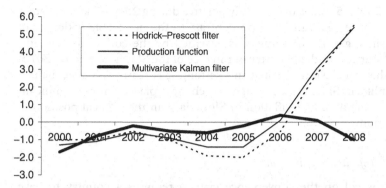

Figure 7.3: Output gap estimates for Slovakia by alternative methods,
2000–8 (% of potential output)
Source: Konuki (2010).

gap that existed during 2003–5 closed and the output gap turned mildly
positive. However, because of lags in the impact of changes in the output
gap, there was no significant increase in inflation in 2006. Econometric
evidence in the Banerjee and Shi (2010) study suggests that, contrary to
Slovakia, the output gap was by far the most important determinant of
inflation in Slovenia. Impulse-response analysis shows that the response
of inflation to a 1 per cent change in the output gap was 8 times greater
than a 1 per cent change in the exchange rate. Also, the output gap
effect lasted twice as long as the exchange rate effect. Thus, with pri-
macy given to exchange rate stability upon ERM II entry and exchange
rate adjustment no longer a policy option for disinflation, the persistence
of a negative output gap during much of the ERM II period played a
critical role in bringing inflation down towards the Maastricht criterion
level. The pick-up in inflation after entering the Eurozone reflected, *inter
alia*, an increasing positive output gap during 2006–7.

The presence of demand-side pressures in Slovakia is the subject of debate. Conventional estimation methods (production function
approach and HP filter) show a significantly negative output gap during 2000–5 that narrows sharply in 2006 and turns drastically positive
in 2007 and 2008. But developments in other indicators such as trade
deficit and wage growth show little signs of overheating. Konuki (2010)
has argued that conventional approaches for estimating output gaps cannot capture a structural shift of the potential growth path driven by a
supply-side impetus, as was the case in Slovakia. He considers the multivariate Kalman filter method to be more appropriate under such situations. Under this method, demand-side pressures are found to be absent
in Slovakia: as Figure 7.3 shows, the output gap is marginally negative

during 2003–5, turns only slightly positive during 2006–7 and becomes negative once again in 2008 (in contrast to the noticeable widening of the positive gap in the same year provided by the conventional methods). Estimates of the Ministry of Finance of the Slovak Republic (2010) share this conclusion. Against this setting, it is reasonable to conclude that, unlike in Slovenia, exchange rate changes played a more significant role in bringing down inflation in Slovakia than the cyclical position of the economy.

2.3   Inflation sustainability

The Protocol on the convergence criteria requires a country to have achieved price stability that is sustainable. This implies that inflation convergence should not reflect the influence of temporary factors that will not be present after the adoption of the euro.[5] Regarding Slovenia's medium-term inflation prospects, the European Commission (2006: 68) concluded favourably that 'the disinflation process in Slovenia has been driven by factors which could be expected to underpin a low inflationary environment in the medium term, including the reform of the wage-setting mechanisms associated with wage moderation, increase of competition, exchange rate stabilisation and fiscal consolidation'.

In the event, as in the earlier experiences of Italy, Ireland and Spain following their entry into the euro area, Slovenia experienced a pick-up in inflation and a widening of its inflation differential *vis-à-vis* the euro area average within a short period from euro adoption in 2007. Surti (2010) notes that the differential *vis-à-vis* the euro area widened in part because increases in global food and commodity prices had a stronger impact on Slovenian inflation, reflecting differences relative to the euro area in consumption baskets and the shares of EU countries in Slovenian imports. However, the most important determinant was a rising positive output gap associated with faster growth of business investment and private consumption. With European Central Bank (ECB) monetary policy determined on the basis of average Eurozone inflation, real interest rates in Slovenia became negative and in turn spurred credit growth. With Eurozone entry assured, the policy discipline and flexibility required to mitigate inflation pressures in the short to medium term were lacking. Fiscal policy, instead of counteracting the demand boom, was procyclical and contributed to the overheating of the economy. In addition, wages and nominal unit labour costs increased strongly

---

[5] See European Commission (2006: 58).

in 2007—8, in a reversal of the slowing trend during the pre-euro adoption period.

The sustainability issue was scrutinised by the ECB and European Commission more critically in the case of Slovakia in view of the role that special factors were deemed to have played in dampening inflation during the ERM II period and given the upsurge in inflation in Slovenia in 2007 following euro adoption. The ECB (ECB 2008: 185) had 'considerable' concerns regarding the sustainability of inflation convergence in Slovakia. The Commission (EC, 2008: 176) also considered the upside risks to inflation to be 'considerable'. One concern was that the restrained increases in regulated prices may have been lower than those dictated by underlying cost pressures and could not be repeated to the same extent in the future without negative consequences for the delivery of services and investment. However, as Dalgic (2008) notes, this concern appears to have been misplaced. Regulated prices do not appear to have been artificially suppressed when benchmarked against unregulated prices of similar goods and services, against price levels and developments in the EU measured in a common currency and against underlying price pressures from commodity prices. However, regulated price adjustments benefited from exchange rate appreciation, which helped keep domestic costs of rising world energy prices in check.

A second concern was that inflationary pressures were likely to pick up once nominal appreciation of the Slovak koruna ceased upon euro adoption. The dampening effect of exchange rate appreciation on import price increases would be absent in the Eurozone, though the pass-through of earlier appreciation on inflation would continue for a while. In addition, the underlying real appreciation trend, a reflection of the catching-up process and other equilibrium effects, would manifest itself in higher inflation.

Since Slovakia entered the Eurozone in the midst of the global financial crisis, the factors that prompted an upsurge in inflation in Slovenia did not come into play. Moreover, the lagged carry-over effect of a significantly appreciated conversion rate of the koruna continued to have a moderating impact on inflation. Decreasing energy and food prices during the financial crisis helped as well, as these items have higher weights in the consumer basket in Slovakia than in other euro area countries. Thus, inflation during the crisis was significantly below the euro area average. It remains to be seen whether there will be sufficient resolve and ability to adopt an appropriate counter-cyclical fiscal policy stance once economic growth rebounds and signs of a rising positive output gap emerge.

Table 7.3: *Policy dilemma in new member states*

Conflict in new member states	
Impossible trinity	*Maastricht criteria*
Free capital flows	Stable exchange rate
Independent monetary policy	Low inflation
Exchange rate stability	Sound public finances
Addressing this conflict	

Policy option 1 Fixed exchange rate/currency board/crawling peg		*Policy option 2* Flexible inflation targeting	
Risk	Policy option	Risk	Policy option
High inflation (Balassa–Samuelson effect)	Wage restraint; significant fiscal tightening; labour market flexibility	Exchange rate instability	Interventions
Asset price bubbles	Tighter regulation	Competitiveness	Interventions; wage restraint; flexible labour markets
Credit boom/foreign currency lending	Tighter regulation; restrictive fiscal policy	Harder transition to euro	Structural reforms

Source: Authors.

3   Monetary policy frameworks and meeting the exchange rate stability criterion

In the pre-ERM II phase, the primary focus of monetary policy in both countries was on disinflation, but their monetary policy frameworks differed from each other. While Slovenia's policy framework was unconventional and involved exchange rate depreciation, that of Slovakia involved tolerance of exchange rate appreciation.

In ERM II, monetary policy faced multiple objectives: controlling inflation, keeping the exchange rate competitive and meeting the exchange rate stability criterion. In an environment of open capital accounts, the potential for conflicts between these objectives was considerable. The countries could go for 'corner solutions' – adopting a hard peg regime or a floating rate regime – to overcome the impossible trinity and give markets unambiguous signals about how the exchange rate would respond to exogenous or policy-induced shocks. Each 'corner solution' has its own advantages, but both are subject to vulnerabilities and require supportive fiscal, wage, and structural policies (Table 7.3). Although a ± 15 per cent band around the central parity seemingly provided some flexibility, it was not clear in advance how the European Commission and ECB would interpret exchange rate stability. Against this background, Slovenia opted to operate within an undisclosed narrow exchange rate band around a central parity, but did not face any conflicts with the inflation objective as there was no pressure in the foreign exchange market from capital inflows. In contrast, there was no material change in Slovakia's monetary policy framework upon ERM II entry. It continued to experience appreciation pressures owing to strong capital inflows and, notwithstanding interest rate adjustments and substantial foreign exchange market interventions, two revaluations of the central parity in the run-up to conversion became unavoidable. In the event, exchange rate appreciation was judged by the European Commission and ECB to be in line with economic fundamentals[6] and consistent with the exchange rate stability criterion.

3.1   The monetary policy framework in Slovenia

In April 2001, the Bank of Slovenia adopted a new monetary framework bearing some of the hallmarks of inflation targeting. The Bank chose a medium-term inflation target consistent with meeting the Maastricht criterion, and sought to steer inflation toward this goal by keeping a grip on liquidity. Toward this end, the Bank targeted a certain level of real interest rates and, to discourage interest-elastic capital inflows, closed the risk-adjusted interest differential between euro- and tolar-denominated instruments by exchange rate depreciation. As inflation slowed down or euro area interest rates were cut, domestic interest rates and the rate of depreciation were reduced in a manner that did not open up interest parity with abroad. An outcome of this strategy was a high degree of real exchange rate stability, which contributed to maintaining the external equilibrium of the economy (Figure 7.4).

The operational success of this framework was facilitated by a contractual agreement between the Bank and the commercial banks, which provided the banks with unlimited access to tolar liquidity through euro swaps, in exchange for their obligation to trade the euro at a given exchange rate if the Bank wanted to signal a particular exchange rate path.[7] While the swap instrument enabled the banks to efficiently manage their forex liquidity, it did not allow them to use these short-term assets fully as a basis for longer-term credit expansion, because of the prudential constraint imposed by the liquidity ratio instrument. The excess

---

[6] Labour productivity differentials played by far the most important role in this.
[7] See Kozamernik and Žumer (2011) for a detailed description of Slovenia's monetary framework.

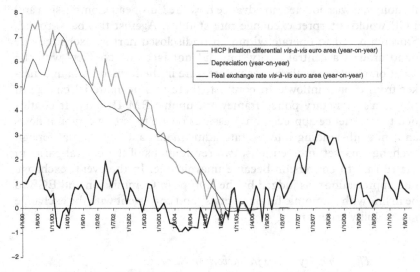

Figure 7.4: Real exchange rates: Slovenia, 2000–10 (% change)
Source: Bank of Slovenia, Eurostat.

liquidity was placed by the banks in Bank bills. The possibility of managing their forex liquidity through access to swaps with the Bank acted as a strong exchange rate smoother, which was highly desirable given the shallow tolar market.

Upon ERM II entry in June 2004, the Bank ended its depreciation policy, and the ERM II central parity was set at SIT 239.64 per euro, close to the then-prevailing market rate, because the authorities considered the corresponding level of the real exchange rate to be close to the equilibrium exchange rate. To have the maximum scope for limiting exchange rate volatility in ERM II, the Bank continued its contractual cooperation with commercial banks on exchange rate policy operations and the use of foreign exchange swaps. In the event, the deviation of the actual exchange rate from the central parity throughout the ERM II period was extremely small, and the final conversion rate was the same as the central parity. There was hardly any pressure in the foreign exchange market on account of capital inflows. A clearly defined monetary policy framework, enhanced policy coordination between the Bank and the government (which included restructuring of the public debt by switching from foreign to domestic debt instruments and holding privatisation proceeds as deposits with the Bank), the small size of the fiscal deficit and a relatively thin government securities market helped avoid exchange rate volatility.

3.2   The monetary policy framework in Slovakia

Slovakia's monetary framework was a hybrid set-up in which the main emphasis was on disinflation but an eye was also kept on exchange rate developments. Initially, the National Bank of Slovakia did not target inflation formally but announced benchmark ranges for headline and core inflation which were often revised mid year, depending on economic developments. The National Bank did not have any explicit commitment to a range for the exchange rate, but the goal was to avoid sharp oscillations in the exchange rate and to avoid erosion of competitiveness. In December 2004, in anticipation of ERM II entry, the National Bank slightly modified its policy framework and announced explicit end-year inflation targets for 2005−7. Following ERM II entry in November 2005, the National Bank also faced the explicit constraint of keeping the exchange rate within a ± 15 per cent band and meeting the exchange rate stability criterion.

Foreign exchange market conditions in Slovakia changed fundamentally in mid 2002. Until then, owing mainly to political uncertainties, Slovakia experienced periodic depreciation pressures in the foreign exchange market, which the National Bank resisted through verbal interventions and direct interventions in the foreign exchange market. From mid 2002 onward, monetary policy was challenged by appreciation pressures. A clear outcome in the September 2002 elections, invitations to join the EU and NATO and sovereign rating upgrades reduced the perceived risks on Slovak assets and spurred capital inflows. Thereafter, announcements of new foreign direct investment (FDI) projects, continued productivity gains in excess of the euro area and positive investor sentiment about the region perpetuated strong capital inflows. The National Bank accommodated a moderate appreciation of the koruna as some of the appreciation was deemed to reflect productivity-driven equilibrium real appreciation and as it would also help restrain inflation. However, the National Bank was concerned about the negative effects of a rapid exchange rate appreciation on the competitiveness of traditional manufacturing firms as well as small and medium-sized enterprises (SMEs), where productivity gains were lower. Thus, on several occasions during 2002−5, the National Bank responded through a combination of verbal intervention, direct intervention in the foreign exchange market, temporary caps on the size of weekly repo tenders (the most common National Bank instrument to absorb liquidity) which forced banks to post funds at an overnight facility with a substantially lower interest rate, and reductions in the policy rate. At the time of ERM II entry in November 2005, the central parity was set at the then-prevailing market rate of Sk38.4550 per euro (Figure 7.5).

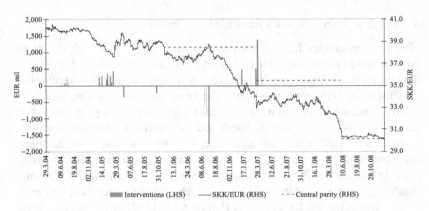

Figure 7.5: Exchange rate and forex interventions: Slovakia, 2004–8
Source: National Bank of Slovakia.

In ERM II, uncertainties about how the exchange rate stability criterion would be interpreted posed a dilemma for the authorities. As Šramko
(2008) notes, this issue was discussed frequently with European Commission and ECB officials. On this basis, National Bank officials considered it likely that real exchange rate appreciation generated by structural
factors would be taken into account in the assessment of exchange rate
stability (though accurate quantification of this factor is inherently difficult in transition economies), but that nominal appreciation seen as part
of a deliberate policy to reduce inflation would be frowned upon. When
the exchange rate began to appreciate following ERM II entry in November 2005, the National Bank did not intervene in the foreign exchange
market to counter the appreciation, with an eye to the inflation objective. Instead, it was oriented towards signalling to the market through its
communications its support for a more appreciated koruna. However,
subsequently, on 31 January 2006, the National Bank announced pub-
licly, probably following instructions from the European Commission
and ECB, that it would no longer comment on exchange rate developments. Thereafter, concerns about a negative inflation outlook prompted
the National Bank to increase its key policy interest rate in four steps in
the first three quarters of 2006 by a total of 175 basis points.

Appreciation pressures intensified significantly from 2006Q4, with the
release of impressive growth figures and news about new foreign investment projects, and as market participants became more optimistic about
the prospects of euro adoption. At the end of December, as the koruna
approached the upper edge of the ERM II ±15 per cent band, the
National Bank began countering appreciation pressures through verbal

and direct interventions and prolonged rejection of bids during regular repo auctions, which drove interbank interest rates down below policy rates. Eventually in mid March 2007, with appreciation pressures persisting, the central parity was revalued with the approval of the EU member states by 8.5 per cent to Sk35.4424 per euro – below the prevailing market rate. The National Bank continued to counter appreciation pressures after the parity revaluation by reducing policy rates twice by a cumulative 50 basis points, at end-March and in April. Thereafter, the koruna fluctuated between 6 and 7 per cent above the new central parity for the remainder of the year. Further appreciation may have been held back by reduced universal market appetite for risk in the context of the global financial turmoil.

The European Commission and ECB determined that the revaluation of the central parity of the koruna was justified by Slovakia's improved economic fundamentals. The productivity growth differential *vis-à-vis* the euro area had widened in 2006, and a sizeable part of the upward pressure on the exchange rate reflected productivity-driven equilibrium real appreciation.

There was a renewed tendency towards appreciation from late January 2008 until the negotiations on the conversion rate in May. The underlying factors were favourable GDP growth data, optimistic investor confidence and, especially, statements by the authorities regarding the conversion rate. The conversion rate of the koruna became a political issue as Prime Minister Fico pushed for the 'best exchange rate for the people' – perhaps on the basis that a significantly appreciated conversion rate would help moderate inflationary pressures in the post-Eurozone entry period. The damage an overappreciated conversion rate could do to competitiveness was deemed to be small as it was considered likely that there would be a further increase in competitiveness in the future. Ultimately, in late May, the central parity of the koruna was revalued for the second time to Sk30.1260 per euro, a rate which was higher than the prevailing market rate and corresponded to the top edge of the ± 15 per cent exchange rate band under the previous central parity. The revised parity was subsequently adopted as the final conversion rate in July 2008. Thus, the final conversion rate of the koruna was some 22 per cent more appreciated than the central parity set at the time of ERM II entry.

Slovakia's experience in ERM II demonstrated emphatically that investor sentiment could quickly turn sour if commitment to euro adoption was seen to be weakening or policy slippages were likely. In the wake of uncertainties around the parliamentary elections in June 2006 and unclear communications from the new government after the elections regarding whether it would stick to the objective of Eurozone entry in

2009, the koruna depreciated sharply and the exchange rate dropped below the central parity under ERM II in June and in July. Since the informal lower limit on the depreciation side of the ERM II band was considered to be 2.25 per cent, the National Bank engaged in three significant interventions in the foreign exchange market, selling a total of 3.085 billion euros, and increased the policy interest rate in order to stem the depreciation pressures. Market conditions calmed only after the Prime Minister and Finance Minister declared their support for the original target Eurozone entry date of January 2009.

4   Fiscal policy

The tasks of fiscal policy on the road to euro adoption are deemed to be several. First, fiscal policy has to be geared toward meeting the Maastricht criterion of a headline general government deficit not greater than 3 per cent of GDP. Second, the fiscal stance under ERM II should be appropriate for supporting disinflation and reducing the likely tensions between the inflation and exchange rate stability objectives in ERM II. Third, fiscal policy should aim at increasing flexibility in the public finances for absorbing asymmetric shocks (e.g. demand booms) in the absence of monetary policy once the country is inside the euro area. Since it is difficult to shift the stance of fiscal policy rapidly, especially when discretionary spending is a small share of total expenditure, fiscal balances need to be positioned well in advance of such potential shocks. Thus, fiscal consolidation prior to and after Eurozone entry should ideally create a safety margin against breaching the Stability and Growth Pact (SGP) 3 per cent deficit threshold in case of adverse cyclical conditions.

In both Slovenia and Slovakia, fiscal policy was narrowly focused on meeting the Maastricht deficit criterion. Although there was close coordination of policies between the central bank and Ministry of Finance, the fiscal stance was expansionary in several years, though to a limited extent. Moreover, the expenditure structure became increasingly rigid in both countries and, unless further systemic reforms of the pension and health sectors are undertaken, there are risks with regard to long-term sustainability of the public finances. Both Slovenia and Slovakia face a substantial rise in age-related expenditures because of rapidly aging populations, low average retirement ages and high pension-to-wages ratios. According to the European Commission (2009), both countries show substantial fiscal gaps and, as Velculescu (2010) documents, intertemporal net worth is significantly negative in Slovenia and Slovakia.

Table 7.4: *Fiscal indicators, 2000–9 (% of GDP)*

	2000	2001	2002	2003	2004	2005	2006	2007	2008	2009
Slovenia										
General government balance	−3.7	−4.0	−2.5	−2.7	−2.2	−1.4	−1.3	0.0	−1.7	−5.5
Total revenue	43.0	43.6	43.9	43.7	43.6	43.8	43.2	42.4	42.6	44.4
Total expenditure of which:	46.7	47.6	46.3	46.4	45.8	45.2	44.5	42.4	44.3	49.9
Compensation of employees	11.3	11.8	11.6	11.7	11.6	11.5	11.2	10.5	11.1	12.6
Intermediate consumption	6.6	6.6	6.8	6.3	6.1	6.2	6.2	5.6	6.0	6.5
Social benefits	16.0	16.0	15.9	15.9	15.9	15.7	15.3	14.4	14.7	16.8
Cyclically adjusted balance	−3.7	−3.6	−2.2	−1.9	−1.5	−0.8	−1.3	−1.5	−3.8	−3.8
General government debt	26.8	26.8	28.0	27.5	27.2	27.0	26.7	23.4	22.6	35.9
Slovakia										
General government balance	−12.3	−6.5	−8.2	−2.8	−2.4	−2.8	−3.5	−1.9	−2.3	−6.8
Total revenue	39.9	38.0	36.9	37.4	35.3	35.2	33.5	32.5	32.5	34.0
Total expenditure of which:	52.2	44.5	45.1	40.2	37.7	38.0	36.9	34.4	34.8	40.8
Compensation of employees	8.8	8.9	9.1	8.9	8.1	7.3	7.4	6.8	6.6	7.8
Intermediate consumption	6.8	6.9	6.2	6.2	5.7	5.0	5.7	4.6	5.0	5.3
Social benefits	13.6	13.6	13.7	11.9	12.3	12.4	11.9	11.6	11.3	13.6
Cyclically adjusted balance	−11.8	−6.3	−8.2	−2.7	−2.1	−2.2	−3.1	−2.1	−3.0	−5.6
General government debt	50.3	48.9	43.4	42.4	41.5	34.2	30.5	29.3	27.7	35.7

Sources: Eurostat, Ministry of Finance of the Slovak Republic, Bank of Slovenia.

4.1   Fiscal policy in Slovenia

Slovenia had already met the Maastricht fiscal deficit criterion when the authorities adopted the euro adoption strategy in 2003. The headline general government deficit (ESA-95 definition) continued to decline in subsequent years, reaching broad balance in 2007 when Slovenia entered the Eurozone. The improvement in the fiscal position mainly involved expenditure restraint. Measures were taken to lower the debt service burden and reduce the growth in the public sector wage bill, pensions and outlays on goods and services. As a result, government expenditure as a ratio to GDP declined by a total of 4 percentage points during 2003–7. However, a part of this impact was offset by measures introduced in 2006 to restructure individual income taxes and reduce payroll taxes. After remaining broadly stable during 2003–5, total revenue as a ratio to GDP suffered a cumulative drop of about 1.5 percentage points during 2006–7 (Table 7.4).

Because of the tax reduction measures and a reversal of the earlier restraint on pension indexation, the cyclically adjusted fiscal stance became expansionary in the last year of ERM II and immediately after euro adoption. Without these measures, the general government budget would have recorded a substantial surplus in 2007. Thus, fiscal policy added to domestic demand instead of counteracting the private demand boom and mounting inflationary pressures. Since the tax cuts were initiated without offsetting structural cuts in spending, they resulted in a permanent deterioration in the structural fiscal position. At that time, Ministry of Finance officials were not convinced of the need to adopt a neutral fiscal stance, given uncertainties about the cyclical position of the economy, and they also saw political constraints to further expenditure rationalisation in the near term. It can perhaps be argued that, with Eurozone entry secured and with the headline budget deficit below the SGP limit, there was little pressure on the authorities to orient fiscal policy to manage the inflationary effects of the demand boom.

The rigidity of Slovenia's budget expenditure structure is greater than the average for the EU-15 and other new EU member states, and rigidity has increased since euro adoption.[8] The restraint in public sector wage growth during 2004–6 was partly the result of delays in the conclusion of negotiations on a new public sector wage structure aimed at reducing wage dispersion. The implementation of the eventual wage agreement will cost more than previously estimated and raised the wage bill substantially during 2008–10. There is now even more need for expenditure-based fiscal consolidation, following a near-doubling of the public debt-to-GDP ratio in 2008–9 associated with the economic downturn triggered by the global financial crisis, and for space to be created for rising age-related expenditures. But, as yet, there is no political consensus for systemic expenditure reforms.

4.2   Fiscal policy in Slovakia

The orientation of fiscal policy in Slovakia shifted markedly in 2003 with the adoption of the programme for a fast-track entry into the Eurozone. The headline general government deficit declined sharply from above 8 per cent of GDP in 2002 to about 2.75 per cent of GDP in 2003. Thereafter, the deficit remained below the 3 per cent Maastricht criterion threshold until Eurozone entry, except for a temporary breach of the limit in 2006 mainly owing to a structural increase in the cost of the newly introduced second-pillar pension scheme. The authorities

---

[8] European Commission (2008). Rigid expenditures are those not dependent upon the discretion of the authorities in the short term. These include social benefits, subsidies, interest payments and compensation of employees.

implemented a major tax reform in 2004 featuring *inter alia*, a single rate of 19 per cent for the VAT and personal and corporate income taxes as well as a substantial increase in excise duties. The tax reform made the economy more market-oriented and fostered investment and growth. Revenues increased strongly as economic growth picked up progressively but, reflecting the increasing contribution to growth of investment and net foreign demand which do not directly enter the tax bases, the revenue-to-GDP ratio declined over time. On the expenditure side, reforms were initiated during 2003–4 to contain public health expenditure and curtail untargeted spending on social benefits and social assistance. Efforts were also directed to restraining the growth of the public sector wage bill and outlays on goods and services. However, expenditure on all these categories increased in real terms, although they declined as a ratio to GDP.

The strong economic growth was not fully exploited by the authorities for deeper fiscal consolidation and to prepare for a strong performance in the monetary union. Throughout the period, revenues exceeded the budgeted levels as growth in the underlying bases was stronger than assumed in the budget, and co-financing of EU-funded projects was underspent because of shortfalls in the drawdown of funds from the EU. However, only a part of the revenue overperformance and co-financing cushion was devoted to ensuring a better-than-budgeted fiscal deficit outturn. A greater part was devoted to expenditure additional to the budgeted levels on goods and services, pension and health benefits and subsidies to the transport sector.

European Council opinions and IMF staff repeatedly advised the authorities to adhere to the budgeted nominal expenditure targets and secure a deeper fiscal consolidation. While the actual fiscal outturn was generally supportive of the disinflation objective – there was a withdrawal of fiscal stimulus in all years except for 2004 and 2006, when the stance was slightly expansionary – a stronger counter-cyclical fiscal policy would have helped in fending off appreciation pressures, ensured greater budgetary flexibility for absorbing asymmetric shocks once in the Eurozone and contributed to the sustainability of the public finances in the long term. However, the authorities' rationale for the emphasis on higher social spending was to make the benefits of growth more socially inclusive.

The allocation of revenue overperformance toward socially oriented current spending increased the rigidity of the public expenditure structure and made the task of expenditure-based fiscal adjustment more challenging. An added problem with Slovakia's three-year budget framework, especially during the ERM II years, was that it did not identify how the announced social expenditure policy priorities would be funded beyond the current year. The authorities' expectation was that these expenditures would be accommodated through stronger revenue performance and restrained government spending in other areas. As long as economic growth and revenue collections were stronger than budgeted, this approach did not create any problem. However, when economic growth turned negative in 2009 and revenue underperformance ensued, there was little that fiscal policy could do to restrain the widening deficit and Slovakia became subject to the Excessive Deficit Procedure (EDP). The task of articulating a credible expenditure-based adjustment strategy to exit from the EDP has become challenging because of the rigid expenditure structure, and the authorities are now considering a combination of revenue and expenditure measures.

5   Lessons for future Eurozone entrants

Given the potential for inconsistency between some of the Maastricht criteria, the risks inherent in a major regime change and the vulnerabilities to swings in market sentiments, countries need to prepare well-articulated strategies for meeting the Maastricht criteria and implementing structural reforms aimed at enhancing the flexibility of the economy to withstand shocks. To ensure a successful transition to the Eurozone, close coordination between the central bank and the government, and broad political and public support are essential. The policies should be clearly communicated to markets and the public, and focused on the objective of smooth integration into the euro area. Otherwise, there is a risk of the momentum getting derailed on account of the electoral cycle and a possible change in government. As the experience of Slovakia after the June 2006 elections shows, even the slightest lack of clarity regarding commitment to euro adoption is likely to be punished severely by the market. Of course, this sensitivity of the market could tie politicians' hands if the euro entry date was close enough. A streamlined and committed policy of adopting the euro has to be implemented in a short period. Otherwise, there may be considerable costs caused by the postponement of policy measures. Long stays in ERM II with policies that are not in line with the requirements for euro adoption would test the mettle of almost any policy framework.

Slovenia and Slovakia spent close to the minimum required period of two years in ERM II, and their experience seems to have been relatively easy. There was an element of good luck for both countries. In the case of Slovenia, the luck was manifested in the domestic economic cycle: the persistence of a negative output gap facilitated meeting the inflation criterion. In the case of Slovakia, the luck factors were the market's confidence in the exchange rate appreciation and decreasing world energy and food prices in 2008. Without good luck, a transition country with faster growth of real GDP and productivity than the EU average would always be confronted with the impossible trinity. An alternative option to not relying on luck factors would be to achieve durable real convergence, as Austria did before achieving nominal convergence.[9] From this point of view, the role of ERM II is less akin to the original idea of a 'training room' for participation in the euro area and more like a 'waiting room' for which sound fundamentals are vital before entering and while staying in the waiting room.

The Slovak experience has shed further light on the interpretation of the exchange rate stability criterion which reduces the potential for inconsistency between this criterion and the inflation criterion. The Slovak case shows that it is not necessary to maintain the exchange rate close to parity and that substantial appreciation of the currency in ERM II may be acceptable to the European Commission and the ECB as being consistent with 'stability'. However, an important caveat is that the appreciation should be in line with economic fundamentals and equilibrium real appreciation. Productivity differentials *vis-à-vis* the euro area are the single most important indicator to monitor in this regard. Since there are no clearly written rules and there is a substantial amount of discretion when evaluating exchange rate stability, it would be important for countries that choose a hybrid monetary framework of inflation targeting and exchange rate targeting to maintain close communication with the Commission and ECB with regard to how exchange rate developments and interventions in the foreign exchange market would be subsequently interpreted. In the Slovak case, direct interventions in the foreign exchange markets were deemed appropriate by the Commission and ECB, but verbal communications signalling support for a more appreciated koruna were deemed problematic.

In countries where the scope for productivity-driven appreciation is limited, the traditional interpretation of exchange rate stability is likely to be applied. In these cases, meeting the Maastricht inflation criterion will require strong fiscal and wage policies, unless the ERM II period coincides with a cyclical downturn, as was the case in Slovenia. However, a risk in such a case is that when the demand cycle reverses, inflation is likely to pick up sharply, as happened in Slovenia in 2007–8 immediately after euro adoption. Slovenia's experience has caused the ECB and the Commission to give greater scrutiny to inflation sustainability, and

[9] See Hochreiter and Tavlas (2005).

future entrants may well encounter more investigation of this issue in the assessment of compliance with the Maastricht criteria.

If the inflation dynamics are strongly affected by the output gap, one needs good estimates of the potential supply and the output gap to calibrate the appropriate policy response. However, adequate and timely information is difficult to obtain. Estimates of the output gap are sensitive to the methodology applied. In addition, the non-inflationary potential output may fluctuate during the process of monetary integration for reasons associated with accelerations in productivity. For example, as noted above, Slovenia experienced a demand boom in the post-euro adoption period whereas Slovakia's strong growth was likely driven by supply-side factors. Thus it will be important to come up with the best possible estimate of the output gap which takes account of the specificity of the individual member states, instead of using a common methodology for all countries as the European Commission currently does.

In designing a macroeconomic policy framework, it is important to keep in mind the long-term perspective of participating in the euro area, not only the 'end-game' ERM II context. This can reinforce the credibility of the macroeconomic framework in place if it is successful in stabilising inflation. Stronger credibility in turn helps stabilise inflation with lower costs, by anchoring inflation expectations and thus limiting second-round effects. Credibility comes out of a successful past policy, from a permanent learning process that generates a positive or negative reputation of the policy framework in place. From this perspective, the absence of a decisive response to counter the inflationary cycle in the post-euro adoption period in Slovenia was a missed opportunity in establishing the credibility of the macroeconomic policy framework. The slippage in the fiscal stance probably eroded credibility further. The lesson here is that the policy discipline that ensured a successful ERM II experience should not be relaxed as soon as the euro is adopted. Both countries and potential new entrants need to give consideration to having an appropriate framework for countering inflationary cycles while in the Eurozone. Prior to euro adoption, the disinflation strategy in Slovakia relied heavily on a large exchange rate appreciation. But this is no longer a policy option.

Keeping in mind the long-term perspective of participating successfully in the euro area requires securing a strong and flexible fiscal policy at an early stage. It is not sufficient to orient fiscal policy to meet the Maastricht criterion, but it should also be adapted prior to Eurozone entry for countercyclical use. Although the topic was discussed and identified in the preparation of the euro adoption strategy, in neither Slovenia nor Slovakia was fiscal policy adjusted sufficiently to enable it to be used with the required flexibility in responding to changing circumstances after euro adoption. The desired response from fiscal policy may be more demanding for new member states if the consistency of the ECB monetary policy stance with domestic needs is low. If new member states have a larger share of more volatile elements in the HICP basket or they experience domestic demand shocks, there is likely to be an amplification of inflationary pressures as monetary policy is geared to the euro area average. This is because nominal interest rates are eroded by higher inflation, thus decreasing the real interest rates and further spurring demand and inflationary pressures.

Future Eurozone entrants should aim to build up a reserve buffer to enable a fiscal stimulus without breaching the SGP limit in the event of a cyclical downturn in normal times. The SGP's constraint of 3 per cent of GDP on the cyclically adjusted budget deficit indeed requires a more ambitious adjustment towards a fiscal surplus in 'good times'. This recommendation has, of course, more general validity and also applies to the post-euro adoption period. A low level of public debt is another key requirement. The crisis has taught us that only those small countries which had low debt levels were able to roll over their debt without significant problems. In addition, several other structural fiscal reforms, if undertaken well before euro adoption, could help alleviate inflation persistence and facilitate economic adjustment after inflationary shocks. These include reducing the rigid and formula-driven indexation of social transfers and public sector wages, and reforming healthcare expenditure and the pension system. In addition, increases in excise duties and regulated prices must be contained to avoid cost-push shocks to inflation. In general, expenditure-based adjustment is preferable to revenue-based consolidation (Alesina and Ardagna, 2009). Finally, EU funds must be oriented towards enhancing potential GDP, and if and when domestic budget resources are freed up they should not be devoted to increasing government consumption.

Significant adjustments should also be undertaken in the domain of wage policies to prevent inflation persistence, losses in competitiveness and persistent unemployment gaps after economic shocks. Wage flexibility and nominal wage restraint are needed to absorb asymmetric shocks and ensure labour cost increases in line with productivity gains over the medium term. This is why attempts were made to move away from wage indexation towards forward-looking wage-setting in Slovenia prior to ERM II. Unfortunately, wages reacted sharply to inflation increases after 2007, stimulated by buoyant economic activity and resulting in high unit labour cost increases and corresponding loss in competitiveness.

References

Alesina, A. and S. Ardagna (2009). 'Large changes in fiscal policy: taxes versus spending', National Bureau of Economic Research Working Paper, No. 15438

Banerjee, B. and H. Shi (2010). 'Determinants of inflation in Slovenia on the road to Euro adoption', in V. Bole and L. MacKellar (eds.), *From Tolar to Euro*, Ljubljana: Center of Excellence in Finance

Bole, V. and L. MacKellar (eds.) (2010). *From Tolar to Euro*, Ljubljana: Center of Excellence in Finance

Cigan, H., A. Jevčák, P. Pradelle and P. Žáková (2008). 'Exchange rate pass-through to inflation in Slovakia', *ECFIN Country Focus*, 5

Dalgic, E. (2008). 'Inflation performance in Slovakia', unpublished paper, International Monetary Fund, April

European Central Bank (ECB) (2008). *Convergence Report May 2010*, Frankfurt, www.ecb.int/pub/pdf/conrep/cr201005en.pdf

European Commission (2006). '2006 Convergence Report on Slovenia', *European Economy*, Special Report, No. 2, http://ec.europa.eu/economy_finance/publications/publication485_en.pdf

(2008). 'Convergence Report 2008', *European Economy*, No. 3, http://ec.europa.eu/economy_finance/publications/publication12574_en.pdf

(2009), 'The 2009 Ageing Report', *European Economy*, No. 2

Hochreiter, E. and G.S. Tavlas (2005). 'Two roads to the euro: the monetary experiences of Austria and Greece', in S. Schadler (ed.), *Euro Adoption in Central and Eastern Europe: Opportunities and Challenges*, Washington, DC: International Monetary Fund

Konuki, T. (2010). 'Estimating potential output and the output gap in Slovakia', *Eastern European Economics*, 48: 39–55

Kozamernik, D. and T. Žumer (2011). 'Monetary policy and the disinflation on the way to the euro in Slovenia', *International Journal of Monetary Economics and Finance*, 4: 21–48

Ministry of Finance of the Slovak Republic (2010). 'Output gap and NAIRU estimates within state–space framework: an application to Slovakia'

Schadler, S., P. Drummond, L. Kuijs, Z. Murgasova and R. van Elkan (2005). *Adopting the Euro in Central Europe: Challenges of the Next Step in European Integration*, International Monetary Fund Occasional Paper, No. 234

Šramko, I. (2008). 'Slovakia's road to the euro: lessons learned and challenges ahead', in K. Liebscher, J. Christl, P. Mooslechner and D. Ritzberger-Grünwald (eds.), *Currency and Competitiveness in Europe*, Cheltenham: Edward Elgar

Surti, J. (2010). 'What drives inflation in Slovenia?', in V. Bole and L. MacKellar (eds.), *From Tolar to Euro*, Ljubljana: Center of Excellence in Finance

Velculescu, D. (2010). 'Some uncomfortable arithmetic regarding Europe's public finances', IMF Working Paper, No. 10/177

8 Is the euro really a 'teuro'? The effects of introducing the euro on prices of everyday non-tradables in Slovakia

*Miroslav Beblavý**

1 Introduction

When euro notes and coins were originally introduced in January 2002, consumers in the member states of the Eurozone experienced a sharp spike in perceived inflation, which translated into a permanent perception that the switch to the new currency was associated with a one-time inflation shock. As evidence of this, the synthetic indicator of perceived inflation over the previous twelve months compiled by the European Commission from consumer surveys showed a jump from 27 in December 2001 to 60 in September 2002 and remained above 50 for most of 2002. The most succinct summary of this view was coined in Germany, where the euro was promptly dubbed 'teuro' (from *teuer*, meaning 'expensive' in German).

For consumer prices as a whole, the perception was largely disproved by the actual data on the development of consumer prices during the relevant period. Prices in January 2002 rose by 0.09 per cent in the Eurozone according to the harmonised index of consumer prices (HICP) and the annual inflation rate during 2002 was also similar to 2001 and 2003, oscillating between 2 per cent and 3 per cent (although there was an unusual jump at the beginning of 2002, attributed mainly to the weather). Therefore, the explanations of discrepancies between the perceived and the actual inflation tended to focus on either purely psychological interpretations of how individuals could experience higher inflation at the time of a change in currencies without any basis in reality, or interpretations combining higher-than-normal changes in specific prices, which

* The author would like to thank David Cobham for the discussion that led to this chapter, Hans Wolfgang Brachinger for agreeing to be the discussant for the original paper and his patience in waiting for the draft, and Soňa Urbančíková and Katarína Lovrantová for invaluable help in preparing the chapter. The draft version of this chapter was published as CEPS Working Document, No. 339 by the Centre for European Policy Studies in Brussels.

Table 8.1: *Answers by respondents in the Eurozone as a whole to the question: 'For each of the following, do you personally have the feeling that, in the conversion to the euro in area X, prices have been . . .' (%)*

	Always rounded up	Most often rounded up	Most often rounded down	Always rounded down	All in all, they cancel each other out	Do not know
Restaurants/cafés	40.8	43.4	3.2	0.4	4.2	8
Services (hairdressers/taxis)	36.5	42.4	3.8	0.8	6.2	10.4
Small food shops	30.3	48.4	4.1	0.5	8.6	8.2
Other small shops	28.4	47.1	4.8	0.6	8.6	10.4
Cinemas/swimming pools	25.9	36.2	4.3	1.3	7.5	24.8
Supermarkets	24.2	43.7	11.1	2	15	4.1
Public transport	24.1	31.2	8.7	1.4	11.6	22.9

Source: European Commission, Eurobarometer, No. 171, Brussels, May 2002.

are likely to form anchors of consumer experiences, with psychologically based misconceptions.

Both explanations build on the fact that Eurozone consumers perceived differentiated levels of price hikes according to the kind of product and establishment. If we look at Table 8.1, we can see a certain subset of frequently purchased non-tradables (restaurants, taxis and hairdressers) that could possibly have been behind the teuro phenomenon. The introduction of the euro in Slovakia in 2009 is an opportunity to revisit this discussion in a new environment.

In the context of inflation perceptions and realities, Slovakia presents an interesting case. Slovakia has had two decades of experience with rigorous monetary policy and moderate inflation, and also with repeated price shocks stemming from changes in administratively set prices, indirect taxes and other transition phenomena. Like the Czech Republic, and unlike Hungary and Poland, it has had a 'German' monetary policy, but without the German experience of monetary stability.

Slovakia also joined the euro at the end of a long period of economic boom, but just as the global financial and economic crisis fully hit the European economies. It adopted the single currency with a very strong exchange rate based on the assumption of further rapid growth, indeed a possibility of overheating after the switchover. There was also the expectation that the lower price level and the Balassa–Samuelson effect would lead to higher inflation once the option of adjusting the real effective exchange rate through nominal appreciation was exhausted.

This chapter looks at the Slovak experience with euro adoption from the point of view of perceived vs. actual inflation, with a focus on a specific set of non-tradable prices. It uses both official price data and an original data set of prices at the enterprise level, examining whether Slovak consumers experienced an unusual price jump at the time of euro adoption. Additionally, this chapter proposes what could be a possible explanation for such a phenomenon, building on the literature concerning previous instances of switches to the single currency.

The chapter starts with a review of the state of the art in the area and then presents the methodology of the chapter. It continues with empirical findings, dealing in turn with the HICP data, data on inflation perceptions and expectations and the enterprise-level price data and their interpretation. Some preliminary conclusions are presented at the end.

2   Inflation shocks during euro adoption: literature survey

In this section, we look briefly at the literature dealing with the two topics most relevant to the chapter. The first and most important body of literature deals with the topic of why the euro's introduction was associated with an inflation hike in the minds of consumers across the Eurozone. This sets the stage for our own research on the introduction of the single currency in Slovakia. The second topic concerns the frequency and (a)symmetry of price changes at the enterprise level and should enable us to better place our micro research in context.

2.1   Euro as 'teuro'

Theoretically, the euro changeover should have had almost no effect on consumer behaviour: the exchange rates were fixed long before the new currency was introduced (Mastrobuoni, 2004), and in the twelve months prior to May 2002 the European inflation rate exhibited the same level as had been recorded right before the introduction of euro notes and coins in the Eurozone (Brachinger, 2006). Even though a strong increase in overall inflation in the Eurozone was observed at the beginning of 2002, this was, as the European Central Bank (ECB) reported, largely owing to exceptional and short-lived factors, such as adverse weather conditions in some parts of the euro area (ECB, 2002, quoted in Ercolani and Dutta, 2007: 384).

Prior to mid-2001 in all EU countries, the gap between perceived and actual inflation was close to zero. The perception gap appeared in all EU countries only a few months before and after the euro changeover. In the countries that did not join the euro area, the trend level of this gap remained close to zero, implying that the departure of perceived inflation from actual inflation was indeed related to euro introduction (Hüfner and Koske, 2008).

Brachinger (2004, 2005a and 2005b) developed the so-called 'index of perceived inflation', showing that in the period around the introduction of euro notes and coins, the average perceived inflation in Germany was approximately four times higher than the official inflation rate (Brachinger, 2006). Mastrobuoni's (2004) findings, based on Eurostat and a consumer survey, present a similar overall picture, with the mean difference between standardised perceived and actual inflation oscillating between 0.32 and 1.23 percentage points among the countries, after the euro changeover. Additionally, Brachinger (2005b) claims, on the basis of the theory of loss aversion, that customers' perceptions about inflation are more influenced by price rises than by price decreases because they weigh purchasing power loss more heavily than purchasing power gain.

Importantly, though, while showing that the perception of increased inflation was markedly overrated, some authors have also stressed that frequent – albeit moderate – price increases did occur at the introduction of the new currency. Stix (2005) notes that most of the goods contained in the micro and mini baskets became more expensive which, in line with the ECB's conjecture that, after the introduction of the euro, consumers based their estimation of price increases on goods that are purchased more frequently (ECB, 2002), partly explains the bias of the euro towards the teuro (Kirchler, 2005).

Mastrobuoni (2004) provides a similar explanation, but rather than presenting it as a partial conclusion, he uses it as a starting point to analyse the causes of differences in inflation patterns for different goods. He does this on the premise that 'the changeover to a new currency reduces the information about prices available to the customer', suggesting that 'the reason for higher inflation among cheap goods is the cost of obtaining information'. The price growth is therefore 'correlated with consumers' ability to adapt to the new currency' – a theory confirmed by the fact that the three countries with the strongest euro effect on prices (Spain, Italy and France) were the countries with the highest percentage of consumers who tended to judge the price appropriateness using their old currency.

Even though Mastrobuoni uses Eurostat's monthly HICP (in combination with the data collected by the Economist Intelligence Unit, EIU), he stresses the bias of relying solely upon the macro indices in testing the level of a possibly euro changeover-induced inflation, perceived or real. Brachinger (2006) similarly points out that the major drawback of 'an expenditure-weighted price index such as the CPI is [that it is] insensitive to the appearance of inordinately high price increases of frequently purchased goods and tends to mask such inflation structures'.

Similar methodological drawbacks are a starting point of the analysis of Ercolani and Dutta (2007), who hypothesise that 'the euro changeover generated inflation that was not detected by official statistics'. While the 2002 ECB statement affirmed that 'no evidence of a euro-changeover-induced increase in aggregate prices could be found and that any variation in food prices was due to seasonal factors', it also conceded there *may* have been price increases for some specific items in the service sectors that 'could have been related to the changeover' (quoted in Ercolani and Dutta, 2007: 384). What the authors thus subsequently attempt to show is that the overall 'weak evidence of a slight temporary increase in aggregate inflation in January 2002 for the countries that did join the euro' played out variably at the individual level of specific sectoral items. At that level, the euro changeover-induced price changes ranged from statistically insignificant and quantitatively small to quantitatively large and statistically crucial – as was specifically the case in the restaurant sector.

The analysis in this chapter focuses on micro data collection as a key to observing the varying price movements for non-tradables. Combining micro and macro data and indices offers an overall picture of the euro adoption process in Slovakia.

2.2   Frequently experienced prices

Inevitably related to the effects of euro changeover as documented by this chapter is the experience of price-setting behaviour at the level of firms and enterprises, concerning which the following aspects are of particular relevance:
- The frequency of price reviews/changes
- The scope of price changes
- The symmetry of this behaviour.

Past surveys have shown that the vast majority of firms review their prices a maximum of three times per year (that is, 57 per cent of firms in the euro area as a whole), while 26 per cent review prices more than twelve times a year, and 17 per cent do so four to eleven times a year (Fabiani *et al.*, 2005). The frequency of the price change, though, is relatively low: micro evidence from the Inflation Persistence Network (IPN) shows that prices in sectors covered by the consumer prices index (CPI) remain unchanged on average for four to five quarters. In addition, the frequency is somewhat lower in the retail sector compared with the producer sector, where the median firm changes the price of its goods once a year. It has also been found that prices change less frequently for products with a larger share of labour input and with a smaller share of intermediate energy inputs (Altissimo, Ehrmann and Smets, 2006).

The price-setting behaviour is thus heterogeneous across the product categories: the IPN micro evidence shows that while changes are very frequent for energy and unprocessed food, they are relatively infrequent for non-energy industrial goods and especially services (Altissimo, Ehrmann and Smets, 2006).

Looking at the magnitude of price changes, it turns out that price increases as well as decreases are sizeable compared with the inflation rate. Price reductions and price increases have a similar order of magnitude, although price reductions are on average larger: the average price increase is found to be of the order of 8 per cent and the average price decrease slightly larger than 10 per cent (Altissimo, Ehrmann and Smets, 2006).

Some sectors – unprocessed food, processed food and energy – are characterised by almost perfect symmetry between price increases and price decreases; the difference is much larger in the services sector, where an asymmetry exists between the frequency of increases and decreases, as only two price changes out of ten are price decreases (Altissimo, Ehrmann and Smets, 2006).

3   Methodology

This chapter is based on comparing price datasets at both the macro and micro levels. In addition to the general price index, we focus on prices in restaurants/cafés, in hairdressing salons and for taxi services.

At the macro level, we compare HICP data collected for Eurostat by the national statistical agencies for three entities – the euro area, Slovakia and the Czech Republic. We use overall inflation as well as three subsets that are closest to what we measure in the micro data:

- Passenger transport by road (reference group for taxis)
- Restaurants, cafés and the like (reference group for all meals and drinks served in restaurants)
- Hairdressing salons and personal grooming establishments (reference group for a haircut).

At the macro level, we also utilise data on perceptions based on consumer surveys collected by Eurostat on a monthly basis. The time series measures consumer experience with inflation (based on the question, 'How do you think that consumer prices have developed over the last 12 months?'). In this case, we also use data for other new member states that have adopted the euro (Cyprus, Malta and Slovenia).

The third set of macro-level data comes from Eurobarometer surveys specifically concerning the introduction of the euro. In the case of Slovakia, these are survey Nos. 240, 249 and 259 (European Commission, 2008a, 2008b, 2009). We compare answers from those surveys with the results of similar surveys done at the introduction of the euro in Slovenia in 2007 and in Cyprus and Malta in 2008, as well as the introduction in the original Euro12 countries in 2002.

At the micro level, we compare datasets collected specifically for this research in Bratislava (the capital of Slovakia) and Brno (the second-largest city in the Czech Republic). The reason for choosing Brno as an analogous case study to Bratislava is the shared Czecho-Slovak history, a comparable size and the geographical proximity (130 km) of the two cities. In this sense, Brno and, at the macro level, the Czech Republic, serve as 'control groups' for Bratislava and Slovakia. The Czech Republic has not adopted the euro or entered the exchange rate mechanism (ERM II) yet and its currency floats vis-à-vis other currencies.

At the micro level, we collected data for eight specific services in three categories. For cafés and restaurants, we collected price data for the most common main course and side dish listed on all menus – schnitzel and boiled potatoes – and the two most frequently drunk kinds of coffee – cappuccino and Viennese coffee. For hair salons, we collected one dataset on basic haircut prices (for a female customer, washing, cutting and styling the hair). For taxis, we collected the price for flagging a taxi, a price per km and a price per minute of waiting.

The micro-level datasets were collected in two snapshots. The first took place in July 2008 and the second in July 2009. In both cases, the prices of specific services were collected from individual service providers based on a combination of prices posted on the internet and prices provided on request by telephone. In the case of Slovakia, the euro prices from July 2009 were compared with the Slovak koruna prices from July 2008 using the official final conversion rate of 30.126 koruna = 1 euro.

The two periods were chosen to eliminate seasonal effects and to capture the overall effect of transition to the euro. In other words, the aim was *not* to measure price jumps (or lack thereof) *exactly* at the time of the switch, but to capture the overall change associated with euro adoption. The net was thus cast relatively widely, in order to measure price developments for the period of six months prior to and after the change.

The data analysis proceeds in the following steps. First, we begin by examining the actual inflation data at the macro level, comparing developments in the HICP for the euro area, Slovakia and the Czech Republic for all prices and for the three subsets identified above. The objective

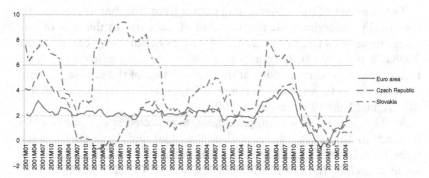

Figure 8.1: HICP inflation: euro area, the Czech Republic and Slovakia, 2001–10 (year-on-year) (%)
Source: Eurostat.

of the initial exercise is to provide a basic picture of the price developments in Slovakia during the 2000s and particularly during the run-up to euro adoption – with regard to both general prices and those that are the specific focus of the chapter.

This is followed in the second step by the analysis of perceptions, using similar tools for the time series analysis, but complementing them with comparison of one-time data gleaned from the Flash Eurobarometer surveys.

In the third part of the data analysis, we look at the micro data from Bratislava and Brno. We examine the distribution of the price increases through an analysis of mean and variance and by comparing the values for each item for the two cities. We then compare the conclusions from the micro data with the development of reference prices in the same period at the national level to note any discrepancies.

4   Findings

4.1   *Inflation in Slovakia and the euro area: the overall HICP and specific non-tradables*

As we can see in Figure 8.1, prices in Slovakia have oscillated markedly during the last decade, with annual inflation reaching almost 10 per cent in 2003, but then dropping steadily and eventually falling below 1 per cent in 2010. Yet this turbulence relative to euro area inflation was largely induced by administrative steps during the 1999–2001 period and the 2003–4 period, particularly several steep increases in VAT and excise taxes as well as direct increases in administered prices. Once the effects of

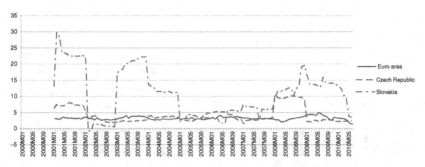

Figure 8.2: HICP inflation for passenger transport: Eurozone, Czech Republic and Slovakia, 2000–10 (%)
Source: Eurostat.

these policy measures had played out by 2005, Slovak inflation decreased to 2 per cent and oscillated between 2 per cent and 5 per cent until the adoption of the single currency in January 2009. At the end of 2006, Slovak inflation began to closely track overall Eurozone inflation and it did not diverge again until mid-2009, when it temporarily spiked.

With regard to non-tradables, notably the services analysed in this chapter, the picture of inflation convergence with the euro is not equally straightforward. Starting with price developments for passenger transport by road, we can observe three sharp spikes in inflation (Figure 8.2). Two of them – in 2001 and 2003 – are directly tied to policy measures (tax changes and price deregulation); however, there is no such obvious explanation for the spike preceding and following the introduction of the euro. After remaining at the 5–6 per cent level during much of 2006 and 2007, the prices of passenger transport by road grew dramatically in 2008, with year-on-year inflation reaching 20 per cent at the end of 2008 and then remaining at around 15 per cent until the end of 2009. Oil prices provide just part of the answer, for there were only weak rises in euro area passenger transport prices during the same period. Moreover, Czech prices did not follow the same pattern (after a spike in 2008 caused by tax measures, this type of inflation dropped dramatically by the end of 2008 towards the Eurozone level).

Similar observations can be made for prices in restaurants, cafés and comparable establishments. As tracked in Figure 8.3, prices also began to diverge from the Eurozone at the end of 2007 and remained at unusually high levels during 2008 and 2009, starting to drop in late 2009. Again, the Czech case confirms the Slovak anomaly, since Czech prices rose during 2008 only as a result of a clearly identifiable set of tax changes, and once these had played out, inflation rapidly decreased and returned

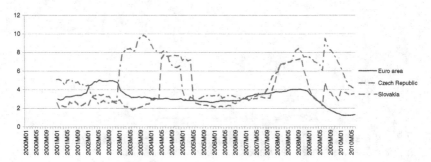

Figure 8.3: HICP inflation in restaurants, cafés and similar establishments: Eurozone, Czech Republic and Slovakia, 2000–10 (%)
Source: Eurostat.

Figure 8.4: HICP inflation in hairdressing salons and personal grooming establishments: Eurozone, Czech Republic and Slovakia, 2000–10 (%)
Source: Eurostat.

to close to the Eurozone level. In the Slovak case, there is a particularly sharp twelve-month hike between July 2008 and 2009, in the period following confirmation of euro entry.

Finally, the price developments for hairdressing salons and personal grooming establishments present an identical picture, including the unusual spike between July 2008 and July 2009 (Figure 8.4).

The rapid increases could of course be a peculiarity of the Slovak case. Given, however, that these prices are those which had already been identified as mostly 'rounded up' in 2002 during the launch of euro notes and coins, it is worth examining whether we are observing a more general trend here.

Table 8.2 presents a summary of price developments during the period surrounding euro adoption. It examines inflation for a given bundle of

Table 8.2: *Inflation in selected areas: July after euro adoption vs. the July prior to euro adoption*

	Overall inflation	Passenger transport by road	Δ	Restaurants, cafés, etc.	Δ	Hair-dressing	Δ	Goods	Δ	Services	Δ
Euro area	2.02	2.38	0.36	4.81	2.79	4.03	2.01	1.15	-0.87	3.23	1.21
Cyprus	5.34	9.46	4.12	6.34	1	6.94	1.6	5.92	0.58	4.43	-0.91
Malta	5.6	1.48	-4.12	5.37	-0.23	2.07	-3.53	5.64	0.04	5.53	-0.07
Slovenia	3.97	2.56	-1.41	8.99	5.02	5.93	1.96	3.39	-0.58	5.09	1.12
Slovakia	0.61	12.44	11.83	5.41	4.8	8.13	7.52	-1.37	-1.98	4.75	4.14

Source: Author's calculations based on Eurostat data.

Table 8.3: *Nominal appreciation/depreciation in the run-up to the single currency*

Appreciation (+)/depreciation (−1)	Slovakia	Slovenia	Malta	Cyprus
Between 12 and 6 months prior to entry	11.2	−0.1	0	−0.9
Between 18 and 6 months prior to entry	11.4	−0.1	0	−0.9

Source: Author's calculations based on ECB data.

goods and services if we compare prices in the July following euro adoption in a given country with the July of the previous year. The years are 2001 and 2002 for the original euro area countries, 2006 and 2007 for Slovenia, 2007 and 2008 for Cyprus and Malta and 2008 and 2009 for Slovakia. It also compares inflation for a given subset of prices with overall inflation, showing the differential between general inflation and the specific bundle.

As we can see, Slovakia exhibits obvious anomalies compared with other countries in this respect. This is true for non-tradables in general (proxied by the prices of services), for which the inflation in Slovakia in the period immediately before and after euro adoption was 4.14 percentage points higher than general inflation, whereas in other countries, the differential was anywhere between −0.91 and 1.21 percentage points.

The same trend can be observed if we compare three specific subsets of the consumer price index examined in the chapter. The differential between changes in the price of a given set of services and the general price index was highest in Slovakia for passenger transport by road (11.83 percentage points) and hairdressing (7.52 percentage points), whereas in the case of restaurants and cafés (4.8 percentage points), it was second highest after Slovenia (5.02 percentage points).

The anomaly is likely to be related to the reliance of Slovakia on nominal exchange rate appreciation to drive down inflation during the qualification period for the single currency, in order to meet the Maastricht inflation criterion. This can be seen from Table 8.3, where the Slovak koruna appreciated by more than 11 per cent in the period preceding entry, whereas the other new member states did not pursue nominal appreciation at all. Rapid nominal appreciation naturally leads to deflation in the prices of tradable goods, thus immediately depressing the overall inflation rate. Yet since the same mechanism does not apply to non-tradable services, in their case inflation can remain higher.

While the effects of nominal currency appreciation could on their own explain some of the unusually high divergence between the inflation of tradable and non-tradable goods in Slovakia, they fail to account for the increase in the rate of inflation we observed during the 2008–9 period with regard to non-tradables. An overheating economy could add some explanatory power, but further increases in late 2008 and the first half of 2009 – when the crisis fully hit Slovakia and unemployment was rapidly growing – make this unlikely. Therefore, there is some *prima facie* evidence of the effects of the changeover on the prices of non-tradables at the macro level.

4.2   Accounting for the Balassa–Samuelson effect

To account for the Balassa–Samuelson effect as a significant factor influencing price appreciation in the non-tradable sector, we analysed differences between price developments for overall HICP inflation and price developments for services as a group and then for several subsets of prices in the service sector, in three periods prior to the introduction of the euro: from eighteen months up to six months, from thirty months up to eighteen months, and from forty-two months up to thirty months prior to the euro changeover (Tables 8.A1–8.A3 in the appendix, pp. 180–182).

Tables 8.A1–8.A3 show that the prices in the non-tradable sector in Slovakia during the period of 1 year up to 3.5 years before introduction of the euro do not reflect any anomaly with respect to other observed countries during the same period. In Slovakia during the observed period, the differential between the prices for the bundle of services and the overall HICP was within the range of –0.94 to 1.21. As a comparison, in the period surrounding introduction of the euro, the differential reached 4.14 percentage points. The same trend is observed comparing three specific subsets of the consumer price indices with the HICP, where the differential was within the range of –1.56 and 4.78. As a comparison, in the period surrounding introduction of the euro, the differential reached 11.83 percentage points (in passenger transport by road). The differentials between the given bundle of services, subsets of services and the overall HICP during the period surrounding introduction of the euro were significantly larger than in the period up to 3.5 years before the changeover. Therefore, we can conclude that the Balassa–Samuelson effect in the observed subsets of services accounts only incrementally towards price appreciation around the euro changeover. The data collected from the period up to 3.5 years before introduction of the euro support our evidence of the effects of the changeover on the prices of non-tradable sectors in Slovakia.

Figure 8.5: Perceived inflation: Eurozone, Czech Republic and Slovakia, 2001–10
Source: Author's calculations based on European Commission data.

4.3   Inflation perceptions vs. reality

In this section, we examine consumer perceptions of inflation in Slovakia compared with the Czech Republic and the Eurozone, and how they relate to actual inflation and to other findings in this chapter.

We start with a simple chart – Figure 8.5 – of perceived inflation in the Eurozone, the Czech Republic and Slovakia during the 2001–10 period. This indicator measures consumer experience with inflation (based on answers to the question: 'How do you think that consumer prices have developed over the last 12 months?'). It is based on the overall balance among answers (there are five possible answers from 'risen a lot' to 'fallen'), with higher values indicating higher perceived inflation.

Figure 8.5 shows that during the last decade, the level of perceived inflation has been higher in the Eurozone than in either the Czech Republic or Slovakia. The peak of perceived inflation in the Eurozone coincided with euro adoption, but it continued at a relatively high level until late 2008, when a steep fall began.

The results indicate that the populations of the Czech Republic and Slovakia have a different benchmark in mind when assessing inflation from that considered by Eurozone consumers. Actual Eurozone inflation was either lower than or equal to Czech or Slovak inflation during nearly the entire period analysed, despite perceptions indicating the opposite. Looking at the Czech and Slovak data, we can see that the 2000s were a period of declining or low perceived inflation with two exceptions:

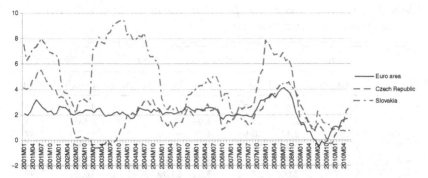

Figure 8.6: Correlation of twelve-month moving sample of the Slovak
HICP with Eurozone and Czech HICP, 2001–10
Source: Author's calculations.

- 2003 and early 2004 in Slovakia, when unification of VAT, an increase
  in excise taxes and other measures resulted in a spike in both actual
  and perceived inflation.
- 2008 for both countries (as well as the Eurozone), when both perceived
  and actual inflation rose due to an increase in commodity prices.

In other words, Slovak consumers (and Czech ones as well) held a fairly
benign view of inflation even prior to euro adoption, and in the absence
of major and visible price shocks, people's perceptions tracked the actual
price developments quite well and tended to converge on price stability.

Based on a visual examination, one could hypothesise that perceived
Slovak inflation began to move in lockstep with the Eurozone (and Czech)
series sometime in 2007. Indeed, analysis of twelve-month correlations in
the developments of Slovak prices relative to Eurozone and Czech prices,
as depicted in Figure 8.6, shows that since late 2007 the correlation
between Slovak prices, on one hand, and either of the two other price
series, on the other, has been very high (in the 0.7–1.0 range).

Still, formal testing of the three price series shows differences in the
characteristics of the series. While the Eurozone and Czech price series
are trend stationary (i.e. they are stationary after removal of a trend),
the Slovak time series is not stationary (i.e. it does not revert to a mean)
and there is no evidence of cointegration between Slovak and Eurozone
prices for either the entire 2001–10 period or the 2007–10 subperiod.

To examine the developments at the time of actual entry into the Eurozone, we compare perceived and actual HICP inflation during the eighteen months surrounding the adoption of the single currency (six months
before and twelve months after). We compare four episodes – 2002,

Table 8.4: *Perceived and actual HICP inflation in the six months prior to and twelve months after euro adoption*

Month	Eurozone		Slovakia		Cyprus		Slovenia	
	Perceived	Actual	Perceived	Actual	Perceived	Actual	Perceived	Actual
$t-6$	36.39	2.55	33.74	4.43	34.37	2.34	13.84	1.93
$t-5$	35.65	2.35	33.28	4.44	42.05	2.24	23.07	3.12
$t-4$	33.30	2.16	30.91	4.55	36.00	2.34	19.20	2.47
$t-3$	29.65	2.25	27.27	4.18	47.01	2.7	22.95	1.54
$t-2$	28.89	1.97	27.58	3.9	51.64	3.2	13.83	2.43
$t-1$	27.27	2.05	24.54	3.54	43.99	3.74	16.24	2.98
t	32.05	2.61	16.72	2.71	38.93	4.07	26.56	2.79
$t+1$	40.16	2.52	15.88	2.39	45.19	4.74	29.00	2.28
$t+2$	42.41	2.50	11.58	1.8	49.39	4.44	22.58	2.63
$t+3$	47.90	2.30	4.46	1.38	41.19	4.35	24.70	2.86
$t+4$	50.19	2.02	−4.56	1.07	60.73	4.64	29.86	3.1
$t+5$	54.64	1.92	−8.64	0.72	67.54	5.21	34.52	3.77
$t+6$	55.74	2.02	−10.11	0.61	68.47	5.34	33.53	3.97
$t+7$	58.98	2.12	−13.02	0.49	70.40	5.07	54.51	3.43
$t+8$	59.91	2.10	−7.65	0.05	67.12	4.99	60.83	3.57
$t+9$	57.97	2.30	−12.26	−0.13	66.98	4.84	72.05	5.11
$t+10$	56.54	2.29	−10.70	0.04	62.56	3.13	74.85	5.74
$t+11$	57.56	2.28	−9.58	0.04	56.51	1.82	77.40	5.7
Correlation	–	−0.24	–	0.98	–	0.60	–	0.88

Note: t is the first month of euro adoption, in practice January of the year of adoption.
Source: Author's calculations based on European Commission data.

when the Eurozone switched to euro bank notes and coins; 2007, when Slovenia adopted the euro; 2008, when Malta and Cyprus did (unfortunately, the relevant survey data are not available for Malta); and 2009, when Slovakia joined.

The results are shown in Table 8.4. We can see that there is a major difference between the Eurozone (2002) and the three other countries in the correlations between actual and perceived inflation. In the period before and after the introduction of euro notes and coins there is correlation between actual and perceived inflation for the Eurozone; meanwhile for each of Cyprus, Slovenia and Slovakia there are relatively high and positive correlations. In the case of Slovakia, this reaches the extremely high value of 0.98.

If one compares *only* perceived inflation, however, there is a high level of correlation between values for the Eurozone, Cyprus and Slovenia (0.8 and higher) and a strong negative correlation between these series

Table 8.5: *Actual and perceived inflation in period of euro adoption: Cyprus, the Eurozone, Slovakia and Slovenia*

Actual/perceived inflation	Low	High
Low	Slovakia	Eurozone
High	–	Cyprus, Slovenia

Source: Author.

and perceived inflation in Slovakia (−0.8 and lower). This indicates that the stylised inflation experience around the time of adoption is one of growing inflation and that Slovakia is an outlier in this stylised picture. These findings lead to the simple typology of the relationship between actual and perceived inflation in the period surrounding euro adoption shown in Table 8.5.

In this simplified version, the original euro area experienced low actual and high perceived inflation, Cyprus and Slovenia experienced high actual and high perceived inflation, and Slovakia experienced low actual and low perceived inflation.

To summarise, inflation as perceived by Slovak consumers has generally been on a downward path during the last decade (with a few exceptions based on exogenous shocks) and euro adoption has not changed this. On the contrary, Slovaks exhibit an extremely high correlation between the actual disinflation during the period surrounding the changeover and their perceptions of declining inflation. This sets them apart from other countries adopting the single currency, which all experienced an increase in perceived inflation during the same period, regardless of whether actual inflation conformed to the same trend.

4.4   *Analysis of the price data at the micro level and comparison with national price data*

In this section, we present an analysis of the price data for selected services collected at the level of individual enterprises in Bratislava and Brno. The point of the analysis is to see whether any anomalies can be observed during the euro adoption period in Bratislava, and to subsequently examine the fit between enterprise-level prices and national price data for similar categories. From this, conclusions are drawn about the impact of the changeover to the euro on these prices in Slovakia.

Table 8.6: *Summary statistics for datasets measuring changes in the prices of selected services: Bratislava and Brno, July 2008 and July 2009*

Service	City	Mean = inflation	Reject Ho of identical means = inflation rates	Variance	Reject Ho of identical variance (dispersion of inflation)	Sample size
Schnitzel	Bratislava	4.38679	No	60.7554	Yes	55
	Brno	5.11667		127.395		30
Boiled	Bratislava	9.13455	No	466.466	Yes	55
potatoes	Brno	8.97333		229.235		30
Cappuccino	Bratislava	5.04364	No	99.4436	No	55
	Brno	4.20667		74.9806		30
Viennese	Bratislava	4.50909	No	71.9001	No	55
coffee	Brno	5.35333		79.3881		30
Woman's	Bratislava	−0.309375	No	2557.08	Yes	32
haircut	Brno	3.45455		234.293		22
Taxi – basic	Bratislava	82.0762	Yes	15061.9	Yes	21
charge	Brno	5.12308		156.382		13
Taxi – 1 km	Bratislava	21.5667	Yes	2302.79	Yes	21
	Brno	1.73077		126.452		13
Taxi – 1 min.	Bratislava	9.5	No	333.816	No	21
waiting	Brno	7.68462		213.248		13

Note: Rejection/non-rejection of Ho is assessed at the 10 per cent probability level.
Source: Author.

The data presented are summary statistics and the results of some basic tests done with the series. For each item, Table 8.6 presents the following information:
- The mean increase in the price between July 2008 and July 2009
- A test of whether we can reject the hypothesis (Ho) of identical means for the Bratislava and Brno series, i.e. confirmation that they are statistically different
- The variance in the increase of the price, i.e. the dispersal of the price changes
- A test of whether we can reject the hypothesis (Ho) of identical variance for the Bratislava and Brno series, i.e. confirmation that they are statistically different.

For cafés and restaurants, we examined four items: a main course (schnitzel), a side dish (boiled potatoes) and two types of coffee. The

Table 8.7: *Distribution of price changes for schnitzel and boiled potatoes: Bratislava and Brno (%)*

	Schnitzel		Boiled potatoes	
	Bratislava	Brno	Bratislava	Brno
Decrease	3.77	13.33	1.81	0.0
No change	50.94	56.67	62.27	66.67
0–10	26.41	6.67	3.63	3.33
10–20	15.09	6.67	16.36	10.0
20–30	1.89	13.33	3.63	6.67
30–40	1.89	0.0	5.45	6.67
Above 40	0.0	3.33	1.81	6.67

Source: Author.

micro data show nearly identical developments in Bratislava and Brno, with inflation broadly in the 4–5 per cent range (with boiled potatoes showing higher inflation at 9 per cent). The dispersion of the prices differs for only two of the four items, notably each time in a different direction. Overall, in this category there does not appear to be any clear difference between the two cities in the mean, but there is a statistically significant difference in the variance for the meals – schnitzel and boiled potatoes – as shown in Table 8.6.

Table 8.7 therefore presents a detailed frequency distribution of the price changes in the two cities for these commodities. In the case of schnitzel, we can observe that the difference in price distribution lies mainly in the fact that Bratislava had a much higher frequency of small to moderate price changes than Brno and very few price decreases, resulting in a higher percentage of upward price changes than Brno: 45 per cent vs. 30 per cent.

For the prices of women's haircuts, there is a similar finding. Here we use only one dataset, but in this case the data for Bratislava exhibit much greater variance, including the unparalleled experience of a majority of establishments in Bratislava cutting their prices, as shown in Table 8.8.

In the case of taxi prices, however, the difference between the two cities is statistically significant, in both the increase in mean prices and in the variance for two of the three items in this category. Bratislava taxi drivers obviously took advantage of the 2008–9 period in terms of what they were charging – with more than an 82 per cent jump in the basic

Table 8.8: *Distribution of price changes for a woman's haircut: Bratislava and Brno (%)*

	Bratislava	Brno
Decrease	40.63	8.7
No change	15.63	47.83
0–10	18.75	8.7
10–20	3.13	21.74
20–30	3.13	4.35
30–40	9.38	4.35
Above 40	9.38	4.35

Source: Author.

Table 8.9: *Frequency distribution of all price changes in the micro dataset, July 2008–July 2009*

	Bratislava	Brno
Decrease	8.63	3.85
No change	49.84	64.84
0–10	14.7	7.69
10–20	13.74	9.89
20–30	3.51	6.59
30–40	3.83	4.95
Above 40	5.75	2.2

Source: Author.

charge and a 21 per cent increase in the price per km. Nothing of this kind happened in Brno during the same period.

In addition to the data collected for every dataset, we also look at the overall frequency of changes in all datasets combined. As shown in Table 8.9, during the period between July 2008 and July 2009, prices were much more stable in Brno than in Bratislava. In Brno, 65 per cent of prices did not change at all, whereas in Bratislava this was true for fewer than 50 per cent of prices. This is a result of higher rates of changes in Bratislava in *both* directions, as Table 8.9 shows.

In the concluding analysis of this section, we compare the data collected at the enterprise level with the official HICP data collected for similar categories. We examine whether similar developments can be

Table 8.10: *Comparison of enterprise-level inflation data: Bratislava and Brno, with national inflation data, year-on-year change, July 2008– July 2009*

Item	Bratislava inflation		Brno inflation	
	Mean	95 per cent Confidence interval	Mean	95 per cent Confidence interval
Schnitzel	4.38679	2.23834–6.53524	5.11667	0.90205–9.33128
Boiled potatoes	9.13455	3.29583–14.9733	8.97333	3.31977–14.6269
Cappuccino	5.04364	2.34779–7.73948	4.20667	0.973292–7.44004
Viennese coffee	4.50909	2.21679–6.80139	5.35333	2.02628–8.68038
HICP cafés, restaurants, etc.	*9.49*	–	*4.71*	–
Haircut	−0.309375	−18.5409–17.9222	3.45455	−3.33204–10.2411
HICP hair salons, etc.	*13.66*	–	*7.84*	–
Taxi – basic charge	82.0762	26.2115–137.941	5.12308	−2.43379–12.6799
Taxi – 1 km	21.5667	−0.276921–43.4103	1.73077	−5.06458–8.52612
Taxi – 1 min waiting	9.5	−1.1399–16.5091	7.68462	1.18331–17.8167
HICP passenger transport by road	*15.79*	–	*2.83*	–

Sources: Author for non-HICP data, Eurostat for HICP data

observed at both levels and, if not, whether the discrepancies might have occurred as a result of the collection process, more specifically whether the data might have been skewed in that process. Table 8.10 thus compares mean price increases for individual items with HICP inflation in the relevant category for the period between July 2008 and July 2009.

To understand and interpret Table 8.10, two caveats are in order. First of all, the individual items are only a fraction of the relevant HICP category and might not include the specific items picked by the national statistical authorities for their surveys. For example, in the Czech statistical index, the cost of a taxi comprises only a small part of the consumer prices for passenger transport by road, which is dominated by public transport. Similarly, the cost of schnitzel is only a small percentage of restaurant and café costs, there is only one type of coffee included and boiled potatoes are not included. For haircuts, a woman's haircut as defined for our purposes is only one of three items included in the relevant HICP category.[1] Second, there might be regional differences in

[1] We could not obtain access to the detailed structure of the Slovak HICP.

prices, so the mismatch between national HICP prices and the micro data for Bratislava and Brno could reflect these rather than any mistakes.

Thus we can only note any major discrepancies between the micro and macro price data. In the case of restaurant/café prices, the price increases at the micro and macro levels do not exhibit an obvious discrepancy. In the case of haircuts, the HICP prices and micro prices for Bratislava are rather different, with enterprise-level prices showing a deflation. Yet given the wide dispersal of prices, it is not possible with certainty to state that the inflation measured for the micro data differs from HICP data. For taxi prices, the basic charge in Bratislava is obviously out of line with HICP prices, but that is of limited value in itself as it is only a part of the overall taxi price. Nonetheless, in the case of taxi prices, we can come closest to stating with confidence that the Bratislava micro data differ significantly from the national data.

5   Conclusion

This chapter has looked at the Slovak experience with euro adoption from the point of view of perceived vs. actual inflation and with a focus on a specific set of non-tradable prices. It has examined whether Slovak consumers experienced or perceived (or both) an unusual price jump at the time of euro adoption and what could be the possible explanations for such a phenomenon, building on the literature concerning previous instances of switches to the single currency. It has utilised both macro-level inflation data and an original dataset of enterprise-level data for specific non-tradables and compared Slovakia not just with the Euro-zone, but also with the Czech Republic – a country with a similar economic policy and inflation history, but which has not joined the single currency.

Our findings can be divided roughly into three groups: developments in actual inflation at the macro level, developments in perceived inflation at the macro level and conclusions concerning enterprise-level prices for selected non-tradables that have been most prone to perceived inflation in previous changeovers to the single currency.

At the macro price level we found that, in Slovakia, the divergence between the prices of tradables and non-tradables became much starker in the period of euro adoption compared with other countries. This finding concerns all services, but even more emphatically the kinds of non-tradables on which the chapter has focused. The anomaly can be most plausibly explained by the reliance of Slovakia on nominal exchange rate appreciation to drive down inflation during the qualification period for the single currency. But even though this can account for some of the divergence between the inflation of tradable and non-tradable goods in Slovakia, it is unlikely to account for all of it. Therefore, there is some *prima facie* evidence of the effects of the changeover on the prices of non-tradables at the macro level.

Looking at perceptions of inflation, Slovak consumers appear to be much more accustomed to inflation shocks and *ceteris paribus* have taken a much more benign view of inflation compared with other Eurozone countries. We have developed a simple typology of inflation perception/reality during the changeover, in which the original euro area experienced low actual and high perceived inflation, Cyprus and Slovenia experienced high actual and high perceived inflation and Slovakia experienced low actual and low perceived inflation. Slovaks exhibited an extremely high correlation between the actual disinflation during the period surrounding the changeover and their perceptions of declining inflation. This accurate perception of real inflation sets the Slovaks apart from other countries adopting the single currency, which all experienced an increase in perceived inflation during the same period regardless of whether actual inflation conformed to the same trend.

With regard to prices, the micro data show that while the mean price increases in Bratislava and its Czech control city Brno are generally indistinguishable (with the exception of taxis, for which Bratislava experienced a huge price increase), Bratislava experienced a much greater variance in price changes. In Brno, 65 per cent of prices did not change at all, whereas in Bratislava this was true for fewer than 50 per cent of prices. This is a result of higher rates of changes in Bratislava in *both* directions.

Our findings point to the following conclusions:

- In terms of both reality and perceptions of general price movements, every adoption is different.
- For Slovakia, euro adoption came at a time of disinflation, which consumers actually experienced, so there does not seem to be any overall 'teuro' perception.
- We can nonetheless observe high inflation for non-tradables at both the macro and micro levels, linked not only to the Slovak strategy of nominal currency appreciation prior to Eurozone entry but also to the changeover itself. In addition there is evidence of greater variance in the prices of non-tradables in Bratislava at the time.

Appendix

Inflation in selected areas prior to euro adoption is shown in Tables 8.A1–8.A3.

Table 8.A1: *Inflation in selected areas, comparing prices eighteen months and six months prior to euro adoption*

	Overall inflation	Passenger transport by road	Δ	Restaurants, cafés, etc.	Δ	Hair-dressing	Δ	Goods	Δ	Services	Δ
Euro area	2.55	4.05	1.50	3.21	0.66	2.37	-0.18	2.53	-0.02	2.48	-0.07
Cyprus	5.34	7.87	2.53	3.12	-2.22	2.22	-3.12	1.2	-4.14	4.18	-1.16
Malta	-0.02	0.00	-0.02	4.02	4.04	1.15	1.17	1.2	1.22	-0.006	0.026
Slovenia	1.93	8.26	6.33	5.52	3.59	6.30	4.37	1.1	-0.83	3.66	1.73
Slovakia	4.42	0.00	4.42	7.61	3.19	7.63	3.21	4.3	-0.12	4.63	0.21

Source: Author's calculations based on Eurostat data.

Table 8.A2: *Inflation in selected areas, comparing prices thirty months and eighteen months prior to euro adoption*

	Overall inflation	Passenger transport by road	Δ	Restaurants, cafés, etc.	Δ	Hair-dressing	Δ	Goods	Δ	Services	Δ
Euro area	2.01	2.04	0.03	2.44	0.43	1.96	−0.05	2.44	0.43	1.39	−0.62
Cyprus	2.34	10.25	7.91	2.19	−0.15	6.46	4.12	3.27	0.93	1.88	−0.46
Malta	3.56	11.01	7.45	2.33	−1.23	1.66	−1.9	4.41	0.85	2.44	−1.12
Slovenia	1.99	0.00	1.99	4.89	2.90	1.44	−0.55	1.97	−0.02	1.99	0.00
Slovakia	1.22	4.86	3.64	3.49	2.27	3.46	2.24	6.00	4.78	2.43	1.21

Source: Author's calculations based on Eurostat data.

Table 8.A3: *Inflation in selected areas, comparing prices forty-two months and thirty months prior to euro adoption*

	Overall inflation	Passenger transport by road	Δ	Restaurants, cafés, etc.	Δ	Hair-dressing	Δ	Goods	Δ	Services	Δ
Euro area	1.07	1.07	0.00	2.02	0.95	1.82	0.75	0.71	−0.36	1.6	0.53
Cyprus	2.84	−0.006	2.84	2.41	0.43	4.52	1.68	9.40	6.56	1.73	−1.11
Malta	1.02	−0.003	1.02	2.45	1.43	0.00	1.02	1.24	0.22	2.4	1.38
Slovenia	3.73	5.90	2.17	4.73	1.00	3.31	−0.42	2.69	−1.04	4.48	0.75
Slovakia	5.01	3.45	−1.56	3.37	1.64	4.99	−0.02	5.44	0.43	4.07	−0.94

Source: Author's calculations based on Eurostat data.

References

Altissimo, F., M. Ehrmann and F. Smets (2006). 'Inflation persistence and price-setting behaviour in the euro area: a summary of the IPN evidence', European Central Bank Occasional Paper, No. 46

Brachinger, H. W. (2004). 'Euro gleich Teuro: Wahrgenommene versus gemessene Inflation', Presentation at Statistik Austria, Vienna, 28 October
  (2005a). 'Euro gleich Teuro: Wahrgenommene versus gemessene Inflation', in G. Greulich, M. Lösch, C. Müller and W. Stier (eds.), *Empirische Konjunktur- und Wachstumsforschung*, Festschrift für Bernd Schips zum 65, Geburtstag, Zürich: Rüegger
  (2005b). 'Measuring perceived inflation: a prospect theory approach', Extended abstract, International Statistical Institute 55th Session, Sydney
  (2006). 'Euro or 'teuro'?: the euro-induced perceived inflation in Germany,' Department of Quantitative Economics Working Paper, No. 5, University of Fribourg

Ercolani, M. G. and J. Dutta (2007). 'The impact of the euro changeover on inflation: evidence from the harmonised index of consumer prices', in D. Cobham (ed.), *The Travails of the Eurozone*, Basingstoke: Palgrave Macmillan

European Central Bank (ECB) (2002). 'Evaluation of the 2002 cash changeover', Technical Report, European Central Bank

European Commission (2008a). 'Preparing for the euro: survey of Slovak enterprises', Flash Eurobarometer, No. 240, Brussels
  (2008b). 'Introduction of the euro in Slovakia', Flash Eurobarometer, No. 249, Brussels
  (2009), 'Euro introduction in Slovakia: *ex post* citizen survey', Flash Eurobarometer, No. 259, Brussels

Fabiani, S., M. Druant, I. Hernando, C. Kwapil, B. Landau, C. Loupias, F. Martins, T. Y. Mathä, R. Sabbatini, H. Stahl and A. C. J. Stokman (2005). 'The pricing behaviour of firms in the euro area: new survey evidence', European Central Bank Working Paper, No. 535

Hüfner, F. and I. Koske (2008). 'The euro changeover in the Slovak Republic: implications for inflation and interest rates', OECD Economics Department Working Paper, No. 632

Kirchler, E. (2005). 'Comment on "Perceived inflation and the euro: why high? Why persistent?"', in *Price Setting and Inflation Persistence in Austria*, Proceedings of OeNB Workshops, No. 8, Österreichische Nationalbank

Mastrobuoni, G. (2004). 'The effects of the euro-conversion on prices and price perceptions', Centre for European Policy Studies Working Document, No. 101

Stix, H. (2005). 'Perceived inflation and the euro: why high? Why persistent?', in *Price Setting and Inflation Persistence in Austria*, Proceedings of OeNB Workshops, No. 8, Österreichische Nationalbank

9   The euro's contribution to economic stability
      in Central, Eastern and Southeastern
      Europe: is euro adoption still attractive?

*Ewald Nowotny**

Both Austria and Slovakia are located in the Central European region – they are part of the Central European family. As a matter of fact, Austria has made effective use of this location in the two decades since the fall of the Iron Curtain. It has become one of the most important investors in its Central European neighbours. Austria's economic links to Slovakia are especially strong, not least because of the short distance between the two capitals, Vienna and Bratislava. Today both countries are also members of the euro area, which strengthens their relationship even further.

The euro was a milestone of European integration (Nowotny, 2010). Against the background of the global financial crisis, it seems to be the right time to discuss and reflect on the euro's development from both a European perspective and from a global angle. In the early stages of its existence, the euro was under heavy criticism. The well-known argument of proponents of the optimum currency area (OCA) theory associates the costs of joining a monetary union with the loss of domestic monetary policy, the well-known argument that 'one size cannot fit all'. Certainly, a currency union becomes costly if the business cycles of its member countries are not synchronised and if domestic adjustment capabilities are limited. In the absence of country-specific monetary policies, an idiosyncratic shock cannot be absorbed through the real exchange rate but has to be digested via flexible wages, fiscal transfers and mobile factors of production.

However this argument is static. Joining a currency area leads to a boost in trade and hence to a convergence of business cycles (Artis, Fidrmuc and Scharler, 2008), which is further supported by fiscal and economic

* Based on the statement delivered at the National Bank of Slovakia's conference on 'The Euro Area and the Financial Crisis' (Panel on 'Is euro adoption still attractive for CEE?'), at the National Bank of Slovakia, Bratislava, 6–8 September 2010, under the auspices of the National Bank of Slovakia, the Heriot–Watt University of Edinburgh and the Comenius University of Bratislava.

policy coordination. Moreover, in the current environment, the question of how costly idiosyncratic shocks are might be less important. The crisis is a shock that has affected all economies. The past ten years have shown that the introduction of a single currency ensured price stability and spurred trade flows across the region (Baldwin, 2006). Although there is no consensus about the magnitude of the trade effect triggered by the creation of a monetary union in Europe, almost all estimates point to a significant increase in trade and also in foreign direct investment (FDI) within the euro area (European Commission, 2008). Correspondingly, Austria profited from the euro's introduction in Slovakia and Slovenia, with its trade with these countries having tripled and doubled, respectively, since 2000 (Ritzberger-Grünwald and Wörz, 2010). The rise in trade has also boosted employment, while inflation has been well below the levels seen in the 1970s and 1980s. Therefore we can say that confidence in the euro is as strong as that in its most stable predecessors used to be.

In its more than ten years of existence, the euro has not only been a great success for its member states but has also continuously enhanced its international role in a gradual fashion. Following Slovakia's entry in January 2009, the euro area currently comprises sixteen member states, with a total population of more than 330 million.[1] This compares with a US population of 304.5 million in 2008. However, the euro area is unique in several ways, given in particular the fact that important policy areas have remained in the member states' domain. The past few years have shown the urgent need for improved cooperation between euro area members. The member states of the monetary union have an obligation to support each other. This is based not only on moral presumptions, but also on real economic grounds. A monetary union can be realised if, and only if, each single member accepts it fully as a 'give-and-take' concept.

This is especially true for challenging times like the recent global financial and economic crisis. The world's worst recession since the 1930s posed a wide range of macroeconomic and political challenges for all affected economies, also bearing on the single currency. High spreads between German government bonds and bonds of other euro area countries as well as diverging credit default swaps (CDS) on government bonds within the euro area were a major concern. Still, Nobel Prize

---

[1] In January 2011, Estonia will become the seventeenth member state of the euro area, whose population will thus expand by about 1.3 million.

winner Milton Friedman's prophecy[2] that 'when the global economy hits a real bump, Europe's internal contradictions will tear [the euro] apart' has proved to be wrong. Quite on the contrary, it is the euro that functions as an anchor of stability and helps weather the storms of the crisis. Still, there are some challenges ahead.

In its early stage, the crisis was confined to advanced economies. Local and foreign banks in Central, Eastern and Southeastern Europe (CESEE) economies held only a negligible amount of so-called 'toxic assets'. Innovative financial products and excessive risk-taking had put major banks under serious stress and brought into question their business model. A post-crisis business model should therefore emphasise the importance of diversification of profit and funding sources, with the latter most reliably provided by deposits. Moreover, Austrian banks holding a major stake in the Central and Eastern Europe (CEE) region must in the near future place a stronger focus on 'traditional' retail banking activities. In particular, the risks of a credit boom (Backé, Égert and Zumer, 2006; Backé and Wójcik, 2008) and especially foreign currency lending (Dvorsky, Scheiber and Stix, 2010) must be adequately taken into account and reflected in their new business model.

With the collapse of the investment bank Lehmans, the crisis reached the CEE economies during the autumn of 2008 and started to fully feed through to the real economy in early 2009. The crisis turned from a financial market crisis into a broad economic crisis throughout the region. Actually, in terms of GDP developments, CEE countries were much harder hit by the financial crisis than the euro area countries (see Figure 9.1a and 9.1b).

The global loss of confidence and the slump in demand for exports almost interrupted the convergence process of most catching-up economies in CEE (with the notable exception of Poland, which continued to display positive growth rates throughout the crisis). What followed were falling stock prices, increasing risk premiums on financial assets and – in some cases – a downward rally of currencies. Import demand from euro area countries, which are the main trading partners of CEE countries, was significantly reduced. Moreover, capital inflows into the region took a severe hit – although the worst-case scenario of a financial meltdown did not occur. Taken together, these developments led to major question marks regarding the medium- and long-term growth prospects of the region. A possibly permanent decline of exports (Francois and Wörz, 2009) and capital inflows (Fidrmuc and Martin, 2011)

---

[2] Quoted as in *Wall Street Journal*, November 29, 2010, http://blogs.wsj.com/source/2010/11/29/milton-friedman-comes-close/.

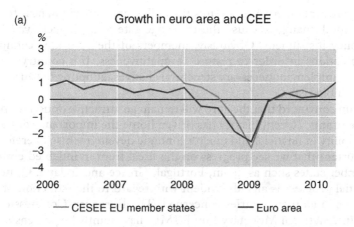

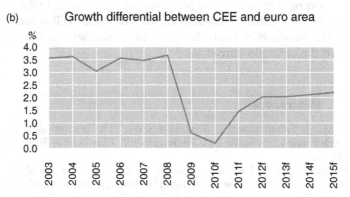

Figure 9.1: (a) Output growth, 2006–10 and (b) output differential, 2003–15: CEE and euro area

Source: Eurostat, IWFO.
Note: f = forecast.

are often seen as factors that could lower the long-term growth prospects of the CESEE region. Since the crisis has severely hit the real economy of the region, the question arises of how long it will take to bring the economies back to a solid growth track. The Conference on European Economic Integration of the Oesterreichische Nationalbank (in mid-November 2010) will focus precisely on this topical issue.

When we reflect on the question of what role the euro can play in this process, we have to keep in mind that being a part of the euro area also entails the obligation to adhere to economic policies that aim at structural changes. Any form of a hard currency policy (including euro area membership) requires the ability and the willingness to effect structural change because the exchange rate is no longer available as a policy instrument. Obviously, members of the euro area cannot use devaluations in order to restore competitiveness. If a country was not able to implement necessary structural changes, adopting the euro would carry a big risk.

I am convinced that the euro will remain an attractive option for potential entrants. Recent history has driven home the importance of the sustainability of financial and macroeconomic developments. Therefore it is important that we see progress on the fiscal front in indebted euro area member states such as Spain, Portugal, Greece and Ireland. Quite substantial progress is already evident with regard to the reduction of fiscal deficits in all the countries concerned. The European Commission and the International Monetary Fund (IMF) have jointly helped ensure that deficit-cutting measures are in place. Structural reforms in the euro area will further strengthen its capacity for growth, which will in turn improve the attractiveness of the euro for those EU countries which have not yet adopted the common currency.

References

Artis, M., J. Fidrmuc and J. Scharler (2008). 'The transmission of business cycles: implications for EMU enlargement', *Economics of Transition*, **16**(3): 559–82

Backé, P., B. Égert and T. Žumer (2006). 'Credit growth in Central and Eastern Europe: new (over)shooting stars?', European Central Bank Working Paper, No. **687**

Backé, P. and C. Wójcik (2008). 'Credit booms, monetary integration and the new neoclassical synthesis', *Journal of Banking & Finance*, **32**: 458–70

Baldwin, R. E. (2006). 'The euro's trade effect', European Central Bank Working Paper, No. **594**

Dvorsky, S., T. Scheiber and H. Stix (2010). 'Real effects of crisis have reached CESEE households: Euro survey shows dampened savings and changes in borrowing behavior', *Focus on European Economic Integration*, Oesterreich-ische Nationalbank, No. **2**, 79–90

European Commission (2008). 'EMU@10: successes and challenges after ten years of Economic and Monetary Union', *European Economy*, **2**

Fidrmuc, J. and R. Martin (2011). 'FDI, trade, and growth in CESEE countries', *Focus on European Economic Integration*, 1:70–89

Francois, J. and J. Wörz (2009). 'The big drop: trade and the great recession', in R. Baldwin (ed.), *The Great Trade Collapse: Causes, Consequences, and Prospects*, VoxEU.org

Nowotny, E. (2010). 'The Euro's contribution to economic stability in CESEE', in E. Nowotny, P. Mooslechner and D. Ritzberger-Grünwald (eds.), *The Euro*

and Economic Stability: Focus on Central, Eastern and South-Eastern Europe,
Cheltenham: Edward Elgar and OeNB

Ritzberger-Grünwald, D. and J. Wörz (2010) 'Wechselkurse und österreichischer
Außenhandel', FIW Policy Brief No. 5, Research Center for International
Economics, Vienna

10   Is the euro still attractive for CEE countries?

Zdeněk Tůma and David Vávra[*]

In this chapter we argue that the attractiveness of the euro for CEE economies has always depended on (1) their willingness and capacity to invest in an independent stabilising monetary policy, and (2) the credibility of the euro project going forward. These are not new criteria, but it is worth recalling that the last decade has dispelled as unfounded the hopes that the euro is a convergence-bringing panacea or a substitute for structural reforms and fiscal discipline. Besides, the crisis and the unfolding fiscal consolidation programmes are reducing the attractiveness of the euro further in the short term. However, it is also worth recalling that the euro has been successful in bringing an important degree of monetary stability to the euro area, and has sheltered its members from many shocks. The attractiveness of the euro project for the Central and Eastern Europe (CEE) countries thus depends on the euro area's ability to build on these achievements. For the CEE countries that have been fixing their currencies, an early euro adoption should be a priority.

The economic debate about euro adoption should be cast in terms of the stabilising role of monetary policy – other considerations may be misleading. At the onset the euro was hoped to improve the long-term macroeconomic performance of member countries, not only in terms of price stability but also in terms of long-term output levels and growth rates. And the arguments portraying the euro as a vehicle of real convergence began to dominate in rationalising the common currency project.

However, the first ten years of the euro project have shown the hopes for the euro as a vehicle of real convergence to be unfounded – at least for now. Real GDP in the euro area has grown equally fast as in the non-euro OECD EU countries (Figure 10.1). Real exchange rates in the euro area have moved heterogeneously and trade imbalances have persisted or widened further (Figures 10.2 and 10.3). The terms of the debate should therefore be firmly set in terms of what monetary policy

---

[*] Dr Tůma was unable to attend the conference, but submitted this statement shortly after it.

190

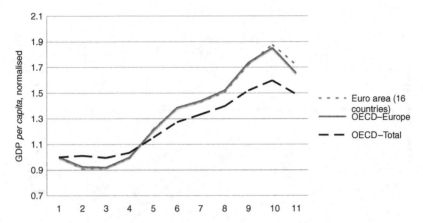

Figure 10.1: GDP *per capita*: OECD country groups
Sources: OECD, own computations.

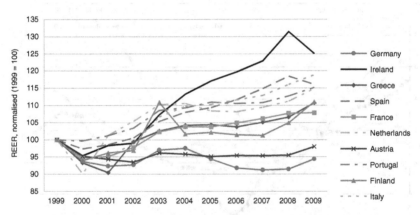

Figure 10.2: Real exchange rates: euro area, normalised, 1999–2009
Sources: Eurostat/OECD, own computations.

is capable of achieving – and that is ensuring long-term nominal stability and reducing macroeconomic volatility.

There, the euro record is mixed. On the one hand, the European Central Bank (ECB) has undoubtedly kept price stability in the euro area as a whole. As a consequence, the euro has strengthened and become a major reserve currency. On the other hand, inflation rates within the euro area have diverged – despite inflation convergence being one of the most important preconditions for membership (Figure 10.4). The ECB has

192   *Zdeněk Tůma and David Vávra*

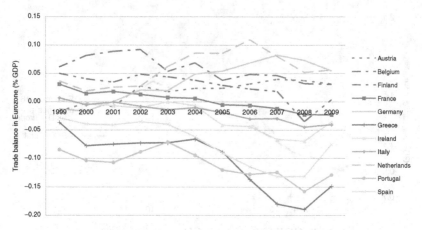

Figure 10.3: Trade balance: euro area (% GDP)
Sources: Eurostat, own computations.

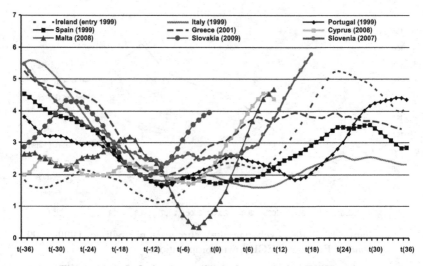

Figure 10.4: Inflation rates (%) before and after EMU entry.
Note: t(0) is the January of the year of entry into the euro area for each
country.
Source: Own computation, inspired by figure in Bulíř and Hurnik
(2009).

recognised its inability to cope with the persisting inflation divergence,
and called for country-specific measures to cope with the issue.

Besides the unconvincing long-term performance, output in the euro
area has suffered heavily in the recent crisis, too. In the Central,

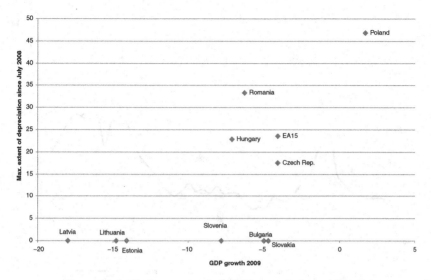

Figure 10.5: Exchange rate and GDP growth during the crisis
Sources: Eurostat, own calculations.

Eastern and Southeastern Europe (CESEE) region, in general, the countries with independent monetary policy and flexible exchange rates – such as the Czech Republic, Hungary, Poland, or Romania – have generally fared better in terms of output growth than fixed exchange rate countries (Figure 10.5). Among the fixed exchange rate countries only Slovenia and Slovakia were members of the euro area at the time, and the deceleration of growth was particularly pronounced in Slovakia – the EU's fastest-growing economy before the crisis. However, much bigger output declines than in Slovakia were recorded in the fixed exchange rate regimes outside the euro – especially in the Baltic region.

This anecdotal evidence suggests that the euro has not contributed much to reducing real economy volatility in the CESEE economies. A similar conclusion was reached in a study on the Czech economy that used a macroeconomic model in estimating the hypothetical impacts of euro adoption on consumption growth volatility (Hurník, Tůma and Vávra, 2010). Indeed, contrary developments were actually observed in Finland (and to a lesser extent in Germany) – a country with a strong monetary stability record before the euro. Volatility of consumption growth in Finland increased after euro adoption more than in Sweden – also a country with monetary stability but staying outside the euro area. However, the sample and period are too limited for any solid conclusions.

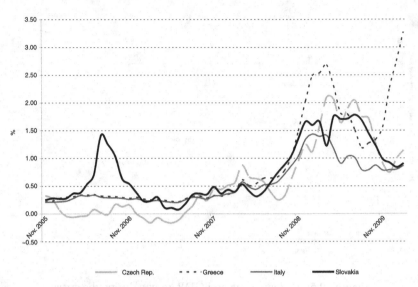

Figure 10.6: Spreads on government bonds
Sources: Eurostat, own calculations.

The evidence that the euro does not help macroeconomic stability much in the face of shocks may come as a surprise. The euro brings low interest rates and risk premiums, which have been seen by some as a shelter from the otherwise unforgiving reactions of the markets to unsustainable domestic policies. However, the recent Greek experience has demonstrated that the sheltering effect is not omnipotent. Besides, the experience of several non-euro area CEE economies – such as the Czech Republic, Poland, or Slovakia (before it joined the EU) – shows that comparable interest rate levels can be achieved outside the euro area despite the fluctuating exchange rate, if monetary policy is credible enough (Figure 10.6).

What is more, the coming period of fiscal consolidation does not bode well for output in the euro area, either. As the recent evidence suggests, fiscal consolidations tend to be contractionary in the short term after all (IMF, 2010). However, the output loss is likely to be lower in economies with independent monetary policy where interest and exchange rates relax to cushion the economy – especially if the consolidation is based on spending cuts.

In summary, the provision of long-term nominal stability is the only tangible economic benefit of the euro project.

At face value, therefore, the economic attractiveness of the euro project for CEE economies seems limited, at least for those that have a credible record of stabilising independent monetary policy. I emphasise the adjective *economic* attractiveness – I am not judging the euro project according to its political economy implications.

However, achieving monetary stability without the euro is easier said than done. It requires large investments in policy credibility. In the Czech Republic, for instance, it took five years of determined efforts before the implementation of adequate decision-making and communication processes, and success in changing the mentality inside the central bank, among the politicians and the public.

Besides the large investments in policy credibility, achieving monetary stability without the euro in the future may be more complicated than in the past. A few years back the prevailing paradigm was an inflation targeting (IT)-like regime based on a flexible exchange rate and interest rate policy transmission. No longer. Foreign exchange interventions, administrative measures and capital controls seem to be standard monetary policy instruments again, although transmission channels are still being investigated. Providing for price stability is often circumscribed by increased concerns for financial stability. As no clear paradigm has yet emerged, the complexities faced by a central bank attempting an independent monetary policy have increased enormously. Against the backdrop of these complexities in the post-crisis world, importing monetary stability from the euro area is still an attractive prospect, especially for the economies in Southeastern Europe that had not achieved enough monetary policy credibility before the crisis – unlike most of the CEE region.

The economies of the CESEE region now fall into two categories: those which are pursuing independent monetary policy based on a flexible exchange rate and those which have fixed their exchange rates. A vast majority of the floaters – mostly concentrated in the CEE region – have been successful in delivering long-term price stability and have reaped the benefits of a flexible exchange rate during the crisis. For these economies, euro adoption is more a political than an economic question.

The group of economies with a fixed exchange rate is facing a different predicament, though. The crisis has unveiled how precarious their position is. They were unable to profit from the sheltering effect of the euro area, while at the same time they could not use monetary policy stabilising channels either. Their post-crisis recovery may therefore be longer than otherwise, because of the time lags in relative price adjustments. A protracted recession is endangering both financial sector stability and the fiscal balance. The fiscal consolidation – which is needed to keep the exchange rates credibly fixed – is going to put further pressure on the economy without the interest rate and exchange rate channels cushioning its contractionary effects.

Moreover, most of the fixed exchange rate CESEE economies have substantial exchange rate mismatches on private sector balance sheets. The financial stability considerations effectively rule out any exchange rate adjustments. But at the same time the current account deficits – necessary symptoms of catch-up growth – require uninterrupted flows of external financing. The survival of these regimes in the future is therefore treading a fine line – in the hope that the recessions are severe enough to reduce the current account imbalances, but not so severe as to destroy the financial sector.

An early euro adoption is therefore the only economically reasonable option for the fixed exchange rate regimes in the region. This has probably always been so, but the crisis has made it an acute priority.

References

Bulíř, A. and J. Hurník (2009). 'Inflation convergence in the euro area: just another gimmick?', *Journal of Financial Economic Policy*, 14(4): 355–69

Hurník, J., Z. Tůma and D. Vávra (2010). 'The Czech Republic on its way to the Euro: a stabilisation role of monetary policy revisited', in E. Nowotny, P. Mooslechner and D. Ritzberger-Grünwald (eds.) *The Euro and Economic Stability: Focus on Central, Eastern and South-Eastern Europe*, Cheltenham: Edward Elgar and OeNB

IMF (2010). 'Will it hurt? Macroeconomic effects of fiscal consolidation', Chapter 3, *World Economic Outlook*, Washington, DC: IMF

Part III

The future of the euro area

11 Why the current account may matter in a monetary union: lessons from the financial crisis in the euro area

Francesco Giavazzi and Luigi Spaventa[*]

1 Introduction

The euro was ten years old in 2008. To celebrate this important birthday the European Commission produced a 350-page report (European Commission, 2008), accompanied by a string of research papers, to evaluate the European Monetary Union (EMU) experience after a decade. Lights and shades emerged from a careful and thorough analysis of the relevant issues, but the overall conclusion was that EMU is 'a resounding success'. Though perhaps more soberly, most observers would have subscribed to this view, ready to shelve some issues that, hotly debated when EMU was first launched, seemed now to have lost relevance: the effects of asymmetric shocks when optimum currency area conditions are not satisfied, the dangers of uncoordinated fiscal policies, the Walters (1986) critique of a 'one-size-fits-all' single monetary policy. One of the questions examined in the report, and at first sight somewhat reminiscent of the issues raised by Sir Alan Walters, was that of persistent differences in growth and inflation between some countries and the rest of the euro area. Misgivings on the sustainability of these trends were expressed here and there, but on the whole the policy conclusion was broadly reassuring:

The performance of [Spain, Ireland and Greece] has ... shown a satisfactory development overall ... The strong performers have been thriving on investment booms spurred by capital inflows attracted by comparatively high rates of return, with the single currency and the integration of financial markets acting as a catalyst ... Overall the divergences in growth and inflation have been long-lasting,

[*] We thank the editor of this volume, participants at the conference on 'The Euro Area and the Financial Crisis', at the National Bank of Slovakia, Bratislava, 6–8 September 2010, under the auspices of the National Bank of Slovakia, the Heriot–Watt University of Edinburgh and the Comenius University of Bratislava, Jacques Melitz in particular, and at seminars at Igier-Bocconi and Banca d'Italia for comments; Giulia Zane for research assistance; Fabio Panetta and Andrea Nobili for providing the data on credit growth.

Table 11.1: *General government balance and debt, 2008–9, % of GDP*

	Balance			Debt	
	Average 2000–7	2008	2009	2008	2009
Euro area	−2.3	−2	−6.3	69.7	79
Ireland	−1.0	−7.3	−14.3	43.9	64
Greece	−6.1	−7.7	−13.6	99.2	115.1
Spain	−1.3	−4.1	−11.2	39.7	53.2
Portugal	−4.1	−3.7	−7.1	66.3	76.8
Italy	−3.1	−2.7	−5.3	106.1	115.8

Source: Eurostat.

involving major shifts in intra-euro-area real effective exchange rates . . . This has been reflected in divergent current account positions across countries. Some, but not all, elements of these differences in inflation, growth and external positions can be attributed to structural convergence in living standards. Even so, not all inflation differentials are harmful; some are merely a sign that competitiveness realignment is doing its job. (European Commission, 2008)

At the time of the publication of the report few would have taken exception to these propositions. When, however, all hell broke loose between the end of 2009 and the beginning of 2010 and the four 'cohesion' countries[1] (the three strong performers as well as stagnant Portugal) came under attack, media and markets, turning those propositions on their head, used them as arguments for the prosecution as the euro was put on trial. True, the proximate cause of the attack was the sudden discovery that the Greek public accounts had been mendacious for years (something of which the Commission had been unaware).[2] But this was not the case for the other three countries, two of which moreover exhibited an enviable and widely praised record of high primary surpluses, low overall deficits (surpluses in some years) and low debt levels up until 2007 (Table 11.1). True, this flattering appearance melted away with the crisis, as the deterioration of public finances in Ireland and Spain in 2008 and 2009 was far greater than in the rest of the euro area; markets and

[1] So defined because at the time of their accession to the EU they were less developed than other countries (GDP *per capita* less than 0.9 of the EU average and large part of their territory with a 'less favoured' region status) and were therefore granted additional financial transfers (cohesion funds).

[2] The Greek general government deficit figures were successively revised from 2.8 to 3.6 to 5.1 per cent for 2007; from 2.1 to 5 to 7.7 per cent for 2008; from 5.1 to 13.6 per cent for 2009. *Sources:* European Commission. Public Finances in EMU, various years and Eurostat.

Table 11.2: *Cumulated current accounts, 1999–2008, % of GDP*

Ireland	−19,2	Germany	31,5
Spain	−59	Netherlands	53,7
Greece	−85,1	Finland	59,1
Italy	−13	France	3,1
Portugal	−90,7	Euro area	22,2

Source: Eurostat.

media were, however, more shocked by the sudden realisation that all four cohesion countries had accumulated high levels of foreign indebtedness, as a result of a long succession of current account deficits (Table 11.2), and of domestic household debt. The relevant data were of course available before, but as long as the going was good those imbalances were considered the natural side effect of a healthy process of convergence; now instead they came to be considered as symptoms of future sovereign insolvency and indicators of the inherent fragility of the whole single currency project. Had the markets been too complacent before or were they now displaying unwarranted pessimism?

The current account position, and hence the savings–investment balance of individual countries, have always been neglected in both the academic debates on and in the policy management of the euro area. In section 2 we shall examine the conceptual reasons provided by the literature that explain this attitude and even, in some cases, offer a normative justification for the persistence of current account deficits. We note, however, that the growth experience of the most dynamic cohesion countries displays some peculiar features which do not fit into the conventional convergence pattern which justifies foreign imbalances. Models establishing the optimality of a succession of current account deficits in a catching-up process implicitly assume that the intertemporal budget constraint is satisfied, so that the accumulation of foreign liabilities is matched by future surpluses. In section 3, by means of a simple two-period, two-good model, we show that fulfilment of that condition constrains the destination of foreign capital inflows even in a currency union. In section 4 we argue that the growth pattern of the countries under consideration was unsustainable because it violated the solvency constraint: the counterpart of the capital inflows (which occurred to a large extent through the borrowing of domestic financial institutions) was a boom of non-tradable residential construction or a growth of consumption. While monetary union removed the external constraint in the short run, a common monetary policy targeting the average inflation rate of the area did nothing (nor could it do much) to prevent the extraordinary growth of credit that fuelled the growing imbalances in the countries under considerations. In section 5 we shall address some policy issues. As our analysis shows, there are indeed fault lines in the construction of the single currency which, previously hidden, became visible under the impact of the world financial crisis. We believe that the euro will survive, but fear that it may not be a healthy survival unless institutional changes are introduced to shelter it from recurrent crises.

2   Convergence and external borrowing

The external payments situation of member states has always been disregarded in both the academic and the policy debate on the conception and implementation of the single currency project. It found no place either in the Maastricht convergence criteria or in the Commission's assessments of individual members' performance; the European Central Bank (ECB) has worried less about current account imbalances and net foreign positions than about the deterioration of some countries' competitiveness. Tellingly, under Article 143 of the Treaty on the Functioning of the European Union (TFEU) only member states with a derogation (those which have not adopted the euro) can receive financial assistance to deal with balance of payments problems.[3]

The literature provides sound justifications for this attitude. Ingram (1973, but see also Ingram, 1962) was perhaps the first to point out that under monetary integration 'the traditional concept of a deficit or a surplus in a member nation's balance of payments becomes blurred' (Ingram, 1973: 13) even from a conceptual point of view. With a common currency, no individual country can be exposed to speculative attacks: 'payments imbalances among member nations can be financed in the short run through the financial markets, without need for interventions by a monetary authority'. Owing moreover to 'the great diversity in circumstances of member nations', it is likely that 'certain member nations may be chronic borrowers in Community capital markets' (Ingram, 1973: 18).

---

[3] 'Where a Member State with a derogation is in difficulties or is seriously threatened with difficulties as regards its balance of payments' and 'if the action taken by the Member State . . . and the measures suggested by the Commission do not prove sufficient . . . the Commission shall . . . recommend to the Council the granting of mutual assistance'. On Article 143 and on the implicit assumption that balance of payments problems were expected to disappear in a monetary union, see Marzinotto, Pisani–Ferry and Sapir (2010).

Modern growth theory elaborates on the 'diversity in circumstances' of nations and predicts convergence at a speed depending on the distance between actual and potential output levels, where potential output depends on total factor productivity (TFP), savings and population growth, as well as on policies – what the literature refers to as 'conditional convergence'.[4] Capital flows to the catching-up countries, attracted by the expectation of faster productivity growth, to finance the current account deficits generated in the convergence to higher output levels. Monetary union facilitates this process by promoting financial integration and reducing the cost of foreign capital thanks to the elimination of the exchange rate premium.

Blanchard and Giavazzi (2002) provide a normative dimension. Considering specifically the euro area, they use an intertemporal model to show that foreign borrowing is optimal for a converging country: the recommended level of external borrowing is higher, and hence savings are lower or investment higher, the greater the country's expected output growth relative to the area average, the lower the wedge between the domestic and the foreign interest rate and the higher the elasticity of substitution between domestic and foreign goods. EMU and the single market have reduced the interest rate wedge and increased the elasticity of substitution between home and foreign goods. For countries at the periphery of the union, with lower initial levels of *per capita* income, the optimal level of external borrowing, and hence the excess of investment over savings, has therefore increased: persistent current deficits are thus a physiological effect of their catching-up process.

Three of the four countries we are considering (the exception being Portugal) seem to conform to this model. They have indeed been 'chronic borrowers' in the capital markets: at first sight with good reason, as their higher growth rates were consistent with the excess of their potential growth over that of the euro area (as later documented in Table 11.4, p. 206). It was indeed the Commission's view (European Commission, 2008) that the EMU years 'can be characterized as displaying a typical convergence pattern': monetary union contributed to this process 'via financial market integration and the elimination of the exchange risk premium' and allowed a smooth financing of the current account deficits caused by higher growth. If this were the case, one should conclude that the fears expressed by the markets were misplaced, or at least grossly exaggerated.

---

[4] See for instance Barro and Sala-i-Martin (2003).

Table 11.3: Per capita *income and labour productivity, 1998, 2000 and 2008*

	GDP *per capita*		Labour productivity per person employed		Labour productivity per hour worked	
	(a)	(b)	(a)	(b)	(a)	(b)
Ireland						
1998	106,1	99,2	108,1	111,4		
2000					94,9	89,0
2008	123,8	116,4	118,7	121,7	104,2	94,7
Greece						
1998	72,8	68,0	78,4	80,7		
2000					64,2	60,2
2008	86,2	81	93,2	95,5	71	64,5
Spain						
1998	83,3	77,9	92,9	95,7		
2000					87,2	81,7
2008	94,5	88,8	94,5	96,9	92,4	84
Portugal						
1998	69,3	64,8	60,4	62,3		
2000					52,9	49,6
2008	71,6	67,2	67,1	68,8	56,2	51,1
Italy						
1998	105,3	98,4	112,2	115,6		
2000					98,5	92,3
2008	93,6	87,9	99,8	102,3	88,8	80,8

Notes:
(a) Euro area = 100.
(b) Germany = 100.
Source: Eurostat.

The picture provided by the available data, however, is not only more complex but also not quite consistent with the 'typical convergence pattern'. Table 11.3 reports country levels of GDP *per capita* and of productivity per person employed and per hour worked, relative to the euro area average and to Germany, in 1998 (2000 for hourly productivity) and 2008. In terms of GDP *per capita*, we can properly talk of convergence only for Greece and Spain: Portugal has hardly moved; in the case of Ireland potential growth, as computed by the Commission, exceeded actual growth but *per capita* income was higher than the average already in 1998. We add Italy, where there was downward divergence, but no systematic accumulation of current account deficits. The changes in relative labour productivity are consistent with those of GDP *per capita* in Greece (upwards), in Portugal (almost flat) and in Italy (downwards). In Ireland the growth of labour productivity (especially hourly productivity) was much slower than that of *per capita* GDP. The case of Spain is extreme: the fast catching-up of *per capita* GDP (11 points with respect to euro area, 10 points with respect to Germany) occurred at an almost unchanged level of relative productivity and appears to be due almost entirely to an increase in employment.

The behaviour of labour productivity deserves attention. Two growth accounting exercises – to be found in the 2008 Commission report and in a 2007 ECB study (European Central Bank, 2007) – provide interesting information.[5] Assuming a technology $Y = Af(K, L)$, with A an index of TFP and $L = (N * Hours)$ the input of labour, depending on labour participation and utilisation, the growth rate of GDP per head can be decomposed as

$$\left(\frac{dY}{Y} - \frac{dN}{N} \right) = a\frac{dK}{K} + (b-1)\frac{dN}{N} + b\frac{dHours}{Hours} + \frac{dA}{A}$$

where a and b are the elasticities of output with respect to capital and labour. The first three terms measure the contribution to the growth of *per capita* GDP of the factors of production, the fourth that of TFP. In the course of the catching-up process, as the first three components converge to the levels prevailing in the more advanced countries, we expect the weight of TFP to increase.

Table 11.4 reports the results of the Commission exercise, showing potential growth rates rising in Greece and Spain in the EMU decade, falling in Portugal and remaining constant at a very high level in Ireland. The Commission notes that the catching-up process was 'heavily geared towards a greater use of...labour and capital'. Actually the picture is more complex, and more interesting. The TFP contribution collapses in Portugal and Spain and declines in Ireland, while the labour contribution rises, particularly in Portugal and Spain. Greece instead displays a performance more in keeping with what a conventional convergence model would lead us to expect, with a rising contribution of TFP and a declining relevance of the use of factors.

The results of the ECB (2007) exercise (Table 11.5) are quite consistent with this pattern. The ECB computes the contributions to actual growth of population and labour utilisation (lumped together in Table 11.5) and of hourly productivity for two five-year periods before and after EMU; the contribution of hourly productivity is in turn split between that

---

[5] The ECB (European Central Bank, 2007), however, cautions against the measurement shortcomings and the theoretical limitations of these exercises.

Table 11.4: *Potential growth and its components, 1989–2008*

	Euro area	Ireland	Greece	Spain	Portugal
Potential growth rate					
1989–98	2,3	6,5	2,1	2,9	3,1
1999–2008	2,2	6,5	3,9	3,7	1,9
% contributions to potential growth rate					
• *Labour*					
1989–98	8,7	20,0	19,0	34,5	9,7
1999–2008	22,7	29,2	15,4	54,1	36,8
• Capital					
1989–98	34,8	16,9	38,1	44,8	41,9
1999–2008	36,4	27,7	33,3	43,2	52,6
• TFP					
1989–98	56,5	58,5	38,1	20,7	45,2
1999–2008	36,4	40,0	48,7	2,7	10,5

Source: European Commission (2008).

Table 11.5: *Determinants of growth, 1995–2005*

	Euro area	Germany	Italy	Ireland	Greece	Spain	Portugal
Real GDP growth							
1995–98	2,3	1,7	1,7	10,0	2,9	3,4	4,2
1999–2005	1,9	1,2	1,2	6,8	4,3	3,7	1,6
% contributions to GDP growth							
• Labour utilisation and population							
1995–98	34,8	−23,5	29,4	40,0	34,5	94,1	14,3
1999–2005	36,8	−25,0	66,7	44,1	14,0	86,5	37,5
• Hourly labour productivity							
1995–98	65,2	123,5	70,6	60,0	65,5	5,9	85,7
1999–2005	63,2	125,0	33,3	55,9	86,0	13,5	62,5
of which:							
• *TFP*							
1995–98	47,8	82,4	41,2	60,0	48,3	5,9	57,1
1999–2005	36,8	83,3	−8,3	39,7	58,1	0,0	−6,3
• Capital deepening							
1995–98	17,4	41,2	29,4	0,0	17,2	0,0	28,6
1999–2005	26,3	41,7	41,7	16,2	27,9	13,5	68,8

Source: European Central Bank (2007).

due to capital deepening and that due to TFP growth. Once more we see that Spanish GDP growth appears to have relied almost entirely on employment growth; in the second period, the modest contribution of hourly productivity is entirely accounted for by capital deepening, as TFP remains flat. Greece, on the contrary, displays a sizeable productivity component, resting on robust TFP developments. Ireland stands in the middle, with a declining contribution of labour productivity and of its TFP component. The low growth rate of Portugal relies to a large extent on capital deepening.

This evidence does not fit easily into the story narrated by a classical convergence model, where capital flows financing current account deficits are prompted by the expectation of faster output growth driven by rising productivity. Though (with the exception of Portugal) growth remained vigorous in the cohesion countries until 2007–8,[6] while current account deficits grew faster,[7] the behaviour of labour productivity and especially the declining role of TFP in three out of the four countries is a signal of lower future growth and therefore not quite compatible with the persistence of foreign capital inflows. Spain earns a distinction for its stagnant labour and TFP. As for Ireland, it is noteworthy that its growth, while export-led and accompanied by hefty current account surpluses in the golden convergence period of the early 1990s, was driven by domestic demand, with declining TFP and growing current account deficits, after 1998.

All this leaves us with two questions. First, we ask in section 3 under what conditions persistent current account deficits, reflecting persistent excesses of investment over savings, are the natural and acceptable consequence of a convergence process. Second, we shall illustrate (in section 4) why developments in Ireland, Greece and Spain in the EMU years were incompatible with those conditions.

3   The intertemporal budget constraint and the composition of output

Ingram (1973) warns that the irrelevance of current account imbalances and of external debt in a monetary union holds only as long as 'the proceeds of external borrowing are used for ... productive purposes':

---

[6] In Italy instead a very low growth rate was consistent with the dismal performance of TFP and labour productivity.

[7] The deterioration of the current account between 2000 and 2007 (by 5.3 percentage points of GDP in Ireland, 6.7 in Greece and 6.0 in Spain) was not accompanied by a decline in the share of the three countries in total euro area exports.

if this is the case, a rise of external debt is sustainable because it is accompanied by a proportional growth of national wealth. Instead – he adds, by way of example – 'to finance unemployment compensations or other income-maintenance programs by external borrowing would be asking for trouble!' (Ingram, 1973: 17–18).

The distinction between productive and unproductive purposes of foreign borrowing on the part of catching-up countries seems to have been lost, at least in the context of EMU. That distinction, and the requirement that national wealth and external debt grow together, can be translated into the condition that the borrowing country must respect an intertemporal solvency constraint requiring that today's liabilities must be matched by future (discounted) current surpluses. This is only possible if foreign borrowing is used to increase the country's productive capacity of exportable goods and services. This important point is overlooked in convergence models (such as Blanchard and Giavazzi, 2002) which assume that all the goods a country produces are tradable and can as such contribute to the achievement, at some future date, of the export surplus required by the solvency condition. As soon as we allow for the existence of non-traded goods and for the possibility that investment can be devoted to the production of either type of goods, that condition becomes more stringent and therefore the current account position may come to matter. A simple model helps to better understand this point.

3.1   Optimal external borrowing in the presence of traded and non-traded goods

In this subsection we analyse a simple model with external borrowing and both traded and non-traded goods. This model is designed to show that introducing both traded and non-traded goods makes the conditions for the sustainability of external borrowing much more stringent. The simple reason is that if a country borrows mostly to finance the production of non-traded goods it will eventually violate its intertemporal budget constraint, since it will be unable to generate the export surplus necessary to satisfy the intertemporal budget constraint. Fagan and Gaspar (2008) also use a model with traded and non-traded goods to analyse macroeconomic adjustment in a monetary union. Their model, however, although it derives optimal consumption decisions from the intertemporal choices of infinitely lived agents, makes one crucial assumption: the flow endowment of traded and non-traded goods is exogenous. Thus the model cannot address the question of what happens if a country decides to invest mostly in the non-traded sector. This is the distinguishing feature of our simple exercise.[8]

The structure of the model is as follows. Agents consume both traded, T, and non-traded, N, goods. We concentrate on the country's intertemporal budget constraint overlooking agents' optimal consumption decisions.

There are two periods, t and $t + 1$, and the economy can exchange traded goods with the rest of the world in each period. At time t, $C_t^N = Y_t^N$, because N goods cannot be traded, while C_t^T can be larger or smaller than Y_t^T (we assume that both Y_t^T and Y_t^N are fixed).

Domestic output of traded and non-traded goods at time $t + 1$ depends on investment at time t. There is no labour and the technology is linear in capital: $Y_{t+1}^N = A^N K_t^N$, $Y_{t+1}^T = A^T K_t^T$, where K_t^N and K_t^T are the amounts invested at time t in the non-traded and traded goods sectors, respectively and A^N, A^T denote productivity in the two sectors.[9] For illustrative purposes we make the extreme assumption that all capital invested at time t is financed by foreign borrowing F. F finances investment in the two sectors, therefore $F = K_t^T + K_t^N$. Along the economy's production possibilities frontier (PPF) (shown in Figure 11.1)

$$Y^N = A^N(F - Y^T/A^T).$$

The optimal allocation of capital, and thus of production, between the two sectors depends on the expected relative prices of traded and non-traded goods $E(P^T/P^N)_{t+1}$ at the time when they are produced $(t + 1)$

$$\left(\frac{dY^N}{dY^T}\right)_t = E\left(\frac{P^T}{P^N}\right)_{t+1}$$

where E denotes expectations as of time t. This equation defines the PP line in Figure 11.1. The higher the expected relative price of non-traded

---

[8] Blanchard (2007a) also studies optimal external borrowing in a model with traded and non-traded goods. In that model, however, there is no capital and labour is the only factor of production. Thus the model, like Fagan and Gaspar (2008), cannot address the effects of alternative allocations of imported capital between the traded and non-traded good sectors. Introducing labour, however, allows wages to be determined so as to clear the labour market, something we obviously overlook in this model. A complete model should have both capital and labour, something for future work.

[9] An alternative interpretation of our assumption about technology is perfect complementarity between capital and labour (fixed coefficients) with constant returns to scale. Nothing of substance would change under such an interpretation. Nor would the substance of our result change if we assumed decreasing returns to K and then used a linear approximation of the technology to solve the intertemporal budget constraint.

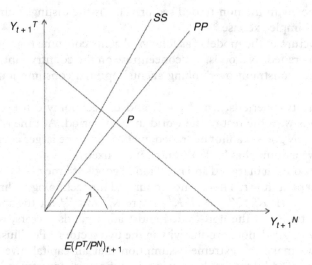

Figure 11.1: The PPF

goods, the more production (and thus capital) is tilted towards the N sector. In Figure 11.1 the optimal production is denoted by P.[10]

Next consider the intertemporal budget constraint of this economy. Net foreign borrowing in period t, F_t, must correspond to a current account deficit in the same period and hence to an excess of consumption over production of traded goods in period t. At time $t + 1$ the intertemporal budget constraint requires that net exports are sufficient to balance the debt incurred the previous period

$$\left(Y_{t+1}^T - C_{t+1}^T\right) \geq F_t \left(1 + R\right). \tag{11.1}$$

Using the production function, the intertemporal budget constraint can be rewritten as

$$\left(\frac{K^N}{K^T}\right)_t \leq \frac{A^T}{(1 + R)}(1 - \frac{C_{t+1}^T}{Y_{t+1}^T}) - 1.$$

The first term on the right-hand side can be assumed to be greater than 1 as $A^T - (1 + R)$, the net marginal product of the capital goods employed in the production of traded goods, can be assumed to be positive. The second term is the share of the production of tradable goods

---

[10] This depends on the fact that in a monetary union there is no exchange rate. If the exchange rate was not fixed a shift in P^N could be partly (and temporarily) offset by a change in the domestic currency price of traded goods.

which is not consumed at home in $t + 1$. For the condition to be fulfilled with a positive value of K^N the productivity in the tradable goods sector must be high enough and/or the share of traded goods not consumed internally must be high enough. Notice that productivity in the non-traded goods sector is also indirectly relevant: for a given demand C_{t+1}^N, the higher A^N the lower the required K^N. The above condition can be rewritten as

$$\left(\frac{Y^N}{Y^T}\right)_{t+1} \leq \frac{A^N}{(1 + R)}\left(1 - C_{t+1}^T/Y_{t+1}^T\right) - 1.$$

In Figure 11.1 this condition (the slope of which is the expression on the right-hand side) defines a region of current account 'sustainability' which corresponds to all points above the SS line. Thus in Figure 11.1, P violates the sustainability condition.

Of course the intertemporal budget constraint as written in (11.1) looks exceedingly stringent: but this is only due to our extreme assumption that all investment at time t is financed by foreign borrowing: it is easily shown that allowing for domestic financing would make the constraint more plausible. Still the message remains the same: an excess of foreign borrowing with the purpose of financing the production of non-traded goods is incompatible with a budget constraint. The intuition behind this result is quite simple. Insofar as non-tradable goods by definition can only be consumed domestically, foreign financing for their production is equivalent to borrowing abroad for consumption purposes.

3.2   Discussion

Before dealing in section 4 with developments in the cohesion countries in the light of the above model, we need to clarify some points.

First, the foreign capital inflow into the country at time t, though matching identically a current account deficit, is not motivated by the financing of that deficit. The channels through which the inflow occurs are either foreign direct investment (FDI), or the sale of domestic debt securities, or the borrowing of home banks abroad, from foreign banks or on the wholesale market. Direct investment consists of the purchase of a physical asset and does not have to be paid back. The net borrowing abroad, mostly by the banks, reflects an excess of investment over savings. If there is this imbalance, an increase in the domestic demand for loans cannot be matched by a corresponding increase of residents' deposits and can only be satisfied if the banks increase their foreign liabilities. Second, the distinction between traded and non-traded goods has a high degree of arbitrariness: any non-exportable good or service – from a haircut to housing services – becomes tradable to the extent to which it is consumed by visiting foreigners. Still, a criterion of prevalence holds: there are goods which are mostly devoted to domestic use, either because they can only be consumed *in loco* or because they cater mostly to domestic tastes.

The third point is more delicate.[11] What is foreign and what is domestic when the currency is the same? Why should the current account balance, and hence a constraint to the foreign net position, be relevant for an individual member state of EMU, while certainly irrelevant for the states of the American federation? Why indeed are current account statistics available for the former, but not for, say, California or Wyoming? As in the case of traded and non-traded goods there is no clear-cut answer. We observe that markets do seem to make a distinction: while European corporate bonds often include a country risk component and are correlated to government bonds, in the US nobody cares about the state where a company operates; more relevantly, as we saw in the recent crisis in Europe, markets did pay attention to the individual countries' foreign position. These facts, however, while corroborating our view that even under a single currency the current account may matter, still do not answer the question of why this does not hold for the dollar. Our tentative answer goes along the following lines. First, there is far greater personal mobility within the US than within Europe, where there are language barriers and administrative obstacles: this by itself reduces the quantity of goods and services which are traded in the sense that they are consumed at home by non-residents. Second, unlike the US, Europe is not a federation but an association of fully sovereign states which, even when accepting a common currency, have delegated their competences to Union law only in some specific matters: not for the national budgets (the Union budget being almost non-existent), not for taxation, not for civil and company laws, not for bankruptcy laws. Even when European legislation holds, it often only sets minimal requirements, as in the case of financial services for which there is no single rule book. In short, each member state of the EU remains a separate jurisdiction with its own legal system and its own entities in charge of enforcement and supervision. (The obvious example is banking, where the recent crisis has brought to light the national fragmentation of supervisory rules and practices.) We conclude that a common currency, while blurring to some extent the notion of a member state's foreign position, is not by itself sufficient to make that notion irrelevant.

---

[11] We are very grateful to George Kopits, our discussant when this paper was first presented, who raised this point forcibly and provided many useful observations.

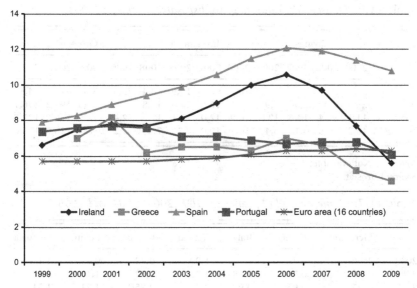

Figure 11.2: Value added in construction, 1999–2009, % of total value added

4   Unsustainable growth

In Ireland and Spain growth was led by a construction boom. The share of construction in total value added rose sharply in those two countries (Figure 11.2), while it declined slightly in Greece and Portugal and remained more or less constant in the euro area. The same happened to construction investment, both as a ratio to GDP and as a share of total investment: housing construction accounts for the rise in that ratio as well as for the increase in the ratio of gross capital formation to GDP which, until 2007, took place in Ireland and Spain, but not in the rest of the euro area.[12]

Table 11.6, reporting the households' saving rate, investment rate and gross debt (as ratios of gross disposable income, GDI), shows the other face of the housing boom. In both Spain and Ireland the households' investment rate rose sharply (to collapse in 2008), but the savings rate declined: the result was an increase in households' gross debt of the order of 80 per cent. A fall in the saving rate caused an increase of debt in Portugal in spite of a decline in the investment rate. Data for Greece are not available now, probably because of ongoing revisions: earlier releases

[12] See the analyses in Martinez-Mongay, Lasierra and Yaniz Igal (2007) and Suárez (2010) for Spain and in Kelly (2010) and Honohan (2009) for Ireland.

Table 11.6: *Households, ratios to gross disposable income, 2000–8*

	Savings				Investment				Gross debt			
	2000	2002	2007	2008	2000	2002	2007	2008	2000	2002	2007	2008
Euro area	..	..	..	..	10,3	9,6	10,9	10,4	75,5	78,0	94,6	94,8
Ireland	..	9,0	7,9	9,9	..	16,8	24,0	15,8	..	107,5	194,2	196,7
Spain	11,1	11,4	10,6	12,9	10,9	12,0	15,1	12,9	72,4	79,2	129,9	127,8
Portugal	10,2	10,6	6,1	6,4	10,7	10,0	7,7	7,6	87,2	99,3	126,2	136,0

Note: .. = Not available.
Source: Eurostat.

Table 11.7: *Domestic credit*, ratios to GDP, 2000, 2004 and 2008*

	Germany	France	Italy	Ireland	Greece	Spain	Portugal
2000	1,06	0,72	0,71	1,00	0,42	0,87	1,10
2004	1,01	0,76	0,78	1,26	0,62	1,11	1,24
2008	0,95	0,95	0,97	2,02	0,85	1,71	1,51

Note: * Outstanding amounts at the end of the period.
Sources: National central banks.

of Eurostat reported negative saving rates. Be that as it may, Greece stands out for its ratio of private consumption to GDP, which is the highest in Europe (about 0.75 as against 0.58 both for the EU and for the euro area).

The housing boom in Ireland and Spain was accompanied by an impressive expansion of domestic credit. Table 11.7 reports the ratios to GDP of domestic credit (loans) to the private sector in the four countries under consideration and in the three major euro area countries. The ratio remained constant in Germany, and grew slowly towards the German level in France and in Italy. In Ireland and Spain, instead, it doubled in eight years, to levels far higher than those of the larger countries. Between 2004 and 2007 loans for housing credit increased by 68 per cent in Ireland and by 65 per cent in Spain, twice as much as in the average of the euro area. Though the ratio of credit to GDP is often taken as an index of a country's financial development, we would find it difficult to interpret the developments in Ireland and Spain in this light. Domestic credit also increased rapidly, though at a less hectic pace, in Greece and Portugal. Everywhere credit growth was fed by foreign borrowing, as domestic banks would tap the interbank market and issue commercial paper or bonds (Kelly, 2010; Suarez, 2010). While

Table 11.8: *Portfolio investment of the four cohesion countries' share of total investment, 2001 and 2008*

	2001	2008
France	10,8	18,3
Germany	10,8	20,3

Source: IMF.

there was little FDI, foreign portfolio investment rose fast. Table 11.8 reports the share of portfolio investment of the four cohesion countries in total foreign portfolio investment from France and Germany: it doubled or almost doubled (it more than doubled in the case of Ireland and Spain).

These developments shed light on several issues. First, EMU created the environment suitable for a credit boom in countries at the periphery of the single currency area. As argued by Lane (2010), by eliminating currency and liquidity risks (and by fostering financial integration), EMU represented a major shock for those countries, as even low yield differentials would attract massive capital flows. But this is, after all, what the convergence model would predict.

The growth pattern in the four countries shows, however, that we are far away from that model. Considering first Ireland and Spain, the growing weight of construction in value added provides an explanation for the disappointing behaviour of TFP in the two countries, as construction is a sector less exposed to productivity-enhancing innovations. More importantly, the output of construction – housing services – is a largely non-traded good. Selling houses to foreigners would be registered as FDI: but direct investment was a small share of total flows. True, housing services can be a tradable outcome of the construction activity to the extent to which houses are rented to foreigners. Appropriately weighting for the period of occupancy, it is however unlikely that housing services to foreigners represent a significant fraction of the total.

Ireland and Spain thus fit into our simple model above. In both countries foreign capital went into the production of non-traded and non-tradable goods to an extent incompatible with the intertemporal budget constraint. Viewed in this light, the current account positions of the two countries became unsustainable even within the convergence model. While recognising that there was a housing price bubble (even more pronounced than in the US), one may ask why foreign investors did not seem to be aware of the sustainability problems. The answer is that to a large extent there were no foreign investors investing specifically in assets earmarked for the financing of the construction activity:[13] foreign banks and investors would lend to, or purchase financial assets from, domestic banking institutions which would then finance the domestic construction industry.

The cases of Greece and Portugal do not fit into the picture of an excess production of non-tradable goods. As for Greece, productivity performance was not unsatisfactory; credit grew, but more slowly than in Ireland or Spain; there was no comparable construction boom. The violation of the budget constraint was at the same time less interesting and more blatant. With a ratio of private investment to GDP near the euro area average (and lower than in Ireland and Spain), but with much higher levels of consumption and high public deficits, Greece was just not saving enough. Real appreciation was not the major cause of the current account problem: foreign capital was financing an excess of Greek consumption.[14] The Portuguese story is sadder. Its imbalances are similar to those of Greece, with high consumption and low households' saving. But in the EMU years Portugal, unlike Greece, remained stagnant, with its GDP *per capita* hardly growing relative to the European average.[15]

The 2009–10 crisis in the euro area was ignited by the discovery of the Greek budget mendacity, but there were deeper causes. In an environment where the current and prospective increase in the supply of public debt by all advanced economies caused investors to be more selective, it is not surprising that the weaker members of the euro area came under attack. First and foremost, investors realised that the pattern followed by some countries over the last decade, with growth driven by domestic demand and financed with foreign borrowing, was unsustainable: the heavy imbalances which had accumulated signalled, as we have argued, the existence of solvency problems. Second, members of EMU are more exposed than other countries with similar problems because they do not have their own central bank which, in troubled times, if need be, can support the national Treasury as 'market-maker of last resort'. From this point of view the sovereign debt of a member of the euro area, though issued in euros, is from other points of view similar to foreign debt,

[13] The circulation of the equivalent of mortgage-backed securities, especially in their most sophisticated version, was far less common than in the US.
[14] Also because the real effective exchange rate appreciated in Greece less than in many other countries. In 2008 the index (1999 = 100) was 107 in Greece, but 136 in Ireland, 118 in Spain, 113 in Portugal, 115 in Italy and 108 in France.
[15] See Blanchard (2007b).

unlike that issued in national currencies by countries with their own central bank.[16]

Finally, for the countries that came under attack the deterioration of the fiscal position caused by the crisis was far greater than for other euro area countries.[17] This also was to some extent the effect of their growth pattern. The remarkable fall in public revenues in Ireland (about 3 percentage points) and in Spain (6 points) is connected to a considerable extent to the collapse of the past growth pattern in the two countries. Honohan (2009) shows that in Ireland there was a systematic shift towards 'fair weather' taxes based on the construction and housing boom. Martinez-Mongay, Lasierra and Yaniz Igal (2007) argued, before the crisis, that the increase in tax revenues recorded in Spain depended very much on the composition of growth rather than on permanent factors. Suarez (2010) reckons that the real estate boom inflated Spanish government revenues by almost 3 per cent. It thus turned out that the surprisingly good past records of budget discipline were not a permanent acquisition.

5   Policy implications

Jaumotte and Sodsriwiboon (2010) run regressions to show that specific EMU/euro effects, in the shape of lower savings, explain most of the (abnormal) deterioration in current accounts in the southern euro area. Though the group of countries is heterogeneous and Ireland is missing, the result is interesting and plausible, but leaves unexplained why there is a geographical partition and has no obvious policy implications. Honohan (2009) argues that EMU membership 'lulled [Irish] policy makers into a false sense of security', especially because the single currency removed the external constraint and made the exchange rate and the interest rate insensitive to domestic developments. Kelly (2010) thinks that the impact of low interest rates allowed by the euro on the Irish construction boom was modest, but Suarez (2010) believes that the ECB monetary policy,

[16] Asset managers have always priced in this possibility when assessing probabilities of default. More importantly, the recent 'quantitative easing' practices of the Fed and of the Bank of England, which have acquired government securities on their balance sheets, show that that possibility is not forgotten. Formally, the Treaty only forbids the ECB from financing governments on the primary market, but its emergency decision in April to intervene on the secondary market to support some countries' sovereign bonds in the presence of 'dysfunctional market conditions' was severely frowned upon: so heavy were the criticisms that its interventions were small and timid.

[17] Between 2006 and 2009 the general government primary balance worsened by more than 16 percentage points of GDP in Ireland, more than 13 points in Spain and more than 9 in Greece.

while consistent with developments in the three bigger countries of the euro area, was unfit for the Spanish conditions of fast output growth and rampant credit expansion. This discussion reminds one of the Walters critique, according to which the project of a single currency for Europe is inherently flawed because of the chronic inability of a common monetary policy to deal with a diversity of cyclical situations in member countries: one size can fit some, but not all. The issue is, however, more complex and goes deeper than the macroeconomic effects of a common monetary policy on countries in different cyclical situations: it reflects weaknesses in the way in which EMU was conceived.

The admission criteria to the common currency were the levels of inflation and interest rates (with respect to the average) and the levels of public deficits (while the public debt criterion was conveniently massaged to fit all applicants). The first two variables were largely endogenous: once a common currency and a common monetary policy are in place, short-term interest rates and to some extent inflation rates are expected to converge. After the start of the euro the attention of European policy-makers and of external observers was exclusively, and at times obsessively, concentrated on public deficits, with the Treaty and the Stability and Growth Pact (SGP) dictating detailed (and often ineffective) procedures to deal with deficits in excess of the limit. Many other variables instead have always been neglected: relative productivity and cost trends; credit and leverage; the savings–investment balance, and hence the current account which, though no longer a short-term binding constraint under a common currency, is an immediate indicator of the existence of output–expenditure imbalances. Whereas the Maastricht variables more or less converged (including the deficit variable, at least until 2007–8), the situation in the euro area was unsettled by the diverging trends of precisely those neglected variables. It is sobering to recall the praise lavished on Ireland and Spain for their deficit and debt performance. It has thus become apparent that the stability of the monetary union depends on a wider set of conditions than compliance with budgetary discipline.

Insuring that those conditions are fulfilled is however a daunting task. In the case of public deficits precise limits can be set (whether they make sense is another matter) and an implementing procedure can be devised (again, whether it is effective or not depends on political factors). Setting a scoreboard of enforceable targets for macroeconomic variables, as envisaged by the European Commission (2010a, 2010b, 2010c), meets instead with conceptual difficulties and with problems of implementation in an association of fully sovereign states, which have only one market, one money and a limited number of laws and rules in common. The identification of imbalances requiring action would be a highly judge-mental operation, open to all kind of objections in a long and compli-cated collegial procedure and with little preventive value. In some cases it would even be difficult to conceive of enforceable remedies – as, for instance, when an external imbalance is caused by falling competitiveness due to unsatisfactory productivity developments.

Any alternative to a fully-fledged macroeconomic programme should be less ambitious in scope, but at the same time be more effective for the prevention of imbalances and easier to enforce. As recent experience shows, the imbalances that matter for the stability of monetary union are the result either of fiscal profligacy – as in Greece and to some extent in Portugal – or of an unchecked credit expansion fuelled by capital inflows and feeding an unsustainable growth of the non-traded sector – as in Ireland and Spain. Fiscal imbalances are, or should be, taken care of by an enhanced version of the excessive deficit procedure (European Commission, 2010d). The problem then is how to deal with credit in the individual member states.

This is not a new issue. Ceilings on total domestic credit used to be a major ingredient of IMF conditionality in the stand-by agreements with countries in need of support because of current account imbalances. But it is a difficult issue in a financially integrated, single-currency area.

Common monetary policy is hardly the appropriate instrument. An augmented Taylor rule (Giavazzi and Giovannini, 2010), even if accept-able and feasible, can hardly deal with divergent credit dynamics within the union: again one size cannot fit all. Macro stability rules – dealing, for instance, with reserve requirements – are also unfit for the purpose: the much-praised Spanish rules on dynamic provisioning did nothing to prevent the credit boom. One must therefore turn to the exercise of spe-cific supervisory and regulatory powers (Bean et al., 2010; Orphanides, 2010): stricter rules on lending (for instance on loan/equity ratios and mortgage refinancing) would have prevented the excesses observed in some countries (and did so in other countries).

Who should be entrusted with these regulatory and supervisory tasks? The Irish, Spanish and British experiences show that national authorities are not always reliable: they may be captured by the regulated (as in Ireland: see Honohan, 2009 and Kelly, 2010) or may be lenient and hesitant to interrupt a boom. In a financially integrated area with a single currency some supervisory and regulatory powers should be entrusted to a supranational body. The Treaty has not given such powers to the ECB. The new bodies which are being set up, implementing the proposals of a report by Jacques de Larosière (de Larosière, 2009) may serve the purpose. The already established new European Systemic Risk Board

(ESRB), and especially the European Supervisory Banking Authority, are potentially in a position to discipline, directly or indirectly, the domestic rules and practices which allowed the excesses leading to a crisis that put the stability of the whole union at risk.

The first decade of the life of the euro deluded policy-makers and observers into thinking that almost all had gone well and was well, perhaps unexpectedly. The recent crisis has shown the fragility of the construction. The ESRB and the European supervisory authorities mark an important institutional development in the Union: they offer an opportunity to improve the stability of the single-currency area.

References

Barro, R. J. and X. Sala-i-Martin (2003). *Economic Growth*, 2nd edn., Cambridge, MA: MIT Press

Bean, C., M. Paustian, A. Penalver and T. Taylor (2010). 'Monetary policy after the fall', Bank of England, mimeo

Blanchard, O. (2007a). 'Current account deficits in rich countries', IMF Staff Papers, *Palgrave Macmillan Journals*, vol. **54**(2): 191–219

(2007b). 'Adjustment within the euro, the difficult case of Portugal', *Portuguese Economic Journal*, **6**(1)

Blanchard, O. and F. Giavazzi (2002). 'Current account deficits in the Euro Area: the end of the Feldstein–Horioka puzzle?', *Brookings Papers on Economic Activity*, **2**: 2002

Clerc, L. and B. Mojon (2011). 'Financial stability and monetary policy: lessons from the euro area', Chapter 14 in this volume

European Central Bank (2007). 'Output growth differentials in the euro area: sources and implications', *Economic Bulletin*, **04**

European Commission (2008). 'EMU@10: successes and challenges of Economic and Monetary Union', *European Economy*, **2**

(2010a). 'Reinforcing economic policy coordination', **COM(2010)250**, 12 May

(2010b). 'Enhancing economic policy coordination for stability, growth and jobs – tools for stronger EU economic governance', **COM(2010)367/2**, 30 June

(2010c). 'Proposal for a regulation of the European Parliament and of the Council on the prevention and correction of macroeconomic imbalances', 29 September

(2010d). 'Proposal for a regulation of the European Parliament and of the Council on enforcement measures to correct excessive macroeconomic imbalances in the euro area', 29 September

Fagan, G. and V. Gaspar (2008). 'Macroeconomic adjustment to monetary union', European Central Bank, Working Paper, No. **946**

Giavazzi, F. and A. Giovannini (2010). 'Central Banks and the financial system', CEPR, Discussion Paper, No. **7944**

Honohan, P. (2009). 'What went wrong in Ireland?', May, mimeo

Ingram, J. C. (1962). *Regional Payments Mechanisms. The Case of Puerto Rico*, Durham NC, University of North Carolina Press

(1973), 'The case for European monetary integration', International Finance Section, Princeton University, Essays in International Finance, No. **98**

Jaumotte, F. and P. Sodsriwiboon (2010). 'Current account imbalances in Southern Euro Area', IMF Working Paper, **WP/10/139**

Kelly, M. (2010). 'Whatever happened to Ireland?', CEPR Discussion Paper, No. **7811**

Lane, P. R. (2011). 'The Irish crisis', chapter 4 in this volume

de Larosière, J. (2009). *Report of the High-Level Group on Financial Supervision in the EU*, Brussels, 25 February

Martinez-Mongay, C., L.A. Lasierra and J. Yaniz Igal (2007). 'Asset booms and tax receipts: the case of Spain, 1995–2006', *European Economy* – Economic Papers, No. **293**

Marzinotto, B., J. Pisani-Ferry and A. Sapir (2010). 'Two crises, two responses', Bruegel Policy Brief, **2010/01**

Orphanides, A. (2010). 'Monetary policy lessons from the crisis', CEPR Discussion Paper, No. **7891**

Suárez, J. (2010). 'The Spanish crisis: background and policy challenges', CEPR Discussion Paper, No. **7909**

Walters, A. (1986). *Britain's Economic Renaissance*, Oxford University Press

12 National fiscal rules within the EU framework

*Daniele Franco and Stefania Zotteri**

1 Introduction

Since the early 1990s many European countries have introduced fiscal rules and procedures which are aimed at either preventing or reducing fiscal imbalances. This development reflects three main factors: the experience of the previous decades, characterised by large imbalances, public debt growth and the implementation of pro-cyclical policies; the creation of the Economic and Monetary Union (EMU) and the introduction of fiscal rules at the European Union (EU) level; and the challenges of ongoing demographic changes.

The reforms have involved three main lines of action: (1) the introduction of numerical fiscal rules; (2) the modification of budgetary procedures, in particular with a view to strengthening the role of the Ministry of Finance and to making budgetary policy more medium-term oriented; and (3) the creation of independent fiscal institutions, which can contribute to macro fiscal forecasting, fiscal analysis, policy design and even implementation.

These national frameworks are rather diversified in the emphasis placed upon numerical and procedural aspects, in the choice of numerical indicators and in the legal foundations. However, there are a few common features. Some countries (Spain, Sweden) target (or used to target, in the case of the UK) the structural budget balance. A similar rule has been implemented also in non-EU countries such as Switzerland; in 2009 Germany moved in the same direction. Other countries (Finland, the Netherlands, Sweden and Switzerland) target expenditure growth.

More recently, the debate has focused on fiscal rules and procedures aimed at the consolidation of public finances after the most severe economic downturn of the post-war period. The recent accumulation of public debt (combined with the pressure that demographic change will

* Banca d'Italia, Structural Economic Analysis Department. The views expressed in this chapter are those of the authors and should not be attributed to the institution to which they are affiliated.

exert on budgets) poses difficult challenges to fiscal policy. Many countries must achieve a sizeable improvement in the budget balance and maintain a sound fiscal position for several years in order to ensure the sustainability of the public finances. Well-designed fiscal rules and procedures are widely considered an essential component of this effort.

The impact of the crisis on the national fiscal framework has been different across countries. In some countries – such as the UK – the crisis led to the suspension of the previous fiscal framework. In others – such as Sweden – the previous framework proved to be effective and has simply been reinforced. In others the crisis has been exploited as an opportunity for introducing significant reforms. This is the case of Germany.

Given the decentralised nature of fiscal policy making in the EU and the need for national ownership of EU fiscal rules, both the September 2010 European Commission proposal for reforming economic governance (European Commission, 2010a, 2010b, 2010c) and that of the van Rompuy task force (van Rompuy, 2010) stress – *inter alia* – the complementarity between the European fiscal framework and national fiscal frameworks. Both reform proposals refer to the need for minimum requirements that national frameworks should meet. More specifically, the reform proposal put forward by the European Commission sets minimum requirements for transparency, medium-term orientation, accounting systems and statistics and numerical fiscal rules.

After briefly reviewing the literature on fiscal rules and fiscal framework developments in some European countries before and after the crisis, this chapter considers the ongoing debate on fiscal rules and, in particular, some of the lessons suggested by the recent German reform and the reform proposal which is at present under discussion in France. It highlights some issues which are left open by both the current debate and the German reform.

2   Fiscal rules: sketching a map

For a long time fiscal rules were generally not written into constitutions and laws. Rather, they were part of an accepted set of attitudes about how government should conduct its fiscal affairs (Buchanan, 1997; Balassone and Franco, 2001). In recent decades, partly also as a result of the high deficits of the 1970s and 1980s, the focus of the debate has gradually shifted to the introduction of formal rules. These are expected to be more difficult to abandon without high reputational costs.

Fiscal rules are primarily about the sustainability of fiscal policy: they are expected to avoid large deficits and growing debt levels. They are also expected to make fiscal policy less volatile, less procyclical and more consistent over time (Kopits and Symansky, 1998; Banca d'Italia, 2001; Kumar and Ter-Minassian, 2007).

A fiscal rule can be defined as '[a] permanent constraint on fiscal policy, typically defined in terms of an indicator of overall fiscal performance' (Kopits and Symansky, 1998: 2). It can also be seen as 'a constraint on fiscal policy with a time-bound character' (Danninger, 2002: 7). Fiscal rules can be designed in different ways. The actual design of a rule depends on the specific goal it pursues, on its coverage (e.g. central government, local governments, overall general government), on how the implementation works (including the authority responsible for monitoring compliance and the presence of error-correction mechanisms), on its time horizon (e.g. one year, the length of the cycle) and on the indicator it refers to (e.g. budget balance, debt).

As to the last aspect, broadly speaking rules can be divided into three groups: (1) budget balance rules (which may refer – *inter alia* – to the overall or the current balance; and to the submitted budget, the approved budget, or the actual budget balance); (2) debt rules (which usually set a limit to the debt level and often complement a budget balance rule); (3) rules which account for the composition of the budget, typically expenditure rules.

While the balanced budget has generally remained the reference point of budget balance rules, the need for exceptions has long been recognised for (1) investment projects, (2) cyclical factors and (3) exceptional events (Pigou, 1928). The last two exceptions are necessary in order to avoid procyclical fiscal policies.

Fiscal rules are typically introduced at the national level. However, there are some supra-national rules, the most well known being those introduced at the European level by the Maastricht Treaty and the Stability and Growth Pact (SGP). Many countries have specific rules for subnational governments, either decided at the national level or introduced by the subnational governments themselves (this is the case for US states and Canadian provinces).

Kopits and Symansky (1998) identify a number of desirable features against which the quality of fiscal rules can be measured. According to these criteria, an ideal fiscal rule should be well defined, transparent, simple, flexible, adequate relative to the final goal, enforceable, consistent and underpinned by public finance reforms. As far as the optimal commitment technology for ensuring compliance is concerned, drawing on his analysis of US states' fiscal rules Inman (1996) indicates four main criteria: (1) the fiscal rule must be complied with *ex post* and not only *ex ante*; (2) it must not be overridden or temporarily suspended by a simple majority vote of the legislature; (3) it must be constitutionally – not statutorily – grounded; and (4) it must be enforced by an open and politically independent – not partisan – review panel or court.

Similar criteria are used in other studies to rank fiscal rules. The Advisory Commission on Inter-governmental Relations (1987) builds an index of strictness of balanced budget rules: a rule gets high marks if it is imposed and there is no deficit carryover; it gets low marks if it is self-imposed and applies only *ex ante* to the budget. The Inter-American Development Bank (1997) provides an index of strictness of borrowing capacity: marks are high if the government cannot borrow at all and has no control on banks or enterprises; marks are low if there is no restriction on borrowing and the government owns banks or enterprises.

While earlier studies noticed that the evidence on the effectiveness of fiscal rules was mixed (Kopits and Symansky, 1998), more recent empirical work is more positive. There is evidence that the strictness of rules is positively related to their effectiveness. Ayuso-i-Casals *et al.* (2007) develop some summary indexes of the strength of numerical fiscal rules in place in EU countries over the period 1990–2005, based on a new dataset built by the authors from questionnaires addressed to country fiscal experts. By estimating fiscal reaction functions, Ayuso-i-Casals *et al.* find that a more extensive use of numerical fiscal rules tends to reduce the size of the deficit and that this relationship is stronger the larger the share of general government covered by the rules and the stricter the enforcement mechanism. They conclude that 'higher values of the Fiscal Rule Index and in the Expenditure Rule Index[1] lead, respectively, to an improvement in the [cyclically-adjusted-primary balance] and to a reduction of primary government expenditure' (Ayuso-i-Casals *et al.*, 2007: 684). They also note that the design of rules may have an impact on the cyclical behaviour of fiscal policy. In particular, multiannual budget balance rules matter.

These results are basically consistent with those obtained by Guichard *et al.* (2007) on OECD data. They note that '[f]iscal rules ... are estimated to have affected several dimensions of fiscal consolidation'; 'the size of fiscal consolidation was significantly larger and the consolidation efforts sustained for longer when such rules [expenditure rules] were present'; 'in general budget-balance rules that are not combined with expenditure rules are less effective' (Guichard *et al.*, 2007: 16, 18).[2]

---

[1] The first indicator refers to all rules, the second to expenditure rules only. Both indexes take into account the share of government finances covered by numerical fiscal rules and the qualitative features of fiscal rules such as the statutory base and whether there is independent monitoring, the nature of the institution responsible for the enforcement of the rule and the existence of predefined enforcement mechanisms.

[2] But there is a causality issue. Wierts (2007: 781–2) notes that '[t]he empirical analysis indicates that the institutional design of the rules reflects political willingness to address

Fiscal rules are usually part of a broader institutional framework. Over the last decade several countries have introduced comprehensive institutional arrangements aimed at improving fiscal policy outcomes (Banca d'Italia, 2001; Kopits, 2007). These arrangements – usually defined as fiscal responsibility laws – usually include both procedural and numerical rules that the government should follow in the design and implementation of fiscal policy. They aim at making fiscal policy more predictable, credible and transparent (Kumar and Ter-Minassian, 2007). Governments are usually requested to commit to a medium-term fiscal policy strategy and to provide extensive information about targets and outcomes. Among the most notable cases are those of New Zealand (Fiscal Responsibility Act, 1994), Australia (Charter of Budget Honesty, 1998), United Kingdom (Code for Fiscal Stability, 1998) and Spain (Budget Stability Law, 2001).

3   The experience of European countries before and after the crisis

In Europe the debate on national fiscal rules has been pervasively affected by the procedural and numerical requirements of the Maastricht Treaty and the SGP. EU members can stick to the European framework either adopting or not adopting complementary national rules. Nevertheless, national rules can help ensure compliance with the EU rules (especially in decentralised countries), allow government to achieve more ambitious targets (for instance, to deal with the budgetary consequences of an aging population) and contribute to the achievement of other targets (among others, those related to the size of government).

The idea of developing adequate national fiscal frameworks has gradually gained consensus. In 2005 the European Council (Council of the European Union, 2005: 21) agreed 'that national budgetary rules should be complementary to the Member States' commitments under the SGP' and considered 'that domestic governance arrangements should complement the EU framework for fiscal surveillance. National institutions could play a more prominent role in budgetary surveillance to strengthen national ownership, enhance enforcement through national public opinion and complement the economic and policy analysis at EU level.'

Over the last decade several European countries have introduced fiscal rules to guide national fiscal policy (Ayuso-i-Casals, 2010). According

high expenditure-to-GDP ratios'. In particular, 'results show that countries with higher initial expenditure to GDP have introduced stricter expenditure rules'.

Table 12.1: *Most common features of national fiscal frameworks in EU countries*

	Indicator	Time-frame	Legal basis	Automatic correction mechanism
General government and central government	Expenditure	Multi–annual	Political agreement	No
Regional and local governments	Budget balance – debt	Annual	Law – Constitution	Yes

Source: European Commission (2006).

to the European Commission (2006), in the EU national rules present some general features which are summarised in Table 12.1.[3]

This issue has returned to the fore in the debate on strengthening the EU fiscal framework that followed the developments of the first months of 2010. In its contributions to the debate the European Commission has stressed (European Commission, 2010a, 2010b) that national fiscal frameworks should better reflect the priorities of EU budgetary surveillance: 'Member States should have in place national fiscal rules ensuring that domestic fiscal frameworks reflect the Treaty obligations' (European Commission, 2010b: 7). It is 'essential that the objectives of the EMU budgetary coordination framework are reflected in the national budgetary frameworks' (European Commission, 2010c: 6). The Commission advocates the need to switch from annual to multiannual budgetary planning and to have comprehensive frameworks, covering the whole of general government. It also plans to propose minimum requirements for the design of national fiscal frameworks.

The impact of the crisis on national fiscal frameworks has been different across countries. In the UK the existing rules – a golden rule and a debt ceiling, both holding over the economic cycle[4] – were disrupted by the economic crisis. With the November 2008 Pre-Budget Report the UK government announced a temporary departure from the existing

[3] In addition, countries following the 'contract approach' (procedures ensuring agreement among policy makers) are more likely to have rules for central government or general government; whereas countries following the 'delegation approach' (which assigns strong powers to the Finance Minister or the Prime Minister) usually have rules for regional and local governments (Ayuso-i-Casals *et al.*, 2007).

[4] According to the latter, over the economic cycle the ratio of net public debt to GDP has to be set at a stable and prudent level, defined by the Chancellor as no more than 40 per cent.

fiscal rules and the implementation of a new temporary operating rule which requires the government 'to improve the cyclically-adjusted current budget each year, once the economy emerges from the downturn, so it reaches balance and debt is falling as a proportion of GDP once the global shocks have worked their way through the economy in full' (HM Treasury, 2008: 4). In addition, in May 2010 an independent authority – the Office for Budget Responsibility (OBR) – was formed. This authority has to make independent assessments of the public finances and the economy, directly control the forecast and make all the key judgements that drive the official projections, while having full access to the necessary data and analysis produced by the Treasury. The OBR also has to present a range of outcomes around its forecasts to demonstrate the degree of uncertainty. Based on these range of outcomes, in each Budget and Pre-Budget Report the OBR has to confirm whether the government's policy is consistent with a better than 50 per cent chance of achieving the forward-looking fiscal mandate set by the Chancellor.

In Sweden the impact of the crisis on the existing fiscal framework was very different: the latter survived basically unchanged. In the light of its effectiveness, in 2010 the government proposed to reinforce its legal basis by making the surplus target statutory via its inclusion in the Budget Act (without specifying the value set for the target; Swedish Fiscal Council, 2010).

The national fiscal framework was introduced in 1997 after the severe budgetary imbalances of the 1990s. It was conceived also as a way of favouring compliance with the EU rules (Fischer, 2005). The framework includes, *inter alia*:

- A surplus objective of 1 per cent of GDP for the general government balance over the economic cycle.
- Multiannual nominal expenditure ceilings for the central government which cover three rolling years. The ceilings do not include interest expenditure and are defined so as to provide contingency margins for unexpected events and forecast errors. Since 2009, the expenditure ceiling has been part of the Budget Act.

The surplus objective is meant to provide room to cope with cyclical developments and with the implications of aging. Overall, the framework has proved to be successful in leading to prudent fiscal policy-making and a medium-term perspective in fiscal policy. In particular, the expenditure ceilings were respected and those set for the succeeding years were not revised upwards over time. Compliance with the spending limits has great political importance. The success of the ceilings may depend on their transparency: compliance can be easily evaluated. It may also depend on the top-down budgetary approach.

In Germany the crisis has been exploited as an opportunity for introducing significant reforms. The new fiscal framework uses some of the features of the Swiss debt brake to build up a setting which is very close to the EU fiscal rules. This Swiss fiscal rule was introduced in 2001 in order to bring debt dynamics under control after the significant increase observed during the 1990s.[5] At that time other rules were already in place: the Constitution called for a balanced budget and even for the elimination of the debt in the medium to long term (Bodmer, 2006). Nevertheless, in practice the absence of any sanction made these rules ineffective.

The debt-brake rule is based on limits to federal spending:[6] each year spending cannot exceed expected revenue times a measure of the cyclical position of the economy (given by the ratio between expected trend GDP and expected GDP).[7] The limit is therefore symmetric over the economic cycle (i.e. it is binding not only in bad times, but also in good times). In other words, the rule requires that:

- If the economy is moving along its trend, there has to be at worst a balanced budget
- In good times (when GDP is above its trend value), there has to be a surplus
- In bad times (when GDP is below its trend value), there can be a deficit.

This means that the expenditure limit can also be interpreted as a budget balance rule: it is very close to requiring a balanced budget over the economic cycle.

To compensate for forecast errors, the expenditure limit is recomputed *ex post*, based on actual revenue and the new assessment of the cyclical position of the economy. If actual expenditure is higher/lower than this *ex post* limit, the difference has to be debited/credited to a fictional account called 'adjustment account' and the balance of the account is subtracted/added to the expenditure limit for the following year. If the balance of the adjustment account is larger than 6 per cent of the previous year's spending, it must be brought under this threshold within three years.

Section 4 gives more details of the new German framework which is at present shaping the debate on national fiscal rules. It also considers the reform proposal currently under discussion in France.

---

[5] The new rule was supposed to come into force in 2003. Nevertheless, given that 2003 was a recession year, it was deemed necessary to introduce an adjustment path mechanism towards the adoption of the actual debt-brake mechanism, to be applied up to 2006.

[6] Some expenditure items may be excluded. In addition, cantons are excluded, but some cantons had already introduced their own debt-brake rules during the 1990s.

[7] If the elasticity of revenue to the output gap is equal to 1, the limit can also be interpreted as being equal to expected cyclically adjusted revenue.

4   Recent developments: the German rule and the French debate

After a long debate, in May 2009 Germany introduced a new fiscal rule which refers to the budget balance in cyclically adjusted terms. A debate on the introduction of a national rule similar to the German one is currently under way in France. The German rule and possibly the one prefigured in France leave open some issues which are dealt with in section 5.

Germany used to have a constitutionally based golden rule. The debate on the pros and cons of such a type of fiscal rule dates back at least to the 1930s. Overall, the cons seem stronger than the pros (Balassone and Franco, 2000; Baumann, Dönnebrink and Kastrop, 2008). In particular – with reference to the German rule embodied in the original draft of Article 115 of the German Constitution[8] – the Deutsche Bundesbank (Deutsche Bundesbank, 2007) stresses two weak points: the broad definition of capital spending (including government subsidies to public entities with limited returns) and the fact that depreciation of public assets and proceeds from asset sales are not deducted from capital spending in order to compute the borrowing limit.

On top of the uneasiness with certain aspects of the previous rule which had not prevented the accumulation of a large public debt, other factors led to the reform of the German fiscal framework: first, the need to have a framework fully consistent with the SGP; second, the request by the Federal Constitutional Court in 2007 for a revision of Article 115 in a ruling on the constitutionality of the 2004 Federal budget.[9] The Committee on the Modernisation of Financial Relations between the Federation and the States – established in March 2007 – was mandated to draft a new fiscal rule. The change in the Constitution was finally adopted by both Houses of Parliament in May 2009 and is complemented by a Federal law dealing with the details of its implementation. According to the rule, the deficit of the general government cannot exceed 0.35 per cent of GDP in cyclically adjusted terms. A transitional period has been defined: the deficit limit for the Federal government must be

---

[8] It stated that: 'Borrowing cannot exceed the total investment expenditure in the budget; exceptions are only allowed to avoid disturbances to the overall economic equilibrium.'

[9] For a description and an analysis of the new German fiscal rule, as well as of its motivation and development, see Baumann, Dönnebrink and Kastrop (2008); Deutsche Bundesbank (2009); Federal Ministry of Finance (2010); OECD (2010). For an analysis of the factors underlying the reform see Deutsche Bundesbank (2005, 2007). Positive and critical views are, respectively, expressed by and Mody and Stehn (2009) and Münchau (2009).

achieved by 2016, while the Länder will be prevented from running a structural deficit from 2020 onwards.[10]

Any error in setting the targets, in the forecasts and in the implementation of the budget has to be imputed as a debit/credit to an account called the control account. When debits exceed 1.5 per cent of GDP, corrective action must be taken.[11] The control account represents the main technical innovation with respect to the SGP: it provides a new answer to the need to run symmetric policies over the cycle.

The new German rule combines a number of traditional features (the objectives of fiscal sustainability and a balanced budget) with new elements (cyclical adjustment, the control and correction mechanism), drawn from the EU framework and from the experience of other countries. It envisages a balanced budget with temporary exceptions for two of the three factors indicated by Pigou (1928): the cycle and exceptional events. It includes mechanisms which should make fiscal policy symmetric over the cycle. It aims at making the German fiscal framework consistent with the EU framework and at combining prudent and sustainable fiscal policies with the need to avoid procyclicality. It focuses on general government, consistently with EU rules.

The new German framework presents several of the positive features indicated by Inman (1996) and Kopits and Symansky (1998):

- It is – *prima facie* (i.e. assuming that a cyclically adjusted balance can be defined precisely and unambiguously) – well defined and simple: the overall government deficit cannot exceed 0.35 per cent of GDP in cyclically adjusted terms.
- It must be complied with *ex post* and not only *ex ante*.
- It envisages some flexibility (for cyclical developments and exceptional events).
- It is constitutionally grounded and highly visible, thereby maximising the reputational costs for governments that do not respect it in the future.
- A qualified majority, although not a very large one (50 per cent of the seats), is required for the approval of special financing needs, which can only apply to exceptional events.
- Enforcement is allocated to the Constitutional Court.[12]

---

[10] Financial transactions (such as proceeds from privatisations) will be disregarded in the computation of the budget balance, consistently with EU fiscal regulations. This aspect is examined in Deutsche Bundesbank (2007).

[11] Article 115 specifies that 'debits exceeding the threshold of 1.5 per cent ... are to be reduced in accordance with the economic cycle'.

[12] It is also expected that the new rule will be underpinned by public finance reforms, in particular by the revision of the structure of the federal budget (Federal Ministry of Finance, 2009).

Some aspects of the reform may turn out to be problematic and deserve further analysis. The new framework envisages a deficit limit which may appear too tight. It abolishes the golden rule (which several economists advocate as the most useful fiscal rule). It is based on cyclically adjusted figures (which have sometimes proved rather problematic). It does not include an expenditure rule (which has been supported by several economists and institutions in recent years and which Guichard *et al.* (2007), deem an important complement to budget balance rules). It does not create a fully independent fiscal council (as advocated by several experts in recent years). These issues will be considered in section 5.

In France the budget balance target was enshrined in the Constitution in 2008. At the beginning of 2010 the French government set up a high-level working group – the Camdessus working group – to design a rule-based framework to achieve this target (Camdessus and Guidée, 2010; Groupe de travail présidé par Michel Camdessus, 2010). The working group outlined a rule which should credibly set medium-term objectives and provide operational tools to achieve them. The key provision is a mandatory multiyear framework for budget programming which would set budget targets also in cyclically adjusted terms: the yearly budget act would have to be consistent with medium-term targets and, in case of slippages, there would be an automatic correction mechanism echoing the German one. Importantly, the rule should apply to the whole of the general government.

The working group suggested that the rule should refer to the discretionary component of the cyclically adjusted balance, i.e. the share of spending and revenue over which legislators have control. Automatic stabilisers should be allowed to operate freely.

The working group also envisaged changes in the implementation of the budget and responses to deviations from the targets. A monitoring procedure would be defined in order to detect slippages during the budget year and specific amendments should then be introduced to compensate for the slippages. In case of detection of deviations from targets at the end of the year, a mechanism for automatically tightening the targets for the following years would be defined.

Given the key role of monitoring, the working group proposed that not only the Audit Court (*Cour des comptes*), but also an independent group of experts in the fiscal field should be in charge. This independent group would inform the public about fiscal developments and, in particular, about the soundness of the macroeconomic and fiscal forecasts on which the medium-term plans are based.

5   Open issues

The German rule and possibly the one prefigured in France leave some issues open concerning the size of the deficit limit, the role of cyclical developments, expenditure rules and independent fiscal institutions.

5.1   The deficit limit

The deficit limit the German rule refers to is close to balance. Given that in the coming years Germany – as well as many other countries – will have to set ambitious fiscal targets to rapidly reduce the debt ratio, a balanced budget or a surplus may be desirable. In this regard a tight limit for the cyclically adjusted balance is undoubtedly appropriate for a certain number of years.

Nevertheless, over a longer time span the deficit limit may turn out to be too tight: the 0.35 per cent limit is consistent with a debt ratio that is asymptotically very low. This outcome is similar to that envisaged by the adoption of the close-to-balance-or-in-surplus target in the context of the SGP. European countries targeting a surplus position would converge to negative debt levels. The policy stance thus implied may often be tighter than what is needed for sustainability by whatever definition: no definition of sustainability actually envisages the abolition of public debt.

The adoption of such an extreme solution in both the EU and in the German frameworks mainly reflects practical considerations. Even with the new rule, it will take some time before the German debt ratio reaches the 60 per cent threshold indicated by the EU fiscal framework. So it is prudent to have a rule aimed at helping the tightening of fiscal policy in the next decade or two when it is most needed, without worrying too much now about the need for adjusting the rule when the debt ratio will actually become too low.

The specific 0.35 per cent threshold has no economic foundation, but it makes German rules fully consistent with the SGP's precept of 'close to balance or in surplus'. It will help Germany to meet the demographic challenges ahead. Obviously, a similar deficit limit would be even more necessary for countries with higher debt ratios or more worrying age-related expenditure projections.

5.2   The role of cyclical developments

The policy debate in the 1990s and the 2000s has largely recognised that in normal circumstances automatic stabilisers ought to be allowed to operate freely and that, in order to avoid excessive debt accumulation, budgetary policy has to be symmetric over the economic cycle. This is one of the implicit core tenets of the EU fiscal framework, but the results have not been satisfactory in several countries. Discretionary fiscal action has generally been considered problematic in view of irreversibility and timing problems and of the uncertainty about its effects (European Commission, 2001). However, during the recession of 2009–10 – recognised as being of exceptional size and gravity – most countries took discretionary action.

In principle the new German rule guarantees full flexibility for the operation of automatic stabilisers. It also allows discretionary policies, provided there is room for manoeuvre in the budget *vis-à-vis* the deficit limit. The decision to use the methodology of the European Commission for estimating potential output increases transparency. However, the use of cyclically adjusted figures has sometimes proved problematic (Larch and Turrini, 2009). In particular, estimates of output gaps have frequently been revised, sometimes significantly (Koske and Pain, 2008; Tosetto, 2008). The OECD (2010) notes that the Commission's estimates for Germany have frequently been revised upwards (i.e. becoming less negative), in particular in the first two years following the budget year. This implies that the cyclical component has been overestimated, with an underestimation of the cyclically adjusted deficit. Revisions would not be problematic if they are symmetric.

Additional problems may arise from the fact that revenues sometimes fluctuate more than would be expected on the basis of the GDP cycle, for instance due to movements in asset and commodity prices (Morris and Schuknecht, 2007). Revenue windfalls and shortfalls – which explain a significant part of the changes in euro area cyclically adjusted budget balances in the period 1999–2007 – were mostly due to fluctuations in profit-related taxes (Morris *et al.*, 2009). These fluctuations cannot be easily dealt with by standard methodologies for cyclical adjustment. Revenue windfalls and shortfalls may offer room for expansionary policies in good times and require procyclical contractionary policies in bad times.

These problems do not suggest the abandonment of cyclically adjusted figures, rather their use with some degree of caution (Balassone and Kumar, 2007; Larch and Turrini, 2009). In particular, they suggest that the success of the new rule will depend on the prudent use of the margins offered by the control account. If the government builds up a safety margin in this account, which would operate as a fictional rainy-day fund (Balassone, Franco and Zotteri, 2009), unexpected revisions in output gaps and unexpected revenue developments would not trigger the need for corrective measures which might be politically and economically undesirable. Safety margins could also absorb errors in forecasts and unexpected increases in public expenditure.[13] Obviously, there is a risk that governments approaching elections may be tempted to reduce the safety margins. This problem is common to all medium-term frameworks, but the design of the German rule can help by making the erosion of the safety margins more evident (and therefore less likely). Independent scrutiny of fiscal policy and good information to the public would also be useful in tackling this problem.

5.3   Independent fiscal institutions

In recent years several economists have suggested that the role of independent agencies and committees in advising and even implementing fiscal policy should be enlarged (Eichengreen, Hausman and von Hagen, 1999; Banca d'Italia, 2001). These proposals draw on the experience of central banks running monetary policy. Like central banks, independent fiscal bodies should aim to deliver both long-term stability/sustainability and flexible short-term stabilisation.

Jonung and Larch (2006) show that in countries where the task of the preparation of the macroeconomic forecast underlying the budget is delegated to an independent authority, the macroeconomic forecasts have no significant bias (Austria, Belgium, the Netherlands) while the bias exists when the government is in charge. The issue was discussed in the debate concerning the reform of the SGP in 2005.[14] In 2010 it again came to the fore as one of the ingredients of the reform of EU governance. In particular, the van Rompuy task force (van Rompuy, 2010: 5) recommends 'the use or setting up [at the national level] of public institutions or bodies to provide independent analysis, assessments and forecasts on domestic fiscal policy matters as a way to reinforcing fiscal governance and ensuring long-term sustainability'.

Wyplosz (2002) suggests allocating to a Fiscal Policy Committee (FPC) the responsibility for setting the target of the budget balance on the basis of a debt sustainability constraint (defined by legislation/parliament) expressed either as an obligation to achieve a certain

---

[13] The relation between budgetary rules and forecasting uncertainty is examined in Deutsche Bundesbank (2007).

[14] In particular, the European Commission advocated independent forecasts (Jonung and Larch, 2006). The forecasts underlying the Stability/Convergence Programmes of some countries have frequently turned out to be optimistically biased (von Hagen, Hallerberg and Strauch, 2004). This can translate into higher-than-projected deficits, since government revenues quickly respond to changes in potential output whereas adjustments on the expenditure side normally require a lengthy process of political decision making.

budget balance over the cycle or to reduce/stabilise the debt ratio in line with the constraint over a given horizon. The FPC would be accountable to parliament, which would then decide which specific tax and expenditure policies were required to reach the target set for a given year by the Committee. Parliament would therefore retain control of the optimal debt level and intergenerational equity as well as of resource allocation and distribution.

Calmfors (2003) considers an alternative solution whereby parliament would delegate to the FPC the right to vary certain tax rates or government expenditure levels within predetermined margins. Parliament would decide the target for the budget balance over the cycle as well as the stabilisation policy objectives.[15]

However, the distinction between setting a target for the budget balance (to be entrusted to the FPC) and the allocative and distributive function (to remain the responsibility of government and parliament) may prove difficult. Decisions about the budget balance affect the composition of expenditure and revenues. All decisions are inherently political. In addition, the issue of the legitimacy of the powers of the committee is obviously very important. Calmfors (2003) examines some solutions to tackle it: appointments of the members of the FPC should be made by the government and be subject to approval by parliament; a high degree of transparency should be required of the FPC; parliament would carry out *ex post* evaluations of the committee's performance and have the possibility of overriding an individual decision by the FPC with a qualified majority.

Debrun, Hauner and Kumar (2007) survey the literature and examine the solutions implemented in a number of countries. They identify two types of bodies: independent fiscal authorities, which implement some aspects of fiscal policy, and fiscal councils, which undertake analysis, provide projections and advise on policy action. They note that so far no independent fiscal authority is in operation. On the other hand, in many countries there are fiscal councils contributing in different ways to the policy-making process.

In several EU countries independent councils contribute to fiscal policy in soft ways (European Commission, 2006). In Belgium the Federal Planning Bureau provides both macroeconomic and fiscal

---

[15] He also considers weaker forms of delegation of fiscal policy decisions aimed at macroeconomic stabilisation – such as, for instance, giving the FPC the power to control only a rainy-day stabilisation fund. This fund could be built up through specific tax receipts in booms and then run down through specific tax rebates in recessions. The committee would not interfere with the normal budget process, which would still be in charge of the allocation and distribution functions.

forecasts concerning the short, medium and long term. Forecasts, methods and models are published. The forecasting performance is assessed. The National Accounts Institute (to which several institutions contribute) coordinates the macroeconomic forecasts for the budget. The High Council of Finance, which is composed of high-level experts (academics, central banks, federal and regional administrations), formulates medium-term objectives for the balance of central government and the regions (Debrun, Hauner and Kumar, 2007). In other countries the macroeconomic forecasts are either prepared independently of government (Austria, the Netherlands) or assessed by independent bodies (Germany, Portugal).

In 2007 Sweden established a Fiscal Policy Council entrusted with the task of assessing the extent to which the government's fiscal policy objectives are being achieved. These objectives include long-run sustainability, the budget surplus target, the ceiling on central government expenditure and the consistency of fiscal policy with the cyclical situation of the economy (Swedish Fiscal Council, 2010). In 2008 Hungary created a Fiscal Council with the task of promoting the transparency and sustainability of the public finances (Kopits and Romhányi, 2010). The Council which conducted economic analysis and forecasting and monitored the consistency of the proposals and decisions of the government and of the parliament with the existing fiscal rules was abolished at the end of 2010. In 2009 with the introduction of the new fiscal rules Germany created a Stability Council (consisting of the Federal Ministers of Finance and Economy and the finance ministers of the Länder),[16] which replaces the Financial Planning Council and is charged with monitoring budgetary developments. Whenever the Council considers that a Federal or state government risks falling into financial distress, that government has to propose corrective measures; the Council is also expected to monitor the implementation of the consolidation plan. As already mentioned, in 2010 the UK set up the OBR to make an independent assessment of the public finances and the economy.

5.4   Expenditure rules

Since the late 1990s several European countries have introduced spending rules (e.g. Sweden, Finland and the Netherlands; see Wierts, Deroose and Moulin, 2005). While fiscal rules of this type may be problematic

---

[16] Even before the 2009 reform Germany had several councils in the fiscal domain mainly with forecasting and advising purposes. According to von Hagen (2010), these councils lack visibility and, more importantly, do not have a mandate for maintaining sustainable public finances and do not have any enforcement powers.

238   *Daniele Franco and Stefania Zotteri*

at the EU level (indeed there is no EU-wide consensus on the size and role of the public sector), they can be an effective national tool for pursuing fiscal discipline and sustainability and also for complying with EU rules. They may allow policy makers to agree not only on the budget balance but also upon the size of government, which especially in high-tax countries can be large.

There are several reasons for having expenditure rules (Banca d'Italia, 2001; Dában *et al.*, 2003; Deroose, Moulin and Wierts, 2006): (1) governments can control annual spending more than revenue and deficit; (2) expenditure rules are easy to explain to the public and to monitor; these features imply that expenditure rules can bring about more transparency and accountability; (3) expenditure rules do not hamper stabilisers on the revenue side, which is consistent with tax smoothing and cyclically adjusted targets; (4) expenditure rules can curb the tendency to increase spending in upturns, making them a useful complement to the SGP, which lacks incentives for fiscal discipline in good times; spending pressure is the main source of procyclicality and of the asymmetry of fiscal policy over the economic cycle (Balassone, Francese and Zotteri, 2010); (5) expenditure rules can link the annual budgetary process to a multiannual policy framework.

The debate on expenditure rules has highlighted a number of problematic features concerning the choice of the reference indicator and of the relevant spending items (Ljungman, 2008). First of all, expenditure rules can refer to a target which can be defined in either nominal or in real terms.[17] Second, expenditure rules can consider either primary or total spending: on the one hand, interest spending cannot be controlled and, on the other, it affects the budget balance and debt dynamics.[18] Third, should only current spending be targeted or also capital spending? The first option may induce the distortions typical of the golden rule. Another option would be to have separate and ring-fenced targets. Fourth, should cyclically sensitive spending be excluded? If it is included, the rule may lead to a procyclical policy. But the exclusion may raise some technical problems: for instance, how should spending for structural unemployment be considered? Fifth, should the rule cover only discretionary spending, thereby excluding entitlements? Pension and health spending are among the most important budgetary items: if they are excluded the

---

[17] The issue is relevant in cases where there are significant errors in inflation projections. The choice depends on the time horizon: nominal spending is probably more relevant over the short term; real spending is more relevant over the medium term.

[18] Again, the choice may depend on the time horizon: primary expenditure is probably more relevant over the short term; total spending is more relevant over the medium term.

spending target would not be very relevant. But if they are included, there may be enforcement problems: achieving the target may require structural reforms.

The fact that an explicit expenditure rule is not part of the German reform framework probably reflects Germany's success in controlling expenditure in recent years. The public expenditure-to-GDP ratio for Germany is now about 3 percentage points below the euro area average. Other countries may consider that the control of public expenditure is relatively more urgent: an expenditure rule can help to make this urgency more visible. As in Sweden, this rule should complement (not replace) the rule for the budget balance.

6   The future

The need to restrain public deficits and debts, the pressure from financial markets and the strengthening of the EU fiscal framework will induce many European countries to modify their fiscal rules and institutions. Reforms are likely to make national frameworks more consistent with European rules and to increase their medium-term orientation. As shown by the debate in France, the new German rule represents a reference point for the policy debate. But solutions can also be different. In countries where budgetary problems largely stem from difficulties in keeping expenditure in check, an expenditure rule can play an important role, in parallel with a balanced budget rule. In some countries independent institutions can supply forecasts, provide advice and monitor fiscal developments. Once rules and priorities are well defined, there is greater room for an independent assessment. Imposing a balanced budget on subnational governments can be part of the solution to intergovernmental coordination problems. But other options are available. For instance, some countries have experimented with Internal Stability Pacts, which usually include sanctions and correction mechanisms.

Fiscal rules can make policies more time-consistent, contribute to fiscal discipline and facilitate stabilisation. But rules are not a magic wand. Governments can choose to override (either explicitly or implicitly) their own rules. A number of factors (cyclical developments, unexpected shocks, structural changes) may require adjustments of the rules, which can endanger their credibility. Rules can only work if they are grounded on a comprehensive fiscal framework and high standards of transparency. They can be successfully implemented over a long period of time only if public opinion considers them a valuable contribution to policy making.

References

Advisory Commission on Inter-governmental Relations (1987). 'Fiscal discipline in the federal system: national reform and the experience of the states', Washington, DC

Ayuso-i-Casals, J. (2010). 'National fiscal governance reforms across EU member states', European Economy Occasional Papers, No. 67

Ayuso-i-Casals, J., D. G. Hernández, L. Moulin and A. Turrini (2007). 'Beyond the SGP: features and effects of EU national-level fiscal rules', in Banca d'Italia (ed.), *Fiscal Policy: Current Issues and Challenges*, Rome

Balassone, F., M. Francese and S. Zotteri (2010). 'Cyclical asymmetry in fiscal variables in the EU', *Empirica*, 37(4): 381–402

Balassone, F. and D. Franco (2000). 'Public investment, the Stability Pact and the golden rule', *Fiscal Studies*, 21(2): 207–29

  (2001). 'EMU fiscal rules: a new answer to an old question?', in Banca d'Italia (ed.), *Fiscal Policy: Current Issues and Challenges*, Rome

Balassone, F., D. Franco and S. Zotteri (2009). 'Rainy day funds: can they make a difference in Europe?', in J. Ayuso-i-Casals, S. Deroose, E. Flores and L. Moulin (eds.), *Policy Instruments for Sound Fiscal Policies*, Basingstoke: Palgrave Macmillan

Balassone, F. and M. Kumar (2007). 'Cyclicality of fiscal policy', in M. S. Kumar and T. Ter-Minassian (eds.), *Promoting Fiscal Discipline*, Washington, DC: IMF

Banca d'Italia (ed). (2001). *Fiscal Rules*, Rome

  (2007). *Fiscal Policy: Current Issues and Challenges*, Rome

Baumann, E., E. Dönnebrink and C. Kastrop (2008). 'A concept for a new budget rule for Germany', CESifo Forum, No. 2

Bodmer, F. (2006). The Swiss debt brake: how it works and what can go wrong', *Schweizerische Zeitschrift für Volkswirtschaft und Statistik*, 142(3): 307–30

Buchanan, J. M. (1997). 'The balanced budget amendment: clarifying the arguments', *Public Choice*, 90: 117–38

Calmfors, L. (2003). 'Fiscal policy to stabilise the domestic economy in EMU: what can we learn from monetary policy?', *CESifo Economic Studies*, 49(3): 319–53

Camdessus, M. and R. Guidée (2010). 'By the rule', *Finance & Development*, 47(3): 38–9

Council of the European Union (2005), *Presidency Conclusions*, Brussels, 22–23 March

Dabán, T., E. Detragiache, G. Di Bella, G. M. Milesi-Ferretti and S. Symansky (2003). 'Rules-based fiscal policy in France, Germany, Italy and Spain', IMF Occasional Paper, No. 225

Danninger, S. (2002). 'A new rule: the Swiss debt brake', IMF Working Paper, No. 18

Debrun, X., D. Hauner and M. S. Kumar (2007). 'The role for fiscal agencies', in M. S. Kumar and T. Ter-Minassion (eds.), *Promoting Fiscal Discipline*, Washington, DC: IMF

Deroose, S., L. Moulin and P. Wierts (2006). 'National expenditure rules and expenditure outcomes: empirical evidence for EU member states', *Wirschaft-spolitische Blätter*, 53(1): 27–43

Deutsche Bundesbank (2005). 'Deficit-limiting budgetary rules and a national stability pact in Germany', *Monthly Report*, 57: 23–37

(2007). 'Reform of German budgetary rules', *Monthly Report*, 59: 47–68

(2009). 'The reform of the borrowing limits for central and state government', *Monthly Report*, 61: 78–9

Eichengreen, B., R. Hausmann and J. von Hagen (1999). 'Reforming budgetary institutions in Latin America: the case for a national fiscal council', *Open Economies Review*, 10: 415–42

European Commission (2001). 'Public finances in EMU', *European Economy*, 3

(2006). 'Public finances in EMU', *European Economy*, No. 3

(2010a). 'Reinforcing economic policy coordination', Communication from the Commission, 12 May

(2010b). 'Enhancing economic policy coordination for stability, growth and jobs: tools for stronger EU economic governance', Communication from the Commission, 30 June

(2010c). 'Strengthening economic governance in the EU: proposals for Council Regulations', 29 September

Federal Ministry of Finance (2009). 'Detailed concept for the new federal budget', www.bundesfinanzministerium.de/nn_4318/DE/Wirtschaft_und_Verwaltung/Finanz_und_Wirtschaftspolitik/Neue_Steuerungsinstrumente/020709_Feinkonzept_1_Zusammenfassung_engl,templateId=raw,property=publicationFile.pdf

(2010). 'German Stability Programme – January 2010 update'

Fischer, J. (2005), 'Swedish budget rules: praise from Brussels, pressure at home', *ECFIN Country Focus*, 2(4)

Groupe de travail présidé par Michel Camdessus (2010). *Rapport – Réaliser l'objectif constitutionnel d'équilibre des finances publiques*, 21 June

Guichard, S., M. Kennedy, E. Wurzel and C. André (2007). 'What promotes fiscal consolidation: OECD country experiences', OECD Economics Department Working Paper, No. 553

HM Treasury (2008). Pre-Budget Report, November

Inman, R. P. (1996). 'Do balanced budget rules work? US experience and possible lessons for the EMU', NBER Working Paper, No. 5838

Inter-American Development Bank (IADB) (1997). *Fiscal Stability with Democracy and Stabilization, Report on Economic and Social Progress in Latin America*, Washington, DC: Johns Hopkins University Press for the Inter-American Development Bank

Jonung, L. and M. Larch (2006). 'Improving fiscal policy in the EU: the case for independent forecasts', *European Economy Economic Papers*, No. 210

Kopits, G. (2007). 'Fiscal responsibility framework', *Public Finance Quarterly*, No. 2: 205–22

Kopits, G. and B. Romhányi (2010). 'Lessons from Hungary', Paper presented to Conference on Independent Fiscal Institutions, Fiscal Council Republic of Hungary, Budapest, 18–19 March

Kopits, G. and S. Symansky (1998). 'Fiscal policy rules', IMF Occasional Paper, No. 162

Koske, I. and N. Pain (2008). 'The usefulness of output gaps for policy analysis', OECD Economics Department Working Paper, No. 621

Kumar, M. S., and T. Ter-Minassian (eds.) (2007). *Promoting Fiscal Discipline*, Washington, DC: IMF

Larch, M. and A. Turrini (2009). 'The cyclically-adjusted budget balance in EU fiscal policy making: love at first sight turned into a mature relationship', *European Economy Economic Papers*, No. 374

Ljungman, G. (2008). 'Expenditure ceilings: a survey', IMF Working Paper, No. 282

Mody, A. and S. J. Stehn (2009). 'Germany's new fiscal rule: a responsible approach to fiscal sustainability', www.voxeu.org, 11 August

Morris, R., C. R. Braz, F. de Castro, S. Jonk, J. Kremer, S. Linehan, M. R. Marino, C. Schalck and O. Tkacevs (2009). 'Explaining government revenue windfalls and shortfalls: an analysis for selected EU countries', ECB Working, Paper, No. 1114

Morris, R., and L. Schuknecht (2007). 'Structural balances and revenue windfalls: the role of asset prices revisited', ECB Working Paper, No. 737

Münchau, W. (2009). 'Berlin weaves a deficit hair-shirt for us all', *Financial Times*, 21 June

OECD (2010). Germany, *OECD Economic Surveys*, 9

Pigou, A. C. (1928). *A Study in Public Finance*, London: Macmillan

Swedish Fiscal Council (2010). 'Swedish Fiscal Policy', 17 May

Tosetto, E. (2008). 'Revisions of quarterly output gap estimates for 15 OECD member countries', OECD, Statistics Directorate, 26 September

van Rompuy Task Force on Economic Governance (2010). *'Strengthening economic governance in the EU'*, *Final Report of the Task Force to the European Council*, Brussels, 21 October, www.consilium.europa.eu/uedocs/cms-data/docs/pressdata/en/ec/117236.pdf

von Hagen, J. (2010). 'The scope and limits of fiscal councils', Paper presented at the conference on Fiscal Councils organised by the Fiscal Council of Hungary, Budapest, 18–19 March

von Hagen, J., M. Hallerberg and R. Strauch (2004). 'Budgetary forecasts in Europe: the track record of stability and convergence programmes', ECB Working Paper, No. 307

Wierts, P. (2007). 'How do expenditure rules affect fiscal behaviour?', in Banca d'Italia (ed.), *Fiscal Policy: Current Issues and Challenges*, Rome

Wierts, P., S. Deroose and L. Moulin (2005), 'National expenditure rules and expenditure outcomes: empirical evidence for EU member states', *Wirtschaftspolitischer Blätter*, 53(1): 27–41

Wyplosz, C. (2002). 'Fiscal policy: institutions versus rules', CEPR Discussion Paper, No. 3238

13   The road to better resolution: from bail-out to bail-in

*Thomas F. Huertas**

1   Introduction

Better resolution forms a key component of the cure against future crises – along with better regulation, better supervision and better macroeconomic policy (Huertas, 2010a). This chapter outlines a possible path toward better resolution for large, systemically important financial firms.

Achieving better resolution of such firms is essential. 'Too big to fail' is too costly to continue, and ways must be found to assure that failing banks can be resolved at no cost to the taxpayer and limited cost to society at large. 'Too big to fail' distorts competition, creates moral hazard and threatens the public finances. The foundations for moving away from 'too big to fail' are being laid: they are the introduction of special resolution regimes for banks and the requirement that banks prepare 'living wills' (recovery and resolution plans). On top of these foundations now needs to be built a means of resolving large, complex cross-border banks without equity support from taxpayers. Bail-in offers the promise of such a solution, and this chapter analyses how that promise might be fulfilled.

Much is riding on the outcome. If bail-in can work, too big to fail can become a relic of the past. If bail-in cannot be made to work, the case for structural solutions (make banks smaller or make banks simpler) would become more compelling, as might the case for taxes on banks to

* The author is Alternate Chair, European Banking Authority (EBA), and Member, Executive Committee, Financial Services Authority (FSA) (UK). The opinions expressed in this chapter are made in the author's personal capacity and do not necessarily represent the views of either the EBA or the FSA. An earlier version of this chapter was presented to the conference, 'The Euro Area and the Financial Crisis', held at the National Bank of Slovakia, Bratislava, 6–8 September 2010, under the auspices of the National Bank of Slovakia, the Heriot–Watt University of Edinburgh and the Comenius University of Bratislava. This revised version benefits greatly from the comments made at the conference by Philip Hartmann as well as from subsequent comments from Stephen Strongin and Michael Krimminger. Stephen Drayson, John Thompson and Matt Lucas have also provided significant inputs into the chapter. All errors are the responsibility of the author.

pre-fund the resolution expenditures that might be required to bail out banks in the future.

2   The probability of bail-out determines risk

For any private sector creditor the risk that the creditor will incur a loss is a product of three things:[1]

(a) The probability that the obligor will (absent a bail-out) have to default on its payments to the creditor (*PD*)

(b) The probability that a bail-out will occur (*PB*)

(c) The loss given either bail-out (*LGB*) or default (*LGD*).

A simple example shows the dramatic impact that the possibility of bail-out can have upon the expected loss associated with a credit. Take the case where there are two borrowers, 'Likely to be rescued' and 'Likely to be abandoned'. Each has a probability of default of 20 per cent and a loss given default of 25 per cent. If a bail-out occurs, the loss given bail-out is zero. The only difference between the two borrowers is the market's estimate of the probability that the authorities will bail out the institution, if intervention is required.[2] For 'Likely to be rescued' the probability of bail-out is 95 per cent. For 'Likely to be abandoned' the probability of bail-out is 5 per cent. For the former the expected loss is 25 basis points; for the latter, the expected loss is 475 basis points. This dramatic difference in expected loss will lead to significant differences in the risk premiums that the two borrowers would have to pay.

This simple example suggests two things: (1) that the analysis of the probability of bail-out is integral to credit analysis; and (2) that changes in the market's estimate of that probability can have significant effects on the spreads that borrowers will have to pay. If the change in the estimate of probability is either sudden or large, the consequent change in the spreads that borrowers would have to pay can adversely affect the economy at large.

3   Estimating the probability of bail-out

The probability of bail-out depends on two factors – the ability and the willingness of a possible guarantor to bail out the borrower in question. In

---

[1] The expected loss may be expressed as $EL = PD \{PB^*LGB + (1 - PB)^*LGD\}$ and the risk premium demanded in the market will be a function of the expected loss. Note that the probability of default and the loss given default (without bail-out) may be positively correlated.

[2] Note that this market estimate may differ from the probability that the authorities themselves would assign to the possibility that they would bail out the institution, should intervention be required.

some cases, legislation attempts to prohibit or limit the scope of guarantors who would be able to bail out borrowers from doing so. Examples are the Maastricht Treaty restrictions on the European Central Bank (ECB) and the Dodd–Frank Act restrictions on the Federal Deposit Insurance Corporation (FDIC) and other US authorities. In other cases legislation mandates that possible guarantors support borrowers, even though one or more of those guarantors might be unable to do so.

But there are limits to the constraints that a legislative authority can impose on its successors. Even if no bail-out rules exist, authorities have found ways to bail out borrowers. Governments have injected equity into banks to prevent their failure/closure; and Eurozone member states have created a financial solidarity pact to underpin the ability of such member states to meet their sovereign obligations.

So it is in order for market participants to conduct some analysis of the authorities' ability and willingness to conduct a bail-out. Ability is a question of relative resources: does the possible guarantor have sufficient resources to provide a bail-out at the time the bail-out might be required? Will the bail-out compromise the ability of the guarantor to meet its own obligations? Such questions can be answered via classic credit analysis under the assumption that the possible guarantor is obliged to bail out the borrower, and such analysis can also shed light on the most cost-effective method for the guarantor to implement the bail-out.

The willingness of the possible guarantor to bail out the borrower is more difficult to analyse. A starting point is a simple extrapolation of past behaviour. If an authority has executed a bail-out in the past, the market is likely to conclude that the authority will act in a similar manner in the future if presented with a similar situation.[3]

Such a simple extrapolation could be expanded to include the cost-benefit analysis (CBA) that the possible guarantor might conduct if presented with the question of whether or not to bail out a borrower. This would compare the benefit of the bail-out with the costs of providing the bail-out. The benefits of bail-out relative to no bail-out are generally considered to be greater financial stability, higher output and higher employment. The costs of bail-out should at a minimum be the financial cost of the bail-out itself. Ideally, however, the costs of providing a bail-out should also include the knock-on effects of the bail-out: reduced financial flexibility for the guarantor, and greater expectation among market participants that bail-outs would become the norm – a factor

---

[3] If market participants do in fact extrapolate past behaviour by the authorities, it is exceedingly difficult for the authorities to pursue a policy of constructive ambiguity. Such a policy assumes that the market is genuinely in doubt as to whether or not the authority would or would not execute a bail-out.

that could actually promote future crises. Focusing solely on immediate benefits and costs (which are more certain and more likely to materialise during the term in office of the official decision-maker) biases the results of the cost-benefit test in favour of bail-outs.

4   The impact of sudden changes in the market's estimate of the probability of bail-outs

Unexpected and sudden reductions in the market's estimate of the probability of bail-outs can have severe and immediate adverse consequences. As our simple example shows, a sudden shift in the estimated probability of bail-out from 95 per cent to 5 per cent would dramatically raise the expected loss (and therefore the risk premium) on credits extended to the firm. This would raise the cost of funding to the firm and reduce the availability of funds to the firm.

Such an abrupt reversal is exactly what happened in September 2008. On 14 September the US authorities ordered the parent holding company of Lehmans to file for bankruptcy (Paulson, 2010: 220). This abruptly reversed the pattern of protecting large systemically important firms that had been established first through the rescue of Bear Stearns (March 2008) and then through the conservatorship of Fannie Mae and Freddie Mac (September 2008).

The resolution of Washington Mutual (WaMu) on 25 September further compounded the situation. Although the FDIC followed US law in applying the least-cost resolution method to resolve WaMu, the resulting losses to unsecured creditors of the bank surprised many market participants,[4] and made investors nervous about placing funds in troubled banks, even on an overnight basis.

Further pressures on funding arose from the introduction of the Troubled Asset Relief Program (TARP). In seeking the funds from Congress, the US administration highlighted that it had exhausted its budgetary authority to save troubled institutions and outlined the dire consequences that would arise if Congress failed to enact the proposal. Yet Congress

---

[4] Although WaMu was a very large bank – with over $300 billion in assets, nearly $200 billion in deposits and 2,200 branches in fifteen different states – the FDIC did not invoke the systemic risk exemption allowable under US legislation (FDICIA) but resolved WaMu under the least-cost resolution method as prescribed by FDICIA. JPMorgan Chase bought the insured deposits as well as certain assets and liabilities of the insured bank subsidiaries of WaMu in an auction conducted by the FDIC. The premium paid was $1.9 billion. Left behind were the assets and liabilities of the parent holding company as well as the unsecured debt of the operating bank subsidiaries, including uninsured deposits over the coverage limit of $100,000. These creditors were exposed to serious loss.

did initially reject TARP on 29 September, creating the spectre that even the US would be too small to save its financial institutions. Congress did finally enact TARP on 3 October, but it then became apparent that the Administration did not have a plan in place to implement TARP quickly.

The reversal in the market's assessment of US intervention/resolution policy was not an example of contagion. The failure of Lehmans did not cause payments, clearing and settlement infrastructures to fail. In fact, they held up rather well.[5] Nor did the failure of Lehmans or WaMu cause losses to other market participants which were in themselves so grave as to deplete the capital and/or liquidity of the counterparty in question. What the failure of Lehmans did do was to underline to market participants that the US government would not necessarily stand behind other broker dealers. What the resolution of WaMu did was to underline that the US government would set a very high bar indeed for invocation of the systemic risk exemption in the Federal Deposit Insurance Corporation Improvement Act (FDICIA) legislation, and that the US authorities would seek to resolve even very large institutions by reference to the cost to the deposit guarantee fund rather than the cost to society as a whole.[6]

Instead of contagion, the failure of Lehmans and the decision to employ the least-cost method to resolve WaMu were more akin to an undersea earthquake that set off a massive tsunami in financial markets. This tsunami had severe knock-on effects on specific institutions, on financial markets as a whole and on the economy at large. The most immediate effect of the Lehmans failure was to underline that the stand-alone investment bank was not viable. If the government let Lehmans fail, it dramatically increased the probability that it would allow other

---

[5] In part, this statement depends on the decision to prop up the US broker dealer subsidiary for a few extra days through emergency liquidity assistance from the Federal Reserve. This allowed Barclays to conduct accelerated due diligence on the assets and liabilities of the US broker dealer and to buy selected assets and liabilities of Lehmans. However, even in the UK, where the subsidiaries went immediately into administration, the infrastructures held up well. LCH.Clearnet, for example, was able to use margin posted by Lehmans to liquidate its positions without having to have recourse to the default fund.

[6] The FDICIA legislation contained a so-called systemic risk exemption that allowed the FDIC to provide open bank assistance to a failing bank provided this was judged necessary by the FDIC, approved by a super-majority of the Board of Governors of the Federal Reserve System and also approved by the Secretary of the Treasury 'in consultation with the President'. The first time this systemic risk exemption was invoked was on the weekend of 26 September in connection with the proposed acquisition of Wachovia by Citigroup. However, this deal was never completed, as Wells Fargo made a superior offer that allowed Wachovia to be resolved without cost to the FDIC. The net result was a lack of clarity as to when the US government would invoke the systemic risk exemption and a lack of clarity as to whether the US authorities would or could stick by deals that were initially struck in a crisis situation.

stand-alone investment banks to fail as well. Consequently, it made sense for investors to move their free cash balances and securities portfolios away from such entities toward entities associated with commercial banks (which were reckoned to have a higher degree of government support).

This started as soon as the markets opened on 15 September and continued throughout the week. The pressure was particularly intense on Morgan Stanley (whose credit default swap spread soared from 245 basis points (bp) on 12 September to 883 bp on 18 September) and Goldman Sachs (whose credit default swap spread rose from 183 bp on 12 September to 548 bp on 18 September). The pressure on Morgan Stanley and Goldman Sachs began to abate only after each had announced new equity infusions from third-party investors and their conversion into bank holding companies subject to oversight and supervision by the Federal Reserve with access to liquidity facilities from the latter.

In contrast, the pressure on Merrill Lynch in the wake of Lehmans was not as great, despite much greater problems at the firm itself than at either Morgan Stanley or Goldman Sachs. The credit default swap rate on Merrills actually fell (from 455 bp to 398 bp) – evidence consistent with the hypothesis that the market expected Bank of America to support Merrills (in line with the merger agreement announced on 14 September) and the Fed, if need be, to support Bank of America.

Although stand-alone investment banks were the institutions most directly affected, the tsunami unleashed by the decision to force Lehmans into bankruptcy caused havoc in financial markets generally. It led to an immediate re-pricing of risk, to a flight to quality and to a run away from institutions judged most likely to require intervention. These runs brought forward the point at which various institutions ran out of liquidity and accelerated the requirement for the authorities to intervene. Immediately after the failure of Lehmans, the LIBOR–OIS spread began to climb into the stratosphere, rising from an already elevated level of 75 bp on 12 September to 116 bp on 18 September. In this environment, institutions such as HBOS and WaMu with challenged credit portfolios and a high degree of reliance on short-term wholesale funding were particularly vulnerable, and they required, one after the other, some type of intervention.

The manner in which the US authorities resolved WaMu (although consistent with FDICIA) surprised the market and further aggravated the situation. The decision to impose losses on unsecured senior creditors and uninsured depositors was akin to a severe aftershock that unleashed a new tsunami. There was a renewed scramble for liquidity, with a flight to quality and away from institutions that had problematic asset and/or funding positions, such as Wachovia in the US, Bradford and Bingley in the UK and Fortis, Dexia, HRE and the Icelandic banks in the European Economic Area (EEA). In the days following the resolution of WaMu, the LIBOR–OIS spread raced further toward the sky, rising from 152 bp on 26 September to 201 bp on 8 October. Together the resolutions of Lehmans and WaMu had substantially reduced the market's estimate of the probability that the authorities would bail out a firm requiring resolution. This created a vast scramble in financial markets for liquidity.

This scramble for liquidity set off a vicious debt–deflation cycle in the economy as a whole. To raise liquidity, banks began to sell off good assets and to contract the amount of credit that they extended. Firms began to run down inventories, slash investment expenditures, curtail production and cut jobs. Consumers stopped spending on durables such as cars, furniture and appliances and cancelled or curtailed vacations, entertainment and dining out. As a result, the world economy went into free fall. Output declined in the fourth quarter of 2008 and the first quarter of 2009 at a rate that was even faster than the rate of deterioration in the economy at the start of the Great Depression.

5   The need for an 'exit strategy'

There is ample recognition that it is unsustainable to continue fiscal and monetary stimulus on the scale implemented in 2008Q4 and throughout 2009. Finance ministries and central banks need to develop an 'exit strategy', and the first signs of this are already apparent (Bernanke, 2010).

But this 'exit strategy' must encompass resolution as well. It is unsustainable for governments to continue to promise that no systemically important institution will be allowed to fail. Such a promise is unsustainable, for two reasons. First, it removes market discipline from such institutions. That increases the probability that systemically important institutions will require intervention and that governments will be required to perform on the guarantee that they have given to such institutions. Second, the promise is unsustainable simply because of the potential expense involved. In many countries, the total balance sheet of the largest financial institutions is a multiple of the GDP of the country in which they are headquartered. Even if governments were willing to shoulder the responsibility of standing behind the liabilities of financial institutions headquartered in their country, they might not have the means to do so and/or they might not secure the political authorisation for the spending that would be required in order to meet such commitments of support.

We must move away from a policy of full support for systemically important financial institutions in a measured, considered way, lest we be forced to do so abruptly and repeat the mistakes made in the case of

Lehmans and WaMu. We need to map out what our long-term resolution policy should be, and consider how we will take steps to move from where we are today to where we need to be.

6   What should our resolution policy be?

Ideally, we want a resolution policy that allows governments to resolve institutions promptly without recourse to taxpayer funds, but at the same time minimises the social disruption that could occur from widespread interruption to deposit, insurance and/or securities accounts. This would allow for maximum continuity in customer-related activities while ensuring that capital providers remain exposed to loss and avoiding the need to give widespread or long-lasting guarantees of the bank's liabilities. Such a solution would also avoid the problems that arise from abruptly unplugging a bank from payments, clearing and settlement infrastructures. It would also allow for deposit accounts to be maintained, and revolving credit arrangements to continue functioning. In effect, such a solution would amount to an accelerated, but solvent, wind down of the bank through rapid sales of certain aspects of the bank's activities to third parties and through a rapid reduction in certain activities. That would leave customers largely unaffected, but impose losses on investors/capital providers.[7]

To ascertain how we can approach this ideal, the authorities have asked a number of large banks to prepare so-called 'living wills', or recovery and resolution plans.[8] With respect to resolution what living wills ask banks to do in advance is to make preparations so that the bank would be able to furnish at short notice the information that the authorities would need in order to make a choice among the resolution methods open to the authorities to use, should the condition of the bank deteriorate to the point where they have to intervene. The actual resolution plan (choice among resolution methods) is for the authorities to develop.

Although the pilots are not yet complete, it is perhaps not too early to draw some tentative hypotheses about what should be concluded.

6.1   *The task remains important*

As outlined above, it is unsustainable to continue 'too big to fail'. We need to move away from the notion that large systemically important firms will

---

[7] For a fuller discussion of the difference between customer and investor capital see Merton and Perold (1993) and Huertas (2010c).

[8] For a fuller discussion of living wills see Huertas (2010b).

always be rescued. The market must come to expect that resolution, not rescue, is the probable outcome, if a bank's condition deteriorates to the point where intervention is required.

Such a change in the market's view must be well prepared. Simply switching over a weekend from 'bail-out' to 'no bail-out' will not work. The US tried that with Lehmans, and it brought the world economy to the brink of meltdown. We have to develop a method of resolving large, complex financial institutions that will not involve either significant taxpayer support or massive social costs, and it has to be accepted in advance that the authorities will employ this method to resolve such a firm, should the firm no longer meet threshold conditions (minimum regulatory requirements).

If resolution is not a realistic option for large systemically important firms, then it must be questioned as to whether firms should be allowed to become so large or so complex that they become systemic. That would point toward measures (surcharges on capital and liquidity requirements, taxes, limits on size and/or activity, etc.) that would force firms to become smaller and/or simpler. Conversely, if resolution is a realistic option, the need for structural reform would diminish and possibly disappear.

6.2   *A special resolution regime is essential*

Banks are not well suited to be resolved under normal corporate bankruptcy or insolvency procedures. Unlike non-financial corporations there is no ready way for a bank to continue to operate while in bankruptcy. This means that normal bankruptcy procedures in the case of a bank effectively amount to the liquidation of the bank – a process that almost always implies significantly higher costs than a resolution process that allows the firm to continue to operate.

For this reason it makes sense to impose a special resolution regime for banks. This has two aspects:
(a) Determination of the trigger point: this should be the point at which the supervisor determines that the bank no longer has adequate resources (e.g. capital, liquidity) to meet its obligations.
(b) Choice and implementation of a resolution method: the resolution regime provides the resolution authority with a range of methods that it can use to resolve a bank rapidly, if the supervisor reaches a decision that intervention is required. This allows the resolution authority to act within the time-frame required (at most over a weekend, and possibly overnight).

Table 13.1: *Overview of resolution methods*

	Taxpayer support	Immediate impact/cost	Long-term impact/ cost (moral hazard)	Going/gone concern
Options under SRR				
Liquidation/deposit payoff	None	Very high	Eliminates moral hazard	Gone
Deposit transfer/ bridge bank	Limited	High	Improves market discipline and reduces cost	Gone
Share transfer/TPO	To be decided	To be decided	To be decided	Going
Early equity injection	Very high	Limited	High (increases moral hazard)	Going

Source: Author.
Note: SRR-Special resolution regime.

6.3   *Existing resolution options are insufficient to deal with systemically important firms*

Broadly speaking, there are three methods of intervention/resolution open to the authorities under special resolution regimes, if they reach a determination that they must intervene (Table 13.1). These are liquidation/deposit payoff, deposit transfer/bridge bank and share transfer (temporary public ownership, TPO). Each involves a combination of taxpayer support, immediate impact and long-term market impact. None of the available methods is satisfactory for a large, systemically important bank, and for this reason the authorities opted during the crisis for a fourth method, early equity injection, that lies outside the special resolution regime.

Liquidation and depositor payoff is as yet not readily implementable for a large, systemically important bank, particularly for one with millions of retail deposit accounts and/or very large provision of credit to small and medium-sized enterprises (SMEs). In addition to the differentially higher losses that would result from allowing the bank to become a gone concern, there would be severe knock-on effects from any delay in depositors' having access to their funds[9] and from SMEs having to

---

[9] The speed with which depositors receive their money depends to a large extent on the capability of the deposit guarantee scheme to pay out insured depositors promptly. Under the proposed revisions to the EU Deposit Guarantee Schemes Directive (DGSD) deposit guarantee schemes in member states would have to be able to pay out insured deposits within twenty-one days of the failure of a bank. This will require streamlining the procedures in the deposit guarantee schemes of many member states as well as changes

seek replacements for lines of credit that they had previously obtained from the failed bank. To some extent these immediate costs are reduced if the authorities can put customer activities into a bridge bank and/or transfer deposits to a healthy bank. This allows for continuity of client business and avoids a good portion of the knock-on effects associated with liquidation and deposit payoff. But such a split of activities is very difficult to carry out quickly, particularly for large, complex, internationally active banks with significant numbers of transaction accounts and/or large derivative books. Such a split implies that some portion of the bank becomes a gone concern and that some taxpayer and/or central bank support may be required in connection with assuring that the 'good bank' remains so.

The third method of resolution, share transfer or TPO, preserves the bank as a going concern, but effectively requires the taxpayer to guarantee the obligations of the failed bank and may require the taxpayer to inject new equity into it. This avoids the immediate economic repercussions that the failure of the bank would otherwise have caused, but adds to government obligations and weakens the government's credit standing. This has long-term implications as well. Market participants will regard the intervention as confirming the government's willingness to bail out banks but as weakening its ability to do so, should further banks require assistance in the immediate future.

Early equity injection avoids some of these pitfalls. Under this method the government supports the bank without triggering the special resolution regime, so that the bank does not fail at all. This completely ensures the continued operation of the bank and avoids measures such as closing out derivative transactions that can impose large costs on the bank itself and its counterparties. Formally, the equity injection is also voluntary, in the sense that it is approved by the shareholders of the bank and/or its board of directors. In some cases, the government provides the offer of equity as back-up underwriter – the bank is free to obtain equity from private sources if it can do so. The early equity injection may also avoid the government's having to take full ownership of the bank. This reduces the prospect that the bank's obligations will be fully regarded as government obligations – a factor that enables the government to retain a higher degree of financial flexibility.

However, early equity injection effectively bails out preferred stockholders, subordinated debtholders and other forms of investor capital

to the data management procedures of banks themselves. It will also require assurances that the deposit guarantee scheme has immediate access to adequate funds. For a further discussion see Huertas (2010a: Chapter 8).

such as senior debt that private market participants had provided to banks. The only capital provider to suffer is the common shareholder – s/he suffers death by dilution, and even this may be delayed or avoided if the government provides new equity in the form of preferred stock or a similar instrument that the bank may subsequently redeem. Under an early equity injection, the taxpayer effectively takes the risk that the bank will not recover, rather than the private providers of non-equity capital to the bank. This weakens market discipline and creates moral hazard as well as potentially undermining the public finances.

6.4   Minimising the social cost of resolution depends on preserving customer activity

The social costs associated with the failure of a large, complex financial institution depend critically on whether or not the institution remains able to meet its customer obligations, such as payments on deposits and settlements on foreign exchange (FX), securities and derivative transactions.

Such customer liabilities should be distinguished sharply from what might be called 'investor capital'. Some investor capital is plainly labelled as capital. Preferred stock and subordinated debt are examples. The motivation for such an investment is the return on the instrument relative to the reward that the instrument provides. There are no services associated with the instrument, and the instrument does not provide the investor with protection against other risks (as derivatives would do). Arguably, long-term senior debt is also 'investor capital', although this is in most cases *pari passu* with some or all customer liabilities.

6.5   Speed counts

In resolving systemically important firms, speed counts. There is a very narrow window between the close of business on one day and the opening of business on the next when business stops and the books of a large, systemically important firm can potentially be closed. At weekends this window may extend to as much as thirty-six hours – the time between the close of business in North America on Friday and the opening of business in Asia on Monday (Sunday in Europe and North America).

As a practical matter, the authorities have to implement their choice of resolution method within that window. If the resolution method is attempting to assure continuity in customer obligations, this has to be made clear to the market prior to the opening of business on the morning after the authorities have intervened. Once the authorities have made the decision to intervene, delay in announcing the resolution method or lack of clarity in how customers will be treated will begin to impose significant social costs on customers and society at large.

6.6 Bail-in of investor capital may provide a mechanism to resolve systemically important banks

Given all of the above, bail-in of investor capital may provide the most effective means to resolve a large systemically important bank. By 'bail-in' we mean a process that effectively amounts to a pre-packaged recapitalisation of the bank so that it can remain a going concern and continue to service all its customer obligations.

7 How would a bail-in work?

Bail-in effectively transforms certain non-equity obligations into equity at the point of intervention (but prior to formal declaration of insolvency) so that the bank can absorb the losses that led to the need for intervention and continue to operate as a going concern. This avoids the need to liquidate the bank or to split it into a good bank and a bad bank. It also avoids the need for equity support from taxpayers such as would be provided under the option of early equity injection.

Conceptually, bail-in would work as follows. Upon a finding by the supervisor that the bank no longer met threshold conditions (the intervention point), bail-in would be triggered. Bail-in consists of two steps:

- A conversion of 'back-up capital' into equity
- A write-off of losses.

There are five main preconditions for success, as shown in the following subsections.

7.1 The result of bail-in

The result of bail-in should be a bank with a clean balance sheet (i.e. one with no apparent losses remaining to be taken) and a strong balance sheet (i.e. one with an equity capital ratio substantially above minimum requirements). To achieve this, the bank has to have a sufficient amount of back-up capital available to bail-in.

The first and most obvious precondition is that there has to be enough back-up capital available to bail in. Unless this is the case, the bank will not have sufficient capital to recapitalise itself and write down or off doubtful assets. At the end of the bail-in process the bank has to have both a clean balance sheet and a strong balance sheet.

'Back-up capital' should consist of all forms of capital that would be eligible to be bailed in upon a finding that the bank no longer met threshold conditions. At a minimum this would include all non-equity forms of capital (non-core Tier 1 capital such as preferred stock, Tier 2 capital such as subordinated debt, etc.). It might also include certain forms of senior debt (see below).

The aggregate amount of back-up capital should be sufficient to completely replace the minimum required common equity of the bank. Anything less than this amount could prove insufficient to absorb the losses that the bank requiring intervention might have incurred. Ideally, the back-up capital would also be sufficient to restore the buffer above the minimum to the target level designated by the authorities. This suggests that back-up capital should be at least 5 per cent of risk-weighted assets (RWAs) and ideally on the order of 10 per cent of RWAs.

7.2   Strict seniority should be respected

For bail-in to work, it has to expose back-up capital to the possibility of loss, through either write-down or conversion at the point of intervention. These losses have to be imposed in a manner consistent with strict seniority, if bail-in is to reinforce market discipline.

7.3   The bail-in process must be capable of rapid implementation

For bail-in to work, it must be capable of being implemented quickly and with a high degree of certainty. As outlined above, the relevant time-frame for a large systemically important bank will be no longer than thirty-six hours.

7.4   Bail-in should preserve the bank as a going concern

For bail-in to work, the bank has to remain a going concern. This implies that bail-in itself should not be permitted to trigger close-out on derivative contracts or cross-default on instruments that are not subject to bail-in. In particular, this implies that senior debt subject to bail-in will have to be designated effectively as senior subordinated debt, junior to deposits and other customer obligations that are not subject to bail-in.

7.5   Bail-in may need to be reinforced through liquidity provision from the central bank

It should be recognised that bail-in will not necessarily immediately restore market confidence in the bank. Bail-in may need to be supplemented by recourse to central bank liquidity facilities. These should be on a super-priority basis with a pledge of the bank's unencumbered assets as collateral for any lending that the central bank may provide. To this end arrangements should be made in advance to prepare the logistics (contracts, operations, etc.) that would be required for such a provision of central bank liquidity support. Steps should also be taken to monitor the amount of unencumbered assets that the bank would potentially have available to pledge to the central bank, should a bail-in be required.

8 Two approaches to bail-in

Broadly speaking, there are two approaches to bail-in that might work. The first is a solvent wind-down approach; the second, a conversion approach.

8.1 Bail-in via write-down/solvent wind-down

Upon a determination by the supervisor that the bank no longer met threshold conditions, the resolution authority would take control of the bank. Under the share transfer/temporary public ownership authority, the resolution authority would acquire at zero upfront cost the entire share capital of the bank, all the preferred stock, the subordinated debt and the senior debt subject to bail-in. Contractual payments on such instruments would be suspended, and they would be fully available for loss absorption.

The resolution authority would continue to operate the bank as a going concern. Customer liabilities would continue to be paid, and close-out of derivative contracts would not be triggered. Holders of instruments subject to bail-in would receive certificates entitling them to proceeds from the wind-down/liquidation of the institution. These proceeds would be distributed according to strict seniority, with senior debt being paid first, then subordinated debt, then preferred stock and, if any proceeds remained, common stock.

As an example, take the case where there is a bank with €1,000 in assets, €900 of which are good and €100 of which are doubtful (see Table 13.2). Total RWAs are €500. The bank's liabilities consist of €850 in deposits, €100 in senior debt, €15 in subordinated debt, €5 in preferred stock and €30 in common equity. The €30 in common equity is divided into 30 shares, each with a value of €1.[10] Assume it becomes

---

[10] This will consist of the par value of the stock plus the retained earnings of the bank. Note that this discussion is in terms of the accounting values of the instruments. The market values of the instruments may well differ.

Table 13.2: *Bail-in via write down/solvent wind down*

	Prior to intervention	TPO	Monday Asia opening	Write-down/ distribution of losses during solvent wind down
Assets				
'Good' assets	900	900	900	Remain good and are realised at full value
Doubtful	100	100	100	Are liquidated over time with losses amounting to 75
Total	1,000	1,000	1,000	
RWAs	500	500	500	
Liabilities				
Deposits	850	850	850	Continue to be paid on time
Senior debt subject to bail-in	100	Senior proceeds note (100)	100	Absorbs 25 in loss from realisation of doubtful assets at below book value, but obtains all remaining residual value
Subordinated debt	15	Subordinated proceeds note (15)	15	Absorbs 15 in loss from realisation of doubtful assets at below book value
Preferred stock	5	Junior subordinated proceeds note (5)	5	Absorbs 5 in loss from realisation of doubtful assets at below book value
Common stock	30	First loss note (30)	30	Absorbs first 30 in loss from realisation of doubtful assets at below book value
Total	1,000		1,000	
Immediate loss-absorbing capacity	1,000		150	

apparent that the doubtful assets will not be fully repaid. This prompts the market to cease funding the bank and the supervisor to determine that the bank no longer meets threshold conditions.

Under bail-in via write-down/solvent wind down, the resolution authority steps in. It issues notes to the holders of 'investor capital' (common stock, preferred stock, subordinated debt and senior debt subject to bail-in) equal in amount to their prior holdings. The balance sheet total of the bank does not change, but the immediate loss-absorbing capacity of the bank goes up from 30 (the amount of common stock prior to intervention) to 150 (the total investor capital). At the opening on Monday the bank continues in normal operation as far as its customer obligations are concerned. These continue to be met (although recourse may be needed to central bank liquidity facilities collateralised by the good assets of the bank).

As the wind down proceeds, losses will be realised. These are absorbed first by the first loss note (formerly the common stock), then by the junior subordinated proceeds note (formerly the preferred stock), then by the senior subordinated proceeds note (formerly the subordinated debt) and, finally, by the senior proceeds note (formerly the senior debt). In the example, losses on the doubtful assets are assumed to be 75, so the first loss note, the junior subordinated note and the senior subordinated note receive no payments whatsoever. The senior proceeds note effectively winds up with a claim equal to 75.

To keep the example simple, it may be assumed that at the end of the process the senior proceeds note is converted into common equity, so that the bank winds up with a total balance sheet of €925 and equity of €75. In all likelihood, however, the resolution authority might decide to sell some or all of the bank as a going concern to third parties during the solvent wind down process. This may increase or reduce the proceeds that would ultimately be available to be paid to the holders of the proceed notes.

8.2   Bail-in via conversion

It would also be possible to conduct a bail-in via conversion. Under this approach, the elements of back-up capital would be converted (following a determination by the supervisor that the bank no longer met threshold conditions) into common equity such that a euro of preferred stock (par value) received significantly fewer shares of common stock than a euro of subordinated debt (par value) and a euro of subordinated debt received significantly fewer shares of common stock than a euro of senior debt. Following the conversion of the back-up capital into common equity, the immediately apparent losses that gave rise to the need for intervention would be taken and deducted from the new common equity total.

To illustrate, take a bank that has the same starting position prior to intervention as the one used to illustrate how bail-in via solvent wind down might work (see Table 13.3). The bail-in would work as

Table 13.3: *Bail-in via conversion of back-up capital to common equity*

	Prior to intervention	Conversion	Write-down	Monday Asia opening
Assets				
'Good' assets	900	900	900	900
Doubtful assets	100	100	0	0
Total assets	1,000	1,000	900	900
RWAs	500	500	450	450
Liabilities				
Deposits	850	850	850	850
Senior debt	100	0	0	0
Subordinated debt	15	0	0	0
Preferred stock	5	0	0	0
Common stock	30	150	50	50
Total	1,000	1,000	900	900
Common/RWAs (%)	6	30	11	11
Total reg Cap/RWAs (%)	10	30	11	11

Shares of common attributable to each class of capital

	Conversion ratio	No. of shares post-conversion	% of total post-conversion
Common	30	1	30	0.3
Preferred	0	5	25	0.2
Sub. debt	0	25	375	3.6
Senior debt	0	100	10000	95.9
Total	30		10430	100.0

follows. Each euro of preferred stock would be converted into 5 shares of common equity; each euro of subordinated debt into 25 shares, and each euro of senior debt into 100 shares. Post-conversion total equity would be €150 and the capital ratio (equity/RWAs) prior to write-downs would swell to 30 per cent. The bank would then write off the €100 in doubtful assets, so that the balance sheet would contract to €900, equity would fall to €50 and the capital ratio (equity/RWAs) would fall to 11 per cent – a figure more than double the 5 per cent equity ratio assumed to be the minimum requirement. This is the balance sheet that would be presented to the market at the Monday Asia opening.

From this simple example, a few practical conclusions emerge. First, conversion can be economically practically as effective as write-off/solvent wind down in assuring that common shareholders take first loss. Through conversion, shareholders suffer what might be termed 'death by dilution'. In the example, this is over 99 per cent. Second, conversion can be

Table 13.4: *Bail-in via conversion: timing and decision-maker for conversion ratios*

		Point at which conversion ratio is determined	
		Prior to intervention	At intervention
Decision-maker for conversion ratios	Resolution authority	Possible via statute or regulation but could not be institution-specific and may not be comprehensive	Possible, but would be subject to review/revision
	Bank itself	Possible via contract as part of new issues and/or amendment of old	Not feasible within required time frame

accomplished quickly. It merely requires the establishment of ratios for the different categories of back-up capital. There is no need to conduct a valuation of the entire balance sheet. Valuation corrections can focus entirely on the doubtful asset categories that gave rise to the problem at the bank, and it may be possible to give such doubtful assets a very conservative valuation indeed (i.e. take a large write-off) so as to give the bank post-conversion a clean as well as a strong balance sheet.

There remain the questions of who should establish the conversion ratios and when should they be established. There are two candidates for who should decide the conversion ratios: the resolution authority or the bank itself. And there are two points at which the conversion ratios could be established: prior to intervention or at the point of intervention. This yields a 2 × 2 possibility matrix (Table 13.4). If the conversion ratio is established prior to intervention, this can be done either on a statutory/regulatory basis or on a contractual basis as part of the negotiation of the bank with the providers of capital and senior debt. If the statutory/regulatory approach is adopted, there is a question as to whether this would apply to newly issued instruments only, or to the stock of existing instruments – a factor that has a bearing on how quickly a transition to a bail-in regime might be accomplished (see pp. 254–5).

If the conversion ratios are to be established at the point of intervention, it is really only feasible for the resolution authority to do this, and the resolution authority must have the requisite power to do so under the relevant special resolution regime(s). The bank itself will not be able to negotiate a conversion with the relevant parties within the required time-frame. If the resolution authority is given the mandate to establish the conversion ratios, some provision would in my view need to be made to allow a period of time for the junior classes of securities to buy out the senior classes at a price that would be equivalent to redeeming their unconverted securities at par (possibly plus a premium).[11]

9   From bail-out to bail-in

Much remains to be done before one can say with assurance that bail-in is a reliable method of resolving large, systemically important banks. The key elements in this process are:

9.1   *Ensuring that the authorities have the power under special resolution regimes to implement a bail-in*

In some jurisdictions, special resolution regimes for banks will need to be established. In those jurisdictions where special resolution regimes exist, they will need to be reviewed and possibly amended to ensure that the resolution authority has the power to implement a bail-in. Where such powers already exist under current law, it should be made clear to market participants how the authorities would use such powers.

Arguably, the US is already taking steps in this direction. The FDIC has issued a notice of proposed rule-making (NPR) to implement the orderly liquidation provisions of the Dodd–Frank Act that may be consistent with a bail-in via write-down approach.[12]

9.2   *Ensuring a clear division of responsibilities in advance among home- and host-country authorities in the implementation of bail-in*

Systemically important banks are generally large, complex, cross-border institutions. They are headquartered in a single jurisdiction, but may have branches, subsidiaries and affiliates in scores of different jurisdictions around the world. For bail-in to be implemented at such an institution,

---

[11] In the example given, if the resolution authority had set the ratios at the point of intervention, the old common stockholders would be given the right to buy out the bailed-in shareholders for a total of €125 (plus accrued interest and a possible premium) for a period of time following the bail-in (say one month). If the common shareholders did not exercise this option, the preferred shareholders would have a similar option to buy out the common stock converted from the subordinated debt and senior debt. If the preferred stockholders did not exercise this option, the subordinated debtholders would have a similar option to buy out the common stock converted from the senior debt.

[12] FDIC 12 CFR Part 380 Notice of Proposed Rulemaking Implementing Certain Orderly Liquidation Authority Provisions of the Dodd–Frank Wall Street Reform and Consumer Protection Act, www.fdic.gov/regulations/laws/federal/2010/10propose1019.pdf.

the cross-border aspects need to be clarified and agreed in advance among the relevant authorities.[13]

9.3   Ensuring that banks have sufficient back-up capital available for bail-in, should intervention be required

The Basel Committee on Banking Supervision (BCBS, 2010) has already taken a step in this direction by proposing that all non-core Tier 1 and Tier 2 capital instruments be convertible into common equity or subject to write-down at the point of intervention. Instruments could meet this test either by virtue of statutory provisions affecting such instruments or by contract.

Under the statutory approach the special resolution regime would mandate that non-core Tier 1 and Tier 2 instruments would be subject to convertibility or write-down. Arguably the Dodd–Frank Act, together with proposed rule-making by the authorities to implement the Act, already accomplishes this in the US.

Under a contractual approach the documentation for all new issues of non-core Tier 1 and Tier 2 instruments would require legally binding measures to allow for convertibility or write-down at the point of non-viability/intervention (otherwise the new issues will not qualify as capital). Although this contractual approach may create a flow of instruments that are subject to bail-in, it does nothing to affect the stock of non-core Tier 1 and Tier 2 instruments that do not accord the resolution authority the capability of converting or writing down the instrument at the point of intervention (but prior to a formal declaration of insolvency). To accelerate the possibility of bail-in, it may be necessary to limit or phase out the grandfathering period of existing non-core Tier 1 and Tier 2 instruments. This would increase the flow of new instruments capable of being bailed in, should intervention be required.

---

[13] For example, for a bank headquartered in the home country with branches in one or more host countries, it would seem necessary that the home-country authority decide the point of intervention and activate the bail-in. The host countries would have to refrain from using the intervention by the home country as a cause to put the branch into insolvency or administration proceedings (as might be the case where the host country operated under the territorial principle). For a bank that has subsidiaries in host countries, the question arises as to whether the host country can implement a bail-in of the subsidiary or whether bail-in should be conducted at the group level only and organised by the home-country supervisor. For a banking group organised with a non-bank holding company as parent, the authority of the home-country supervisor would have to extend to the group as a whole. And, for banking groups that issue capital instruments that are governed by laws foreign to the home-country jurisdiction (e.g. a non-UK institution issuing capital instruments under English law), possible conflicts of law would have to be resolved.

Additional factors need to be taken into account if a decision is made to include senior debt as an instrument that would be subject to bail-in. Currently, such debt is in many regimes *pari passu* with deposits and other senior obligations. If senior debt is to be subject to bail-in, this will effectively transform senior debt into 'senior subordinated' debt, senior to Tier 2 capital, but junior to deposits and other customer liabilities that will not be subject to bail-in. Although banks may be able to accomplish this solely through contractual arrangements, it may be necessary to supplement this with changes to regulation and/or statute.

Finally, consideration needs to be given as to whether systemically important banks should be required to hold a minimum amount of back-up capital (i.e. non-equity capital eligible for bail-in), should intervention be required. As indicated above, this minimum should be sufficient to recapitalise the bank (replace the entire amount of the minimum regulatory requirement plus establish a buffer over that minimum).

9.4   Ensuring consistency between bail-in and pre-intervention capital regimes

For bail-in to be effective it has to reinforce the capital regime applicable to banks prior to intervention. This will be the case if the pre-intervention capital regime is phrased predominantly in terms of core Tier 1 capital – capital that is fully able to absorb loss while the bank is a going concern prior to any intervention by the authorities. This is exactly the direction in which the Basel Committee's recommendations are headed.

However, further discussion needs to take place with respect to the role of non-core Tier 1 and Tier 2 capital prior to intervention. It is acknowledged that such capital rarely absorbs loss while the bank is a going concern. It is further acknowledged that introducing loss absorbency could improve the quality of such capital. Many point to contingent capital as a means of doing so and urge that banks be able to, or be required to, issue such capital as a means of reducing the probability that the bank will fail and intervention be required (Huertas, 2010a; Claessens, Herring and Schoenmaker, 2010; Squam Lake, 2010).

What exact form contingent capital should take is still open to considerable debate. Some contend that a market-based trigger is appropriate; others see a regulatory ratio as the best choice for the trigger. There are also differences in how the capital is generated. Some issues convert into common equity; others are written off in part, with the amount of write-off accruing to the bank as earnings and an addition to capital. There are also differences in the 'host' instrument (the instrument that is issued to investors prior to conversion or write-down). In some cases this is preferred stock; in others subordinated debt; and in one case senior debt.[14]

Such 'going-concern' contingent capital (with conversion or write-down prior to the point of intervention) holds considerable promise as a means of reducing the probability that intervention will be required. However, it seems premature at this stage to conclude that a particular form of contingent capital is the right form to the exclusion of all other forms. What is called for at this point is an indication of how regulators will treat such 'going-concern' contingent capital. At this stage, a few principles would seem to suffice:

- There would be no compulsion but also no prohibition on issuing 'going-concern' contingent capital.
- All issues of 'going-concern' contingent capital would be subject to prior regulatory approval to assure that the conversion or write-down feature would be effective.
- Until such point as the instrument is converted or written down, the instrument will be treated for capital purposes according to the characteristics of the host instrument (e.g. if it is subordinated debt as Tier 2 capital).
- If the instrument sets a conversion ratio, the resolution authority will use that conversion ratio for that instrument if the conversion takes place in connection with a bail-in rather than prior to the intervention point.[15]

9.5   *Improving transparency and accuracy of valuation*

Instruments subject to bail-in will potentially be more marketable to investors, the greater the confidence investors have that the authorities will trigger the bail-in in a timely manner, i.e. at the point where the bank has breached minimum requirements but still has positive net worth. This will minimise the loss given bail-in for bail-in via write-down and increase the likelihood that a solvent wind-down would be successful. For bail-in via conversion, such timely intervention would help assure the value of the common stock that the bailed-in investor would receive.

---

[14] Rabobank has issued senior debt that is subject to a write-down of 25 per cent if the bank's core Tier 1 ratio falls below 7 per cent. This write-down accrues to Rabobank as earnings and adds to capital. The remaining 75 per cent of the note is immediately due and payable to the noteholders.

[15] It is possible that the situation of the bank may deteriorate so rapidly (e.g. as a result of suddenly uncovering a massive fraud) that the bank jumps immediately from a position of robust health to the point where it no longer meets threshold conditions and intervention is required.

To create such investor confidence, banks may wish to take steps to value their portfolios more accurately and become more transparent with both supervisors and investors.

10   Conclusion

Many of the above steps can be taken over the coming months. In particular, it is key that the Basel Committee confirm that non-core Tier 1 and Tier 2 capital is subject to conversion or write-down at the point of intervention. This should be supplemented by a requirement that banks (or at least systemically important banks) maintain a minimum amount of back-up capital. With such a framework in place, it can be anticipated that banks will seek to issue large amounts of going-concern contingent capital on conversion or write-down terms that would be more favourable to shareholders than would be the case if conversion or write-down were delayed to the point of intervention. Effectively, much of the road to bail-in would be on a contractual basis and much of that road could be travelled fairly quickly. If so, this would significantly reduce the threat that 'too big to fail' poses to financial stability and government finances.

References

Basel Committee on Banking Supervision (BCBS) 2010. 'Proposal to ensure the loss absorbency of regulatory capital at the point of non-viability', consultative document: www.bis.org/publ/bcbs174.pdf

Bernanke, B.S. (2010). Statement prepared for the Committee on Financial Services, US House of Representatives, February 10, 2010, www.federalreserve.gov/newsevents/testimony/bernanke20100210a.htm

Claessens, S., R. Herring and D. Schoenmaker (2010). *A Safer World Financial System: Improving the Resolution of Systemic Institutions*, Geneva: International Centre for Monetary and Banking Studies, Geneva Reports on the World Economy, 12

Huertas, Thomas F. (2010a). *Crisis: Cause, Containment and Cure*, London: Palgrave Macmillan

(2010b). 'Living wills: how can the concept be implemented?', Remarks before the Conference on Cross-Border Issues in Resolving Systemically Important Financial Institutions, Wharton School of Management, University of Pennsylvania, 12 February

(2010c). 'Improving bank capital structures', Paper presented to LSE Financial Markets Group seminar on 'Modigliani–Miller in Banking', 18 January, www.fsa.gov.uk/pages/Library/Communication/Speeches/2010/0118_th.shtml

Merton, Robert C. and André Perold (1993). 'Theory of risk capital in financial firms', *Journal of Applied Corporate Finance*, **6**(3): 16–32; reprinted in Donald H. Chew (ed.), *Corporate Risk Management*, New York: Columbia Business School Publishing, 2008

Paulson, Henry M., Jr. (2010). *On the Brink: Inside the Race to Stop the Collapse of the Global Financial System*, New York: Business Plus

Squam Lake (2010). K. French, M. Baily, J. Campbell, J. Cochrane, D. Diamond, D. Duffie, A. Kashyap, F. Mishkin, R. Rajan, D. Scharfstein, R. Shiller, H. Shin, M. Slaughter, J. Stein and R. Stulz, *The Squam Lake Report: Fixing the Financial System*, Princeton University Press

14 Financial stability and monetary policy: lessons from the euro area

*Laurent Clerc and Benoît Mojon**

1 Introduction

Central banks are usually assigned two main goals: the most recent one, which has become their priority objective over the last three decades, is price stability; the second one, which is historically their *raison d'être*, is to ensure the integrity of payments.[1] In modern economies, this takes the form of the smooth functioning of interbank exchanges on the money market, which contributes to and depends on the maintenance of financial stability.

In accordance with economic theory, central banks have assigned specific instruments to each of these two objectives. The short-term interest rate has emerged, over the last three decades, as the main instrument with which monetary policy pursues its price stability objective.[2] Central banks support the functioning of the money market through a continuum of instruments, ranging from their marginal standing facilities to the granting of liquidity assistance to troubled money-issuing institutions or lender of last resort (LOLR) to the financial system as a whole. These operations can, however, be sterilised in order to insulate the stance of monetary policy. Looking back at the first twelve years of the euro, this separation in the pursuit of the two objectives, which is consistent with the Tinbergen principle, has not been challenged until recently when short-term nominal interest rates reached their (zero) lower bound in 2009. The Eurosystem then, along with many other central banks throughout

---

* This chapter was prepared for the conference 'The Euro Area and the Financial Crisis', at the National Bank of Slovakia, Bratislava, 6–8 September 2010 under the auspices of the National Bank of Slovakia, the Heriot–Watt University of Edinburgh and the Comenius University of Bratislava. The views expressed in this chapter reflect the personal opinions of the authors and are not necessarily those of the Banque de France or of the Eurosystem.

[1] For an historical perspective on the emergence of modern central banking, see Aglietta and Mojon (2010).
[2] We characterise here the situation of most OECD countries. The US Federal Reserve also has a full-employment objective.

the world, embarked on non-conventional policies. The circumstances of the financial crisis and the great recession blurred the separation between the means mobilised by the euro area central bank in the pursuit of its two objectives.

The full mandate of the Eurosystem is specified in Article 105 of the Treaty establishing the European Community. According to Article 105.1, price stability is the primary objective of the Eurosystem. Article 105.2 lists the other basic tasks to be carried out through the Eurosystem, namely:

(1) to define and implement the monetary policy of the Community;
(2) to conduct foreign exchange operations (. . .);
(3) To hold and manage the official foreign reserves of the Member States; and finally
(4) to promote the smooth functioning of payment systems.

From this, one can see that the Eurosystem's responsibilities for financial stability are limited to the smooth functioning of the money market (1) and of payment systems (4). Effectively, the main contribution of the European Central Bank (ECB) to financial stability is liquidity management. As a complement, emergency liquidity assistance (ELA) to troubled financial institutions is a matter for national central banks.

In normal times, the Eurosystem implements its monetary policy strategy, known as the two-pillar strategy, by cross-checking its assessment of risks to price stability over the short to the medium run, based on a wide array of economic and financial indicators (the so-called economic analysis or first pillar), with its assessment of risks to price stability over the long term based on money and credit aggregate developments (the so-called monetary analysis or monetary/second pillar). As pointed out both by academics and members of the ECB's Governing Council,[3] the monetary pillar might also be useful for detecting, at an earlier stage, the build-up of financial imbalances and therefore also provide useful information on risks to financial stability and some grounds for 'leaning against financial winds'. Indeed, financial booms are correlated in a remarkable number of instances with leverage and credit expansion and as such are likely to show up also in monetary aggregate data. It is important to stress, however, that the Eurosystem monetary policy strategy does not treat monetary or credit aggregates as an intermediate target for monetary policy. The build-up of financial imbalances may, however, raise medium-to-long-run upside or downside risks to price stability, and may, therefore, require changes in the stance of monetary policy.

---

[3] The ECB Governing Council is composed of the six members of the ECB Executive Board and the Governors of the national central banks of the countries of the euro area.

The depth of the financial crisis revived an old debate regarding the optimal choice of policy instruments. In a seminal analysis, (Poole, 1970) money demand instability increases the desirability of an interest rate-oriented policy procedure over a monetary (base) procedure: if money demand is viewed as highly unstable over short-time horizons, greater stability in output can be achieved by stabilising interest rates, letting the monetary base (or aggregate) fluctuate. If instead the main source of fluctuations arises from aggregate demand instability, a policy that stabilises the monetary base will lead to greater output stability. In the context of the financial crisis, the dramatic decrease of short-term interest rates to their (zero) lower bound led a growing number of central banks to resort to unconventional monetary policies. These can be seen as forms of monetary base targeting, echoing Poole's recommendations at a time of heightened uncertainty regarding aggregate demand. Central banks increased their money supply vigorously in the wake of the Lehmans collapse. Their objective was to reduce liquidity and credit risk premia (so-called credit easing policies) or lower the level of the yield curve (so-called quantitative easing policies). In this context, liquidity management has increasingly been used for both financial and monetary stability purposes.

In this chapter, we review the conduct of monetary policy in the euro area since the inception of the euro and the challenges that the Eurosystem faced since the financial crisis erupted in August 2007. Thanks to their unique monetary policy framework, the ECB and the Eurosystem seem well equipped to deal with their monetary and financial stability objectives. Indeed, we show in this chapter that the ECB has fully achieved its mandate of delivering price stability in the euro area. We also show in section 2 that it faced fast monetary and credit growth, largely echoing the rise of real estate prices. However, both the pace of credit growth and that of house price increases in the euro area have been very uneven across countries. Taking a euro area perspective, credit to the private sector increased steadily but nowhere near the steep increases observed in Spain or for US households. We show that the hypothesis that the monetary policy stance had only a limited effect on these developments cannot be rejected, neither with a panel VAR model applied to country level developments nor with an estimated Dynamic Stochastic General Equilibrium (DSGE) model of the area-wide business cycle.

Next, we analyse the Eurosystem's policy response to the financial crisis, before and after the Lehmans collapse. We describe the implications of the fixed rate full allotment procedure which has been implemented since then, and illustrate the role played by liquidity management and the challenges faced by the Eurosystem in trying to achieve both price and financial stability (section 3).

2   The build-up of financial imbalances in the euro area

2.1   Stylised facts

Central banks should always be prepared for turbulent periods that may arise independently from their own actions and, perhaps more importantly, should avoid sowing the seeds of financial and macroeconomic instability. In the case of the 2007–9 crisis, it is obvious that the ECB could do very little to prevent the build-up of financial fragility in the US. The key ingredients of the crisis can be listed as follows:

* Too rapid expansion of credit to US households, including to households that were unlikely to meet their debt obligations.
* Possibly, an overly accommodative monetary policy stance between 2002 and 2004 (Taylor and Williams, 2009).
* Increasing leverage and exposure of the US banking system to real estate risk through undercapitalised vehicles, which effectively rolled over short-term debt to invest in mortgage backed securities (Acharya and Schnabl, 2009).
* Faith that financial innovation always improves market completeness and efficiency (Greenspan, 2008).
* Possibly, letting Lehmans file for bankruptcy.

The broad consensus that these ingredients brought on the crisis can be used as a guideline to evaluate the euro area's situation prior to the event. In so doing we can leave aside the last three factors, which are very much US-specific.

First, what has been the rhythm of credit growth in the euro area? Was it too fast? And, what was the role of the monetary policy stance in the expansion of credit?

Figure 14.1 provides some key facts on these important questions. It reports the evolution of credit over GDP for households, non-financial firms and governments, in the euro area, in the US and across the four largest economies of the euro area. Two results are striking. First, US household indebtedness grew both faster and to much higher levels than that of euro area households. Second, the fast rhythm of credit growth within the euro area was mainly a concern in Spain. There, both households and corporations increased their debt-to-income ratio by a factor of 2 in less than a decade. There is little controversy that such credit growth was favoured by Spain's participation in the euro area. This implied that Spanish nominal interest rates declined dramatically after the adoption

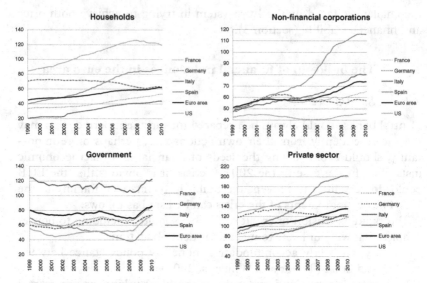

Figure 14.1: Indebtedness of non-financial sectors: US and in the euro area, 1999–2010 (debt to GDP ratios, private sector debt is the sum of households and NFC)
Source: Borgy, Clerc and Renne (2009).

of the euro when the exchange rate risk premia vanished in the late 1990s and took Spanish real interest rates to very low levels. Moreover, the flow of foreign capital financed the housing boom in Spain. Spain's current account deficit was consistently around 9 per cent of GDP in the mid 2000s, that is, even higher than the US deficit which has received so much attention.

While some argue that capital inflows are highly correlated with domestic asset price bubbles (Bernanke, 2010), we should also recall that *ex ante*, even in the case of Spain, the identification of a bubble was not easy. First, it has been argued that Spanish prices, of both real estate and the consumer basket, were bound to catch up with the levels observed in other parts of the euro area. Second, an increasing number of Europeans (including, for instance, over 1 million UK residents) could afford to invest in second homes in Spain, in part thanks to the emergence of low-cost airlines. Last but not least, the population in Spain increased rapidly, from 41 million inhabitants in 2000 to over 46 million in 2008. Hence, part of the increase of real estate prices and credit in Spain corresponded to what were by any standard changes in 'fundamentals'.

Taking the perspective of the euro area as a whole, of which Spain accounts for 15 per cent of the population, credit growth to the private sector remained, however, relatively fast even if much slower than in

Spain. In Figure 14.1 the bottom right chart shows the trend of credit to the private sector over GDP. Over the last decade, it has increased on average by 3.6 per cent of GDP per annum in the euro area and by nearly 5 per cent per annum in the US (and as much as 10.4 per cent in Spain).

A positive trend in credit over GDP seems to be a pervasive feature in the OECD (Alessi and Detken, 2009; Borgy, Clerc and Renne, 2009). This trend is sustainable if not too rapid. With the hindsight of the crisis, credit clearly grew too fast in the US and in some parts of the euro area, most notably in Spain. For the euro area as a whole, the case is much less clear.

The next questions, however, are about the role of monetary policy in the expansion of credit. John Taylor has repeatedly criticised the Federal Reserve for failing to raise interest rates fast enough in 2003 and 2004. This is apparent from the Taylor rule benchmark applied to the US, which we report in Figure 14.2a. We repeat the exercise for the euro area in Figure 14.2b.

The short-term interest rates have indeed been well below their Taylor benchmarks. They are defined as:

$$rr + 2^{\%} + 1.5^*(inflation_t - 2^{\%}) + 0.5^*d(gdp_t)$$

where inflation and GDP growth are year-on-year growth rates. It appears clearly that in the US, and to a much lesser extent in the euro area, the price of liquidity has been lower than suggested by the Taylor benchmark with no smoothing. This may be seen as evidence that the stance of monetary policy in the euro area has been overly accommodative, at least from 2003 to 2005.

However, the stance of monetary policy cannot be narrowly defined as the deviation from an ad hoc benchmark. Given the ECB's mandate to maintain price stability and its strategy to stabilise inflation close to 2 per cent from below over the medium run, the success of its monetary policy needs to be evaluated by the distance of realised inflation from its objective. Figure 14.3 reports euro area HICP inflation since the launch of the euro in 1999. HICP inflation has been 1.98 per cent on average and its deviation from the pre-announced inflation objective has been very small with the exception of the period from 2006 to 2009, when the oil price cycle peaked at $147 per barrel in July 2008 and dropped below $40 in January 2009. Such fluctuations in relative prices should not be blamed on (local) monetary policy conditions, provided they are short-lived. Prior to the boom-bust oil price cycle, inflation had oscillated around 2.1 per cent between 2000 and 2007. While this inflation level was a few basis points above the ECB's own definition of price stability, close to 2 per cent from below, it is clear from Figure 14.3 that deviations

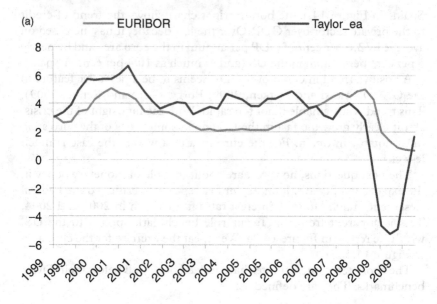

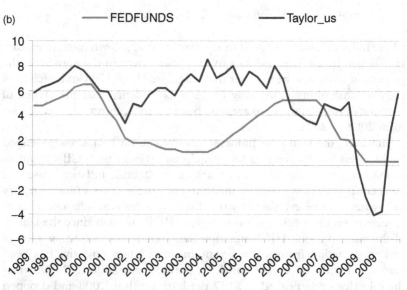

Figure 14.2: Short-term interest rates and Taylor benchmarks: (a) euro area, 1999–2009 (%), (b) US
Source: ECB.

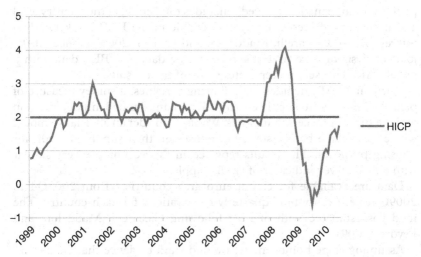

Figure 14.3: HICP inflation: euro area, 1999–2010 (% year-on-year growth rate)
Source: ECB.

of consumer price inflation from this definition of price stability remained small and showed no persistence.

Hence the stance of the ECB's monetary policy in the euro area has been quite successful with respect to its primary objective of price stability. We may nevertheless investigate whether another policy stance would have implied a slower pace of credit growth. We propose to carry out this evaluation with two complementary modelling tools. First, we use a reduced-form panel VAR model of credit, interest rates and the business cycle in euro area countries. The main advantage of this approach is that it can evaluate the potency of monetary policy with respect to credit for the relatively short period of the new monetary policy regime, thanks to the cross-section of country data. A standard time series approach, would, with twelve years of data in the new regime, have only a very small number of observations to estimate such a model.

Second, we will use a DSGE model of the euro area estimated by Antipa, Mengus and Mojon (2010) to evaluate the contribution of monetary policy shocks to credit developments. This model is a Iacoviello (2005) economy, estimated on euro area data from 1985 to 2010.

2.2   *A panel VAR-based analysis of credit growth in the euro area*

In this subsection, we use a euro area country-panel VAR to analyse the joint dynamics of credit, the business cycle and the stance of monetary policy. Our information on credit includes total credit at the country level and indicators of credit supply as available in the ECB Bank Lending Survey (BLS). Ciccarelli, Maddaloni and Peydro (2009) pioneered the joint analysis of euro area macroeconomic data and BLS data with a panel VAR. This section replicates some of their results.

Our panel VAR includes the following variables: a survey measure of banks' willingness to supply credit,[4] GDP, banks' total lending, inflation and the Euribor three-month rates. We also consider an alternative model where we include banks' survey responses on their supply of credit for housing purposes. The results reported in this section are very similar with either survey indicator of credit supply.

Data are available for eleven euro area countries[5] from 2002Q4 to 2009Q4, i.e. twenty-nine quarterly observations for each country. The model is estimated with one lag following Ciccarelli, Maddaloni and Peydro (2009).

Assuming slope homogeneity, we find stark evidence that changes in credit supply have a strong impact on GDP and inflation (see the top panel of Figure 14.4). Moreover, an unexpected shock to the short-term interest rate has a sizeable impact on credit supply (an increase means a tightening of credit standards by banks). This tightening affects credit volumes, GDP and inflation. However, the scale of the effects of changes in the stance of monetary policy on credit is very small. This can be seen in the bottom panel of Figure 14.5 where the contribution of these shocks to the variance of total loans growth is inferior to 1 per cent. According to our model, most of the variance of total credit growth in the euro area is due to credit specific shocks.

Taken altogether, this first set of estimates indicates that a different monetary policy in the euro area could have had only a very limited impact on credit growth. In contrast, having a higher interest rate for the sake of reducing credit growth would have meant lower GDP growth and lower inflation, perhaps to a degree that would have put inflation too far below the announced objective of price stability.

2.3   *A DSGE-based analysis of the financial cycle in the euro area*

The most widely used analytical tools to describe the effects of alternative monetary policies on the business cycle and inflation are the so-called

---

[4] This measure is the country-level response to question 1 of the ECB Bank Lending Survey: 'over the last 3 months how did your standard for the supply of credit or line of credit to enterprises evolve?'

[5] Austria, Belgium, Finland, France, Germany, Greece, Italy, Ireland, the Netherlands, Portugal and Spain.

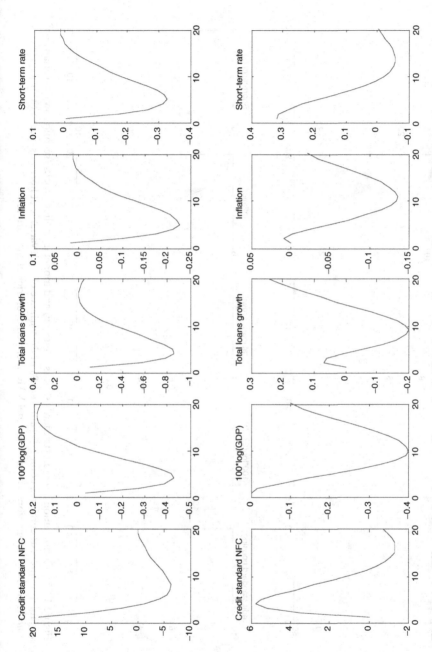

Figure 14.4: Effects of shocks to credit standards (first row) and stance of monetary policy (second row): euro area countries (responses in % are drawn for horizons one to twenty quarters)

Source: Authors' estimations based on a panel VAR of eleven countries of the euro area.

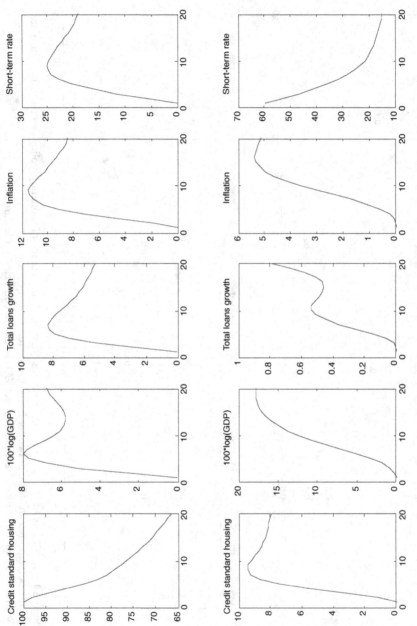

Figure 14.5: Contribution of credit standards shocks (first row) and monetary policy shocks (second row) to variance of variables of interest: euro area countries (units are % of the variance of each variable at horizons one to twenty quarters) *Source:* Authors' estimations based on a panel VAR of eleven countries of the euro area.

DSGE models. These build on the assumption that the key decisions of consumers and firms can be described as intra temporal and intertemporal optimisation of their utility and profits given their preferences and the state of technology.

Households supply labour and allocate their income to consumption and investment. Firms combine labour and capital into output. It is typically assumed that prices cannot be reset every period (prices are said to be sticky) because of menu costs. This nominal rigidity opens the way to the non-neutrality of monetary policy. The most attractive feature of such models is that their behavioural building blocks are independent of public policies. They can therefore be used to compare alternative monetary policies, or the interplay of macro-prudential policies.

These models have a number of limitations. Their dynamic properties, and therefore the relative performance of alternative policies, depend on parameters of which the estimates remain somewhat uncertain. More to the point of this chapter, only recently have these models had a description of the financial sector embedded in them.

Credit is modelled as a determinant of either physical capital accumulation or housing investment because of some form of asymmetric information that limits loanable funds. Hence, borrowers can issue credit only up to the value of their collateral (Iacoviello, 2005). The availability and the cost of credit can influence demand, the output gap and inflation. One can therefore use such models to analyse how monetary policy and financial sector shocks govern the dynamics of credit and the business cycle.

This subsection uses the DSGE model of Antipa, Mengus and Mojon (2010) to analyse the determinants of the euro area credit cycle. This model is a Iacoviello (2005) economy with patient households that lend to impatient households and entrepreneurs. These have a higher discount rate than the patient households and they borrow up to the limit of a collateral constraint either to buy a house (households) or to invest in physical capital (entrepreneurs). The model is otherwise a standard Christiano, Eichenbaum and Evans (2005) DSGE model with nominal rigidities in wages and prices à la Calvo and standard real rigidities (habit formation, adjustment costs to investment, etc.). Its estimation follows the approach introduced by Smets and Wouters (2003). The euro area version of the model is estimated to fit the dynamics of seven observable quarterly time series: GDP, consumption, investment, housing price inflation, total credit, inflation and the three-month Euribor. We conduct a Full Information Bayesian estimation in Dynare on the variables detrended with an HP filter. Our priors for the model's parameters and their posterior estimates are consistent with those of Smets

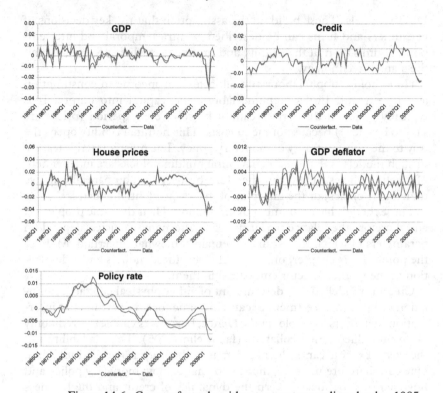

Figure 14.6: Counterfactuals without monetary policy shocks, 1985–2009
Source: Simulations using the Antipa, Mengus and Mojon (2010) model.

and Wouters (2007) and Barthélemy, Marx and Poissonnier (2010). As a result, the impulse responses to the main shocks of the model are quite similar to the ones reported in these papers.

We invert the model to represent (in Figure 14.6) GDP, total credit, house prices, inflation and the interest rate as well as the trajectory these variables would have had if there had not been monetary policy shocks. Altogether, monetary policy shocks have had a very small impact on credit, house prices and GDP.

To conclude this section, we would like to stress that the pace of credit growth in the euro area has been very uneven across countries. Taking a euro area perspective, credit to the private sector increased steadily but nowhere near the steep increases observed in Spain or for US households. In addition, two very different methodologies, a reduced-form-panel VAR model and an estimated DSGE model, concur in rejecting the proposition that the stance of monetary policy has made a significant contribution to the fast pace of credit.

3 The Eurosystem and the financial crisis, or the challenging task of managing both price and financial stability[6]

We turn now to the conduct of monetary policy since the beginning of the financial crisis, in August 2007. Up to the failure of Lehmans in September 2008, the conduct of monetary policy did not change from the previous period. The Eurosystem continued its tightening cycle, even when confronted by increased volatility in the money market. It used liquidity management to ensure the smooth functioning of the money market and avoid the disruption of the payment system. However, the unprecedented situation that arose after Lehmans filed for bankruptcy led the Eurosystem to adopt non-standard measures and implement them on a grand scale. This shift created unprecedented disturbances to the implementation of monetary policy and the guidance of the money market. As a consequence, from October 2008 the separation principle, which had guided Eurosystem policies until then, was *de facto* set aside.

3.1 Easing liquidity up to Lehmans (August 2007–September 2008)

The financial crisis struck in August 2007 while the Eurosystem was still pursuing the upward cycle of its key interest rates initiated in December 2005. The last increase in the corridor of money market interest rates controlled by the central bank had taken place in June 2007.

The euro area economy had indeed entered a phase of accelerating activity in a context of growing inflationary pressures (rising oil prices and signs of tension in the job market). On 9 August 2007, the sudden drying up of liquidity caused BNP Paribas to freeze the activity of three mutual funds operating on the Asset Backed Securities (ABS) market. The Eurosystem intervened immediately by launching a tender at a fixed rate of 4 per cent, thereby injecting nearly €95 billion overnight. It repeated overnight fine-tuning operations in the days that followed, gradually withdrawing the liquidity that had been injected. From 15 August onward, it used its main refinancing operations to insulate money market interest rates from this new type of stresses to liquidity.

At the same time, the ECB's Governing Council underlined the distinction between monetary policy, aimed at price stability, and liquidity

---

[6] This section draws heavily on Bordes and Clerc (2010).

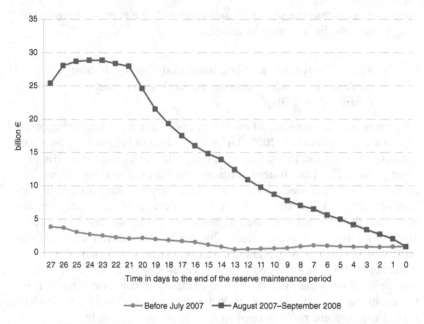

Figure 14.7: Average daily amount of excess reserves (€ billion)
Source: Cassola, Holthausen and Würtz (2008).

management. Its communication stressed that a further tightening of monetary conditions, i.e. increases in the interest rate at which it conducted its main refinancing operations, could arise, if required to maintain price stability.

From August 2007 onward, the Eurosystem gradually implemented its 'credit enhancement policy'. The proportion of central bank money lent through long-term refinancing operations increased to 66 per cent, more than twice the percentage before the crisis. In addition, the Eurosystem began to inject a greater quantity of money than normally required at the start of the reserve maintenance period in order to reassure banks that their access to central liquidity was secure.

As a result, the average amount of excess reserves remained basically unchanged at the end of the maintenance periods (indeed, it was equal to that observed before the onset of the crisis, see Figure 14.7). By using fine-tuning operations more frequently, the ECB succeeded in controlling the money market rate, which continued to fluctuate around the minimum bid rate for its main refinancing operations until October 2008 (Figure 14.8).

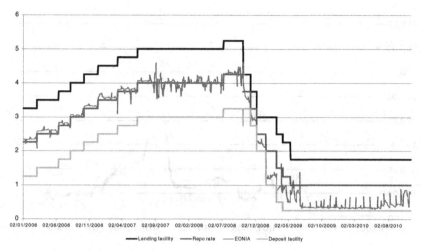

Figure 14.8: ECB key rates, 2006–10
Source: ECB.

Despite an especially tight situation in the money market, particularly at the end of each quarter when the banks published their profit and loss accounts, the ECB succeeded in holding to its course. It even tightened monetary conditions again in July 2008 by increasing its key rates by a further 25 points when the oil price reached its historic high of $147 per barrel, which pushed HICP inflation to 4 per cent and created a palatable threat to medium-run price stability.

Thus, throughout this first-year crisis period, the Eurosystem dissociated the monetary policy stance from liquidity management, aimed at contributing to financial stability, very effectively. The money market rate remained in line with the minimum bid rate for main refinancing operations. Liquidity management operations ensured that the overnight rate volatility was not transmitted along the yield curve.

3.2   Dealing with a financial crisis post-Lehmans: moving to non-conventional policies

The situation suddenly worsened in the week of 7–14 September 2008. The announcement of the federal takeover of major US mortgage corporations Fannie Mae and Freddie Mac on 7 September was followed, on 14 September, by the failure of Lehmans, the purchase of Merrill Lynch by Bank of America and an increasing number of distress signals from Washington Mutual (WaMu) and AIG. It rapidly became apparent that several market segments had virtually seized up, particularly the credit

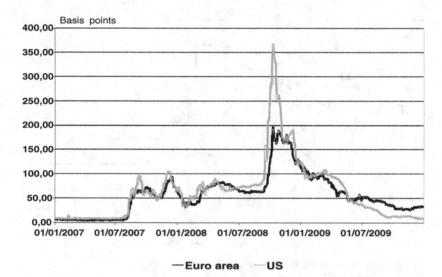

Figure 14.9: Spread between three-month interbank and overnight indexed swap (OIS) rates: euro area and US, 2007–9
Source: Bloomberg.

market where yield spreads reached prohibitive levels. While the crisis struck in the US financial markets, it instantaneously spilled over onto the world's financial markets, including the euro area money markets (Figure 14.9).

The reaction of the central banks was immediate. Massive injections of liquidity at the end of September were followed by currency injections, especially in one-week repos in dollars, and a doubling of the amount of dollar swaps with the Fed.

Gearing short-term interest rates

On 8 October 2008, the Eurosystem joined the Federal Reserve, the Bank of England, the Bank of Canada, the Swiss National Bank and the Riksbank (central bank of Sweden) in reducing its key interest rate by 50 basis points, thus reversing the cycle of rising interest rates.

This decision, the coordination of which was unprecedented, was accompanied by a major operational change: liquidity would henceforth be allocated through fixed rate tenders with full allotment, i.e. fully meeting the total demand for reserves from the banks.

The main aim of this measure was to reduce uncertainty with regard to the supply and cost of liquidity and hence free up the money market. The second aim was to limit the effects of ballooning liquidity and counterparty risk premia on the cost of bank credit. The latter represents over 85 per cent of the debt of non-financial corporations in the euro area. It was essential that the cost of bank refinancing be kept as low as possible at the time when the euro area entered its worst recession since the Second World War.

This full allotment policy was the first non-standard measure adopted by the Eurosystem. Initially forecast to last as long as circumstances required and until at least the start of 2009, this measure was subsequently extended until at least October 2010. Under this measure, the ECB undertook to meet the entire demand for reserves from the banks at prevailing interest rate conditions within a time-frame of up to six months ahead. The implications of this measure were highly significant.

First, the Eurosystem increased its role as intermediary in the money market and, given the very attractive conditions at which it supplied this liquidity, became the main or even the only supplier of liquidity for the maturities covered by its operations (i.e. one week–six months). Moreover, these injections of liquidity were no longer sterilised after October 2008. This resulted in a significant increase in the size of the Eurosystem's balance sheet, which more than doubled.

The Eurosystem was in a difficult situation. It took over the intermediation function of an ailing interbank market while, at the same time, hoping to reactivate it. The effects of this measure compounded the impact of the decision to narrow the money market interest rate corridor. The abundant supply of liquidity put a downward pressure on the Euro Overnight Index Average (EONIA). The latter, which until then had hovered around the minimum bid rate, suddenly peeled off by some 40 to 50 basis points before it converged to near the deposit facility rate (cf. Figure 14.8). The fall in the EONIA was passed on in full to the short-term yield curve, thereby easing the stance of monetary policy. The market rate has since then (meaning until the end of 2010 when this chapter was written) moved closer to the deposit facility rate.

These measures enabled the ECB to lower the effective short rate significantly and therefore to reduce the cost of financing the economy. *De facto*, the monetary policy stance was no longer signalled by the main refinancing rate, which bottomed at 1 per cent, but rather by the marginal deposit facility rate.

Implementing non-standard measures

As from October 2008, the structure of the Eurosystem's balance sheet was modified in important ways (Figure 14.10). This first reflected the softening of the criteria for eligibility for access to its main refinancing

286   *Laurent Clerc and Benoît Mojon*

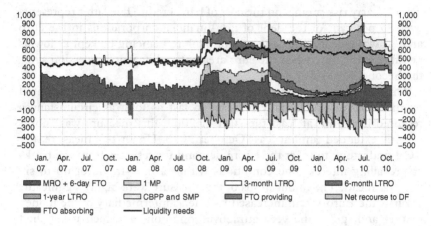

Figure 14.10: Provision and liquidity absorption by Eurosystem, 2007–10 (€ billion)

Notes: CBPP = Covered bond purchase programme; DF = Deposit facility; FTO = Fine-tuning operations; LTRO = Long-term refinancing operations; MP = Maintenance period (monetary policy) operations; MRO = Main refinancing operations; SMP = Securities market programme.
Source: ECB.

operations. After 22 October 2008, the threshold for accepting securities lodged as collateral with the Eurosystem was lowered from A– to BBB–, with the notable exception of ABS. This loosening of collateral standards accompanied the decision on full allotment of liquidity at a fixed rate. It enabled counterparties to double their refinancing potential.

Second, the proportion of long-term refinancing operations continued to increase to the detriment of one-week operations. At the beginning of October, the ECB finalised the Term Auction Facility (TAF) signed a year previously with the US Federal Reserve, which enabled it to lend dollars to banks in the euro area, in operations to lend unlimited quantities of fixed rate dollars at maturities of 7, 28 and 84 days.[7] Though this facility had no direct impact on financing conditions in the euro area, it nevertheless contributed to improving overall refinancing conditions.

On 7 May 2009, the Governing Council of the ECB announced three additional non-standard measures in order to further reduce the cost of financing the banks and hence the euro area economies:
(1) Covered bonds issued by the banks were purchased in a total amount of €60 billion. This measure was designed to dispel some of the uncertainty that impeded the medium-term financing of the banks.

[7] The Bank of England and the Swiss National Bank signed similar agreements with the US Federal Reserve.

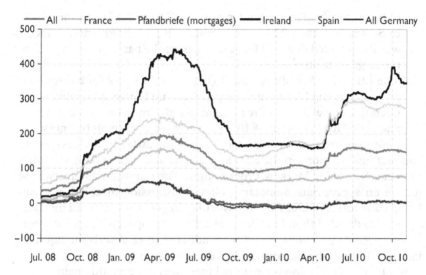

Figure 14.11: Covered bond spreads against five-year swap rate, 2008–10 (basis points – iBoxx indices)

Notes: Pf and briefe = German Covered bond model.
Source: Markit.

Thus, the measure aimed to reduce risk premia on medium-term maturities and create an incentive for the banks to finance new loans in the euro area. It had a major impact on the covered bond market as soon as it was announced (cf. Figure 14.11).

(2) The maturity of refinancing operations conducted as fixed rate tenders with full allotment was extended to one year. Three operations of this type were conducted in 2009, the first two in June and September at a rate of 1.0 per cent, the last in December at a revisable rate corresponding to the average minimum refinancing rate over the maturity of the operation. Thanks to the very advantageous conditions at which the first operation was executed (at the time 1 per cent for twelve months appeared cheap), an exceptional amount of €442 billion was allocated to the banks. The amounts allocated in the next two operations, €75 billion in September and €97 billion in December – were much smaller, in part because the excess liquidity of the banking system put the EONIA way below 1 per cent. The variable rate of the December twelve-month auction introduced uncertainty as to the cost of the refinancing operation, especially as the ECB also carried out two other refinancing operations in December, at a fixed rate of 1.0 per cent and with three- and six-month maturities. This partly explains the decrease in the number

of banks involved in the tender, which fell from 1,121 in June to 589 in September, then 224 in December. The other explanatory factor was the reduced demand for reserves from the banks, especially from the large institutions.

(3) The European Investment Bank (EIB) was accepted for a three-year period as an eligible counterparty to the main Eurosystem refinancing operations. It was generally thought that this measure could generate additional loans of some €40 billion to euro area small businesses.

These measures were completed on 10 May 2010 by the decision to conduct interventions in the euro area public and private debt securities markets (Securities Markets Programme). The purpose this time was to restore an appropriate monetary policy transmission mechanism, insulating bank interest rates from the volatility in government bond markets. It was also decided that, in order to sterilise the impact of these interventions, specific operations would be conducted to re-absorb the liquidity injected through the Securities Markets Programme.

While this set of non-conventional measures has certainly helped sustain bank activity in the euro area, and avoided a major financial and economic collapse, it should be stressed that this policy route is not without risks. At the macroeconomic level, economic agents may draw the conclusion that the Eurosystem has relinquished its key goal, which is to ensure medium-term price stability, in favour of maintaining very short-term financial stability. This perception is likely to increase moral hazard by investors and lead to excessively risky behaviour. Another risk is that banks delegate their liquidity management to the central bank and become accustomed to this easy access to liquidity. Incentives to manage liquidity prudently may weaken. This phenomenon is reinforced for the more fragile banks, for whom refinancing is no longer possible on the market, and who therefore depend exclusively on the unlimited fixed rate refinancing policy adopted by the ECB.

Hence there is a need to exit from the set of non-conventional liquidity management measures adopted in reaction to the financial crisis as soon as the euro area banking system resumes its resilience.

4   Conclusion

The Eurosystem entered the financial crisis with a remarkable record of price stability, fully complying with its monetary policy mandate. This track record is likely to have helped keep inflation expectations anchored throughout the most severe financial crisis in eighty years, limiting the risks that either a deflation spiral or an inflation spiral might take off. It is also important to stress that, as we showed in this chapter, this price stability orientation of monetary policy has had only a limited impact, if any, on the growth of the euro area-wide credit aggregates.

The task of conducting monetary policy became increasingly difficult when the US financial turmoil spilled over world-wide after September 2008. The unconventional measures described in this chapter led to increasing interference between monetary policy, aimed at delivering price stability, and the liquidity management contribution to financial stability assigned to the Eurosystem in the Maastricht Treaty.

Several proposals to change, improve or complete the ECB's monetary policy strategy and mandate have emerged. Blinder (2010) has called for a realignment of central banks' duties, and argued that they should monitor and regulate systemic risks besides ensuring price stability. Other academics, among those who questioned the monetary pillar of the strategy and doubted its practical usefulness in assessing the risks to price stability, noted that monitoring monetary and credit developments would be helpful for financial stability purposes. They therefore called for the rethinking of this pillar as a 'financial stability pillar' (see, for instance, Gali, 2010).

Recent proposals have been made to complement monetary policy with macro-prudential policies. The EU launches the European Systemic Risk Board (ESRB) in January 2011. The ESRB, which will be based in Frankfurt, will draw heavily on the knowledge and experience of the Eurosystem. The ESRB will, however, be distinct and separate from the ECB and its inception will not change in any way the mandate or the functioning of the ECB or any central bank in the EU.

This separation will preserve the credibility of the Eurosystem's monetary policy. However, the Eurosystem will play a pivotal role in the new framework. The Governors of all EU central banks will have a seat on the General Board of the ESRB, and the ESRB Chair will be the President of the ECB. This governance will facilitate collaboration in the design and implementation of monetary and macro-prudential policies. The ECB will provide the ESRB with analytical, statistical, administrative and logistical support. National central banks and supervisors will also provide technical advice, which will constitute an important input into the work of the ESRB.

Overall, the financial crisis has led to the introduction of macro-prudential policies that should prevent and limit systemic risks. The success of the parallel conduct of monetary and macro-prudential policies, in the euro area and elsewhere, will be very difficult to assess. The fact that, as the crisis has showed, financial imbalances can build up in times of price stability raises new analytical challenges. It is for this reason that the Banque de France is investing heavily in improving the analytical tools that will enable us to better understand how the financial system and the business cycle interact.

References

Acharya, V. and P. Schnabl (2009). 'How banks played the leverage "game"', in V. Acharya and M. Richardson (eds.), *Restoring Financial Stability: How to Repair a Failed Financial System*, Hoboken, NJ: Wiley

Aglietta, M. and B. Mojon (2010). 'Central banking', Chapter 9 in A. Berger, P. Molineux and J. Wilson (eds.), *The Handbook of Banking*, Oxford University Press

Alessi, L. and C. Detken (2009). 'Real time early warning indicators for costly asset price boom/bust cycles: a role for global liquidity', ECB Working Paper, No. **1039**

Antipa, P., E. Mengus and B. Mojon (2010). 'Would macroprudential policies have prevented the great recession?', Banque de France, mimeo

Barthélemy, J., M. Marx and A. Poissonnier (2010). 'Trends and cycles: an historical review of the Euro area', Banque de France Working Paper, No. **258**

Bernanke, B. S. (2010). 'Monetary policy and the housing bubble', Paper presented at the Annual Meeting of the American Economic Association, Atlanta, Georgia, 3 January

Blinder, A. (2010). 'How central should the central bank be?', *Journal of Economic Literature*, **48**(1): 123–33

Bordes, C. and L. Clerc (2010). 'L'art du *central banking* de la BCE et le principe de séparation', *Revue d'Économie Politique*, **120**(2): 269–302

Borgy, V., L. Clerc and J.-P. Renne (2009). 'Asset-price boom-bust cycles and credit: what is the scope of macro-prudential regulation?', Banque de France Working Paper, No. **263**

Cassola, N., C. Holthausen and F. Würtz (2008). 'Liquidity management under market turmoil. Experience of the European Central Bank in the first year of the 2007–2008 financial market crisis', ECB, mimeo

Christiano, L. J., M. Eichenbaum and C. L. Evans (2005). 'Nominal rigidities and the dynamic effects of a shock to monetary policy', *Journal of Political Economy*, **113**(1): 1–45

Ciccarelli, M., A. Maddaloni and J. L. Peydro (2009). 'Trusting the bankers: a new look at the credit channel of monetary policy', ECB Working Paper, No. **1228**

Gali, J. (2010). 'The monetary pillar and the great financial crisis', Universitat Pompeu Fabra, mimeo, June

Greenspan, A. (2008). 'Testimony to the Congress', 23 October

Iacoviello, M. (2005). 'House prices, borrowing constraints and monetary policy in the business cycle', *American Economic Review*, **95**(3): 739–64

Poole, W. (1970). 'Optimal choice of monetary policy instruments in a simple stochastic macro model', *Quarterly Journal of Economics*, **84**(2): 197–216

Smets, F. and R. Wouters (2003). 'An estimated dynamic stochastic general equilibrium model of the euro area', *Journal of the European Economic Association*, **1**(5): 1123–75

    (2007). 'Shocks and frictions in US business cycles: a Bayesian DSGE approach,' CEPR Discussion Paper, No. **6112**

Taylor, J. B. and J. C. Williams (2009). 'A black swan in the money market', *American Economic Journal: Macroeconomics*, **1**(1): 58–83

15   Is there a case for price-level targeting?

*Boris Cournède and Diego Moccero**

1   Introduction

There is widespread recognition among academics and policy-makers that monetary policy should aim at price stability. A large number of economies have adopted inflation targeting (IT) as the main objective of monetary policy, aiming at maintaining low and predictable inflation rates as a way of preserving the purchasing power of money. Evidence abounds that targeting inflation has been successful in anchoring and stabilising inflation rates and inflation expectations, with no apparent increase in output volatility, from the end of the 1980s to the beginning of this century (Mishkin and Schmidt-Hebbel, 2001, 2007). Moreover, there is mounting evidence that inflation targeting contributes to keeping inflation low and predictable (Fatás, Mihov and Rose, 2006; Angeris and Arestis, 2008; Benati, 2008; Calderón and Schmidt-Hebbel, 2008).

Nonetheless, current monetary policy frameworks have been brought into question by the frequency with which deflation has taken hold of or threatened OECD economies. Japan went through a period of deflation in 2000–6 while the US was perceived to be exposed to a deflation risk in 2001 and again in 2003. A consequence of the current financial and economic crisis is that deflation has once more emerged as a risk, this time in many OECD countries, while it has taken hold of Japan again. While monetary policy frameworks may need to be reassessed with a

* The authors are members of the Macroeconomic Policy Division of the OECD Economics Department. This work was presented to the conference 'The Euro Area and the Financial Crisis' at the National Bank of Slovakia, Bratislava, 6–8 September 2010, under the auspices of the National Bank of Slovakia, the Heriot–Watt University of Edinburgh and the Comenius University of Bratislava. The authors are indebted to Sebastian Barnes, Hervé Boulhol, David Cobham, Andrea De Michelis, Jørgen Elmeskov, Romain Duval, David Haugh, Peter Hoeller, Michal Horvath, Jens Høj, Jeremy Lawson, Robert Price, Jean-Luc Schneider, Klaus Schmidt-Hebbel, Luke Willard, Eckhard Wurzel and participants in the Bratislava conference for their useful comments. The authors are grateful to Catherine Lemoine for statistical assistance and Susan Gascard and Veronica Humi for secretarial assistance. The opinions expressed in this chapter are those of the authors and are not necessarily shared by the OECD or its member countries.

view to reducing deflation risk, any changes should occur only once current objectives are attained, for fear of undermining confidence in central banks. Against this background an alternative interpretation of price stability has attracted increasing attention from policy-makers in the recent past (Ambler, 2009; Parkin, 2009): it is the notion of *price-level* stability, where the monetary authority aims at stabilising an aggregate price level around a pre-specified path, instead of its rate of change. A principal advantage of price-level targeting is that it is more consistent with the objective of preserving the long-run purchasing power of money. For instance, following a temporary inflation spike, such as that observed in 2005–7, inflation targeting regimes will leave the purchasing power of money permanently below what would have transpired if inflation targets had been met. A successful price-level-based framework would also avoid a permanent increase in the real value of debt after a period of deflation. Practical experience of price-level targeting is, however, restricted to one historical episode, in Sweden during the 1930s (discussed on p. 312).

Against this background, the present chapter analyses whether, and in what circumstances, targeting the price level would have economic advantages over IT for output and price stability. There appear to be pros and cons, the main four benefits of price-level targeting identified in the chapter being:

- Depending on a minimum share of firms and households behaving in a forward-looking manner, a price-level targeting regime can act as a built-in stabiliser by reducing the need for large moves in policy interest rates in response to shocks. For instance, faced with a price-level fall, agents would expect inflation to rise to bring the price level back to its target path, which would reduce the long-term real interest rate, thereby working to support activity and pushing up prices.[1]
- Insofar as the expectations channel reduces the need for large shifts in policy interest rates, the economy will be less likely to fall into a liquidity trap.
- A credible price-level targeting mechanism can have a positive effect on capital accumulation and steady-state growth insofar as it reduces the cost of long-run nominal contracts by protecting the long-run purchasing power of money. In particular, the inflation-risk premium embedded in equilibrium long-term interest rates can be expected to be lower.
- Targeting the price level could also mitigate the risk of price shocks passing through to wages, by protecting against the redistributive

---

[1] Similarly, an increase in inflation would imply lower inflation expectations and therefore higher real interest rates, in turn damping demand and inflation.

effects of unanticipated inflation and reducing the incentive to index wages.

On the other hand, price-level targeting is not without cost or risks, which reduce its practical application:

- IT is better at protecting against welfare losses than price-level targeting when there is strong uncertainty about the presence of a sufficient minimum degree of forward-looking behaviour by economic agents.
- The self-regulating capacity of price-level targeting may be undermined if central banks are not fully credible. An initial lack of credibility may force central banks to choose too short a policy horizon, inducing output gap and nominal interest rate volatility.
- If the IT regime is sufficiently aggressive it may replicate a number (but not all) of the beneficial stabilising features of a price-level targeting monetary framework.

Weighing the pros and cons of price-level targeting, there is no clear-cut case for a change in the monetary regime. This is especially the case since the transition costs for moving from one regime to the other (for example, in terms of communication strategy and the compromising of credibility) may be significant. More practical experience is needed before one can definitely conclude that price-level targeting constitutes a worthy alternative to current monetary frameworks.

Section 2 presents the main advantages of price-level targeting. Section 3 discusses the drawbacks. Section 4 then addresses implementation issues, in particular regarding the time-frame over which the monetary authorities aim to reach the target, before discussing the Swedish experience with price-level targeting and concluding in section 5 with remarks about the hypothesis of price-level targeting in the euro area.

2   The benefits of price-level targeting

2.1   *A built-in stabilisation mechanism*

A key benefit of price-level targeting is the automatic stabilisation that results from changes in inflation expectations. Whenever a shock hits the price level, a credible price-level targeting regime will prompt a change in expected inflation that goes in the opposite direction. The resulting change in the *ex ante* real interest rate will cause aggregate demand to adjust in such a way that output and employment are partly stabilised. For instance, in the case of an unexpected cost-push shock that causes inflation to deviate from target at the end of the period, under inflation targeting next-period expected inflation does not change, unless the target changes. In contrast, under price-level targeting, the sum of future inflation rates has to match the negative of the actual inflation gap (the percentage difference between the price level and the target): if the inflation gap is positive and high today, inflation should undershoot in the future. To the extent that they are forward-looking, households and firms will anticipate that the central bank will tighten monetary policy in order to bring the current price level in line with the target. For a given policy interest rate, the reduction in expected inflation will increase the *ex ante* real rate, which will help contain aggregate demand and help to equilibrate output and prices.[2]

2.2   Protection against a liquidity trap

Price-level targeting may reduce the probability of falling into liquidity traps when economic agents are forward-looking. The reason is that, as mentioned above, a credible regime will be self-stabilising and therefore require smaller moves in nominal interest rates, reducing the probability of hitting the zero lower bound.[3] Simulation results show that, in both a benchmark model with forward-looking agents and a variant including significant backward-looking behaviour, credible price-level targeting is a powerful cure against the risk of falling into a liquidity trap (Box 15.1).[4] The results also suggest that moving to price-level targeting is more effective than raising the inflation target to reduce the risk of hitting the zero lower bound of nominal interest rates. Furthermore, moving to price-level targeting with a slope equal to the previous inflation target probably also involves lower transition costs and smaller risks to central bank credibility than making the inflation target substantially higher or dependent on past output gaps, as suggested by Svensson (1997).

A related but distinct question is which monetary policy regime is better equipped to help the economy get out of a liquidity trap. If price-level targeting is introduced once the economy is already 'trapped', the stabilising real interest rate effect may not materialise, because households and firms may question the credibility of the announced long-term commitment to the new regime. Even if credibility is ensured, the stabilising properties of price-level targeting may be diminished because the

---

[2] The case where the monetary authorities are not fully credible is analysed later in the chapter.

[3] In doing so, price-level targeting automatically mimics optimal intertemporal policy, which in the face of a deflationary shock calls for the central bank to pre-commit to keeping inflation above target for some time in the future (Eggertsson and Woodford, 2003).

[4] Cover and Pecorino (2005) obtain the same result in a dynamic IS–LM model that incorporates a significant degree of backward-looking consumption behaviour.

Box 15.1: Price-level targeting vs. higher inflation targets as protection against hitting the zero lower bound

Price-level targeting can help avoid hitting the zero lower bound on interest rates when faced with very weak demand. Under price-level targeting, when a negative demand shock brings inflation down or even into negative territory, households and firms expect that the monetary authorities will credibly generate high inflation in the future, after the economy has exited the demand deficit situation, in order to get back to the target path for the price level. This automatic mechanism implies that *real* interest rates will automatically fall after a negative demand shock under price-level targeting, which helps to offset part of the shock. This automatic stabilisation mechanism is absent under IT where, because 'bygones are bygones', the central bank cannot credibly commit to keeping inflation above target in the future after the economy is out of the situation of weak demand. To reduce the risk of hitting the zero lower bound while remaining under IT, another option that has been considered is to raise the inflation target (Blanchard, Dell'Ariccia and Mauro, 2010).

A simple DSGE model can be used to illustrate how markedly the two regimes can differ in this respect, at least when households and firms are forward-looking. The model is based on profit-maximising firms and utility-maximising households in an environment where firms produce differentiated goods and have pricing power but only a fraction of firms can reset their prices in each period. In this setting, and with a credible positive long-run inflation target $\bar{\pi}$, actual inflation π_t and the output gap y_t follow a forward-looking New Keynesian Phillips curve (15.1) and a dynamic IS curve (15.2).[1] In these equations, r_t^n is the natural real rate of interest, and μ_t and ν_t are stochastic shocks to prices and aggregate demand. The frequency of price adjustment (θ) is assumed to be invariant to the choice of monetary policy regime. The other parameters are structural: β stands for the discount rate, σ is the coefficient of relative risk aversion and κ is a structural parameter which is a function of β, σ, the elasticity of labour supply (ϕ), the degree of substitutability across differentiated goods (ε) and the equilibrium capital share (α).[2] In this framework, the welfare loss resulting from the presence of partly inflexible prices can be calculated as expression (15.3) in terms of the equivalent loss of steady-state consumption (Woodford, 2003;

Galí, 2008).

$$\pi_t = (1 - \beta)\,\bar{\pi} + \beta E_t\,[\pi_{t+1}] + \kappa y_t + \mu_t \tag{15.1}$$

$$y_t = E_t\,[y_{t+1}] - \tfrac{1}{\sigma}\,(i_t - E_t\,[\pi_{t+1}] - r_t^n) + v_t \tag{15.2}$$

$$W_0 = -\tfrac{1}{2}E_0\left[\tfrac{\varepsilon}{\lambda}\,(\pi_t - \bar{\pi})^2 + \left(\sigma + \tfrac{\phi+\alpha}{1-\alpha}\right)y_t^2\right] \tag{15.3}$$

This framework permits the comparison of different monetary policy strategies, defined as instrument rules relating the policy rate to economic variables. A conventional Taylor rule (15.4) with conventional coefficients is compared to a very soft price-level targeting rule (15.5) where p_t stands for the log-price level, which evolves as $p_t = p_{t-1} + \pi_t$. The values of the structural parameters are set as in Galí (2008) while the estimates by Smets and Wouters (2003) and Galí, Gertler and López-Salido (2007) are used to calibrate the demand and cost-push shocks, respectively.[3] In the cases of the conventional Taylor rule and soft price-level targeting, a value of $\bar{\pi} = 2$ per cent is assumed for the inflation target and the slope of the targeted price-level path, respectively. In another simulation, undertaken to study the option considered by Blanchard, Dell'Ariccia and Mauro (2010), the inflation target $\bar{\pi}$ is raised to 4 per cent.

$$i_t = r_t^n + \bar{\pi} + 1.5\,(\pi_t - \bar{\pi}) + 0.5 y_t \tag{15.4}$$

$$i_t = r_t^n + \bar{\pi} + 0.2\,(p_t - \bar{\pi}t) + 0.5 y_t \tag{15.5}$$

The simulation results shown in Box Table 15.1 illustrate the powerful stabilising effect of price-level targeting in the model for an economy hit by persistent cost-push and demand shocks. Even under the very soft price-level targeting rule studied here, where the coefficient on price deviations is quite small, the policy rate is much more stable than under a standard Taylor rule. As a result, the zero lower bound is never hit. In contrast, with a Taylor rule monetary policy regime, nominal interest rates are negative 10 per cent of the time. The greater stabilisation power of price-level targeting also leads to a sizeable reduction in the welfare costs of fluctuations compared with IT in the simulations (even assuming, as is implicit in the model, that negative nominal rates are practically feasible). Simulation results suggest that raising the inflation target also reduces the chance of hitting the zero lower bound, but not to the same extent as price-level targeting.

It should be noted, however, that the model involves strong assumptions. In particular, all firms consider that the inflation target will

Box Table 15.1: *Compared simulated effects of IT and price-level targeting*

	Standard inflation target	Soft price-level target	4 per cent IT
% of time when short-term nominal interest rates are negative	10.0	0.0	2.3
Standard deviation of nominal interest rate	0.8	0.2	0.8
Standard deviation of real cost of capital	0.3	0.2	0.3
Standard deviation of inflation	0.5	0.2	0.5
Standard deviation of output	0.6	0.7	0.6
Welfare loss due to output and inflation fluctuations (equivalent cut in steady-state consumption, %)	16.0	3.0	16.0

Note: Each simulation has been run over 10,000 quarters using random draws of the shocks and solving as in Blanchard and Khan (1980).

Box Table 15.2: *Simulation results with backward-looking behaviour*

	Standard inflation target	Soft price-level target	4 per cent IT
% of time when short-term nominal interest rates are negative	9.2	0.0	1.6
Standard deviation of nominal interest rate	0.7	0.2	0.7
Standard deviation of real cost of capital	0.3	0.2	0.3
Standard deviation of inflation	0.5	0.2	0.5
Standard deviation of output	0.2	0.4	0.2
Welfare loss due to output and inflation fluctuations (equivalent cut in steady-state consumption, %)	2.8	1.1	2.8

Note: See note to Box Table 15.1.

be met on average in the long term and form their price expectations accordingly in a purely forward-looking way. This assumption is relaxed in an extension where, following Woodford (2003: 213–16), in each period, 60 per cent ($\gamma = 0.6$) of firms that do not reassess their prices let them increase in line with past inflation π_{t-1} instead of the long-run inflation target $\bar{\pi}$. In this setting, the Phillips curve becomes the hybrid specification (15.6) and the welfare loss due to fluctuations is given by (15.7). The results in Box Table 15.2 indicate that the conclusions reached under the benchmark, forward-looking model still obtain in the extended model: interest rates are more variable and the zero lower bound is hit more frequently under inflation targeting.

$$\pi_t = \frac{\gamma\pi_{t-1} + (1-\beta)(1-\gamma)\bar{\pi} + \beta E_t[\pi_{t+1}] + \kappa y_t + \lambda\mu_t}{1+\beta\gamma}$$

(15.6)

$$W_0 = -\tfrac{1}{2}E_0\left[\tfrac{\varepsilon}{\lambda}(\pi_t - (\gamma\pi_{t-1} + (1-\gamma)\bar{\pi}))^2 + \left(\sigma + \tfrac{\phi+\alpha}{1-\alpha}\right)y_t^2\right]$$

(15.7)

The hybrid model incorporates strong implicit assumptions such as flexible wages and complete financial markets. While wage rigidities, nominal or real, would be likely to narrow the welfare gap between IT and price-level targeting (because they imply a greater weight of output gap deviations in the loss function), they would probably not qualitatively alter the results on the frequency at which the zero lower bound is hit. The reason is that adding wage rigidities amounts to incorporating more persistence and the base model is already quite persistent because of the high autocorrelation of the shocks, while the extended model incorporates a lot of additional inertia because of indexation. In contrast, it may be conjectured that relaxing the assumption of complete financial markets by including liquidity-constrained households would partly reduce the benefit of price-level targeting, because the stabilising feedback from the price-level target on real interest rates would only influence unconstrained households. Another valuable extension would be to compare the two regimes in an open-economy setting. A last extension would consist in making some of the parameters regime-dependent, starting with the frequency of price adjustment.

The capacity of price-level targeting to protect against the zero lower bound could also be used to lower the slope of the targeted path, and therefore the long-term average rate of inflation, as a way of reducing the economic cost of inflation.[4] Simulations with the two simple models presented above suggest that the slope of the targeted path for the price level can be reduced to very low equilibrium inflation rates without creating any significant risk of hitting the zero lower bound (Box Table 15.3). In contrast, IT regimes quickly lead to unacceptably high chances of hitting the zero lower bound in the two models.

Box Table 15.3: *IT vs. price-level targeting at very low equilibrium inflation rates: % of time when short-term nominal interest rates are negative*

	Benchmark model		Model with 60 per cent backward-looking indexation	
	Standard Taylor rule	Soft price-level target	Standard Taylor rule	Soft price-level target
2 per cent equilibrium inflation	10.0	0.0	9.2	0.0
1 per cent equilibrium inflation	18.0	0.05	17.0	0.05
0.5 per cent equilibrium inflation	23.0	0.13	22.0	0.16
Zero equilibrium inflation	28.0	0.84	22.0	0.84

Note: See note to Box Table 15.1.

Notes

1. The inflation target $\bar{\pi}$ is credible in the sense that firms that do not re-examine their price in the light of future demand in a given period instead increase their prices at the rate $\bar{\pi}$ as in Yun (1996). See Woodford (2003: 213) for the expression of the New Keynesian Phillips curve in the presence of a positive inflation target. The derivation of the welfare loss function (15.3) in this setting is an exact parallel of the proof of Proposition 6.5 in Woodford (2003).
2. $\kappa = \lambda(\sigma + \frac{\phi+\alpha}{1-\alpha})$ where $\lambda = \frac{(1-\theta)(1-\beta\theta)(1-\alpha)}{\theta(1-\alpha+\alpha\varepsilon)}$.
3. The corresponding values are: $\beta = 0.99$, $\theta = 2/3$, $\alpha = 1/3$, $\varepsilon = 6$, $\sigma = 1$, $\phi = 1$. The shocks are AR(1) with standard deviations $\sigma(\mu_t) = 0.1$ and $\sigma(\nu_t) = 0.297$ and autocorrelations $\rho(\mu_t) = 0.88$ and $\rho(\nu_t) = 0.93$. Finally, $r_t^n = 2$ per cent.
4. For a discussion of the optimal rate of inflation, see for instance Cogley (1997), Schmitt-Grohé and Uribe (2010) and Coibion, Gorodnichenko and Wieland (2010) for a focus on the consequences of the zero lower bound.

elasticity of demand with respect to the real interest rate is likely to be smaller in a liquidity trap, where the traditional monetary policy transmission mechanism is weakened (Aoki and Yoshikawa, 2006). Unconventional monetary policy actions, such as expanding the central bank balance sheet and altering the composition of its assets, may be more appropriate in this situation (Bernanke and Reinhart, 2004).

2.3   *A stable nominal anchor for planning and contracting*

Price-level targeting also has the advantage of eliminating uncertainties about the future purchasing power of money, because it better anchors long-run price levels. A price-level targeting regime ensures that the actual price level fluctuates around the long-run trend implied by the target path. A valuable consequence is that the variance of the price level does not increase with the time horizon. In contrast, under IT, shocks affect the price level used as a base for the inflation target in the succeeding period. Since the central bank does not compensate for deviations in this base – 'bygones are bygones' – the price level follows a random walk with drift process. In other words, one-off shocks to inflation have a permanent effect on the price level under IT. In addition, the variance of the price level therefore increases over time, implying that the purchasing power of money becomes more and more uncertain as the time horizon extends further in the future.

Model simulations suggest that sizeable differences can emerge in the purchasing power of money between a price-level and an IT regime. Figure 15.1 shows that, in the benchmark model presented in Box 15.1, the same shocks result in very different trajectories for the price level even if both monetary regimes target the same steady-state inflation rates. In particular, even a 'soft' price-level target such as the one used in the benchmark model pins down the price level on its target path quite strongly.[5] The fact that, in contrast, shocks have permanent effects on the price level under IT, which is evident in the model simulations shown in Figure 15.1, is also visible in historical data. As an illustration, Figure 15.2 compares the historical price level in the four largest OECD economies to the trajectory that it would follow if inflation remained constant on its *de jure* or *de facto* target rate.

The variability of inflation will also differ between the two monetary regimes. The conventional wisdom maintains that short-run inflation volatility should increase under price-level targeting, because unexpected increases in the price level should be followed by attempts to reduce inflation. This applies where shocks are purely random or have a very low degree of persistence; price-level targeting can then require that past

---

[5] The fact that the long-term slope coefficient of the price level is lower under price-level targeting than IT in Figure 15.1 is purely a result of the non-stationary nature of the price level under IT and the configuration of the random draws of the shocks in the particular simulation shown. Under commitment in monetary policy, the log of the price level will exhibit the same long-term slope coefficient under both monetary policy regimes when averaged across different draws of the shocks. In contrast, if monetary policy is conducted in a discretionary fashion, the log of the price level will exhibit a steeper slope under IT than price-level targeting (Svensson, 1999).

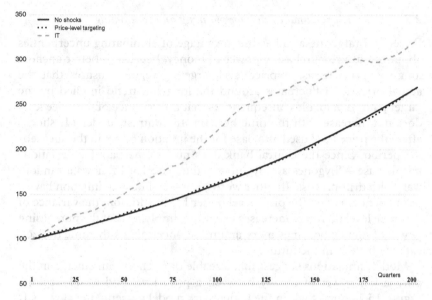

Figure 15.1: Prices over long periods: price-level targeting vs. IT in model simulations

Note: The paths for the price level are simulated for the same shocks with the same benchmark dynamic stochastic general equilibrium model presented in Box 15.1 under two different rules for monetary policy: a standard IT Taylor rule and a soft price-level rule.

Source: Calculations by the authors.

deviations be offset. However, when shocks are highly auto-correlated, as historical experience suggests is the case,[6] price-level targeting will reduce the short-term variability of inflation, both when monetary authorities can commit to a rule (as in the benchmark model presented in Box 15.1) and when they act in a discretionary manner (as in Svensson's later model, Svensson, 1999). Again, the expectation channel is at the origin of this effect. For instance, following a persistent cost-push shock, expected inflation will fall under price-level targeting, which will work via the Phillips curve to reduce actual inflation, thereby partly offsetting the effect of the continued shock. The same reasoning applies following a persistent demand shock.

Guaranteeing the future purchasing power of money can have important consequences for the economy. A direct consequence is that it would facilitate long-term planning by reducing the price risk in long-term

---

[6] See, for instance, Smets and Wouters (2003).

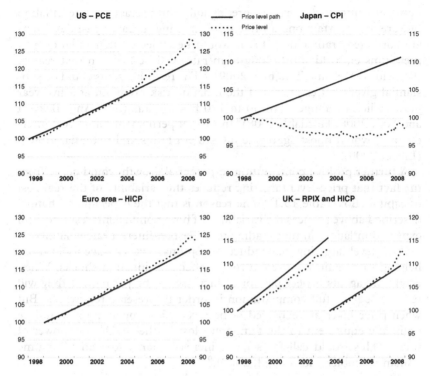

Figure 15.2: Price index and price-level target path: selected countries, 1998–2008

Note: For the US, the price stability target path assumes an implicit inflation rate of 1.9 per cent. The sample period starts in 1998 for the sake of comparability with other countries. For Japan, the price stability target path assumes an implicit inflation rate of 1 per cent. The sample starts with the enactment of a new Bank of Japan Act (1997) stating price stability as the goal of monetary policy. For the euro area, the price stability target path assumes an implicit inflation rate of 2 per cent. The sample period starts with the irrevocable fixing of the member countries' exchange rates. For the UK, the price stability target path assumes an implicit inflation rate of 2.5 per cent until December 2003, and 2 per cent thereafter. The price index targeted by the monetary authorities is the retail price index (RPI) excluding interest payments (RPIX) until December 2003 and the consumer price index (CPI) thereafter. The sample starts with the new monetary policy framework by which the monetary authority sets interest rates to meet the inflation target.
Source: Bureau of Economic Analysis (BEA) for United States, Datastream for Japan, Eurostat for euro area and Office for National Statistics (ONS) and Eurostat for UK.

nominal contracts.[7] Furthermore, as long-run averages of the inflation rate are more certain under price-level targeting (because past deviations are corrected) rather than IT, it would be expected that inflation risk premiums embedded into long-term rates will be lower in that regime (Crawford, Meh and Terajima, 2009).[8] The resulting gains could be substantial given that estimates of the inflation risk premium at a five-year horizon lie in a range from 30 to 110 basis points (bp) (Ang, Bekaert and Wei, 2008; Hördahl, 2008). In turn, a permanent fall in real interest rates would boost aggregate investment ratios and potential growth (Lilico, 2000).

A further positive contribution to potential growth would come from the fact that price-level targeting reduces the variability of the real cost of capital (Box Table 15.1). The reason is that the expectation channel described above reduces the variability of both nominal interest rates and expected inflation, in turn leading to lower real-interest rate volatility.

Price-level targeting may reduce the optimal level of wage indexation, helping to contain the second-round effects of inflation shocks. When economic agents expect past price increases to be permanent they will tend to request full compensation in order to preserve real wages. But when price hikes are expected to be reversed, compensation would be optimally equivalent to the temporary loss in the purchasing power of wages. This would call for a lower increase than under an IT regime (Amano, Ambler and Ireland, 2007).[9]

Unanticipated inflation will lead to smaller redistributive effects under price-level targeting rather than IT (Box 15.2). The main reason is that economic agents differ in terms of their portfolios, in particular as the young and poor are overrepresented among net borrowers.

2.4   A reduced probability of asset-price bubbles?

There are some grounds for supposing that asset-price fluctuations may be easier to avoid under price-level targeting than IT. That would be the case, for example, in a monetary policy easing phase of the cycle in which interest rates can be below neutral for a sustained period of time, for instance following a negative demand shock. As illustrated in

---

[7] The size of this benefit is probably limited in practice, because if benefits were greater than the transaction costs of indexing, indexed contracts would be more common. However, it should be noted that indexation, especially in wage-setting, entails real rigidities which reduce welfare.

[8] This result of course assumes that monetary policy is fully credible under price-level targeting.

[9] The potential benefit arising from buffering the second-round effects of inflationary shocks through the attenuation of wage increases is to be gauged against actual indexation practices. Where indexation is not widespread, then this potential advantage will be small.

Box 15.2: Redistributive effects under inflation and price-level targeting

Because inflation shocks can erode the long-term real value of nominal assets and liabilities under IT but less so under price-level targeting, the choice between the two regimes will have distributive implications. Redistribution effects will reflect differences in the portfolio composition across different groups and sectors in the society. In particular, the young middle-class and the poor tend to be net borrowers (due mostly to mortgage liability holdings), while the rich and the old tend to be net savers (due to pension and long-term bond holdings). Across sectors, in many developed nations the government tends to be a net borrower while the household sector, as well as the foreign sector, tends to be a net lender.

Because price-level targeting provides a stable nominal anchor in the long term, gains and losses on long-term nominal claims will be attenuated relative to those under an IT regime. Meh, Ríos-Rull and Terajima (2008) find that redistributive effects can be substantial under IT. In a model calibrated for the Canadian economy, a one-time positive 1 per cent price-level shock leads to a gross redistribution among households of 5.5 per cent of GDP. As mentioned before, on average, the winners are the young poor and the young middle-class, while the middle-aged workers, the old and the rich are the losers. Moreover, the household sector net wealth loss against the government amounts to 0.4 per cent of GDP under IT (and is almost three times bigger than under price-level targeting).

Meh, Ríos-Rull and Terajima also analyse the impact on output and welfare of different fiscal policies transferring to households the government's windfall gain or loss. In particular, they study the case of a reduction in labour taxes, lump-sum transfers and a transfer to retirees when a positive price-level shock improves the government's portfolio. As agents are heterogeneous regarding labour productivity and propensities to work and save, different types of fiscal policy transfers will have non-zero effects, despite the fact that the redistribution shock is zero-sum across agents in the economy. For these reasons, there will be non-zero effects even under price-level targeting. As expected from the arguments presented in the text, the authors find that the impact is much bigger under IT.

Source: Meh, Ríos-Rull and Terajima (2008).

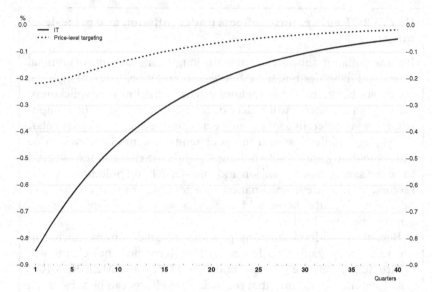

Figure 15.3: Response of nominal interest rate to negative demand shock

Note: The shock is a 1 per cent of GDP negative demand shock. The policy response is calculated in the benchmark model presented in Box 15.1.

Source: Calculations by the authors.

Figure 15.3, the policy easing would be expected to be more aggressive under IT (because changes in *ex ante* real interest rates occur mainly through changes in nominal rates rather than expected inflation, as mentioned on p. 294). In this situation, with substantially lower policy rates over three–five years, an IT regime might potentially be more likely to generate asset bubbles than a price-level-based framework. More generally, including when the economy is also hit by cost-push shocks, price-level targeting reduces the variability of nominal and real interest rates compared with IT (see Box Table 15.1), creating an environment where bubbles might be less likely to develop. Drawing a conclusion about asset-price bubbles based on a premise regarding interest rate movements is highly tentative, however, because bubbles, by definition, occur when prices diverge from fundamentals (of which interest rates are a part) and can arise either in or out of phase with movements in the price level itself.[10]

---

[10] The formation of bubbles cannot be studied inside the model underpinning Figure 15.1. See, for instance, Ahrend, Cournède and Price (2008) for a discussion of the link between low nominal rates and asset-price bubbles and financial market excesses.

3   Main concerns about price-level targeting

3.1   *Greater output volatility*

Central banks are traditionally concerned with the implications of monetary policy for output volatility. Until relatively recently, the dominant view – as expressed, for instance, by Fischer (1994) – was that a price-level targeting regime would induce too much output volatility, implying that an IT regime should be preferred. The intuition was that, under price-level targeting, monetary policy should strongly react to shocks if it is to ensure that the price level reverts to target, inducing interest rate and output volatility. In contrast, under IT, central banks will only partially adjust to changes in the price level.

In fact, theoretical and simulation results on the impact of the monetary policy regime on output gap volatility give mixed results and depend heavily on the model specification and parameters chosen. In the two simple Dynamic Stochastic General Equilibrium (DSGE) models presented in Box 15.1, compared with IT a price-level rule reduces inflation and interest rate volatility but at the cost of greater output variability. Coletti, Lalonde and Muir (2008) obtain the same conclusion in a more comprehensive setting using the Bank of Canada's model for both Canada and the United States. In Svensson's highly stylised model (Svensson, 1999), output gap volatility is not affected by the monetary regime, a fact that can be attributed to the absence of an IS curve in the model. In a model where policy is discretionary (meaning that today's decision only aims at maximising today's welfare), Cover and Pecorino (2005) find that price-level targeting also reduces output volatility compared with IT.

The importance of the degree of forward-looking behaviour by economic agents for the effectiveness of price-level targeting regimes has been extensively analysed in the literature. Williams (2003) studied this issue using the large-scale Federal Reserve Board model for the US economy (FRB/US). The author compares the performance of simple monetary policy rules under commitment and finds that the impact of the monetary regime on the volatility of inflation and output changes with the extent of forward-looking behaviour (i.e. the degree to which price and wage determination are made with rational expectations about the future rather than following rules based on past outcomes). He shows that, under rational expectations, targeting the price level instead of inflation generates little additional output and inflation volatility, because the expectations channel helps stabilise inflation, at the same time reducing output stabilisation costs. Similar results are obtained by Smets (2003), Guender and Oh (2006) and Vestin (2006).

3.2   *Possibly greater vulnerability to model uncertainty*

Price-level targeting may be less robust to model uncertainty than a standard IT Taylor rule. Given that the monetary authorities usually have imperfect information about which model parameterisation provides the most adequate description of the economy, it would be desirable for operational purposes to specify monetary policy rules that are robust to uncertainty in those coefficients. This is particularly the case with respect to the degree of forward-looking behaviour by economic agents which is central for the success of a price-level targeting regime. Jääskelä (2005) studies this issue by assuming that the coefficients of policy rules are optimised with respect to a given benchmark model configuration, when the true model of the economy is described by some other parameterisation. In other words, the monetary authority optimises the coefficients of its policy-reaction function with respect to a different set of parameters than those governing the true economic structure. The author finds that the performance of price-level targeting deteriorates in terms of both inflation and output fluctuations, implying welfare losses, when consumption and pricing decisions are dominated by strong backward-looking behaviour. The result is primarily due to the fact that the beneficial expectation channel inherent in price-level targeting requires a minimum degree of forward-looking behaviour. Under IT the value of the loss function is relatively stable, even when the monetary authorities are wrong with respect to the forward-looking behaviour of economic agents. However, the degree of backward-looking behaviour above which price-level targeting starts to underperform a standard inflation rule is very high.[11] Furthermore, with some forward-looking behaviour, price-level targeting is more robust to changes in or misspecification of shock processes and less prone to indeterminacy (Giannoni, 2010).

Models that combine prevalent backward-looking behaviour with strong exchange rate effects are another illustration of possible situations where price-level rules perform poorly relative to inflation targeting.

---

[11] For instance, in a standard model of price-setting incorporating backward-looking behaviour such as Galí and Gertler's (1999) model with an average duration of prices of three-quarters or less (as apparent in US and euro area data, see Dhyne *et al.*, 2006; Nakamura and Steinsson, 2008), even if all but an infinitesimal fraction of firms are backward-looking, the degree of persistence will *not* be high enough to generate a situation where inflation targeting dominates a price-level rule in Jääskelä's (2005) model. With Galí and Gertler's (1999) structural estimates of the degree of forward-looking behaviour in price-setting, the economy is very firmly in the region where price-level targeting clearly outperforms inflation targeting in Jääskelä's (2005) model. However, some reduced-form estimates of the Phillips curve such as Rudebusch (2002) lie in the range of values where price-level targeting delivers poor results in Jääskelä's (2005) model.

Batini and Yates (2003) study an open economy where the exchange rate enters a strongly backward-looking Phillips curve. In this setting, opening the economy increases inflation and price volatility under both monetary policy regimes, but price-level targeting increases inflation variability relative to IT. This is because in their model with backward-looking behaviour in price-setting and consumption, targeting the price level induces a higher interest rate variance and, through the uncovered interest parity condition (UIP), higher exchange rate volatility than IT. Indeed, model uncertainty and the associated effects of imperfectly calibrated policy rules therefore argue in favour of inflation targeting.

3.3   Higher burden on central bank credibility

The last concern about price-level targeting is that its capacity to maintain price stability by relying on market forces is based on the premise that monetary authorities are fully credible. Using the same argument as before, for expected inflation to rise following a positive supply-side shock, economic agents must believe that the monetary authorities will forcibly reduce interest rates, so that the price level will increase and will converge to the price-level target in the near future. If the price level does not actually converge to the target reasonably quickly, agents may start doubting the commitment or capacity of central banks to achieve monetary policy objectives. If credibility is lost, faced with an unexpected price-level fall, private agents will not revise their expected inflation upwards, and the self-regulating mechanism will fail. Studying a scenario where the central bank moves from inflation to price-level targeting, Kryvtsov, Shukayev and Ueberfeldt (2008) show that the self-regulating mechanism remains weak as long as the public fears that monetary policy could revert to the old regime – that is, when the commitment to the new monetary policy regime is imperfect. In their model, it takes about two-and-a-half years before the new price-level regime acquires a degree of credibility sufficient to deliver welfare gains over IT.

Moreover, if central bank credibility is initially low the authorities may be forced to choose too short a monetary policy horizon, in which case welfare losses will be lower under IT than price-level targeting (Smets, 2003). This is because price-level targeting will induce too much output gap volatility as the policy horizon shortens.

But even if the monetary authorities already enjoy a high degree of credibility, the fact that price-level targeting is a more demanding monetary regime may end by eroding central bank credibility. Taking the example of a small open economy in which exchange rate shocks tend to occur more frequently than in closed economies, achieving a price-level target may be more difficult than reaching an inflation target. This could threaten the credibility of the policy regime, because the path towards a credible price-level target is potentially quite costly. This can be especially the case for developing countries, in which actual and targeted price levels have deviated substantially under IT. Indeed, in some situations and for some countries, especially for small open economies hit by large terms of trade shocks (such as commodity exporters), it can be optimal to let 'bygones be bygones'.

4   Implementation issues

4.1   *The feedback and policy horizon*

Central banks aim at reaching price stability over the medium term rather than instantaneously. This is because the transmission mechanism of monetary policy tends to operate with lags, and trying to counteract short-term shocks to the price level over which the monetary authorities have only little control may result in higher interest rate volatility and output losses. A gradualist response to shocks may avoid such excessive volatility. The question naturally arises of what is the optimal policy horizon for monetary policy – or, in other words, the time-frame over which the monetary authorities should intend to bring inflation back to target. Smets (2003) analyses this issue in a small-scale forward-looking model calibrated for the euro area. In his set-up, the monetary authority acts under commitment and wishes to minimise both interest rate and output gap volatility, subject to the constraint that it should achieve a given price or inflation target over a specific time horizon. The author finds that, for both IT and price-level targeting, setting too short a horizon reduces inflation variability at the expense of increasing output gap and interest rate volatility. The intuition behind this result is that, when the horizon is short, central banks will react promptly to inflationary shocks, making both the monetary tool and the output gap too volatile, but at the same time containing inflationary/deflationary pressures.[12]

Smets (2003) also observes that, for a given policy horizon, the variance of output and interest rates is generally greater under price-level targeting, while the variance of inflation is lower. The reason for the first finding is that bringing the price level back to a path is more demanding

---

[12] It should be noted that the model presented in Box 15.1 does not impose any restriction on convergence to target, in contrast to Smets' model (Smets, 2003). Indeed, the impulse-response functions presented in Figure 15.3 should not be interpreted as indicating any optimal forecast horizon.

than bringing inflation back to target. As for the second finding, it was mentioned on p. 294 that the expectations channel helps to stabilise inflation. Indeed, when comparing the optimal policy horizons for both monetary policy regimes, the author finds that it is longer under price-level targeting than IT. This is because lengthening the horizon improves the trade-off between output gap and inflation volatility.[13]

A related but different concept is the optimal forecast or feedback horizon (Batini and Nelson, 2001). This is the horizon over which central banks form inflation forecasts that enter policy rules, i.e. the horizon at which the central bank reacts to deviation of expected inflation, or the price level, from the target.[14] As before, Coletti, Lalonde and Muir (2008) also find that the optimal feedback horizon is longer when the monetary authority targets the price level. Another implementation issue relates to the choice of an optimal band around the price-level target path.

4.2   When IT and price-level targeting are not that different

In practice, an IT regime could be fashioned in such a way that it would look quite similar in operation to a price-level targeting monetary framework. In particular, price-level targeting can be seen as a more aggressive monetary policy rule than IT in the sense that it magnifies the weight given to correcting inflation deviations. In this respect, Chadha and Nolan (2002) and Coletti, Lalonde and Muir (2008) show that increasing the weight on inflation and reducing that on output in the Taylor rule causes the volatility of output and inflation under IT to converge to that under price-level targeting.

This possible equivalence is important because changing the monetary policy framework can involve large transition costs (for example, in terms of communication strategy and the compromising of credibility). One such communication challenge has to do with announcing different inflation targets for different years. For example, faced with a cost-push shock that causes inflation to overshoot the (implicit or explicit) target, the authorities have to commit to years of inflation below target. This can be especially demanding if fairly large cumulative deviations between the actual and target paths persist over time. To remain credible, the central bank would have to be very clear on its commitment to attain the

[13] In fact, the optimal horizon under a price-level objective will be twice as long as the one for IT, also reducing the strength of the expectations channel.

[14] For example, central banks may react to deviations of expected inflation from the target for the next year, or between the next year and the following one.

target over the medium term. The lack of international experience with price-level targeting, analysed in the next subsection, may also undermine credibility during initial implementation phases because it would increase learning costs. All of this would make the central bank's communication strategy more complex under price-level targeting rather than IT and would require an effective communication policy in order to ensure a smooth transition between the two regimes.

Nevertheless, while the outcomes under both monetary policy regimes can be very similar *ex post*, an aggressive IT policy would lose the *ex ante* automatic stabilisation benefit attached to price-level targeting. As a result, in an environment where a minimum share of decision-makers are forward-looking, aggressive IT can achieve the same price dynamics as price-level targeting only at the cost of greater real-interest rate volatility.

4.3   Limited historical experience[15]

In Sweden, output losses during the monetary experience after the First World War and the world-wide depression that started in 1928 undermined the legitimacy of the gold standard; after leaving the gold standard, a price-level targeting regime was adopted in September 1931. The new monetary programme was widely supported by the economics profession and aimed principally at arresting the fall in prices that was characteristic of the late 1920s. The potential risk of price increases, after the floating of the krona, was not excluded, however.

When the new monetary policy regime was first launched in September 1931, it was accompanied only by a short statement by the monetary authorities that the central bank would aim at preserving the purchasing power of the krona. A fully-fledged programme was completed only in May 1932, after eight months of deliberations among the central bank, leading monetary economists, the parliament and the general public. The main constituent points of the programme were: (1) monetary policy should aim at resisting both inflation and deflation; (2) the objective should be to restore price levels prevailing at the end of 1931: a return to the price level of 1928–9 (before the fall in prices) was not recommended because this would imply too loose a monetary policy, leading, eventually, to inflation and nominal wage spirals[16]; (3) monetary policy should not target any particular price index, so that a simple or formal

[15] See Berg and Jonung (1999) for a more detailed description.
[16] Interestingly, increases in the price level coming from custom duties, other taxes, seasonal price changes, etc. were considered to be consistent with the monetary policy programme and not to require any reaction from the monetary authority.

Table 15.1: *The Swedish experience with price-level targeting*

Feature	Description
Introduction/adoption	Immediately following the suspension of the gold standard (27 September 1931) One sentence declaration
Main reason for adoption	Deflation
Evolution of policy framework	Monetary programme passed by Riksdag (parliament) in May 1932
Legal framework	No change in Charter of Riksbank preceding or following switch of monetary regime
Relevant price index	Weekly CPI and other price indices such as wholesale prices and prices of raw materials
Most important operational target at time of adoption	Average level of consumer goods prices as of September 1931
Caveats	Indirect taxes and seasonal factors
Temporal vs. permanent strategy	Temporary as eventual return to gold standard was envisaged
Policy instrument	Discount rate; operations in foreign exchange market; explicit announcements
Role of exchange rate	Peg of the krona to pound from July 1933 to start of the Second World War
Role of monetary aggregates	No explicit mentioning in monetary programme
Goal independence	Goals were set by Riksdag
Instrument independence	Yes
Accountability	No specific mentioning of sanctions in case policy goal was missed

Source: Guender and Oh (2006).

rule did not appear feasible (the central bank should also monitor the wholesale price index (WPI) and raw materials prices) – nevertheless, for operational purposes, the Riksbank started developing a weekly consumer price index; and (4) it was announced that the floating of the krona was temporary, and a return to gold should be aimed at, as soon as internal and external conditions permitted. Indeed, Sweden became the only country to have a price-level objective. A summary and some more details on price-level targeting in Sweden are presented in Table 15.1.

Both the consumer index and the WPI fell sharply from 1928 until 1932–3 (Figure 15.4). This reflected the transmission of international deflationary pressures from the gold standard mechanism. When Sweden left the gold standard in 1931, it initially adopted a floating exchange rate system. For fear of inflation, the Riksbank initially adopted a tight monetary policy (Figure 15.5), increasing nominal interest rates from 6 per cent to 8 per cent. As a consequence, economic activity fell and

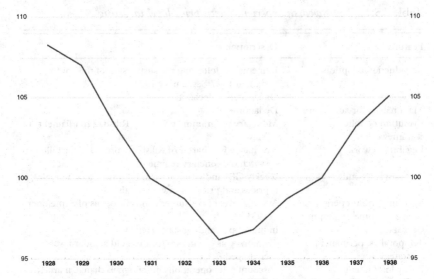

Figure 15.4: The evolution of the CPI in Sweden, before and after
price-level targeting, 1928–38: Index 1931 = 100
Source: Riksbank.

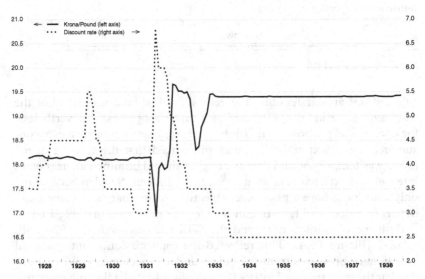

Figure 15.5: Exchange rate and policy discount rate: Sweden, 1928–38
Source: Riksbank.

unemployment rose over the short run. Monetary policy was subsequently eased to counteract the contraction in economic activity, with the policy rate reaching a minimum of 2.5 per cent in 1934, where it remained until the outbreak of the Second World War. Regarding exchange rate dynamics, the krona depreciated through 1932–3, when it became obvious that a return to the gold standard was not a valid alternative, prompting the central bank to peg the krona to the British pound. Wholesale prices increased sharply while consumer prices increased steadily, starting in 1933.

Whether or not the monetary programme was successful in preventing further deflation in Sweden is difficult to gauge given that: (1) there was no commitment to a specific policy horizon against which to evaluate the success of monetary policy; (2) the central bank decided to peg the krona to the pound, raising the question of to what extent the goal of monetary policy was effectively to stabilise the price level: price and exchange rate dynamics in the UK were therefore crucial for the success of the Swedish programme; and (3) interest rate policy seems to have followed other countries like the UK and the US, suggesting that the economic recovery and inflation were driven primarily by global factors.

5   Concluding remarks: price-level targeting and the euro area

In summary, although it comes with a number of challenges, price-level targeting is an option worthy of consideration, especially in an economic environment where the risk of deflation seems to be greater than was thought over past decades. In the euro area, price-level targeting could be adopted under the current treaties, which go only so far as to prescribe that the primary objective of monetary policy should be price stability. The Governing Council of the ECB would simply have to change its definition of price stability. One could even argue that price-level targeting would implement the mandate from the treaties more literally than the current quantitative definition of price stability as 'a year-on-year increase in the harmonised index of consumer prices (HICP) for the euro area of below 2 per cent'. However, even if such a change was implemented, the current inflation criterion for euro accession would remain based on inflation rates, since this prescription is enshrined in the Treaty on the Functioning of the European Union.

In a currency union with multiple countries that are not fully economically integrated, an important aspect of the choice between price-level targeting and IT is the question of which regime will minimise cross-country inflation differentials in the face of shocks. This is essentially the same question as to which of the two monetary regimes will deliver more stable inflation rates. As developed above, while the initial intuition of the first scholars of price-level targeting was that this regime would result in greater inflation variability, most, though not all, current models find that price-level targeting reduces inflation variability thanks to the self-regulating mechanism created by the expectation channel. Besides, at the time of euro accession, even with current treaty-based formal inflation criteria remaining in place, a monetary strategy of price-level targeting would usefully focus attention on the degree of price-level convergence and, in cases of divergence, on the capacity of the candidate country to integrate with the rest of the currency union successfully despite the differential.

Finally, if the euro area adopted price-level targeting, this could create a discrepancy with the US and Japan, where targets for inflation rates currently play an important role in the monetary policy frameworks even though they do not follow strict IT regimes. A difference of this nature could possibly exacerbate the volatility of exchange rate movements following asymmetric shocks as market participants would expect different interest rate responses. However, if a broader set of economies adopted price-level targeting, the associated fall in the variability of policy-controlled interest rates should in principle lead to lower exchange rate volatility. The effects of price-level targeting adoption, unilaterally or more widely, on exchange rate volatility would seem to be worthy subjects for further investigation.

References

Ahrend, R., B. Cournède and R. Price (2008). 'Monetary policy, market excesses and financial turmoil', OECD Economics Department Working Paper, No. 597

Amano, R., S. Ambler and P. Ireland (2007). 'Price level targeting, wage indexation and welfare', Paper presented at the seminar 'New Developments in Monetary Policy Design', sponsored by the Bank of Canada and CIRPÉE, 25–26 October, Montreal, http://tinyurl.com/3alsdaa

Ambler, S. (2009). 'Price-level targeting and stabilization policy: a review', *Bank of Canada Review*, Spring: 19–29

Ang, A., G. Bekaert and M. Wei (2008). 'The term structure of real rates and expected inflation', *Journal of Finance*, **63**(2): 797–849

Angeris, A. and P. Arestis (2008). 'Assessing inflation targeting through intervention analysis', *Oxford Economic Papers*, **60**: 293–317

Aoki, M. and H. Yoshikawa (2006). 'Uncertainty, policy ineffectiveness, and long stagnation of the macroeconomy', *Japan and the World Economy*, **18**: 261–72

Batini, N. and A. Yates (2003). 'Hybrid inflation and price-level targeting', *Journal of Money, Credit and Banking*, **35**(3): 283–300

Batini, N. and E. Nelson (2001). 'Optimal horizons for inflation targeting', *Journal of Economic Dynamics & Control*, **51**: 891–910

Benati, L. (2008). 'Investigating inflation persistence across monetary regimes', *Quarterly Journal of Economics*, **123**(3): 1005–60

Berg, C. and L. Jonung (1999). 'Pioneering price level targeting: the Swedish experience 1931–1937', *Journal of Monetary Economics*, **31**: 525–51

Bernanke, B. and V. Reinhart (2004). 'Conducting monetary policy at very low short-term interest rates', *AEA Proceedings and Papers*, **94**(2): 85–90

Blanchard, O. and C. Khan (1980). 'The solution of linear difference models under rational expectations', *Econometrica*, **48**(5): 1305–11

Blanchard, O., G. Dell'Ariccia and P. Mauro (2010). 'Rethinking macroeconomic policy', IMF Staff Position Note, No. **10/03**

Calderón, C. and K. Schmidt-Hebbel (2008). 'What drives inflation in the world?', Central Bank of Chile, Working Paper, No. **491**

Chadha, J. S. and C. Nolan (2002). 'Inflation and price level targeting in a new Keynesian model', *The Manchester School*, **70**(4): 570–95

Cogley, T. (1997). 'What is the optimal rate of inflation?', *Federal Reserve Bank of San Francisco Economic Letter*, No. **97–27**

Coibion, O., Y. Gorodnichenko and J. Wieland (2010). 'The optimal inflation rate in New Keynesian models', National Bureau of Economic Research Working Paper, No. **16093**

Coletti, D., R. Lalonde and D. Muir (2008). 'Inflation targeting and price-level-path targeting in the global economy model: some open economy considerations', IMF Staff Papers, **55**(2): 326–38

Cover, J. P. and P. Pecorino (2005). 'Price and output stability under price-level targeting', *Southern Economic Journal*, **72**(1): 152–66

Crawford, A., C. Meh and Y. Terajima (2009). 'Price-level uncertainty, price-level targeting and nominal debt contracts', *Bank of Canada Review*, Spring: 31–41

Dhyne, E. *et al.* (2006). 'Price changes in the euro area and the United States: some facts from individual consumer price data', *Journal of Economic Perspectives*, **20**(2): 171–92

Eggertsson, G. and M. Woodford (2003). 'The zero interest-rate bound and optimal monetary policy', *Brookings Papers on Economic Activity*, **34**(1): 139–235

Fatás, A., I. Mihov and A. K. Rose (2006). 'Quantitative goals for monetary policy', European Central Bank Working Paper, No. **615**

Fischer, S. (1994). 'Modern central banking', in F. Capie, C. Goodhart, S. Fischer and N. Schnadt, *The Future of Central Banking: The Tercentenary Symposium of the Bank of England*, Cambridge University Press

Galí, J. (2008). *Monetary Policy, Inflation and the Business Cycle*, Princeton University Press

Galí, J. and M. Gertler (1999). 'Inflation dynamics: a structural econometric analysis', *Journal of Monetary Economics*, **44**: 195–222

Galí, J., M. Gertler and D. López-Salido (2007). 'Mark-ups, gaps and the welfare costs of business fluctuations', *Review of Economics and Statistics*, **89**(1): 44–59

Giannoni, M. (2010). 'Optimal interest-rate rules in a forward-looking model, and inflation stabilization versus price-level stabilization', Columbia University, 28 April, mimeo

Guender, A. and D. Y. Oh (2006). 'Price stability through price-level targeting or inflation targeting? A tale of two experiments', *Journal of Economics and Business*, **58**: 373–91

Hördahl, P. (2008). 'The inflation risk premium in the term structure of interest rates', *BIS Quarterly Review*, September: 23–38

Jääskelä, J. P. (2005). 'Inflation, price level and hybrid rules under inflation uncertainty', *Scandinavian Journal of Economics*, **107**(1): 141–56

Kryvtsov, O., M. Shukayev and A. Ueberfeldt (2008). 'Adopting price-level targeting under imperfect credibility: an update', Bank of Canada Working Paper, No. **37**

Lilico, A. (2000). 'Price-level targeting – the next objective for monetary policy?', *Institute for Economic Affairs*, Oxford

Meh, C. A., J.-V. Ríos-Rull and Y. Terajima (2008). 'Aggregate and welfare effects of redistribution of wealth under inflation and price-level targeting', Bank of Canada Working Paper, No. **31**

Mishkin, F. and K. Schmidt-Hebbel (2001). 'One decade of inflation targeting in the world: what do we know and what do we need to know?', National Bureau of Economic Research Working Paper, No. **8397**

    (2007). 'Does inflation targeting make a difference?', National Bureau of Economic Research Working Paper, No. **12876**

Nakamura, E. and J. Steinsson (2008). 'Five facts about prices: a reevaluation of menu cost models', *Quarterly Journal of Economics*, **123**(4): 1415–64

Parkin, M. (2009). 'What is the ideal monetary policy regime?', *CD Howe Institute Commentary*, No. **279**

Rudebusch, G. (2002). 'Assessing nominal income rules for monetary policy with model and data uncertainty', *Economic Journal*, **112**: 402–32

Schmitt-Grohé, S. and M. Uribe (2010). 'The optimal rate of inflation', National Bureau of Economic Research Working Paper, No. **16054**

Smets, F. (2003). 'Maintaining price stability: how long is the medium term?', *Journal of Monetary Economics*, **50**: 1293–1309

Smets, F. and R. Wouters (2003). 'An estimated stochastic dynamic general equilibrium model of the euro area', *Journal of the European Economic Association*, **1**(5): 1123–75

Svensson, L. E. O. (1997). 'Optimal inflation targets, "Conservative" Central Banks, and Linear Inflation Contracts', *American Economic Review*, **87**(1): 98–114

    (1999). 'Price-level targeting versus inflation targeting: a free lunch?', *Journal of Money, Credit and Banking*, **31**(3): 277–95

Vestin, D. (2006). 'Price-level versus inflation targeting', *Journal of Monetary Economics*, **53**: 1361–76

Williams, J. C. (2003). 'Simple rules for monetary policy', Federal Reserve Bank of San Francisco, *Economic Review*: 1–12

Woodford, M. (2003). *Interest and Prices*, Princeton University Press

Yun, T. (1996). 'Nominal price rigidity, money supply endogeneity, and business cycles', *Journal of Monetary Economics*, **37**(2): 345–70

16 Heterogeneity in the euro area and why it matters for the future of the currency union

*Wendy Carlin**

The euro area's future is troubled because of the heterogeneity of its members. Beneath the surface of satisfactory performance for the euro area as a whole, its first decade was characterised by divergence in key macroeconomic indicators among member countries (e.g. inflation rates, current account positions and real effective exchange rates). This divergence points to the source of the problem. It does not lie with the credibility of the European Central Bank (ECB). Rather, it lies with the difficulties for a number of countries in operating with a single currency. These arise from persistent differences in how labour markets work in member countries and in how different governments have approached the problem of stabilising the national economy within a common currency area (CCA).

The euro area's first decade shows that the choice of monetary regime can affect economic outcomes on the real side of the economy. Expectations that private and public sector agents would change their behaviour once a single currency was adopted proved overoptimistic. Contrary to the expectations of many observers, in the private sector, wage- and price-setters did not modify their behaviour in ways consistent with sustainable growth within a CCA. In the public sector, the need to stabilise national bouts of excess demand was neglected. The markets failed to signal the build-up of these tensions: until the sovereign debt crisis emerged in early 2010, and spreads on the bonds issued by euro area governments remained until then very narrow.

The experience of the euro area suggests that supra-national rules are limited in their ability to change private and public sector behaviour. The problems of the euro area require primarily *national* responses. The incentives for national governments to tackle the roots of the real-side

* I am grateful to Christian Dustmann, Liam Graham, Costas Meghir, Jacques Mélitz, David Soskice, Luigi Spaventa and David Vines for stimulating discussions about these issues and for very helpful comments on an earlier draft of the chapter.

tensions in the euro area and their success in doing so will determine its
long-run future.

I focus on two real-side problems of the euro area. Under the Maastricht policy assignment, member countries are tasked with the 'stabilisation of country-specific shocks subject to fiscal sustainability'. This turns
out to be a difficult problem even in the unrealistic case where there is
a benevolent social planner such as an independent fiscal council with
the power to make fiscal policy decisions. It is a general problem faced
by members of a CCA in the absence of adequate unit cost flexibility.
The second issue relates to the specific problems of the euro area, and
arises because of the institutional characteristics of its largest member,
Germany.

The need for an appropriate macroeconomic policy framework for a
member of the euro area is illustrated by the case where country-specific
inflation deviates from the euro area average (for reasons other than the
Balassa–Samuelson effect). In a country with its own monetary policy, in
the presence of nominal rigidities, the central bank raises or lowers the
interest rate to keep inflation close to its target. The ECB does that job
for shocks that affect the euro area as a whole, but when an individual
country is affected by a shock which pushes up its inflation relative to
the euro area average then domestic policy must respond. Specifically,
fiscal policy will normally have to be used to dampen demand in the
economy.

Ireland's experience provides a good illustration of the failure of
national stabilisation policy (for more detail, see Lane, Chapter 4 in this
volume). Around the time the euro area was created, Ireland's growth
model switched from that of the so-called 'Celtic Tiger' based on the
tradables sector to growth based on non-tradables in the form of a construction boom and property price bubble. Euro area membership was
a source of shocks for Ireland due to the fall in the cost of capital on
entry to the European Monetary Union (EMU), and because of the dis-
proportionate effect on Ireland (owing to its trade pattern) of the initial
depreciation of the euro against the dollar and sterling.

The single nominal interest rate in the euro area also provided a propagation mechanism for shocks. This channel is referred to as the 'Walters'
critique' effect because Alan Walters used it to argue against UK membership of the European Monetary System (EMS) (e.g. Walters, 1990).
The idea is that the common nominal interest rate within EMU would
imply lower real interest rates for countries like Ireland where inflation
was higher than the euro area average. In the context of EMU membership, domestic amplification mechanisms then kicked in via a collateral-
leverage cycle as rising property prices boosted private consumption and

housing investment. This in turn fed into a procyclical fiscal policy as buoyant tax revenue from the construction and property boom fuelled tax cuts and higher government spending. Both of these then fed back into the property boom.

However, these EMU-related effects could have been offset by an appropriate national stabilisation policy. Given that the supra-national rules of the Stability and Growth Pact (SGP) could do nothing to prevent Ireland's destabilising fiscal policy (since Ireland was running budget surpluses and its debt ratio was low and falling), the failure rests squarely with domestic policy and the absence of domestic stabilisation.

One way to think about the national stabilisation problem for a member of a CCA is to begin with the standard New Keynesian approach to this problem in the framing of optimal monetary policy in the context of nominal rigidities in wages and/or prices (e.g. Carlin and Soskice, 2005). We begin with the familiar loss function of a central bank that seeks to minimise the deviations of inflation from target and output from equilibrium, and adapt it to a national policy-maker inside a CCA. In this case, the policy-maker is concerned to minimise the deviation of inflation from the CCA's inflation target, which we call π^*. For simplicity, we assume that the average inflation rate in the CCA is equal to the inflation target. This produces the following optimisation problem and optimal policy rule:

$$\text{Min} \quad L_t = (y_t - \bar{y})^2 + \beta(\pi_t - \pi^*)^2 \qquad \text{National policy-maker's loss function}$$

$$\text{s.t.} \quad \pi_t = \pi_{t-1} + \alpha(y_t - \bar{y}) \qquad \text{Phillips curve}$$

$$(y_t - \bar{y}) = -\alpha\beta(\pi_t - \pi^*) \qquad \text{Optimal output gap}$$

where y_t and π_t are, respectively, output and inflation at time t, $\bar{y}$ is equilibrium output, π^* is the CCA's inflation target, β is the weight on inflation in the policy-maker's loss function and α is the slope of the backward-looking Phillips curve. The optimal output gap tells the policy-maker the output gap it needs to choose (using its stabilisation policy instrument) in response to the observed inflation deviation if it is to guide the economy back to equilibrium output at target inflation.

In the CCA case, the national policy-maker chooses the output gap using fiscal policy in response to its observation of the deviation of the home-country's inflation from the CCA inflation target. In the Irish example, had the Irish government followed this optimal fiscal policy rule, it would have tightened discretionary fiscal policy in response to higher

Irish inflation caused by the shocks described above.[1] The debate about the effectiveness of fiscal policy in affecting output is fierce (Beetsma, 2008). However, new evidence from the UK (Cloyne, 2011) confirms the results of Romer and Romer (2010) that tax changes have a marked and persistent effect on output.

It is important to explore the optimal fiscal policy rule a little further. As we shall see, simply taking over the modified monetary policy rule and using it to choose the optimal output gaps required to guide the economy back to the euro area inflation target at equilibrium output is not sufficient to ensure fiscal sustainability. This can be illustrated using an example of the simplest kind of shock, and comparing the outcomes in the case where *monetary* policy is used to stabilise (a country has an independent central bank) and where *fiscal* policy is used (by a country inside a CCA). We use the experiment of a temporary country-specific inflation shock (arising, for example, from a burst of domestic wage growth). We ask whether in the presence of inflation persistence, fiscal policy in a CCA is a good substitute for monetary policy in a flexible exchange rate regime. Under flexible exchange rates, the central bank and the foreign exchange market forecast the output contraction required to get the economy back to target inflation (see e.g. Carlin and Soskice, 2010). The central bank tightens policy by raising the interest rate and the nominal exchange rate appreciates. This puts the economy on the path to return to equilibrium with target inflation. Once the economy is back at equilibrium, the real variables (output and the real exchange rate) are back at their initial levels; as is the government's primary deficit and the current account.

We now consider an identical, temporary country-specific inflation shock in a member country of a CCA. We assume that fiscal policy is used to implement exactly the same output and inflation path back to equilibrium output and the target – i.e. the CCA – inflation rate. However, once the economy is back at equilibrium, the home-country's real exchange rate has appreciated due to the period of higher (though falling) inflation along the path to equilibrium. Wages and prices are assumed to respond to the period of higher than equilibrium unemployment in exactly the same way as in the flexible rate economy. Consumption and investment are unchanged at equilibrium since the real interest rate is pinned down by the CCA nominal interest rate and by the domestic inflation rate, which is equal to the CCA inflation target. However, net

---

[1] To the extent that a national boom is the outcome of a leverage cycle, the use of a policy instrument specifically targeted at stabilising this cycle (rather than the use of stabilisation policy as normally conceived in Taylor rule macroeconomics) would be appropriate (e.g. Geanakoplos, 2009).

exports are lower because of the appreciated real exchange rate so there must be some combination of higher government expenditure or lower taxation to sustain demand at the level required for equilibrium output. In short, the primary fiscal balance must have deteriorated.

This illustrates that fiscal imbalance can arise in a CCA not only as a result of 'profligacy' on the part of the national government. It can also arise as an unintended consequence of the use of the same 'optimal' policy rule to stabilise the economy in the face of a temporary inflation shock as that chosen by an inflation targeting (IT) central bank in a flexible exchange rate regime. The implications of this result are that optimal policy for a country in a CCA requires 'more than' an IT rule: to leave the primary fiscal balance unchanged following the adjustment to a temporary inflation shock, the *price level* must return to its initial position in order that the real exchange rate is unchanged. In contrast to the situation under flexible exchange rates, it is not sufficient for the *inflation rate* to return to target.[2]

In principle, active fiscal policy can be used to implement a stabilisation policy that is neutral in relation to the structural primary balance (i.e. delivering primary balance at equilibrium output) in a CCA, but it will be at higher output cost than simple IT. The reason for this is that given persistence in the inflation process, a larger cumulative output gap is required to return the price level to its initial position than is required to return the inflation rate to target. If stabilisation policy does not ensure that the cumulative effects on the real exchange rate arising from country-specific shocks are offset, there will be lasting implications for the real exchange rate and for government indebtedness.

In a flexible exchange rate economy, fiscal policy is in principle available to stabilise but in practice its political nature and doubts about its efficacy explain why a government in such an economy normally uses monetary policy. Monetary policy can be delegated to an independent central bank. By contrast, since it involves the use of tax revenues, fiscal policy is inherently political, which is captured by the phrase 'no taxation without representation'. This makes it impossible literally to delegate fiscal policy in the same way as monetary policy. However, an independent, sophisticated fiscal council acting like the social planner in the example above can provide advice and auditing of government fiscal policy against the requirements for macroeconomic stabilisation. Sweden's Fiscal Policy Council and the newly created Office for Budget Responsibility

---

[2] An inflation shock is the simplest to model because the real exchange rate is unchanged in the new equilibrium under flexible exchange rates. Similar issues arise in the more complicated cases of an aggregate demand or supply-side shock.

(OBR) in the UK play this role for EU countries outside the euro area. For a country inside the euro area where monetary policy is not available for stabilisation, the role of such a council is even more important. As the annual reports of Sweden's Fiscal Policy Council make clear (e.g. Swedish Fiscal Policy Council, 2010), its task is not confined to stabilisation but extends to the longer horizon design of fiscal policy to ensure government solvency in the face of demographic and other pressures. These additional demands on fiscal policy make the task of monitoring its use for stabilisation yet more challenging.

Why is the issue of stabilisation policy within the US currency union not discussed? Part of the answer is that through the federal tax and transfer system the federal government insures states against regional income shocks. Although the initial estimates of Sala-i-Martin and Sachs (1991) suggested that a \$1 reduction in a region's *per capita* personal income triggers a decrease in federal taxes of about 34¢ and an increase in federal transfers of about 6¢, more recent estimates using consistent accounting and improved econometric methods show that stabilisation is more modest and lies between 10 and 20 per cent for the US (Mélitz and Zumer, 2002). This is still considerably larger than the negligible stabilisation provided to members by the EU budget. Recent evidence questions the common assumption that it is geographical labour mobility that plays a large role in facilitating adjustment to regional shocks in the US currency union (Rowthorn and Glyn, 2006). In short, puzzles still remain about stabilisation in the US and about the role of a number of factors in accounting for US-euro area differences: the nature and persistence of shocks, wage and price flexibility, factor mobility and stabilisation policy.

If the labour market is perfectly flexible without nominal or real rigidities, then any role for stabilisation policy is much reduced. In the absence of such flexibility, the role fiscal policy plays in macroeconomic stabilisation in a currency union may be shared with or substituted by wages policy (see e.g. Allsopp and Vines, 2008). This possibility depends on institutional arrangements for collective bargaining and is relevant in the euro area because of the use made of it by Germany. This takes us to the second problem that arises from the euro area's heterogeneity. This derives from the specific characteristics of its current members. Germany is the largest euro area member and its institutional characteristics and industrial structure pose particular difficulties for some other member countries.

From a macroeconomic perspective, the attraction of joining a CCA with Germany was acquiring a credible commitment to low inflation. However, as noted above, one outcome has been divergent real exchange

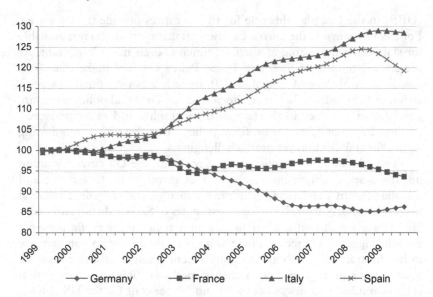

Figure 16.1: Real effective exchange rates, 1999–2009 (1999 = 100)

Notes: Quarterly real effective exchange rates (relative unit labour costs in manufacturing) vs. (the rest of) sixteen euro area countries
Source: European Commission.

rates because inflation rates or, more specifically, growth rates of unit labour costs, did not converge to Germany's.[3] From 2000, Germany was able to effect a substantial real depreciation within the euro area through a combination of restraint in nominal wage growth and more rapid productivity growth than many other member countries. Although this partly reflected the recovery of Germany's competitiveness, which had been depressed by the consequences of reunification, more importantly it demonstrated the country's ability to engineer a real depreciation inside the euro area when required. Figure 16.1 illustrates the divergence in real effective exchange rates among the four large euro area members over 1999–2009.

While it does not have a classical flexible labour market, Germany, like some other northern euro area members (and some EU countries outside the euro area like Sweden and Denmark), has wage-setting institutions that enable it to coordinate nominal wage growth. Unions agreed

---

[3] The dangers arising from this possibility in EMU were highlighted in the contribution of Wendy Carlin and Andrew Glyn to the UK's Treasury's EMU enquiry (Carlin and Glyn, 2003).

to modest nominal wage increases in multiyear deals, and works councils in large companies negotiated over wages and flexibility of hours in exchange for investment by firms in fixed capital and training (e.g. Carlin and Soskice, 2008). Unions play a key role in limiting the bargaining power of skilled workers in the core export sector of the German economy. Its model of export-led growth requires that the exercise of power by wage-setters in the non-tradables sectors be controlled by powerful unions in the tradables sector.

The German model substitutes coordinated wage restraint for the use of stabilising fiscal policy along the lines sketched above. In other words, in the face of a negative aggregate demand shock, Germany is able to achieve a response similar to that under *flexible* exchange rates whereby demand is stabilised by a real depreciation achieved via wage restraint, rather than by a nominal depreciation achieved via lower domestic interest rates. Countries without access to coordinated wage-setting (or a sufficiently flexible labour market)[4] must rely on fiscal policy for stabilisation, with the attendant difficulties that have been discussed. In fact, for countries like Germany where the export sector is the dynamic part of the economy, it can be argued that it is important to limit the use of discretionary fiscal policy for stabilisation since it weakens the incentive of wage-setters to exercise restraint.

For other euro area members that do not have similar or substitute unit cost control mechanisms, the problem discussed above is endemic – instead of a temporary inflation shock, such countries are characterised by a trend rise in relative unit labour costs. This partly reflects the failure of domestic unit cost growth to adjust to the euro area inflation average of just above 2 per cent and partly the success of Germany in achieving unit cost growth below 2 per cent p.a. Given the variation in institutional characteristics and industrial structures of euro area members, it is difficult to see how this problem is to be overcome on a lasting basis.

The first decade of its existence has shown that the euro area's monetary policy framework is essentially sound. But its first crisis brought to the fore the build-up of divergences inside the euro area. Sophisticated fiscal councils may help with delivering stabilisation and sustainability in some members with well-functioning governments. However, even if these were to be introduced successfully, the question remains of how easy it will be for a number of countries to live in a CCA with Germany, with its extra policy instrument of wage coordination.

---

[4] Interestingly, East Germany achieved a substantial real depreciation against West Germany after 2000 through labour market flexibility rather than by using the traditional German model of wage coordination (Carlin, 2010).

References

Allsopp, C. and D. Vines (2008). 'Fiscal policy, intercountry adjustment and the real exchange rate within Europe', *European Economy Economic Papers*, **344**

Beetsma, R. (2008). 'A survey of the effects of discretionary fiscal policy', Working Paper, University of Amsterdam

Carlin, W. (2010). 'Good institutions are not enough: ongoing challenges of East German development', CESifo Working Paper, No. **3204**

Carlin, W. and A. Glyn (2003). 'British exports, cost competitiveness and exchange rate arrangements', in HM Treasury, *Submissions on EMU from Leading Academics*, Stationery Office, Chapter 5: 57–61

Carlin, W. and D. Soskice (2005). 'The 3-equation New Keynesian model – a graphical exposition', *Contributions to Macroeconomics*, **5**(1), Article 13, www.bepress.com/bejm/contributions/vol5/iss1/art13

   (2008). 'German economic performance: disentangling the role of supply-side reforms, macroeconomic policy and coordinated economy institutions', *Socio-Economic Review*, **7**(1): 67–99

   (2010). 'A New Keynesian open economy model for policy analysis', CEPR Discussion Paper, No. **7979**

Cloyne, J. (2011). 'What are the effects of tax changes in the United Kingdom? New evidence from a narative evaluation', CESifo Working Paper, No. 3433

Geanakoplos, J. (2009). 'The leverage cycle', *National Bureau of Economic Research Macroeconomics Annual*, Chicago University Press

Lane, P. R. (2011). 'The Irish crisis', Chapter 4 in this volume

Mélitz, J. and F. Zumer (2002). 'Regional redistribution and stabilisation by the center in Canada, France, the UK and the US: a reassessment and new tests', *Journal of Public Economics*, **86**(2): 263–86

Romer, C. and D. Romer (2010). 'The macroeconomic effects of tax changes: Estimates based on a new measure of fiscal shocks'. *American Economic Review*, **100**: 763–801

Rowthorn, R. and A. Glyn (2006). 'Convergence and stability in US employment rates', *Contributions to Macroeconomics*, **6**(1), Article 4

Sala-i-Martin, X. and J. Sachs (1991). 'Fiscal federalism and optimum currency areas: evidence for Europe from the United States', National Bureau of Economic Research Working Paper, No. **3855**

Swedish Fiscal Policy Council (2010). *Report of the Swedish Fiscal Policy Council 2010*, Stockholm

Walters, A. (1990). *Sterling in Danger*, London: Fontana

17   The euro area: how to regain confidence?

*Vítor Gaspar**

Athanasios Orphanides in his opening keynote address affirmed that the global crisis revealed fault lines in the governance of the euro area. He concentrated on the new architecture for financial stability in Europe. In my brief contribution I want to focus on fiscal sustainability and budget discipline.

1   Demographic transition, the global crisis and debt levels

Before focusing on the specific case of the euro area I want to comment very briefly on a crucial evolutionary driver that will shape budgetary trends for the next several decades: demographics. The world is experiencing a fundamental demographic transition: according to the latest demographic projections, made available by the United Nations (2009), world population will stop growing by 2050, when it will have reached about 9 billion people (compared to almost 7 billion in 2010). This will interrupt a trend of pronounced population growth recorded for centuries. This constitutes an epochal transition, with profound impacts on economic, political and social balances.

The transition will happen first in advanced countries. For example for the twenty-seven member states of the EU the population is projected to decline slightly in the four decades from 2010 to 2050 (notwithstanding significant migration flows). The share of EU27 in world population is projected to decline from 7.2 per cent to 5.4 per cent.[1] All other things equal, a slowdown in population growth increases the implicit public debt burden associated with the operation of health and pension systems. Moreover, public debts in OECD countries have doubled since the mid 1970s and the global crisis accelerated the trend. The evolution

---

* Special Adviser Banco de Portugal. I am grateful to Isabel Gameiro and Paul Hiebert for comments and corrections. The remaining errors are my responsibility. The views expressed are my own and do not necessarily reflect those of the Banco de Portugal or the Eurosystem's.
[1] In 1950 the relevant percentage was 14.8 per cent.

was marked by the functioning of automatic stabilisers, discretionary expansion and the costs of intervention to stabilise the financial system.[2] Such accumulation of public debt is unprecedented in peacetime. Therefore, the sustainability of public finances is a central challenge that the global crisis has made even more pressing.

2   Budgetary rules and procedures in the euro area

The economic constitution of the euro area reflects the view that stability-oriented macroeconomic policies provide the groundwork for the proper functioning of a market economy with unfettered competition leading to sustainable growth. The primary goal of monetary policy is price stability and the conduct of monetary policy was entrusted to the independent European Central Bank (ECB). The Lisbon Treaty (TFEU) includes provisions protecting the central bank from encroachment from the fiscal authorities. Article 123 prohibits monetary financing and Article 124 rules out privileged access to financial institutions. Moreover, Article 125 excludes the responsibility of the EU or of other member states for financial commitments assumed by one member state, and Article 122 limits financial assistance to cases in which a member state 'is in difficulties or is seriously threatened with severe difficulties caused by natural disasters or exceptional occurrences beyond its control . . . '. Notoriously, Article 143 does not foresee mutual assistance for the case of members of the euro area.[3]

A fundamental question is whether, given the prohibition of monetary financing, privileged access and bail-out, market discipline can be expected to be sufficient to ensure fiscal discipline. The question was addressed more than twenty years ago in the Delors Report (1989: 24):

To some extent market forces can exert a disciplinary influence . . . However, experience suggests that market perceptions do not necessarily provide strong and compelling signals and that access to a large capital market may for some time facilitate the financing of economic imbalances . . . The constraints imposed by market forces might either be too slow and weak or too sudden and disruptive.

---

[2] As Trichet stressed, in his address to the 2010 Jackson Hole Conference, in the euro area, public debt to GDP shot up by more than 20 percentage points in a period of just four years starting in 2007 (see Trichet, 2010).
[3] The point is made by Marzinotto, Pisani-Ferry and Sapir (2010).

In a companion piece, Lamfalussy (1989) argues that there is indeed reason to be sceptical about the effectiveness of market-imposed discipline for countries participating in a monetary union.[4] The conclusion in the Delors Report was that participation in the single market and in the single currency implied that member states had to accept corresponding policy constraints. This view is reflected in relevant provisions in the TFEU. Specifically Articles 120 and 121 prescribe that member states conduct their economic policies as a matter of common concern and with a view to achieving the objectives of the union. In case a member state does not behave in conformity with the Broad Economic Policy Guidelines (BEPGs) or risks jeopardising the smooth functioning of economic and monetary union, it is subject to the possibility of warnings from the European Commission and recommendations from the EU's Council. Moreover, Article 126 imposes on member states participating in the euro area the legal obligation to avoid excessive deficits. The TFEU provisions were completed by the Stability and Growth Pact (SGP).[5] The SGP made clear a distinction between the *preventive arm*, based on the surveillance of budgetary positions, and the *corrective arm*, based on the excessive deficit procedure. The preventive arm is covered by Regulation EC 1466/97 (amended by Regulation EC 1055/2005). The corrective arm, in turn, is covered by Regulation EC 1467/97 (amended by Regulation EC 1056/2005).[6] Paragraph 11 of Article 126 of the TFEU foresees the possibility of sanctions in the case of non-compliance.

3   Sovereign debt market behaviour

The creation of the euro area has been associated with the emergence of an integrated market for sovereign debt. Capiello, Engle and Shephard (2006) find that the correlation between bond returns issued by governments participating in the euro area approached unity shortly after the start of the euro area in 1999. In most of the first decade of the euro area sovereign spreads have been low (rarely exceeding 30 basis points and averaging much lower).[7]

The situation changed dramatically with the global crisis. Spreads widened slowly and gradually and the process speeded up after the bankruptcy of Lehmans, in September 2008. In 2009 there was a

---

[4] Empirical evidence and further discussion are provided in Restoy (1996), Bernoth, von Hagen and Schuknecht (2006) and Schuknecht, von Hagen and Wolswijk (2008).

[5] For the genesis of the SGP, see Stark (2001) and Costello (2001).

[6] A useful source for the relevant secondary legislation texts is http://europa.eu/legislation_summaries/economic_and_monetary_affairs/stability_and_growth_pact/index_en.htm.

[7] As documented by, for example, Gerlach, Schulz and Wolff (2010).

period when the situation seemed to be on a path of gradual easing. However, from the Autumn onwards spreads widened again and credit default swaps (CDS) premiums increased, reflecting bond market tensions driven, to a large extent, by idiosyncratic factors. Euro area bond markets were in turmoil in early May 2010 and stabilised only after the announcement of strong collective action at the European level. At the current time (September 2010) tensions persist in bond markets.

Schuknecht, von Hagen and Wolswijk (2008, 2010) importantly show that bond yield spreads can be largely explained on the basis of economic fundamentals before and after the financial market turmoil and the crisis. The ability of these authors to find a systematic relationship between spreads and fundamentals before and after the market turmoil and the crisis has important policy implications. In particular market discipline has been present throughout the whole period, albeit in a much stronger way in the recent past.

The evidence shows a clear pattern in which market discipline was 'too slow and weak' before the global crisis and became, more recently, 'too sudden and disruptive'. The SGP and the other provisions in the TFEU and secondary legislation failed to prevent the very pattern of market behaviour they were designed to avoid. Such failure requires major adjustments in the governance of the euro area. The issue is central for macroeconomic stability, in general, and for financial stability, in particular.

4   The work of the van Rompuy task force

The problem identified above was already clear in March 2010. On 26 March the European Council gave a mandate to the van Rompuy task force on economic governance (van Rompuy, 2010) to examine the relevant issues and to present measures leading to an improved crisis resolution framework and better budgetary discipline.[8] The approach of the task force includes three elements:
- First, strong surveillance over national fiscal policies and more effective prevention and correction of excessive levels of public deficits and public debt
- Second, effective monitoring of countries' competitiveness positions aimed at the correction of macroeconomic imbalances
- Third, a crisis management framework.

In their contribution to the work of the van Rompuy task force, the Governing Council of the ECB (ECB, 2010) stresses the importance

---

[8] European Council conclusions (2010), 26 March.

of mechanism design to contain the moral hazard associated with the crisis management framework. As Jean Tirole has said: in crisis, policy-makers often have their options narrowed to choosing between 'the bad and the ugly'.[9] The only way around the problem is to design *ex ante* institutions to shape incentives to ensure prudent behaviour. To do so it is necessary to ensure that financial support will be made available only at penalty rates and under strict conditionality. The rules that apply in extreme crisis situations are crucial for shaping incentives at all times. The European Commission put forward a package of legislative pro-posals on 29 September 2010 (European Commission, 2010), and the van Rompuy task force issued a final report (including a specific set of recommendations) on 21 October.

The global crisis has demonstrated an unprecedented degree of inter-national interdependence. Nowhere are linkages stronger than in the euro area. An institutional response is required, consistent with this increased interdependence. The construction of the euro area is work in progress. If it is successful it will lay the stability-oriented economic policy framework of the euro area on stronger institutional foundations.

References

Bernoth, K., J. von Hagen and L. Schuknecht (2006). 'Sovereign risk premiums in the European government bond market', SFB/TR Discussion Paper, No. 150.

Capiello, L., R. Engle and K. Shephard (2006). 'Asymmetric dynamics of cor-relation of global equity and bond markets returns', *Journal of Financial Econometrics*, 4(4): 537–72 (an earlier version of the paper was released as European Central Bank Working Paper, No. 204)

Costello, D. (2001). 'The SGP: how did we get there?' in A. Brunila, M. Buti and D. Franco (eds.), *The Stability and Growth Pact: The Architecture of Fiscal Policy in EMU*, New York: Palgrave Macmillan

Delors Report (1989). Committee for the Study of Economic and Monetary Union, *Report on Economic and Monetary Union in the European Community*, Luxembourg: Office for Official Publications of the European Communities

European Central Bank (ECB) Governing Council (2010). *Reinforc-ing Economic Governance in the Euro Area*, www.ecb.int/pub/pdf/other/reinforcingeconomicgovernanceintheeuroareaen.pdf

European Commission (2010). 'A new EU economic governance – a comprehen-sive package of proposals', COM (2010) 522, final; COM (2010) 523, final; COM (2010) 524, final; COM (2010) 525, final; COM (2010) 526, final;

---

[9] Jean Tirole's contribution to the conference 'Portuguese Economic Development in the European Area', organised by Banco de Portugal, Tirole (2010).

COM (2010) 527, final, http://ec.europa.eu/economy_finance/articles/eu_economic_situation/2010-09-eu_economic_governance_proposals_en.htm

European Council Conclusions (2010), 26 March 2010, www.consilium.europa.eu/ueDocs/cms_Data/docs/pressData/en/ec/113591.pdf

Gerlach, S., A. Schulz and G. Wolff (2010). 'Banking and sovereign risk in the euro area', Centre for Economic Policy Research Discussion Paper, No. **7833**

Lamfalussy, A. (1989). 'Macro-coordination of fiscal policies in an economic and monetary union', in Committee for the Study of Economic and Monetary Union, *Report on Economic and Monetary Union in the European Community*, Luxembourg: Office for Official Publications of the European Communities

Marzinotto, B., J. Pisani-Ferry and A. Sapir (2010). 'Two crises, two responses', *Bruegel Policy Brief*, 01

Restoy, F. (1996). 'Interest rates and fiscal discipline in monetary unions', *European Economic Review*, **40**: 1629–46

van Rompuy Task Force on Economic Governance (2010). 'Strengthening economic governance in the EU', Final Report of the task force to the European Council, Brussels, 21 October, www.consilium.europa.eu/uedocs/cms_data/docs/pressdata/en/ec/117236.pdf

Schuknecht, L., J. von Hagen and G. Wolswijk (2008). 'Government risk premiums in the bond market: EMU and Canada', European Central Bank Working Paper, No. **879**, published in *European Journal of Political Economy*, **25**, 2009: 371–84

(2010). 'Government risk premiums in the EU revisited: the impact of the financial crisis', European Central Bank Working Paper, No. **1152**

Stark, J. (2001). 'The genesis of a pact', in A. Brunila, M. Buti and D. Franco (eds.), *The Stability and Growth Pact: The Architecture of Fiscal Policy in EMU*, New York: Palgrave Macmillan

Tirole, J. (2010). 'Monitoring the indebtedness of banks and countries: reflexions on regulatory reforms and international institutions', 14 May, www.bportugal.pt/pt-PT/EstudosEconomicos/Conferencias/Documents/2010DEP/jeantirole.pdf

Trichet, J.-C. (2010). Lunch address on 'Central banking in uncertain times: conviction and responsibility', Jackson Hole Conference on 'Macroeconomic Challenges: The Decade Ahead', www.ecb.int/press/key/date/2010/html/sp100827.en.html

United Nations (2009). *World Population Prospects: The 2008 Revision, Population Database*, New York: United Nations, http://esa.un.org/unpp/

18   How to regain confidence in the euro area?

Stefan Gerlach

How can we strengthen public confidence in the euro project following the Greek public debt crisis? To do so, it is crucial to remove the risk of a full-blown sovereign debt crisis, which could easily trigger a banking crisis, in the euro area. This requires us to resolve the conflict between national fiscal policy and supra-national monetary policy by reinforcing the institutions underpinning fiscal policy.

To my mind, three sets of measures need to be adopted: we need to strengthen the Stability and Growth Pact (SGP); we must ensure that fiscal policy is subject to stringent surveillance and supervision; and we have to make sure that there is a permanent and credible crisis resolution mechanism that provides incentives for investors not to lend, and for governments not to borrow, excessively.

1   Strengthening the SGP

With the benefit of hindsight, it is clear that the SGP was subject to a number of shortcomings that impaired its effectiveness. Several changes in its design appear crucial.

First, there is a need to ensure more automaticity in the application of the Excessive Deficit Procedure (EDP). The SGP was intended to function with peer pressure as a lubricant. However, fiscal policy impacts on the distribution of income and wealth and is therefore politically extremely sensitive. As a consequence, governments refrained from commenting on each other's fiscal policies in the hope of receiving reciprocal treatment. Moreover, since they interact constantly on a range of issues with many opportunities for horse trading, it was always unlikely that a country would push for the rules to be applied to someone else.

Second, the sanctions of the SGP must be graduated. The fact that the EDP came into play discretely at a deficit of 3 per cent of GDP was problematic since it required governments to tighten fiscal policy in a situation in which the economy was already weak. This made fiscal policy procyclical and it was therefore difficult to enforce this rule.

Furthermore, since a government running a deficit a little smaller than 3 per cent of GDP could soon find itself above the limit, it had little incentive to enforce the rule. Moreover, the fact that it is difficult to know whether an excessive deficit reflects bad policy or bad luck – that is, too expansionary budget plans or a fall in tax revenues due to an unexpected weakening of the economy – also made governments hesitate to enforce the SGP.

Third, there should be greater focus on the level of debt than on the size of the deficit. A government with a debt-to-GDP ratio of 100 per cent but a deficit of 2.5 per cent of GDP plainly does not have its fiscal house in order.

Fourth, there should be a greater focus on creating incentives for good fiscal policy, rather than rules and 'lines-in-the-sand'. In particular, incentives must be put in place to replace the market discipline that has been lacking since investors and borrowers alike (correctly) expected to be bailed out if the debts grew too large.

2   Fiscal surveillance

In order to reduce the role of peer pressure, a European Financial Stability Agency (EFSA) should be created to provide surveillance of fiscal policies across the euro area and to ensure compliance with the SGP. It will prepare annual reports on fiscal policy developments; furthermore, it will determine what countries should enter the 'surveillance regime', 'enhanced surveillance regime' and 'strict surveillance regime' of the SGP that I propose below.

Such an institution must be small and not afraid to take controversial positions. In turn, this requires it to be independent from euro area governments, the European Commission and the European Parliament (and any other EU organs). Since determining whether a country is in compliance with the SGP involves judgement and not a mechanical application of rules, that decision should be taken by a committee of experts of no more than nine members, rather than a single person, through majority voting. The committee members, who must be recognised experts in the area of banking, fiscal policy or monetary policy, may not be civil servants or hold political office and may not seek or take advice from the outside.

Of course, an alternative to establishing a euro area wide-fiscal surveillance agency would be to rely on national fiscal councils. However, few euro area countries have such bodies and it might therefore be easier simply to introduce a single European institution.

3   Sanctions

Rather than having a single trigger point for sanctions at a deficit of 3 per cent, the new regime should have several trigger points for increasingly stringent sanctions. This requires the SGP to come into play at much smaller deficits. Moreover, greater focus should be given to debt levels than is presently the case.

As an illustration, countries experiencing deficits greater than, say, 1.5 per cent of GDP and/or a public debt greater than 60 per cent of GDP should enter a 'surveillance regime'. This regime would require them to provide the European Commission, the European Central Bank (ECB) and the EFSA with data on budget outcomes and budget plans for fiscal consolidation. However, there would be no presumption that any immediate policy action needed to follow.

If the budget deficit was greater than, say, 3 per cent, or the public debt was greater than 90 per cent of GDP, the country would enter an 'enhanced surveillance regime'. This would require governments to present plans to reduce deficits and debt. These plans would be reviewed and commented upon by the European Commission, the ECB and the EFSA.

If the budget deficit exceeded, say, 5 per cent of GDP, or the public debt was greater than 110 per cent of GDP, the country would enter a 'strict surveillance regime'. Moreover, national budgets would need to be presented to the Commission, the ECB and the EFSA for public comment before adoption. Under this regime, the Commission and the EFSA would send resident representatives to follow public finance developments on site and in real time. Few governments will welcome the growing involvement of European institutions, and the resulting public debate. This will provide incentives for better fiscal policy.

4   A fiscal stability charge

Since market discipline did not function in the run-up to the Greek crisis, a new mechanism must be found to provide firm incentives to reduce debt. The introduction of a Fiscal Stability Charge (FSC) that equals 1 per cent of the stock of public debt above 60 per cent of GDP should be explored. Under this regime, a country with a debt stock of 90 per cent of GDP would pay $(0.90-0.60)*0.01 = 0.003$ or 0.3 per cent of GDP. The charge will be paid by national governments to the European

Commission, which will return to it to the euro area governments on a pro rata basis. The net cost will thus be zero: the scheme will simply redistribute income from countries that have borrowed excessively to countries that have pursued more prudent fiscal policies.

Given the weak state of public finances currently, the rules would only apply to debt issued after 1 January 2011. Since only a fraction of public debt is rolled over annually, it will take several years before the 60 per cent limit is reached. However, if the charge is credible, governments will already now have incentives to reduce debt so as to decrease the charge when it becomes applicable.

5   Strengthening the European Financial Stability Facility (EFSF)

But even if a revised and strengthened SGP, coupled with stricter surveillance through the new EFSA and the incentive effects of the FSC, will reduce the likelihood of a public debt crisis in Europe, some risk will always remain. While the EFSF has been established to deal with a sovereign debt crisis, it has been designed to be operational for only three years. This raises the risk that borrowers and lenders alike will assume that, after this period is over, we will return to the pre-crisis situation in which there is implicit bail-out insurance.

Rather than relying on constructive ambiguity to limit deficits, it would be much better to make crystal clear that a bail-out will be available but only on politically and economically very unattractive terms so that no government or investor would want to run the risk of a sovereign debt crisis.

For instance, euro area governments could agree that financial support would be available to any government that asks for it from the EFSF but any request would trigger an automatic write-down of the outstanding debt by 30 per cent. If credible, this condition would make investors hesitant to lend to governments who are facing fiscal problems. Similarly, any support would come with strict conditionality and would require budgets to be pre-approved by the European Commission and the EFSA. These conditions would raise the political costs of borrowing and provide better incentives for fiscal prudence than the present arrangements. However, for such a regime to be credible, the EFSF must be permanent.

6   Conclusions

Restoring confidence in the euro area requires the tension between national fiscal policy and supra-national monetary policy to be resolved.

The SGP must be made more automatic and changed to entail a series of sanctions of increasing severity. The political costs of large deficits must be increased in order to provide disincentives to borrowing and investors must be discouraged from lending to governments whose fiscal policies are in disarray. To achieve this, stronger institutions are needed. It is time to go back to the drawing board and create these.

19   How to save the euro? Lessons from the US

Jacques Mélitz

The problems of the euro area brought to light some failures of the system. Nevertheless, the resulting drop in confidence in the system has gone further than one could expect. Questions have even arisen about the system's survival. Yet monetary systems do not tend to dissolve simply because of faulty performance. On the contrary, as a rule they endure even when they function very badly. It takes a political *force majeure* to bring about the break-up of a single currency area, typically without connection to its monetary performance. Why, then, has the possible default of a country engaged in irresponsible fiscal policy and accounting for only 3 per cent of the euro area's GDP raised questions about 'saving the euro' and the survival of the Eurozone? The issue has not received the attention it deserves. It is often simply taken for granted that the departures from the Stability and Growth Pact (SGP) provide a sufficient reason for the earthquake that has shaken the whole currency area. Yet if we look around the world past and present, the mismanagement of finances by regional governments has no particular tendency to bring down entire monetary systems, far from it. In line with the usual – I think superficial – diagnosis of the ailment, proposed remedies for the euro area centre on strengthening the SPG, increasing joint political control over fiscal policy and providing joint insurance against government default, or some mixture of the three. But what if a vital element of the problem is really the official doctrine that sovereign default is incompatible with the euro? What if the scale of the crisis that took place has resulted from financial markets' conviction, based on that doctrine, that the future of the euro was at stake? What if assuring the long-run sustainability of the euro means convincing those markets, quite differently, that nothing as manageable as a Greek default can upset the euro area? That is precisely what the US example would suggest and what I will defend. In that case, the right road ahead looks quite different. It means shifting the emphasis away from avoiding government defaults toward assuring the stability and the solvency of the banking system at all times, regardless of the financial difficulties of some member governments.

340

In the US, default on state and municipal contractual obligations is very much a possibility whenever lower-level governments are in financial trouble; bail-out cannot be taken for granted. New York City defaulted in 1975; the biggest default of all by a lower-level government unit since the Second World War took place in 1983 when the Washington Public Power Supply System went into bankruptcy; Orange County defaulted in 1995. Various municipal governments have been on the verge of default at times in the last few decades, including Philadelphia and Cleveland. There is also no SGP in the country. Yet financial discipline is considerably higher in the US at the state government level than in the European Monetary Union (EMU) at the national level. All states except Vermont have balanced budget rules; but these rules are self-imposed. It is easy to argue that this difference in fiscal discipline on the two sides of the Atlantic is related to the fact that when push comes to shove in the US and a lower-level government unit cannot or will not meet its debt obligations, the lenders can expect to take a big part of the hit.

Some rudimentary analysis is relevant. Consider any government unit unable to print money and without any prospect of a bail-out. Theory tells us that credit rationing is very much a possibility. As the interest rate that such a government offers on its debt goes up, extra lending dries up completely at some point as the expected rate of return on the government debt falls. This must happen because higher nominal interest rates impair the government's solvency and bring default nearer. Risk aversion simply lowers the interest rate at which credit rationing begins.

Suppose we compare the situation in the US and the EMU since the 2007–9 financial crisis in this light. The crisis brought about dire financing problems for many lower-level government units in the US and some national governments in EMU. According to the spreads on credit default swaps, California and Illinois now (September 2010) have a higher probability of non-performance on public debt than Portugal and Spain. This has been true for months. Consider next the difference in response in the US and Europe. Illinois simply stopped paying $5 billion of bills. In June 2009, California issued vouchers for wage payments. In addition, savage cuts in public services have begun and are now threatened in various states in difficulty, not only these two. Nevada has made startling reductions in spending on higher education and welfare. In the case of Portugal and Spain, nothing so drastic has happened thus far. There have been occasional spikes in interest rate spreads over German bunds of 100 to 200 percentage points above usual levels. Both Spanish and Portuguese governments have also been forced to plan greater austerity and reduced government deficit spending, but they have been able and willing to keep borrowing.

Part of the explanation may be, and probably is, that Portugal and Spain are more able to raise tax revenues than US states. But another part is the higher probability of a bail-out in Europe. The example of Greece is to the point. Greece has been able to continue borrowing in 2010 at interest rates typically around 200 percentage points above Portugal and Spain on ten-year government bonds (and since May 2010 more than 500 percentage points higher than German bunds). If you do the maths, it is clear that this could never have happened without a high probability of a bail-out. In fact, you do not need to do the maths: there have been occasions in February–March and particularly May 2010 when some Greek issues would clearly have failed without the assurance of public lending and ECB support. If Greece can borrow on the probability of a bail-out so could Portugal and Spain.

Based on this evidence, the current EMU strategy of treating government default as anathema permits member governments to sink into deeper waters, weakens the forces that would otherwise exist in favour of self-imposed budget restraints and thereby raises the probability of a bail-out. But an actual bail-out is perhaps the most likely setting for the breakdown of the euro area. If taxes ever need to rise all over the euro area in order to bail out a member government, one can easily imagine a pullout by Germany, followed by the Netherlands and Austria (if no others), in order to form a separate monetary union.[1]

What are the dangers of the opposite strategy of mimicking the US instead and moving towards heavier reliance on markets to discipline member governments and to price sovereign risk? The answer lies in the external effects of government default on the payments system and the banks, and this problem would be aggravated by contagion. But those dangers exist in the US as well. If the US federal government were to allow Illinois or California to default on state government debt in today's circumstances of widespread financial difficulties across the states, there is a serious threat that interest premia would go up on the debt of most state governments and a wave of state defaults would follow. For this reason, the federal government might well step in. But if we look at the *institutional* manner in which the US deals with the problem, we find the answer to lie in country-wide prudential rules for banks and

---

[1] Many would say that Greece has already been bailed out. But so far no holder of Greek debt has yet suffered a credit event. Further, no one outside of Greece has yet paid any taxes to fulfil a claim on Greek debt. Thus, according to my usage, no bail-out has happened. However, none of the argument hinges on this choice of words.

central bank powers of lender of last resort (LOLR). There is no general announcement that state government default is incompatible with the dollar. Instead there is a strict separation of the issue of joint support of the financial system and joint support of financing by the subgovernment units in the country. Would Europe not be wise to adopt the same strategy and to cease to conflate the two issues?

What this would mean, of course, is adopting EMU-wide prudential rules on banks, providing the ECB with full LOLR powers and, very significantly, dismissing the idea that the SGP is the pillar on which the whole Eurozone project stands. This idea is highly perilous.[2] Markets believe it, and at times of financial precariousness, what markets believe is extremely important. According to my proposal, the SGP could still be upheld as a code of good behaviour which improves public finances in Europe and facilitates the task of the ECB. But the basic philosophy would be that if any individual member government in the Eurozone engages in irresponsible fiscal conduct, contrary to the SGP, the creditors and its taxpayers would bear the brunt of the consequences. Everything would be done to assure the stability of the financial sector in the euro area and the lack of repercussions on the risk premiums that the more financially responsible member governments need to pay. Banks might be bailed out but not governments. Any aid to member governments, if it came, would not concern the euro system but the International Monetary Fund (IMF), or if any aid did come from the EU it would be part of a programme that could as well have existed had the euro never appeared, and would be clearly sealed off.

Reference

Reinhart, C. and K. Rogoff (2009). *This Time is Different: Eight Centuries of Financial Folly*, Princeton University Press

---

[2] If we really think that a government default would bring the euro down, we must conclude that the euro has no long-run future ahead; it is doomed. A reading of Reinhart and Rogoff (2009) should convince any one.

Index

Printed in the United States
By Bookmasters